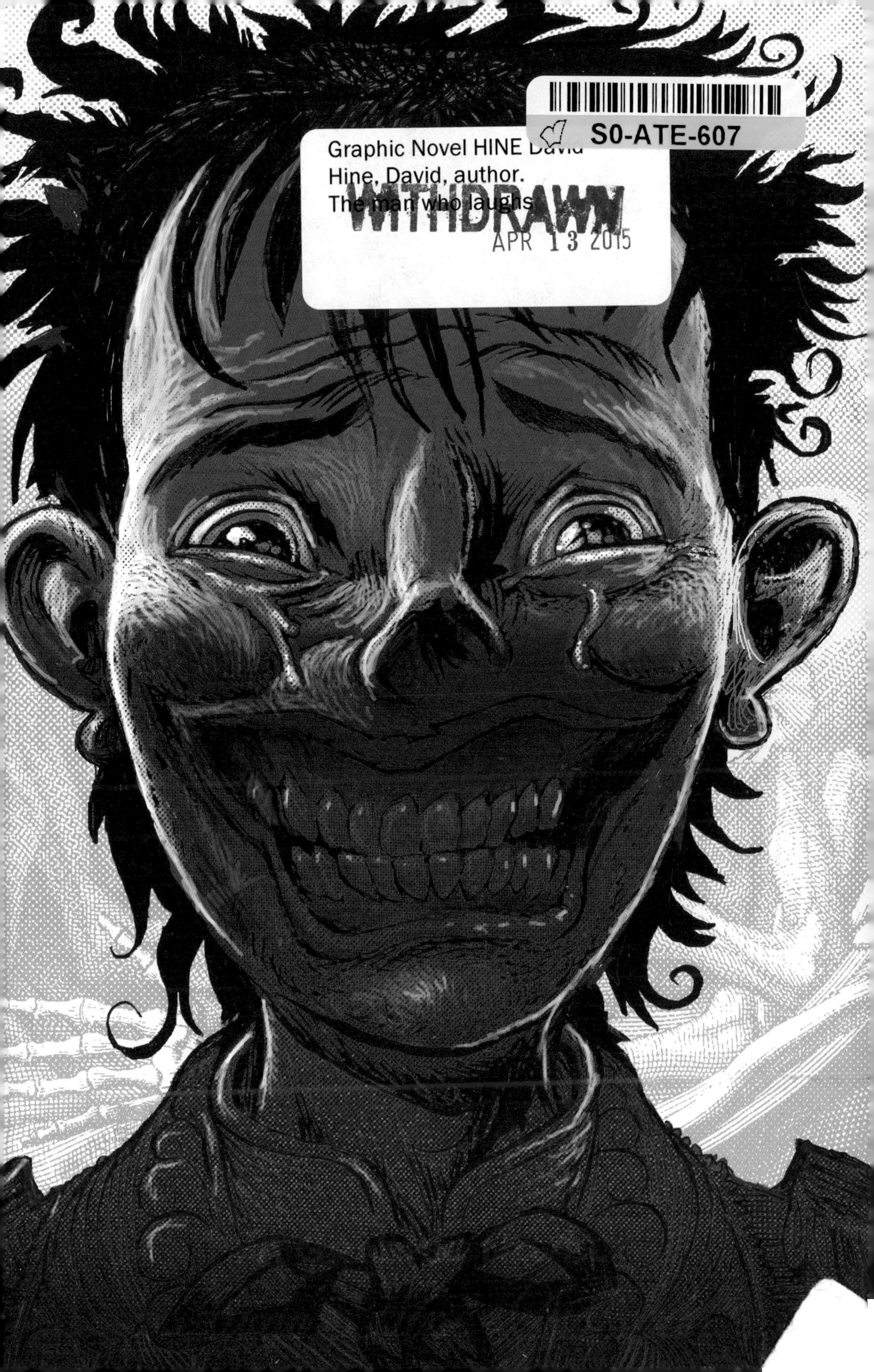

The Man Who Laughs

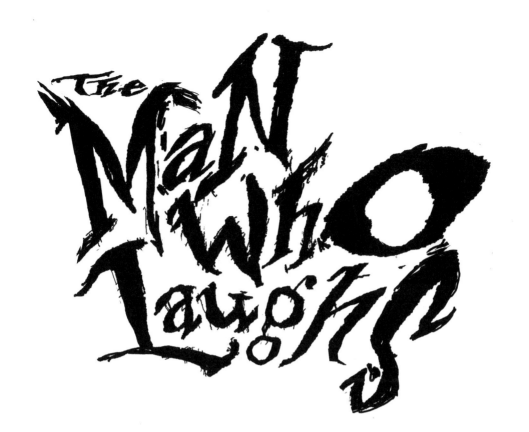

First published 2013
by SelfMadeHero
139–141 Pancras Road
London NW1 1UN
www.selfmadehero.com

This edition printed 2014
© 2013 SelfMadeHero

Adapted by David Hine
Illustrated by Mark Stafford
Lettering by Lizzie Kaye

Editorial & Production Manager: Lizzie Kaye
Sales & Marketing Manager: Sam Humphrey
Publishing Director: Emma Hayley
With thanks to: Paul Smith, Jane Laporte and Nick de Somogyi

A CIP record for this book is available from the British Library

ISBN: 978-1-906838-58-4

10 9 8 7 6 5 4 3 2

Printed and bound in China

ADAPTED FROM
THE NOVEL
"L'HOMME QUI RIT"
BY
Victor Hugo

WRITTEN BY
David HINE

ILLUSTRATED BY
Mark Stafford

SELF
MADE
HERO

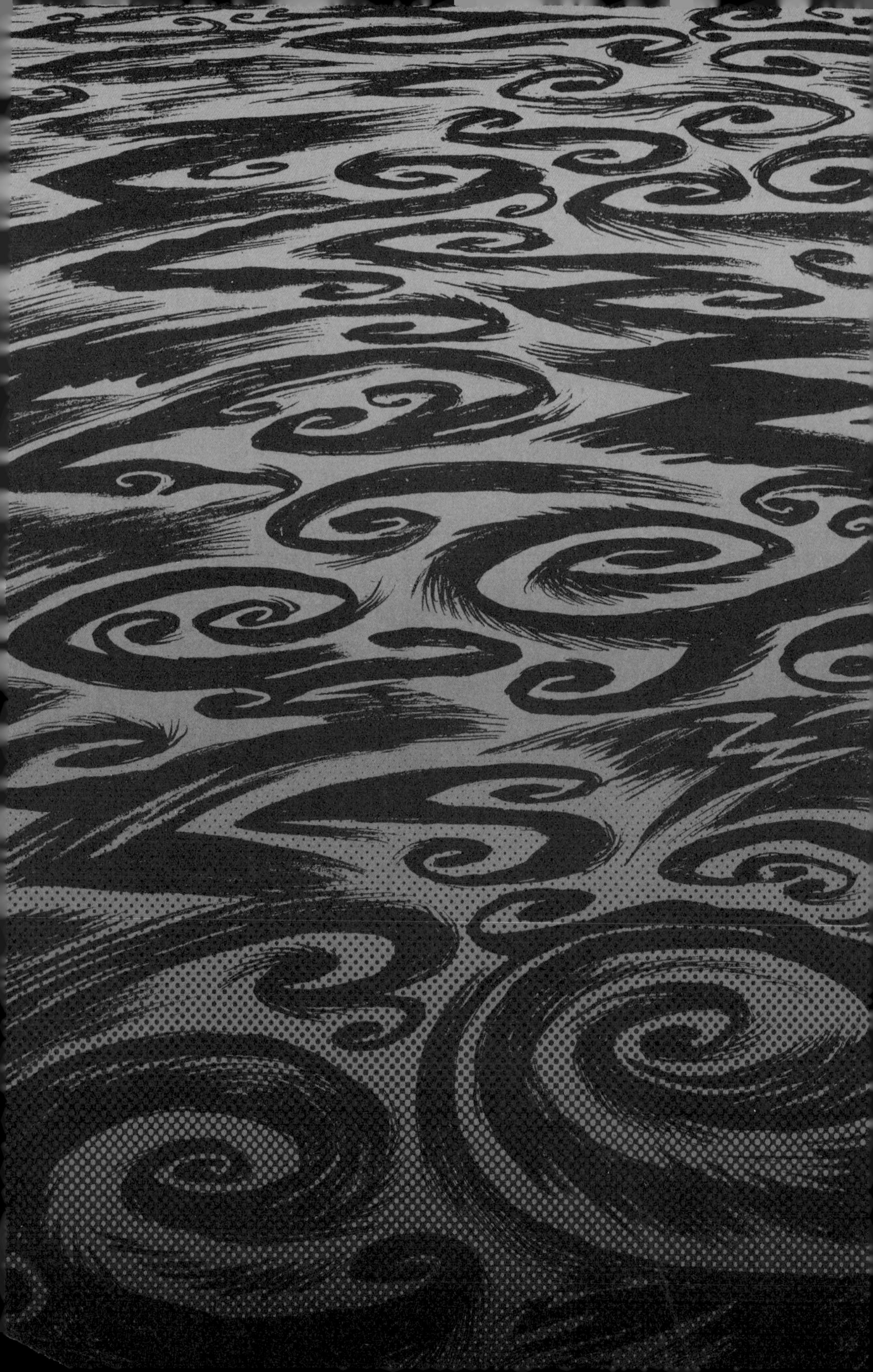

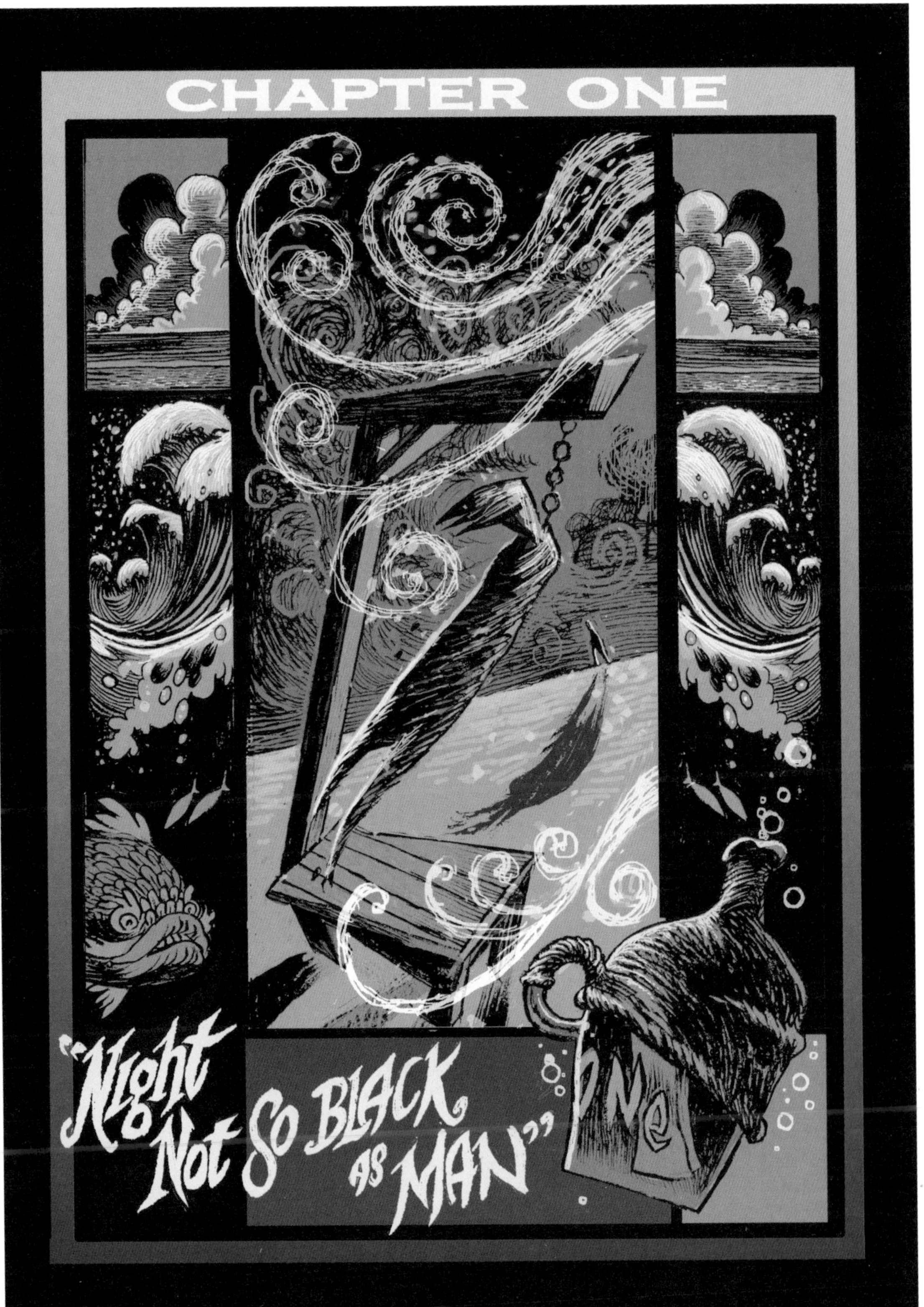
CHAPTER ONE
"Night Not So Black as Man"

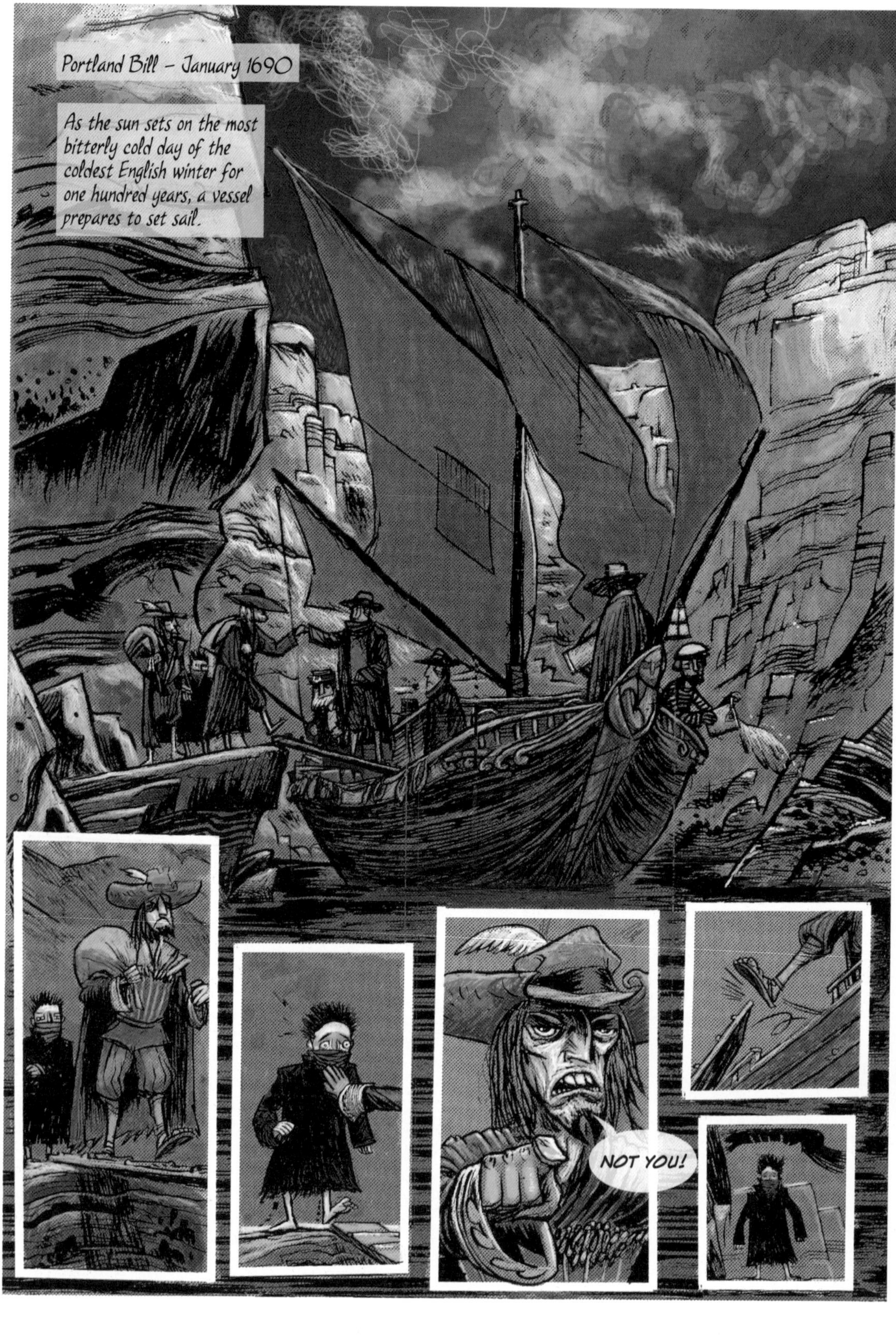
Portland Bill – January 1690
As the sun sets on the most bitterly cold day of the coldest English winter for one hundred years, a vessel prepares to set sail.
NOT YOU!

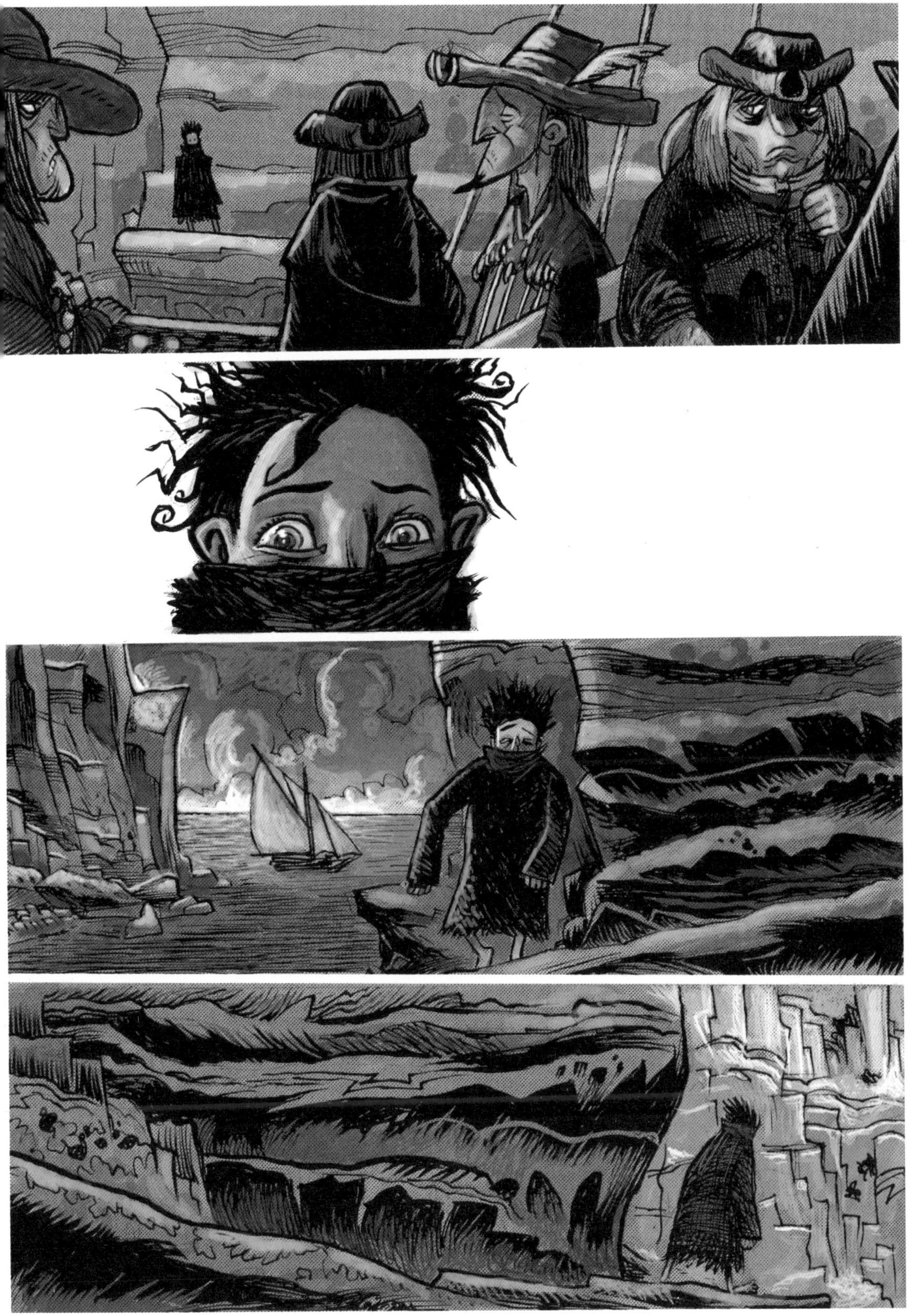

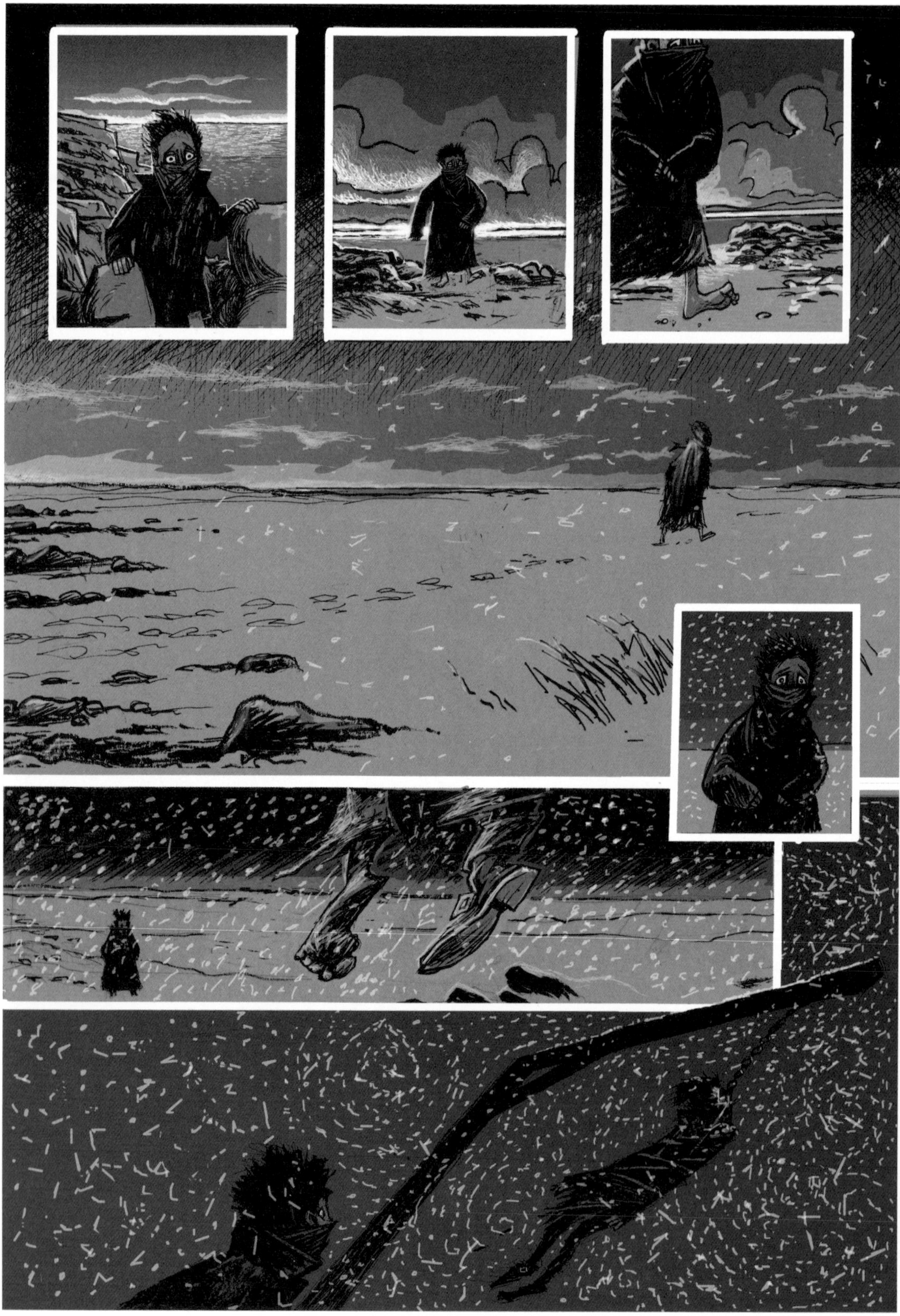

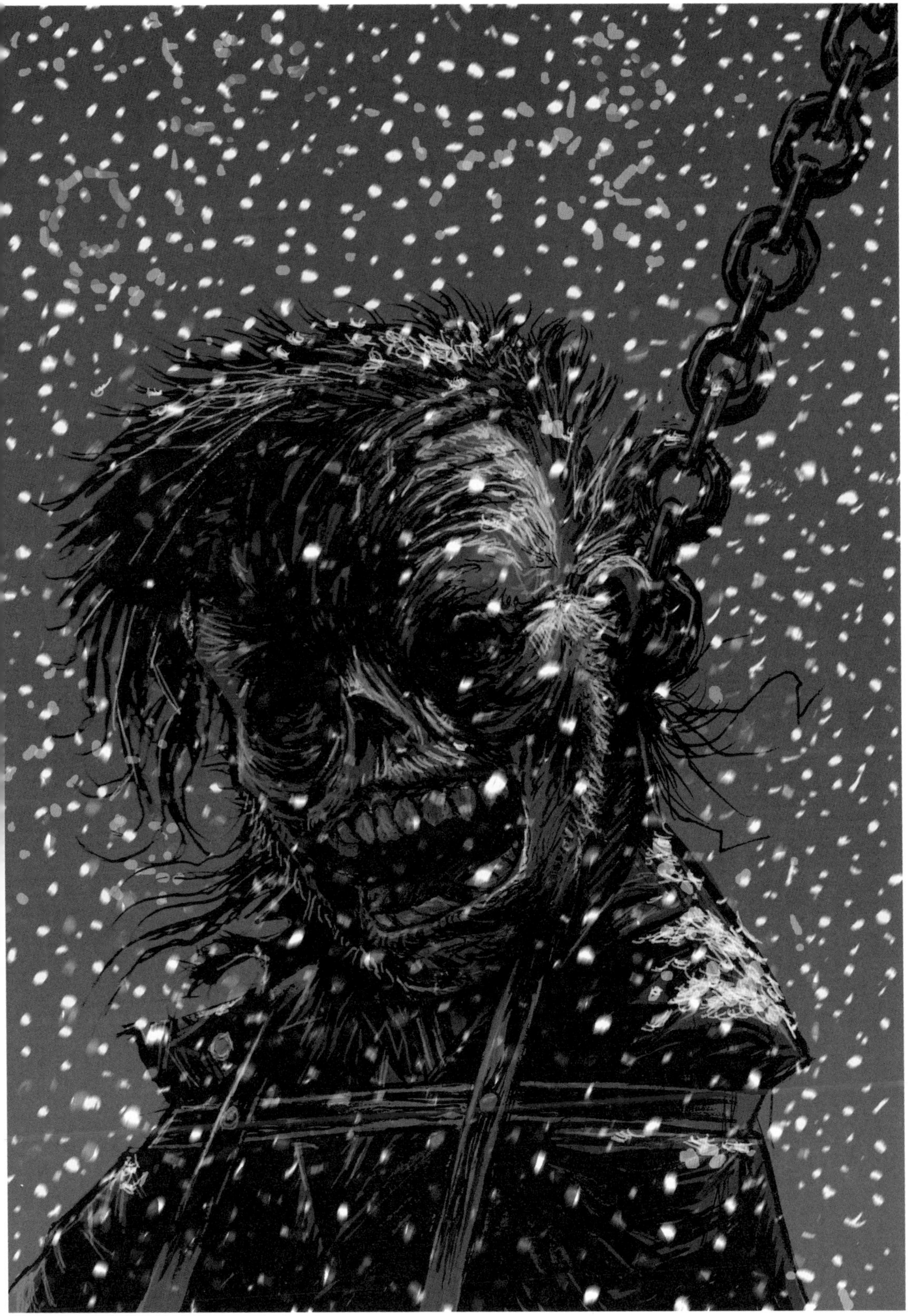

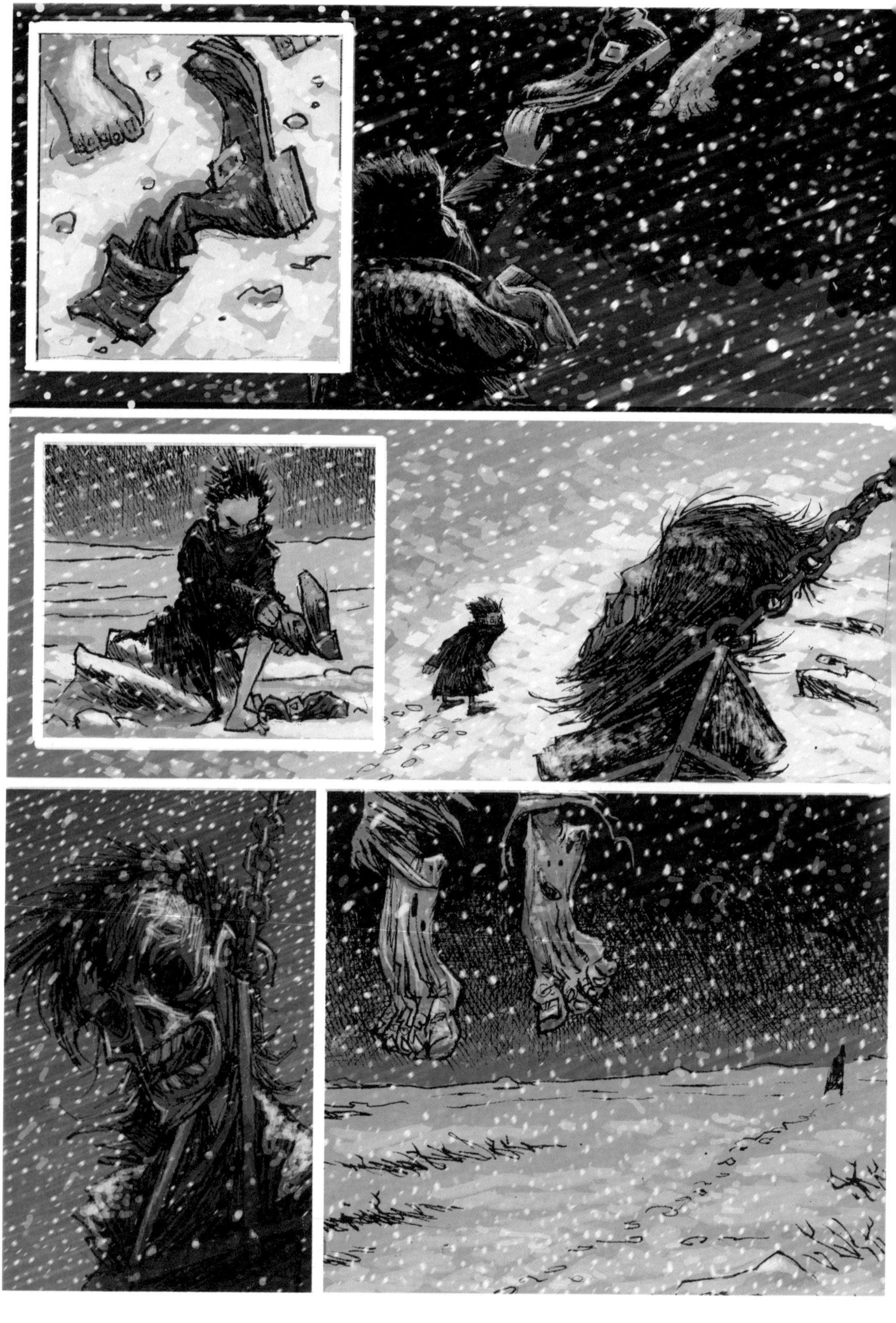

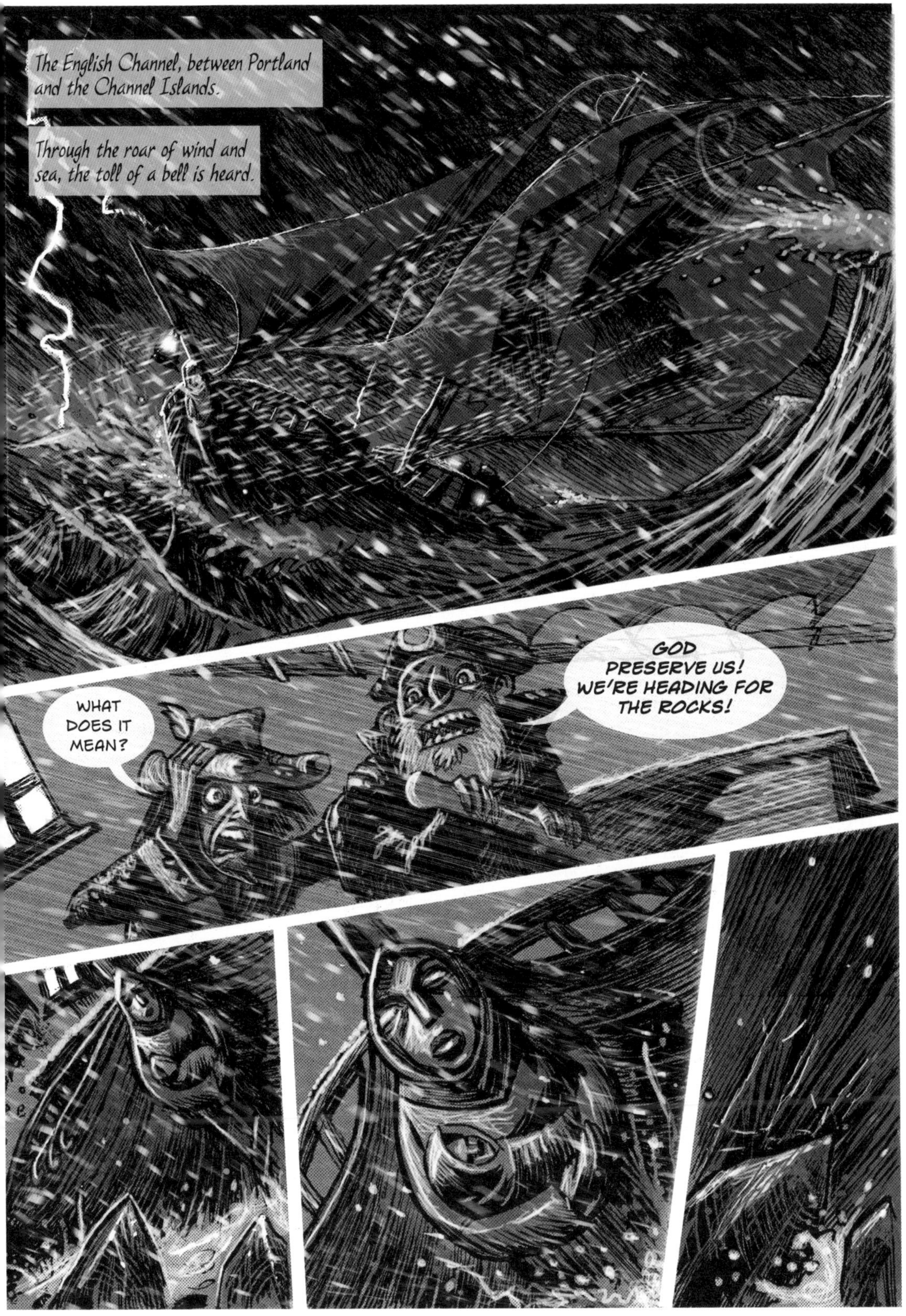
The English Channel, between Portland and the Channel Islands.
Through the roar of wind and sea, the toll of a bell is heard.
WHAT DOES IT MEAN?
GOD PRESERVE US! WE'RE HEADING FOR THE ROCKS!

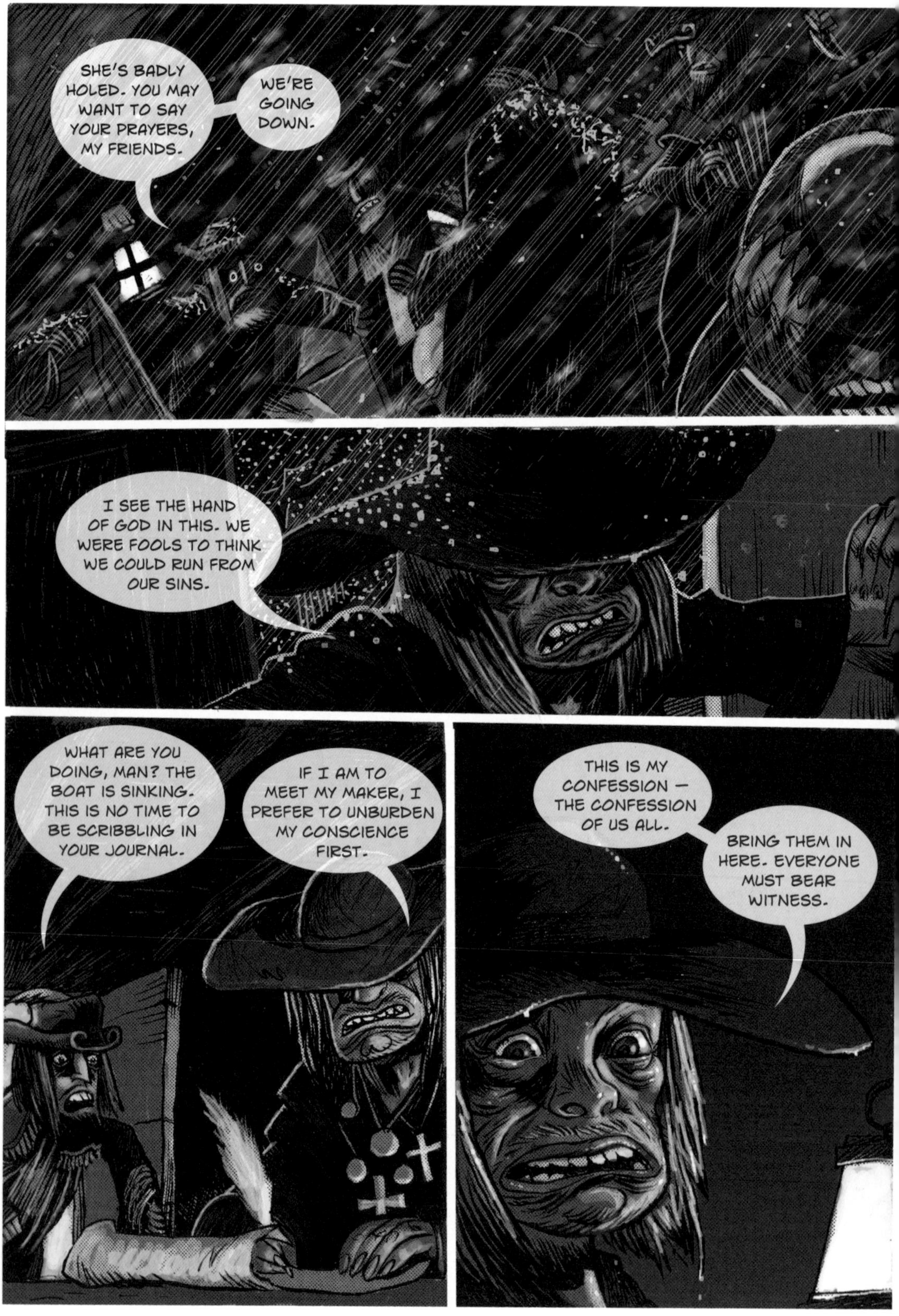

SHE'S BADLY HOLED. YOU MAY WANT TO SAY YOUR PRAYERS, MY FRIENDS.
WE'RE GOING DOWN.
I SEE THE HAND OF GOD IN THIS. WE WERE FOOLS TO THINK WE COULD RUN FROM OUR SINS.
WHAT ARE YOU DOING, MAN? THE BOAT IS SINKING. THIS IS NO TIME TO BE SCRIBBLING IN YOUR JOURNAL.
IF I AM TO MEET MY MAKER, I PREFER TO UNBURDEN MY CONSCIENCE FIRST.
THIS IS MY CONFESSION — THE CONFESSION OF US ALL.
BRING THEM IN HERE. EVERYONE MUST BEAR WITNESS.

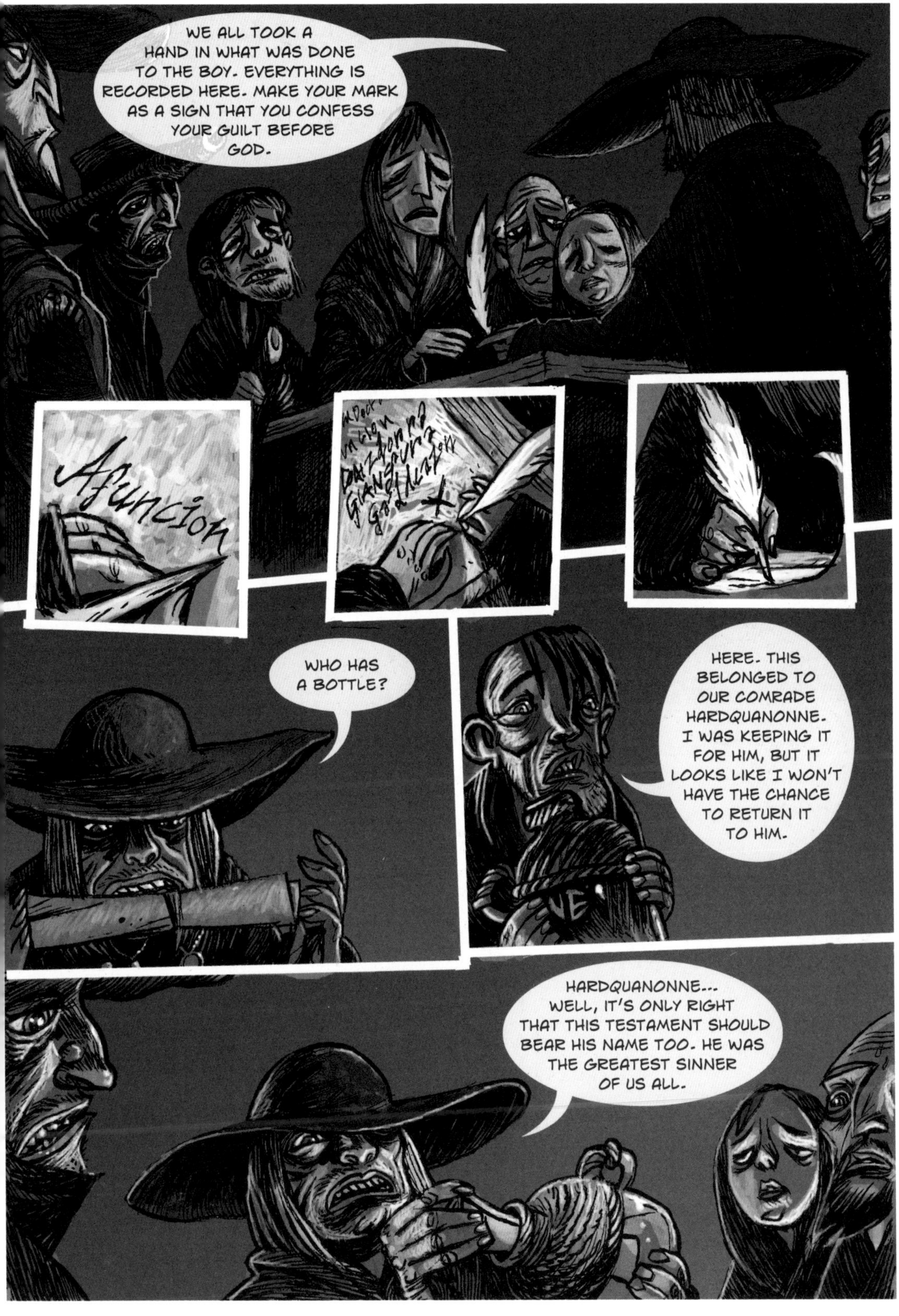
WE ALL TOOK A HAND IN WHAT WAS DONE TO THE BOY. EVERYTHING IS RECORDED HERE. MAKE YOUR MARK AS A SIGN THAT YOU CONFESS YOUR GUILT BEFORE GOD.
Afuncion
WHO HAS A BOTTLE?
HERE. THIS BELONGED TO OUR COMRADE HARDQUANONNE. I WAS KEEPING IT FOR HIM, BUT IT LOOKS LIKE I WON'T HAVE THE CHANCE TO RETURN IT TO HIM.
HARDQUANONNE... WELL, IT'S ONLY RIGHT THAT THIS TESTAMENT SHOULD BEAR HIS NAME TOO. HE WAS THE GREATEST SINNER OF US ALL.

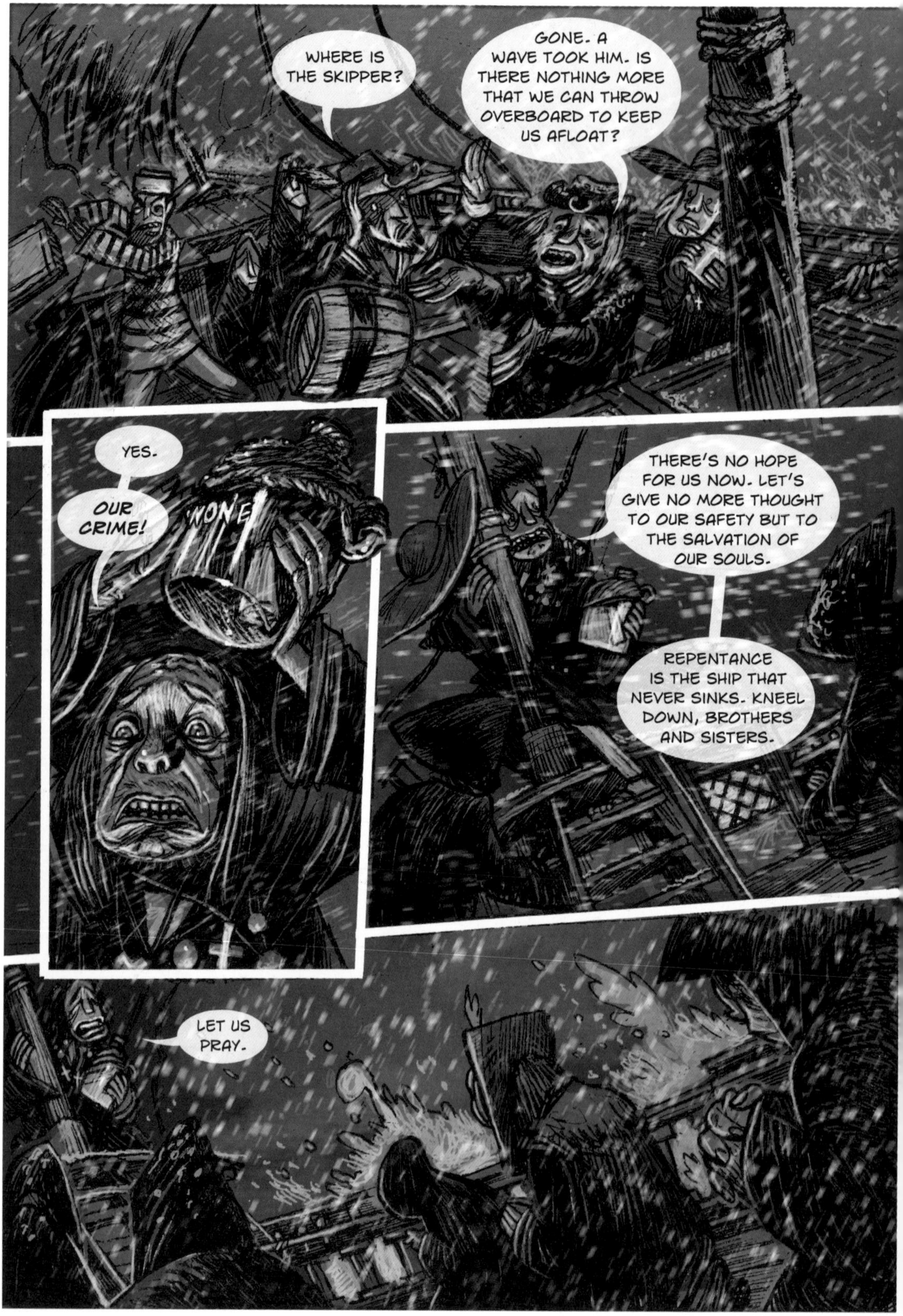
WHERE IS THE SKIPPER?
GONE. A WAVE TOOK HIM. IS THERE NOTHING MORE THAT WE CAN THROW OVERBOARD TO KEEP US AFLOAT?
YES.
OUR CRIME!
THERE'S NO HOPE FOR US NOW. LET'S GIVE NO MORE THOUGHT TO OUR SAFETY BUT TO THE SALVATION OF OUR SOULS.
REPENTANCE IS THE SHIP THAT NEVER SINKS. KNEEL DOWN, BROTHERS AND SISTERS.
LET US PRAY.

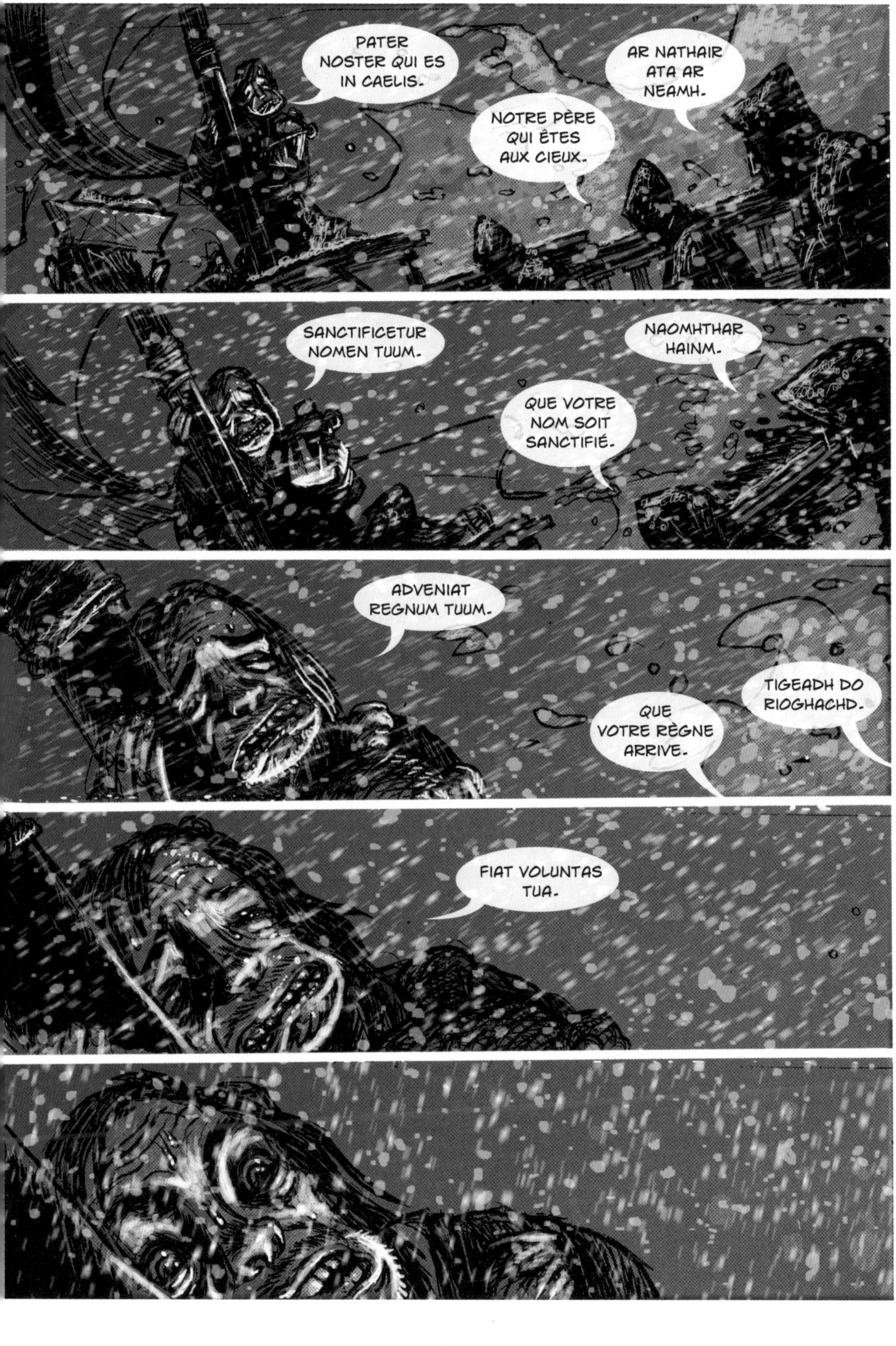
PATER NOSTER QUI ES IN CAELIS.
AR NATHAIR ATA AR NEAMH.
NOTRE PÈRE QUI ÊTES AUX CIEUX.
SANCTIFICETUR NOMEN TUUM.
NAOMHTHAR HAINM.
QUE VOTRE NOM SOIT SANCTIFIÉ.
ADVENIAT REGNUM TUUM.
TIGEADH DO RIOGHACHD.
QUE VOTRE RÈGNE ARRIVE.
FIAT VOLUNTAS TUA.

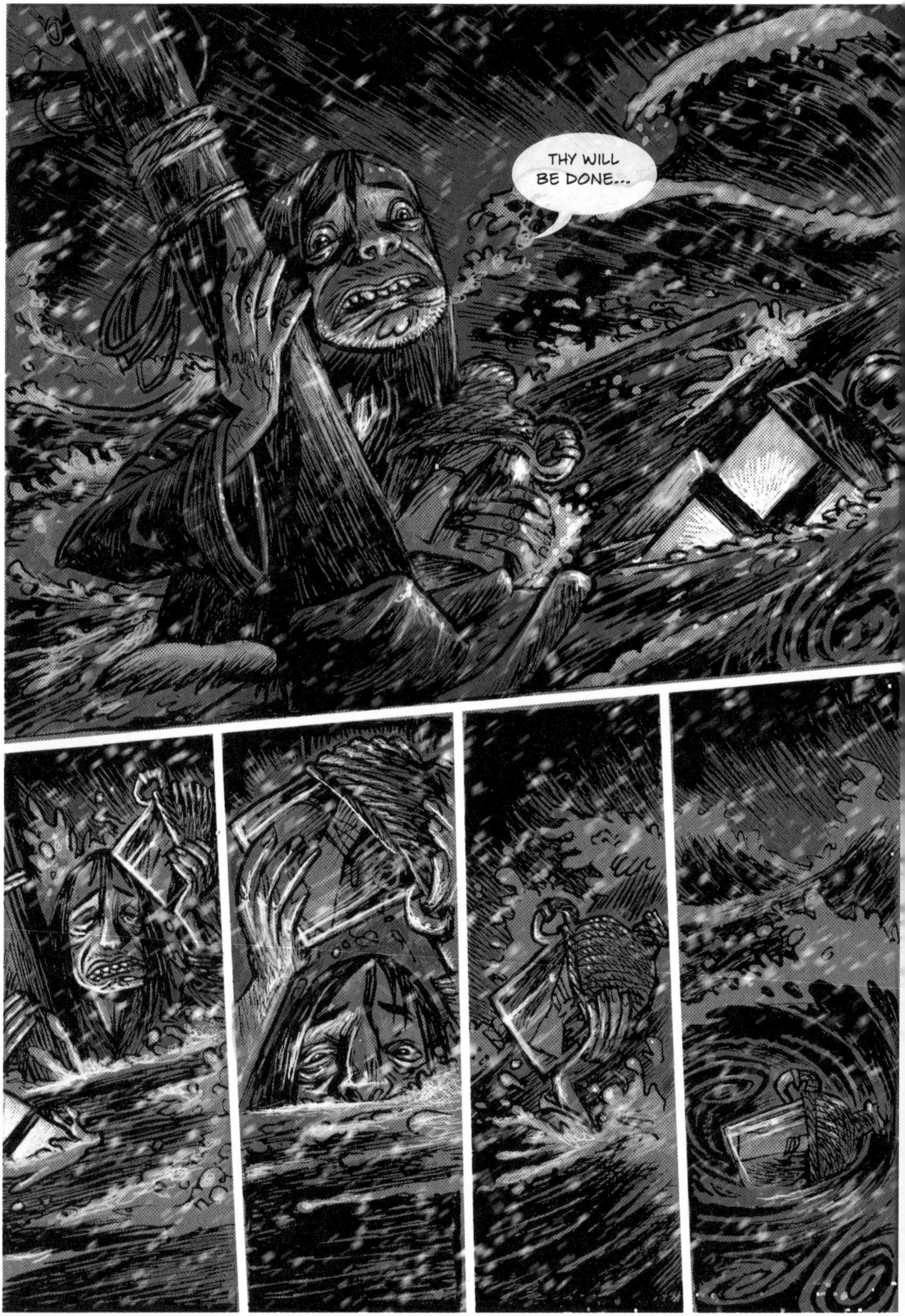
THY WILL BE DONE...

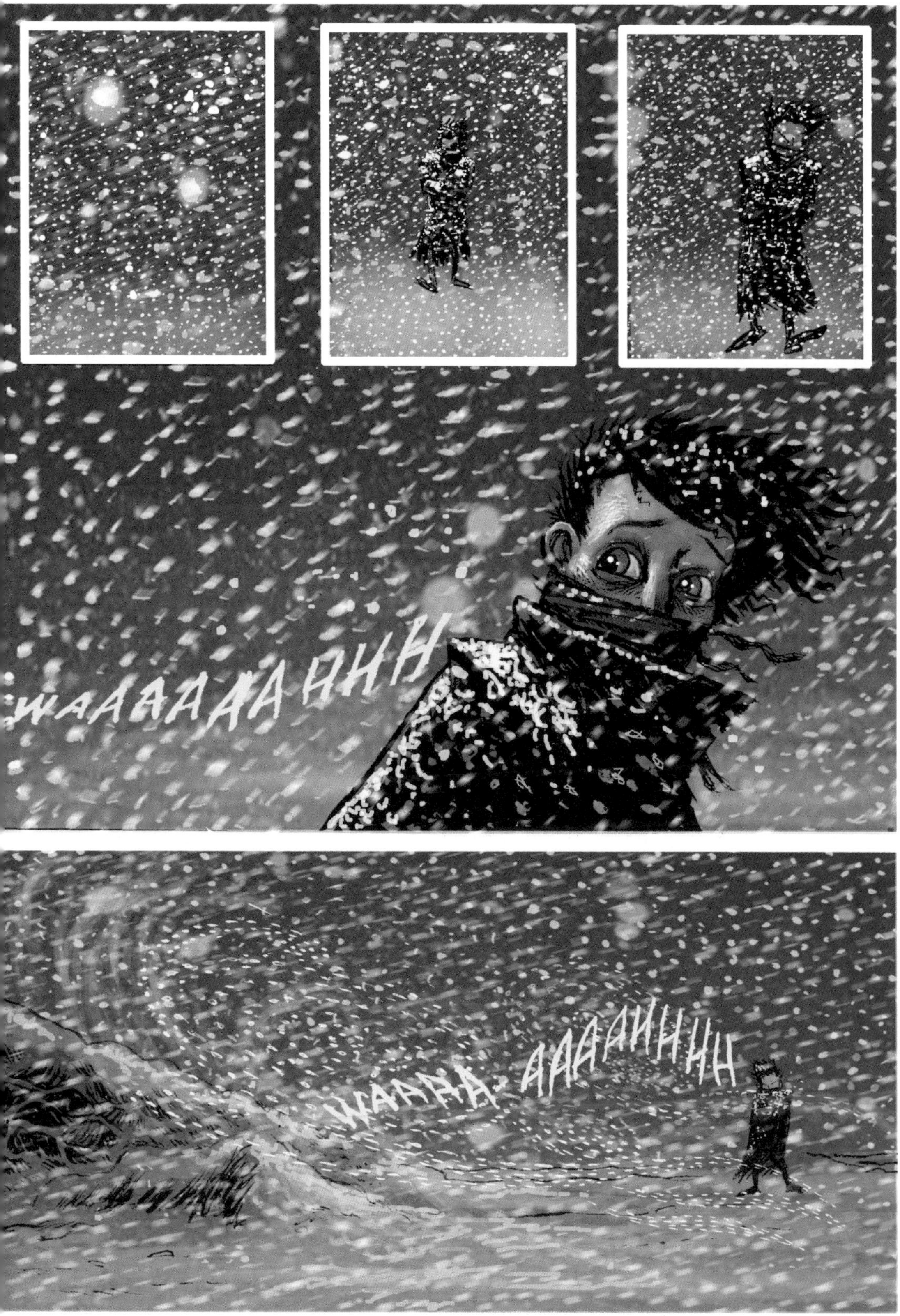
WAAAAAAHHH
WAAAA AAAAHHHH

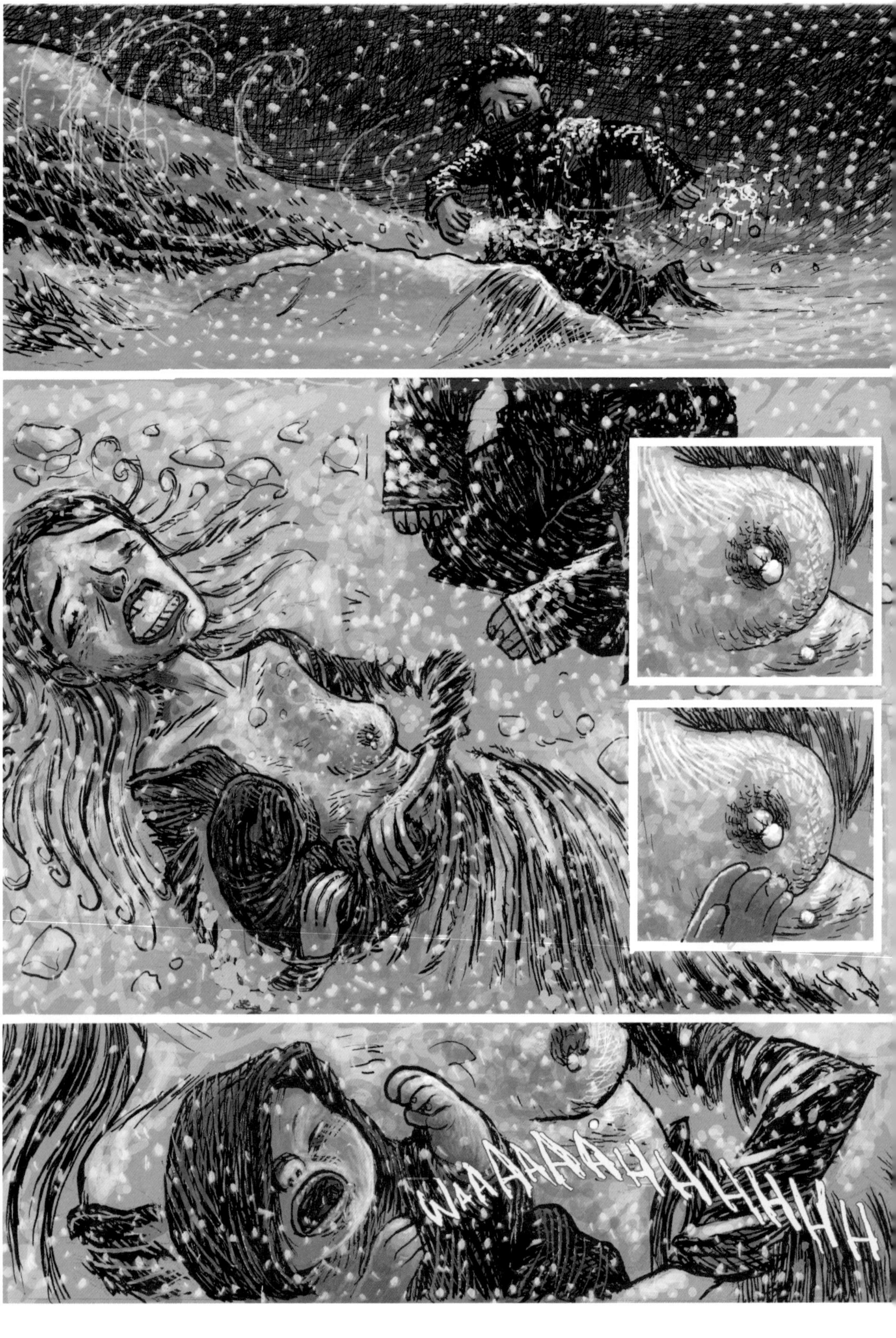
WAAAAAAHHHHHHHH

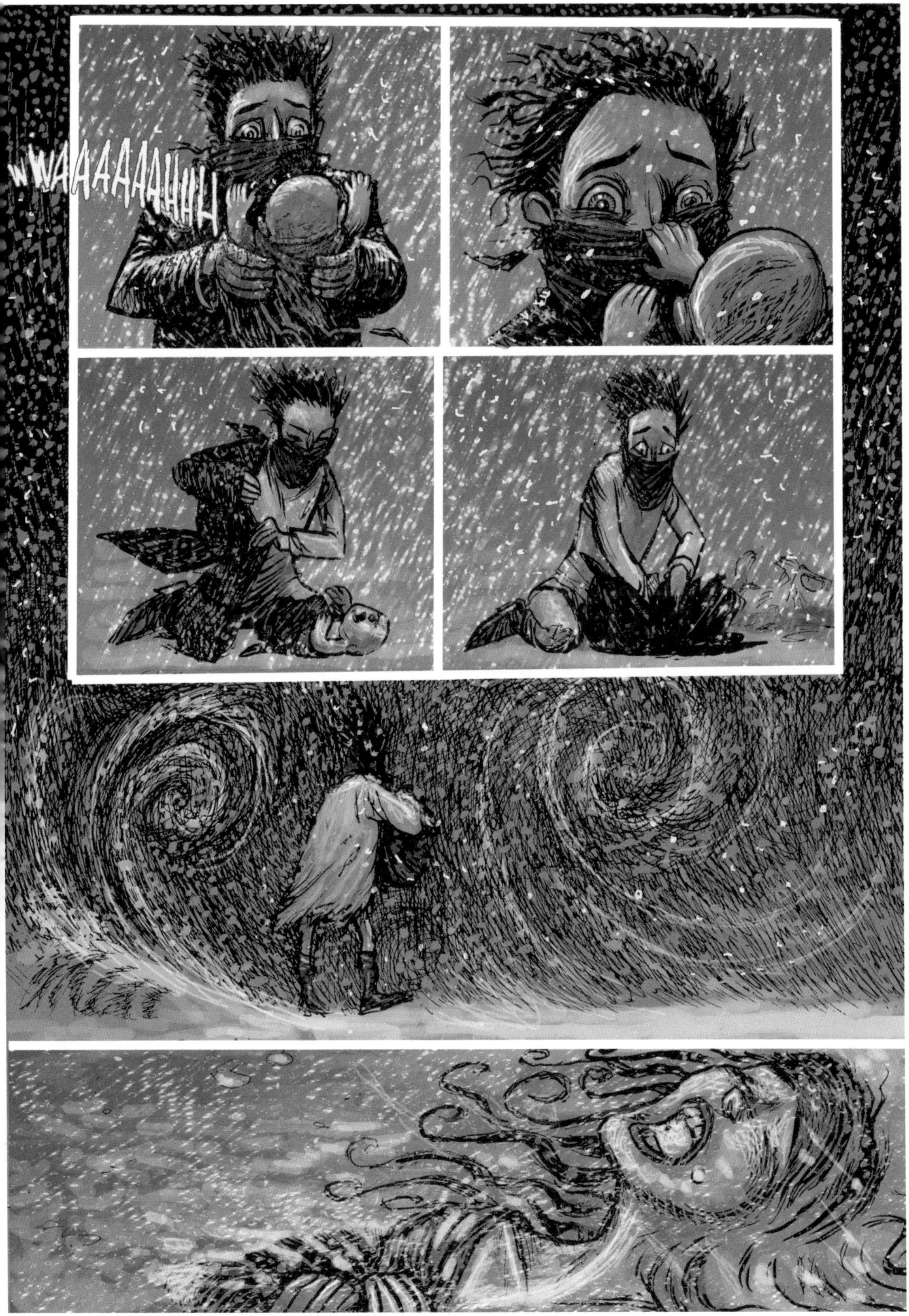
WWAAAAAAHHH

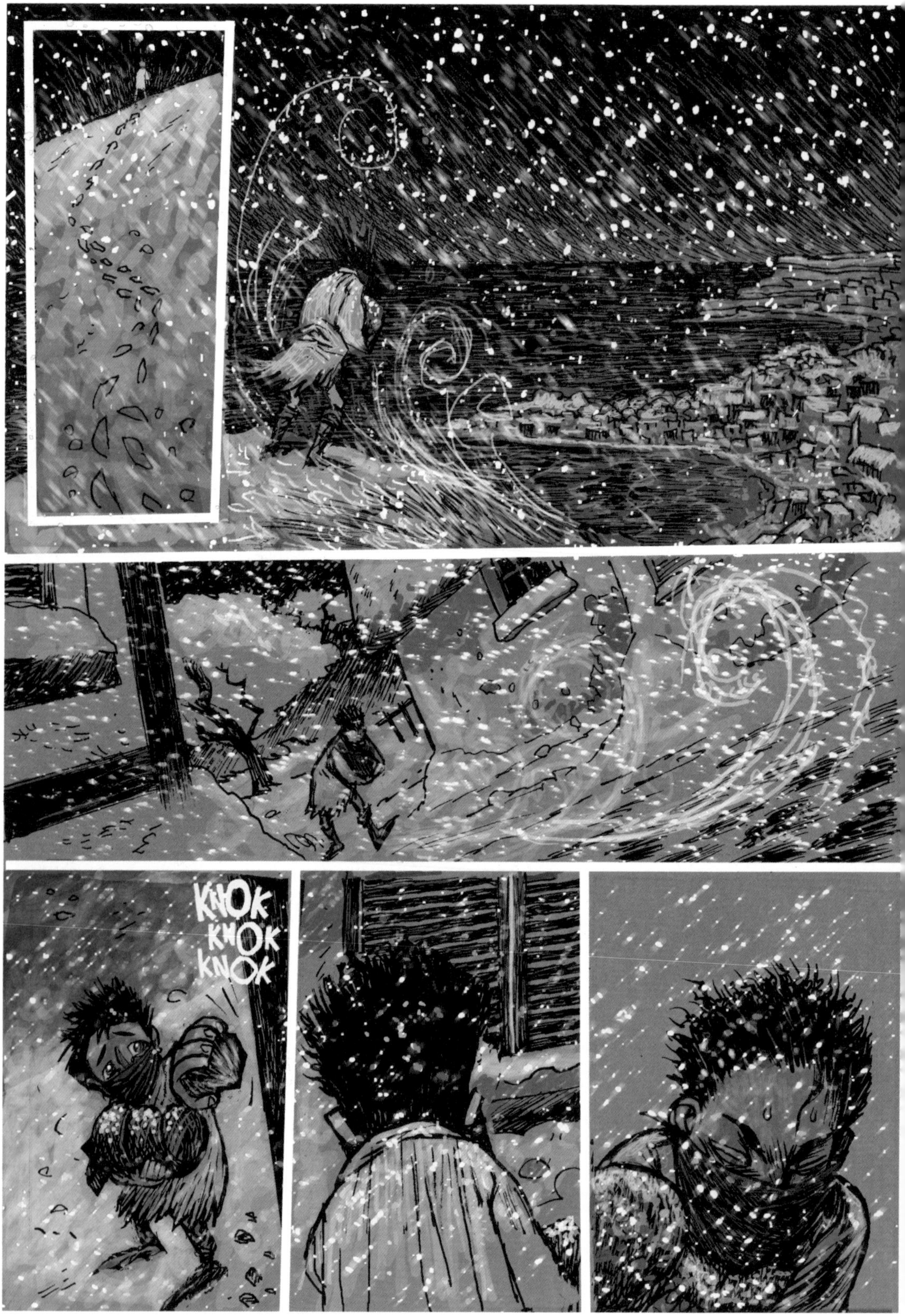
KNOK
KNOK
KNOK

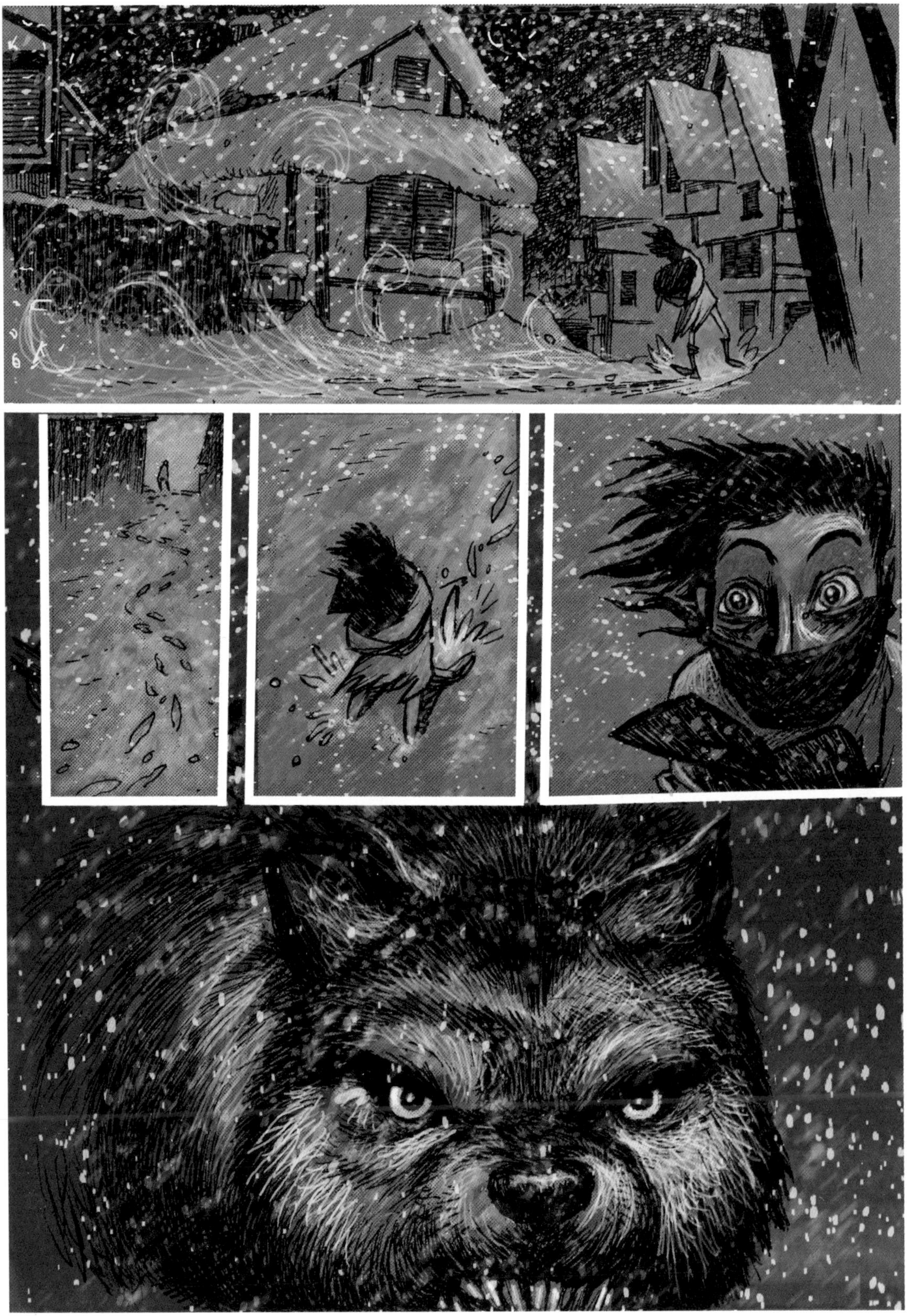

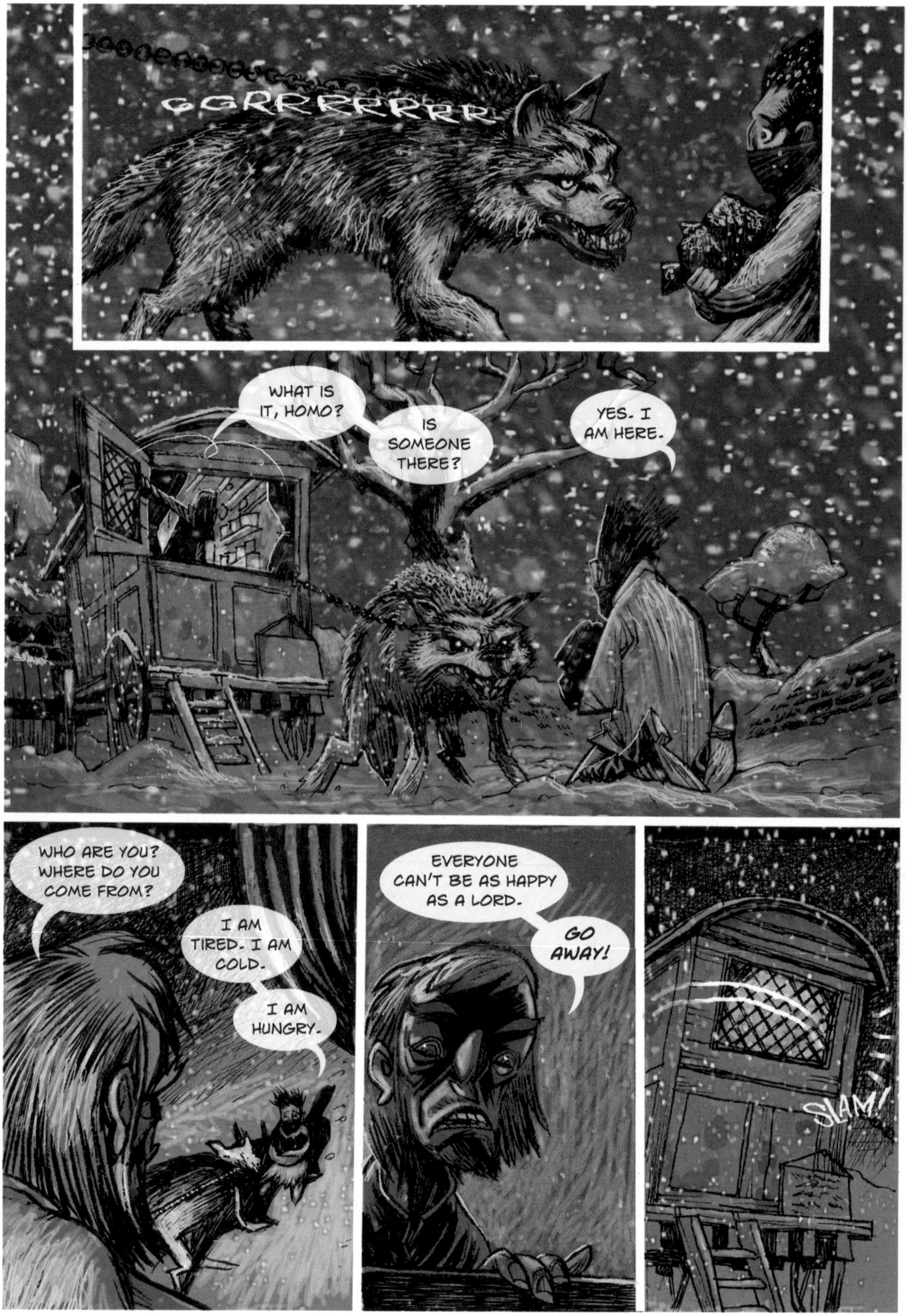
GGRRRRRRRR
WHAT IS IT, HOMO?
IS SOMEONE THERE?
YES. I AM HERE.
WHO ARE YOU? WHERE DO YOU COME FROM?
I AM TIRED. I AM COLD.
I AM HUNGRY.
EVERYONE CAN'T BE AS HAPPY AS A LORD.
GO AWAY!
SLAM!

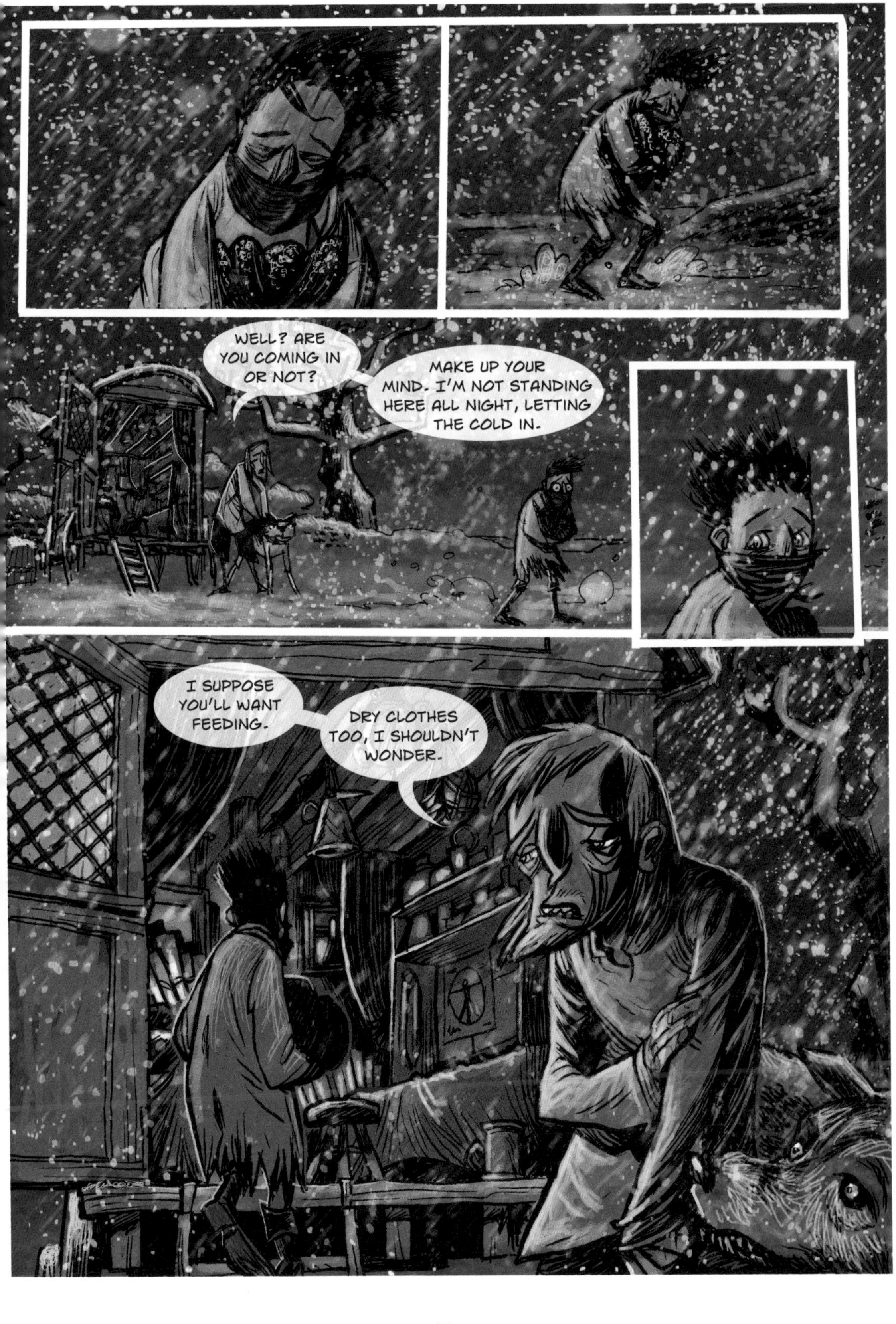
WELL? ARE YOU COMING IN OR NOT?
MAKE UP YOUR MIND. I'M NOT STANDING HERE ALL NIGHT, LETTING THE COLD IN.
I SUPPOSE YOU'LL WANT FEEDING.
DRY CLOTHES TOO, I SHOULDN'T WONDER.

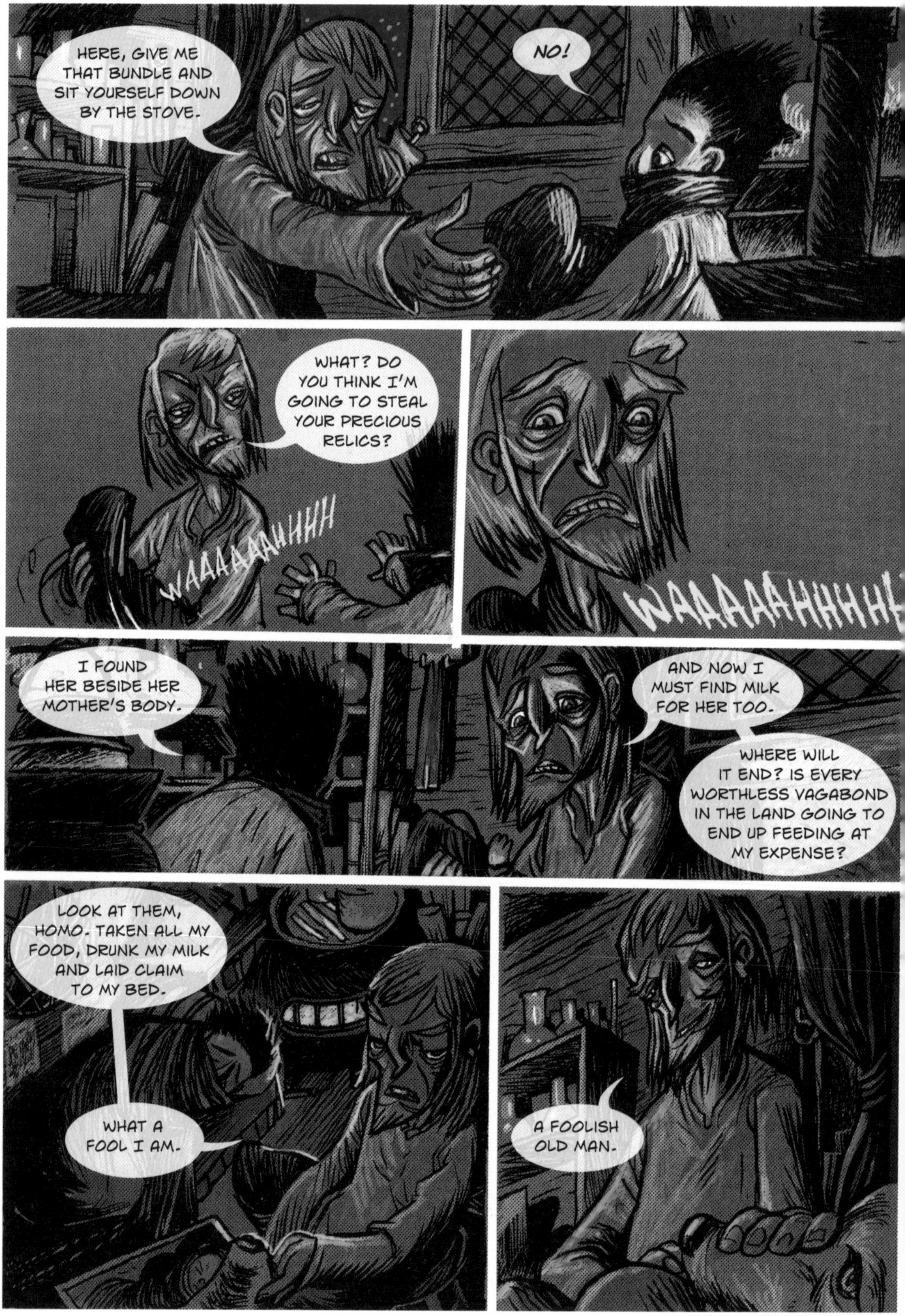
HERE, GIVE ME THAT BUNDLE AND SIT YOURSELF DOWN BY THE STOVE.
NO!
WHAT? DO YOU THINK I'M GOING TO STEAL YOUR PRECIOUS RELICS?
WAAAAAAHHHH
WAAAAAHHHHH
I FOUND HER BESIDE HER MOTHER'S BODY.
AND NOW I MUST FIND MILK FOR HER TOO.
WHERE WILL IT END? IS EVERY WORTHLESS VAGABOND IN THE LAND GOING TO END UP FEEDING AT MY EXPENSE?
LOOK AT THEM, HOMO. TAKEN ALL MY FOOD, DRUNK MY MILK AND LAID CLAIM TO MY BED.
WHAT A FOOL I AM.
A FOOLISH OLD MAN.

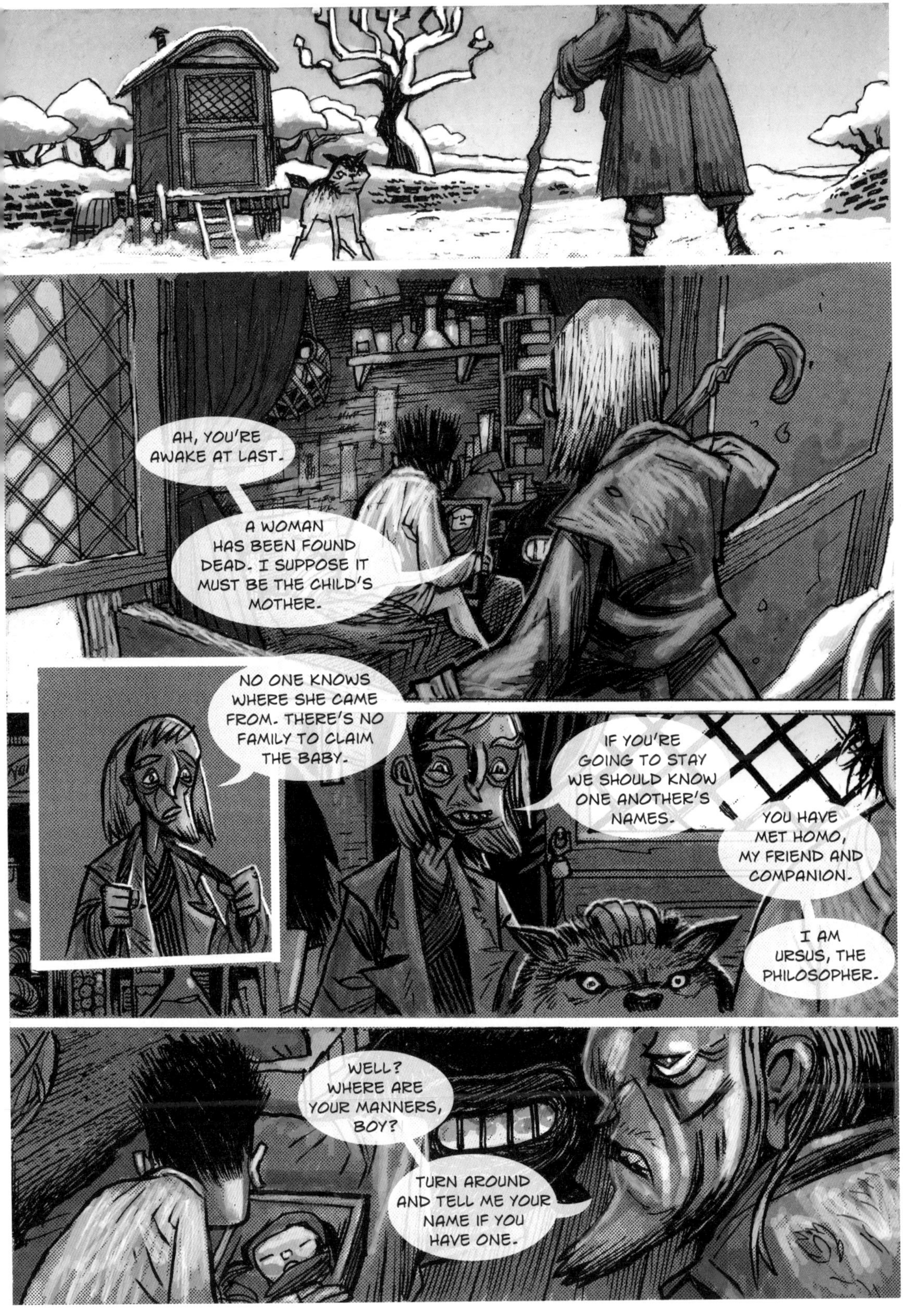
AH, YOU'RE AWAKE AT LAST.
A WOMAN HAS BEEN FOUND DEAD. I SUPPOSE IT MUST BE THE CHILD'S MOTHER.
NO ONE KNOWS WHERE SHE CAME FROM. THERE'S NO FAMILY TO CLAIM THE BABY.
IF YOU'RE GOING TO STAY WE SHOULD KNOW ONE ANOTHER'S NAMES.
YOU HAVE MET HOMO, MY FRIEND AND COMPANION.
I AM URSUS, THE PHILOSOPHER.
WELL? WHERE ARE YOUR MANNERS, BOY?
TURN AROUND AND TELL ME YOUR NAME IF YOU HAVE ONE.

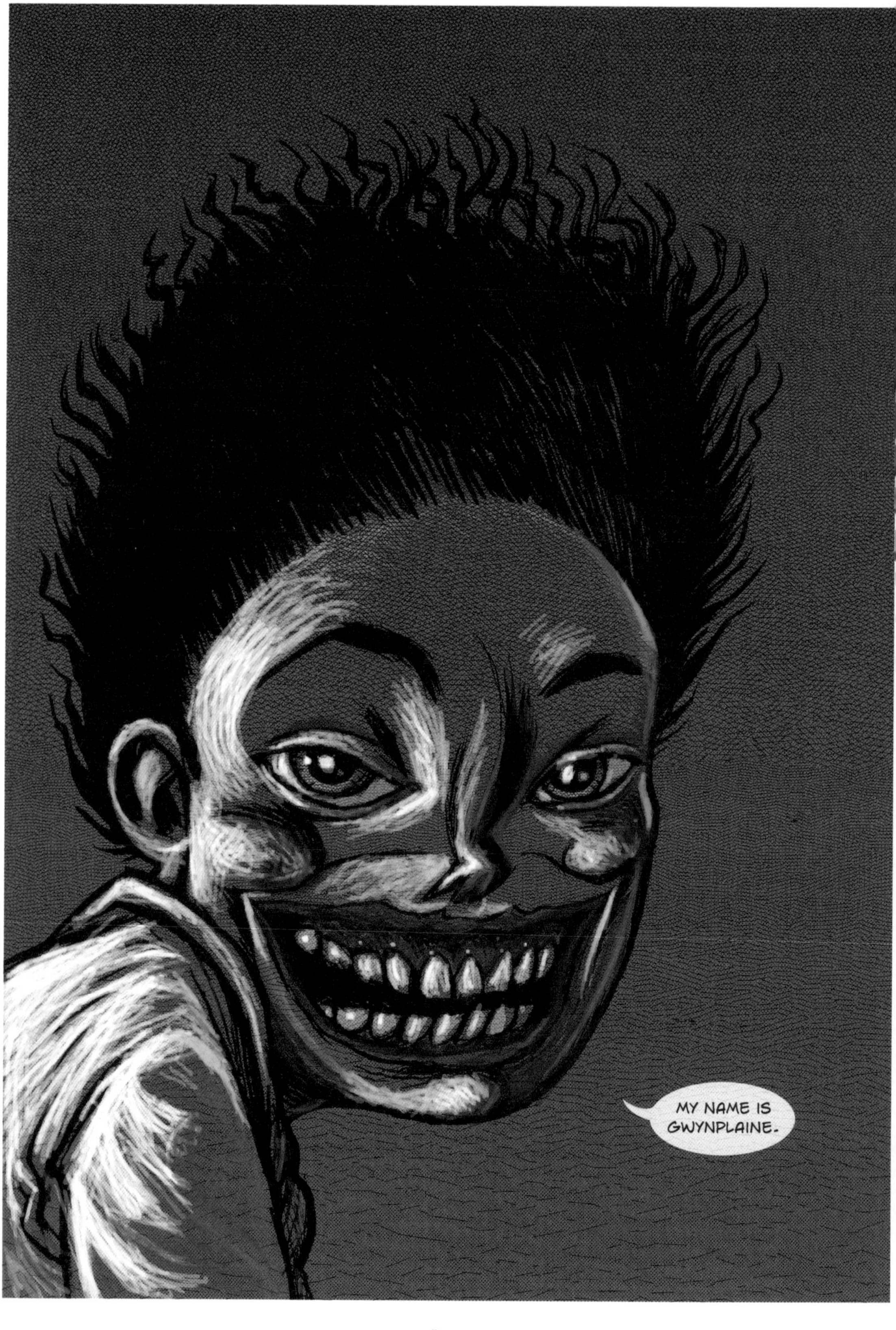
MY NAME IS GWYNPLAINE.

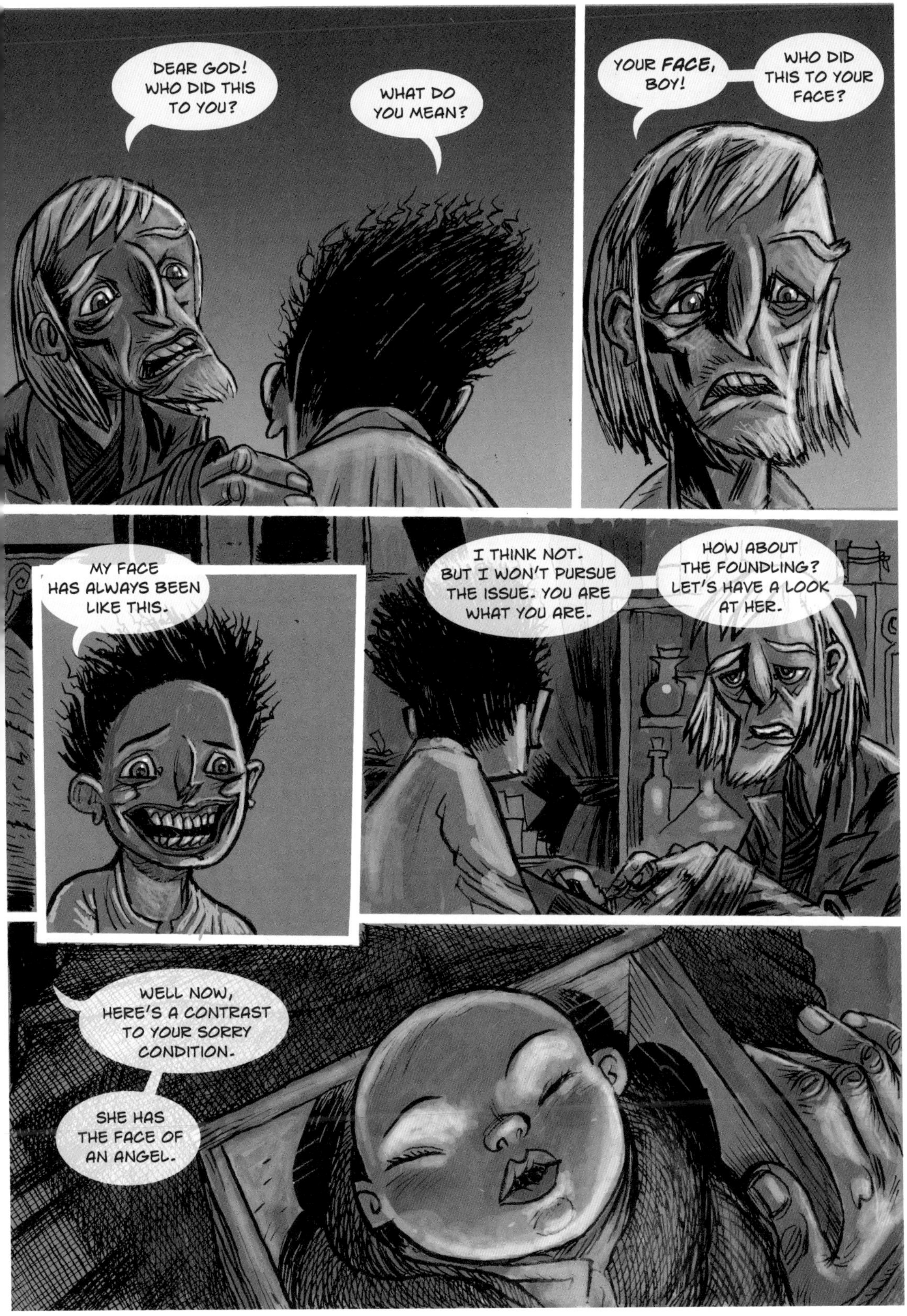
DEAR GOD! WHO DID THIS TO YOU?
WHAT DO YOU MEAN?
YOUR FACE, BOY!
WHO DID THIS TO YOUR FACE?
MY FACE HAS ALWAYS BEEN LIKE THIS.
I THINK NOT. BUT I WON'T PURSUE THE ISSUE. YOU ARE WHAT YOU ARE.
HOW ABOUT THE FOUNDLING? LET'S HAVE A LOOK AT HER.
WELL NOW, HERE'S A CONTRAST TO YOUR SORRY CONDITION.
SHE HAS THE FACE OF AN ANGEL.

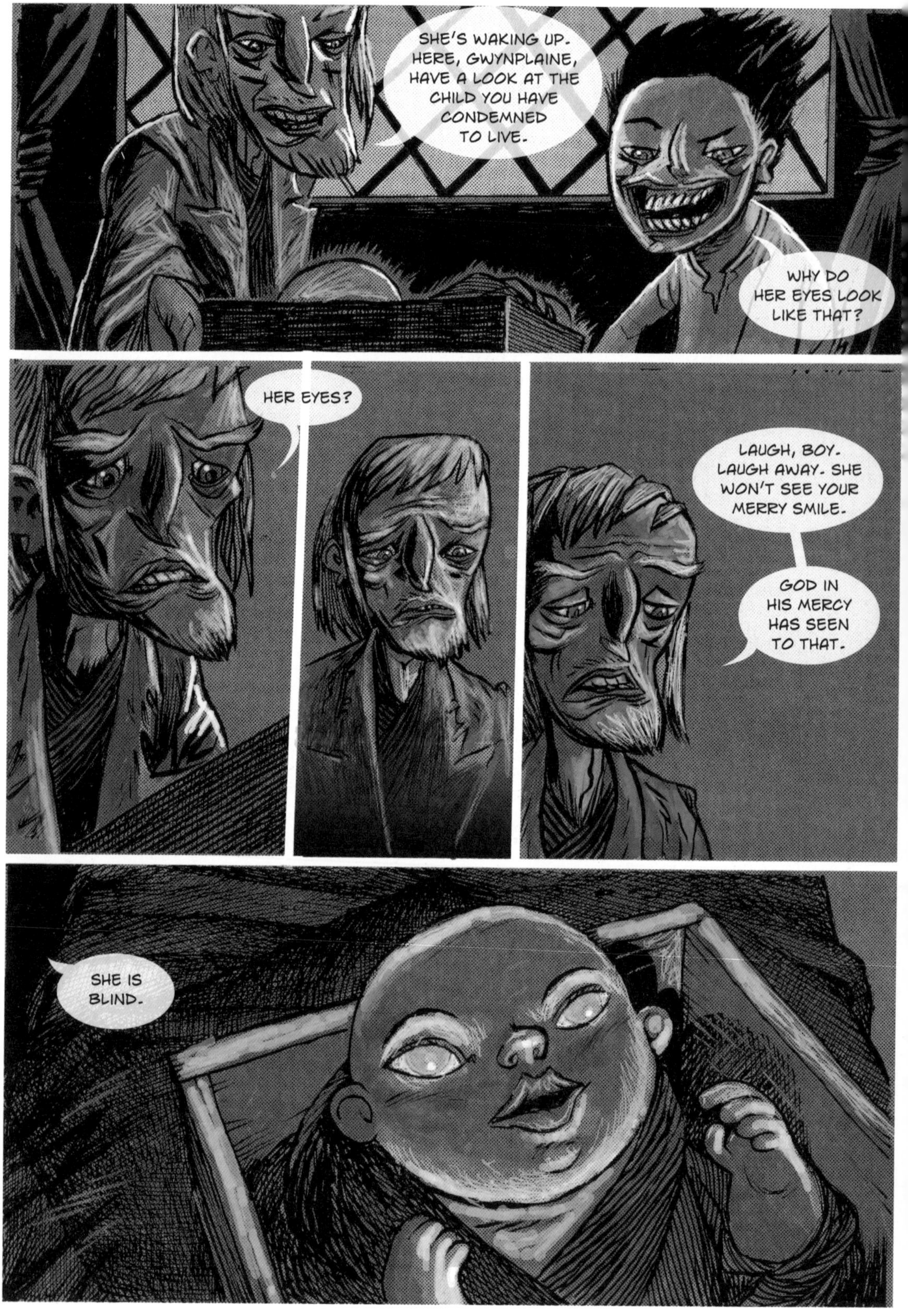
SHE'S WAKING UP. HERE, GWYNPLAINE, HAVE A LOOK AT THE CHILD YOU HAVE CONDEMNED TO LIVE.
WHY DO HER EYES LOOK LIKE THAT?
HER EYES?
LAUGH, BOY. LAUGH AWAY. SHE WON'T SEE YOUR MERRY SMILE.
GOD IN HIS MERCY HAS SEEN TO THAT.
SHE IS BLIND.

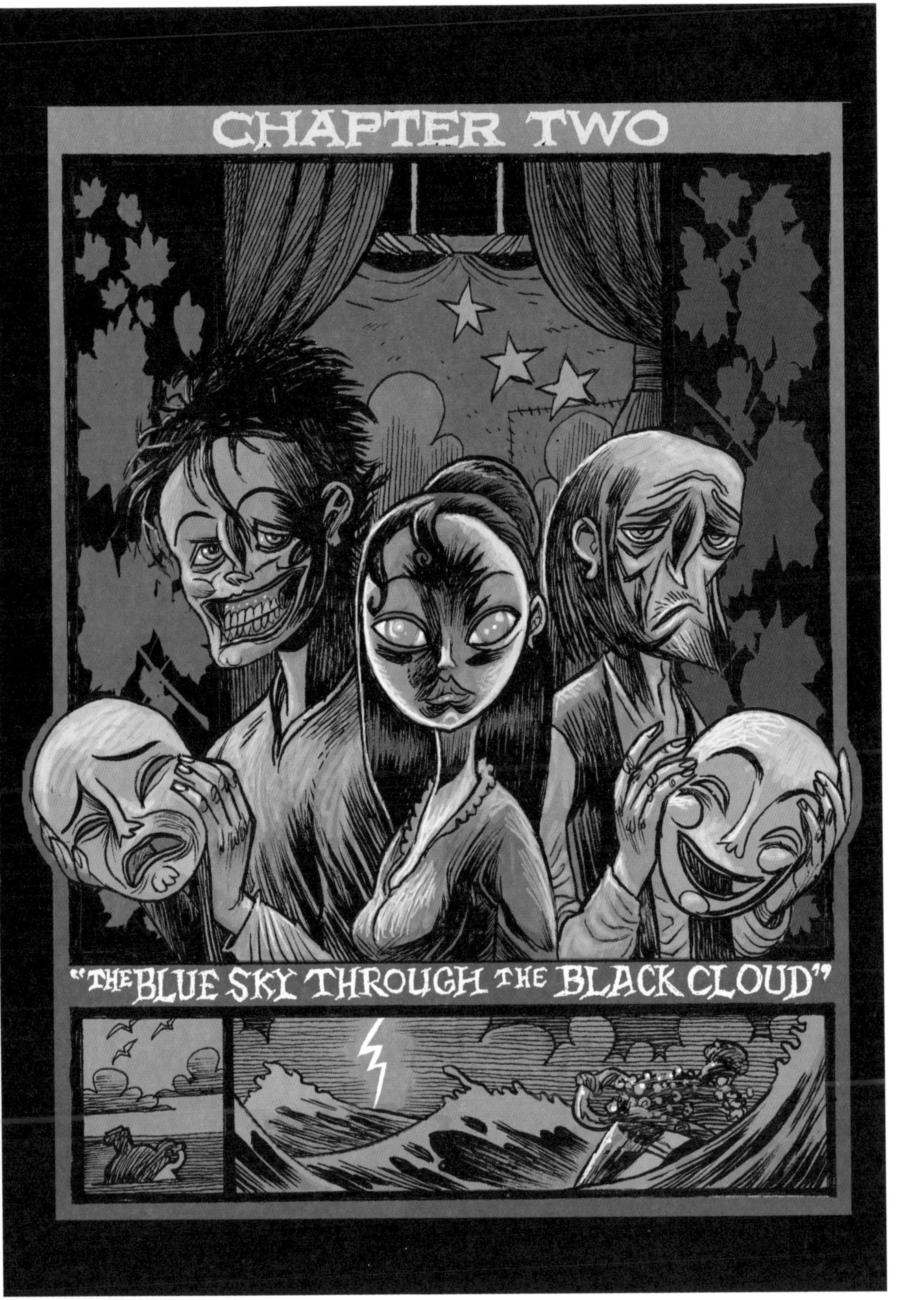
CHAPTER TWO
"THE BLUE SKY THROUGH THE BLACK CLOUD"

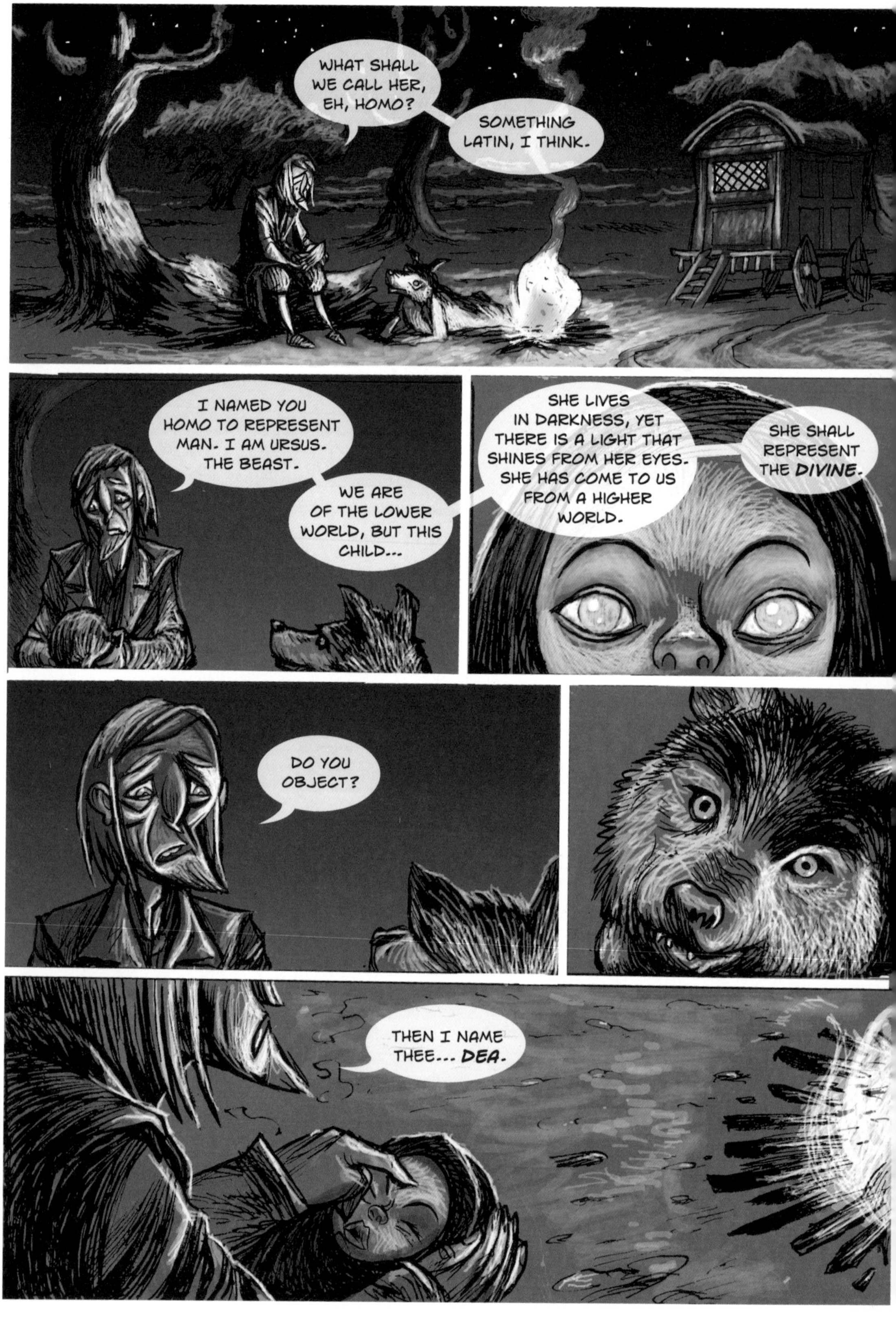
WHAT SHALL WE CALL HER, EH, HOMO?
SOMETHING LATIN, I THINK.
I NAMED YOU HOMO TO REPRESENT MAN. I AM URSUS. THE BEAST.
WE ARE OF THE LOWER WORLD, BUT THIS CHILD...
SHE LIVES IN DARKNESS, YET THERE IS A LIGHT THAT SHINES FROM HER EYES. SHE HAS COME TO US FROM A HIGHER WORLD.
SHE SHALL REPRESENT THE DIVINE.
DO YOU OBJECT?
THEN I NAME THEE... DEA.

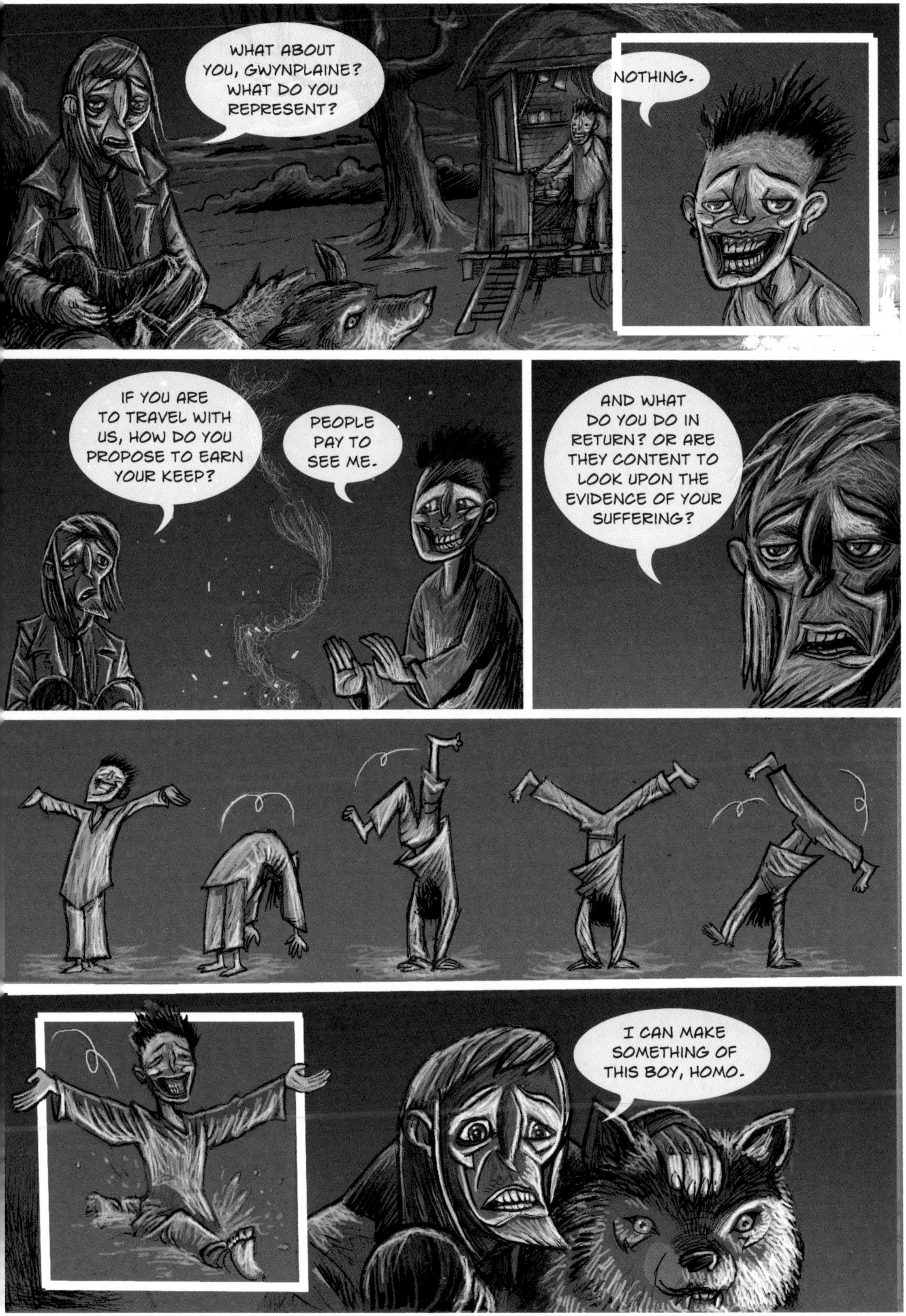
WHAT ABOUT YOU, GWYNPLAINE? WHAT DO YOU REPRESENT?
NOTHING.
IF YOU ARE TO TRAVEL WITH US, HOW DO YOU PROPOSE TO EARN YOUR KEEP?
PEOPLE PAY TO SEE ME.
AND WHAT DO YOU DO IN RETURN? OR ARE THEY CONTENT TO LOOK UPON THE EVIDENCE OF YOUR SUFFERING?
I CAN MAKE SOMETHING OF THIS BOY, HOMO.

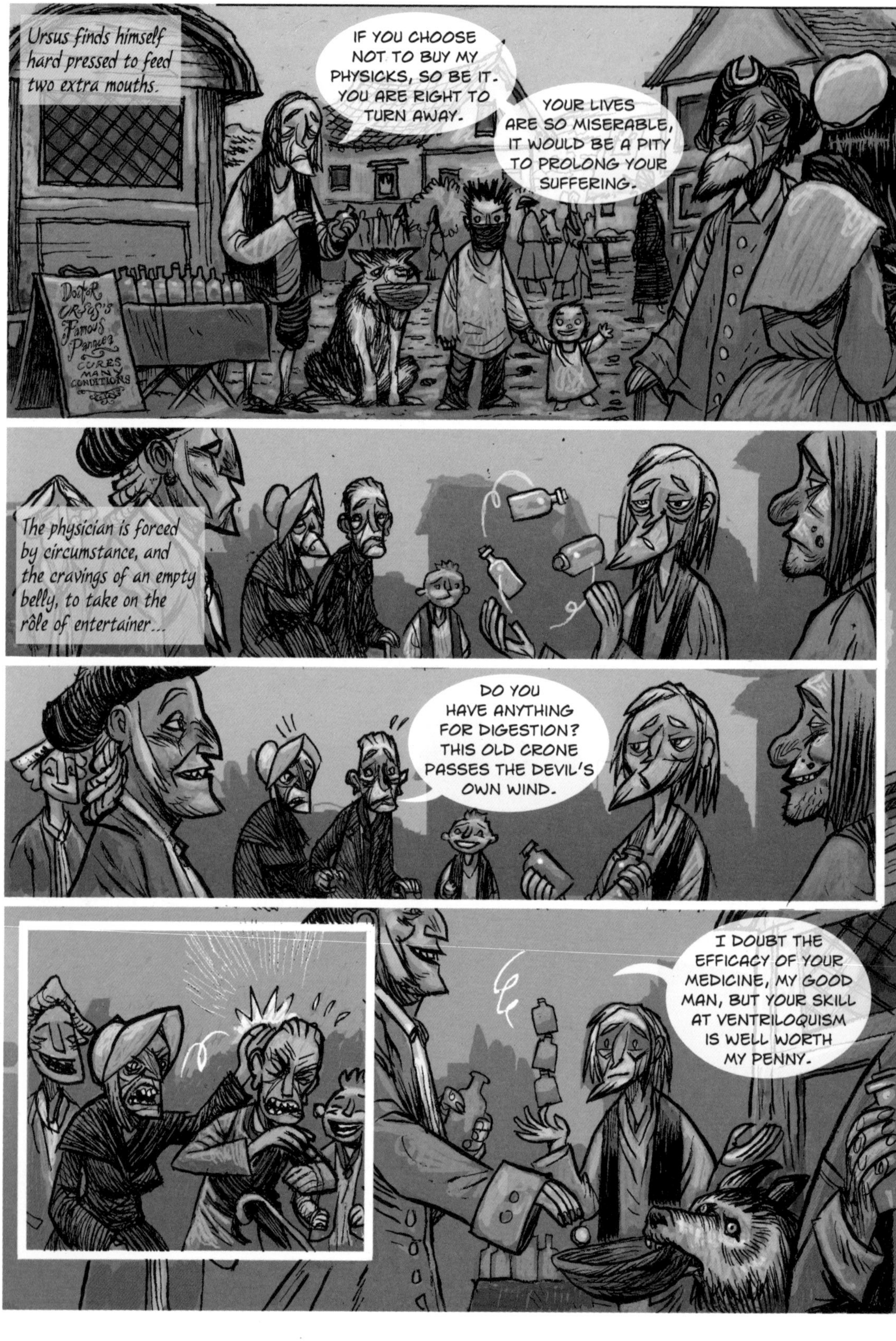
Ursus finds himself hard pressed to feed two extra mouths.
IF YOU CHOOSE NOT TO BUY MY PHYSICKS, SO BE IT. YOU ARE RIGHT TO TURN AWAY.
YOUR LIVES ARE SO MISERABLE, IT WOULD BE A PITY TO PROLONG YOUR SUFFERING.
CURES MANY CONDITIONS
The physician is forced by circumstance, and the cravings of an empty belly, to take on the rôle of entertainer...
DO YOU HAVE ANYTHING FOR DIGESTION? THIS OLD CRONE PASSES THE DEVIL'S OWN WIND.
I DOUBT THE EFFICACY OF YOUR MEDICINE, MY GOOD MAN, BUT YOUR SKILL AT VENTRILOQUISM IS WELL WORTH MY PENNY.

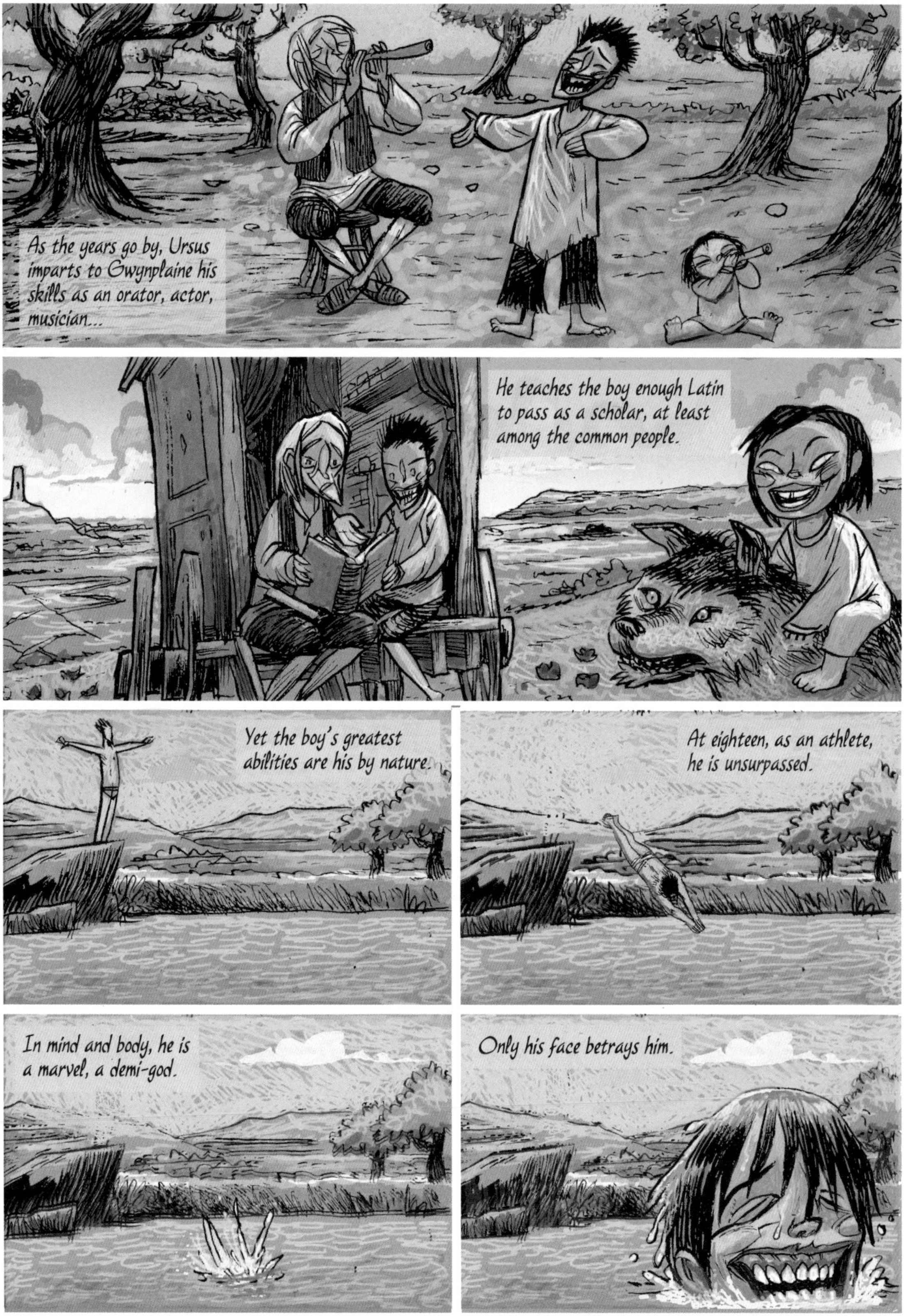
As the years go by, Ursus imparts to Gwynplaine his skills as an orator, actor, musician...
He teaches the boy enough Latin to pass as a scholar, at least among the common people.
Yet the boy's greatest abilities are his by nature.
At eighteen, as an athlete, he is unsurpassed.
In mind and body, he is a marvel, a demi-god.
Only his face betrays him.

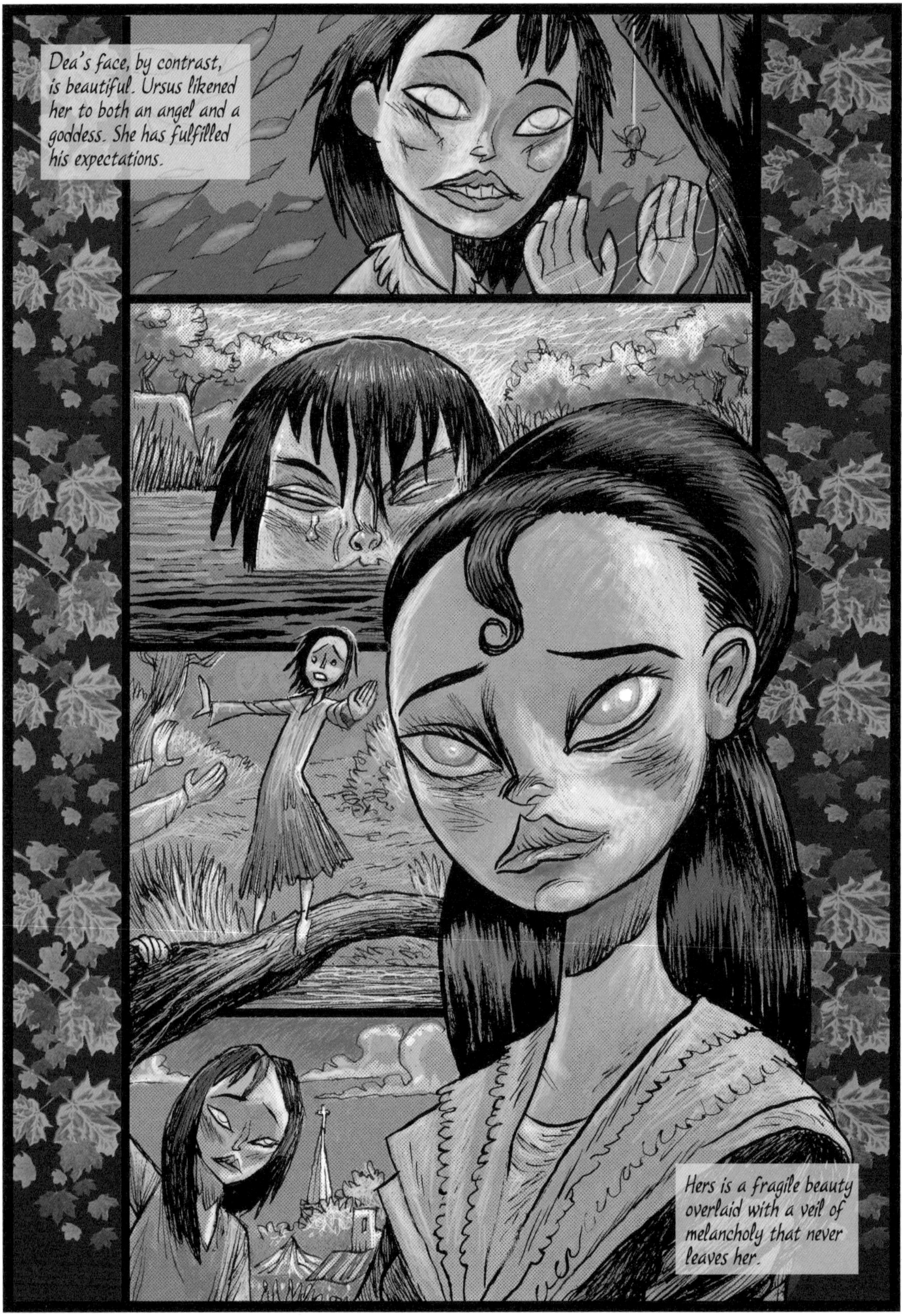
Dea's face, by contrast, is beautiful. Ursus likened her to both an angel and a goddess. She has fulfilled his expectations.
Hers is a fragile beauty overlaid with a veil of melancholy that never leaves her.

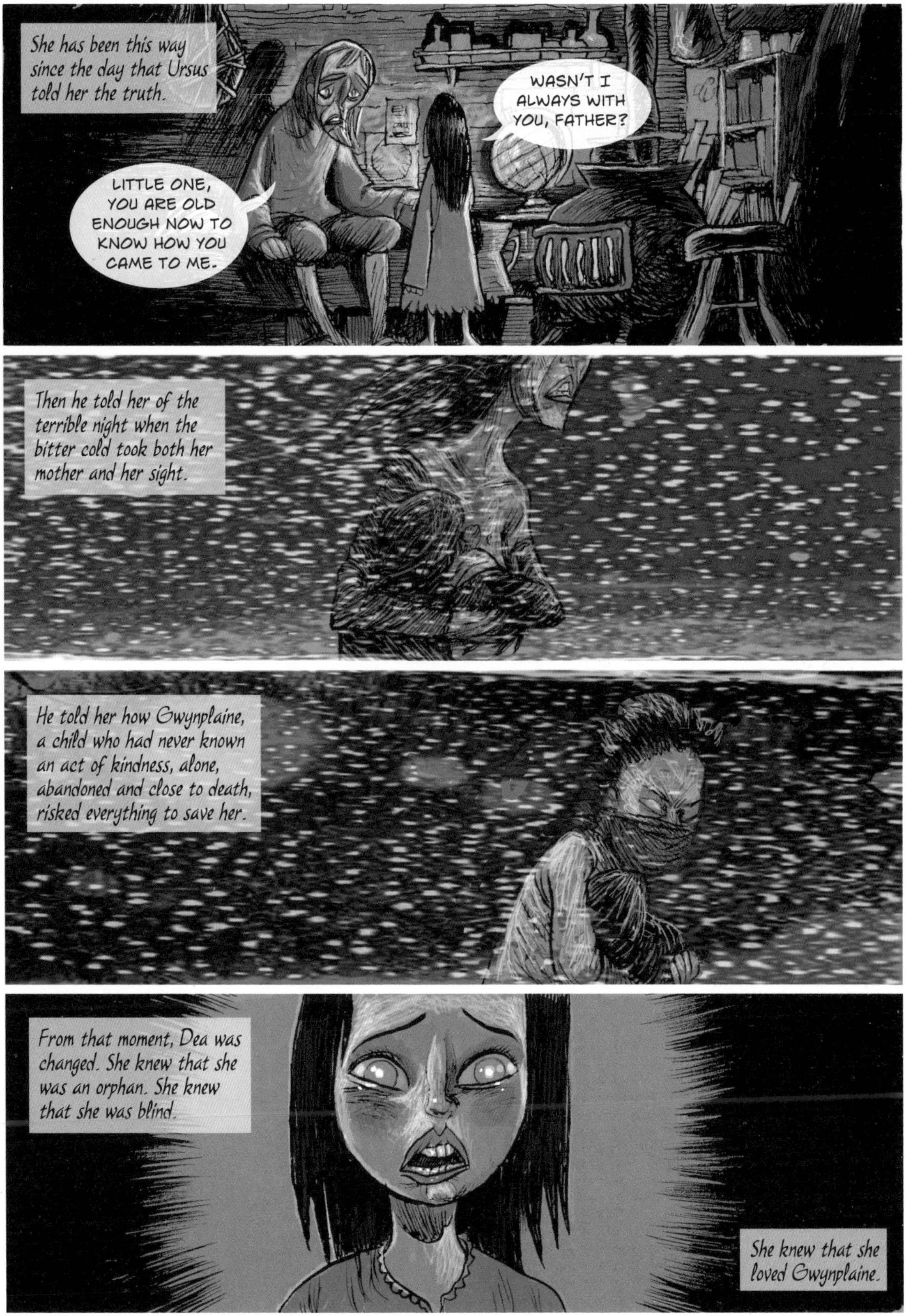
She has been this way since the day that Ursus told her the truth.
LITTLE ONE, YOU ARE OLD ENOUGH NOW TO KNOW HOW YOU CAME TO ME.
WASN'T I ALWAYS WITH YOU, FATHER?
Then he told her of the terrible night when the bitter cold took both her mother and her sight.
He told her how Gwynplaine, a child who had never known an act of kindness, alone, abandoned and close to death, risked everything to save her.
From that moment, Dea was changed. She knew that she was an orphan. She knew that she was blind.
She knew that she loved Gwynplaine.

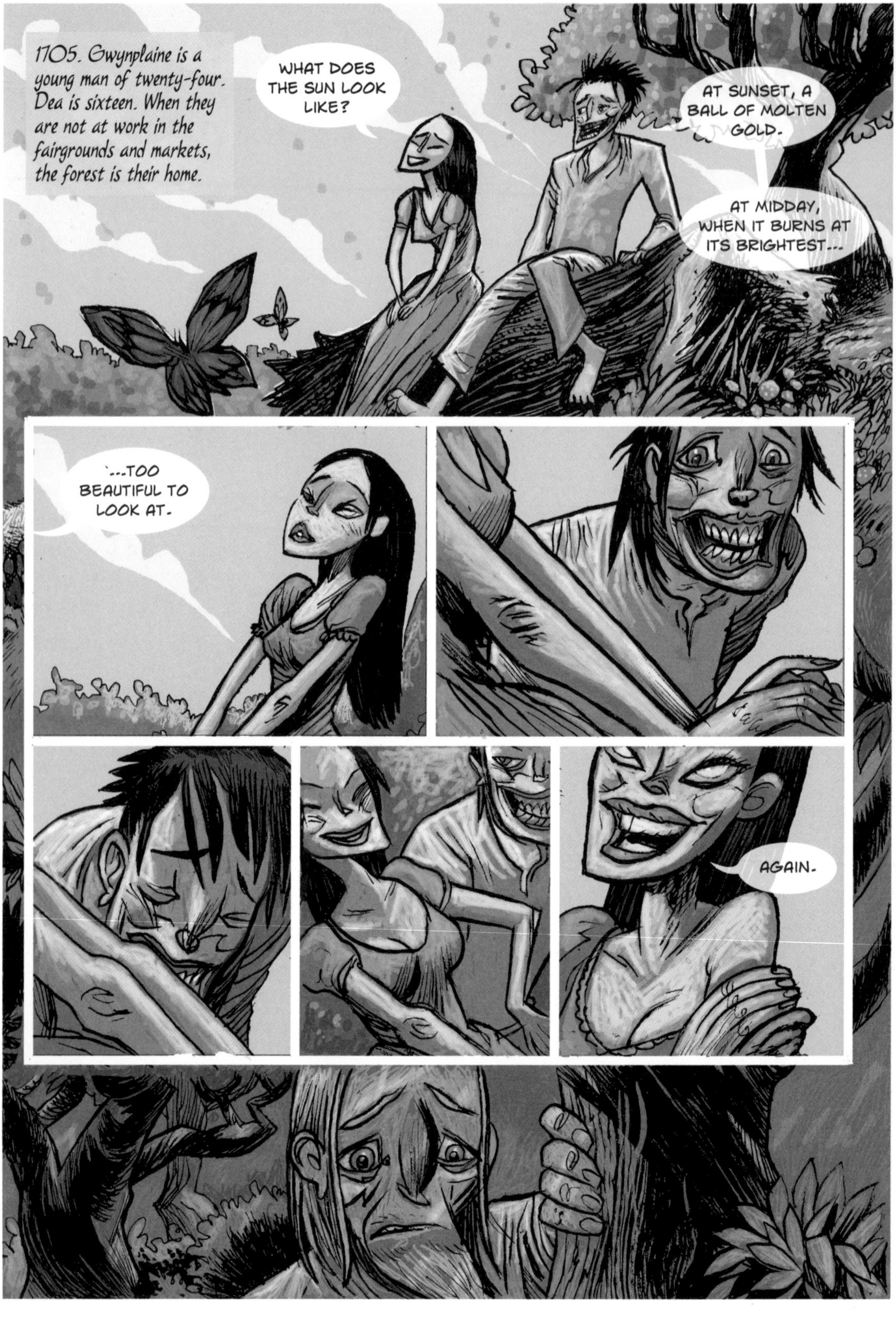
1705. Gwynplaine is a young man of twenty-four. Dea is sixteen. When they are not at work in the fairgrounds and markets, the forest is their home.
WHAT DOES THE SUN LOOK LIKE?
AT SUNSET, A BALL OF MOLTEN GOLD.
AT MIDDAY, WHEN IT BURNS AT ITS BRIGHTEST...
...TOO BEAUTIFUL TO LOOK AT.
AGAIN.

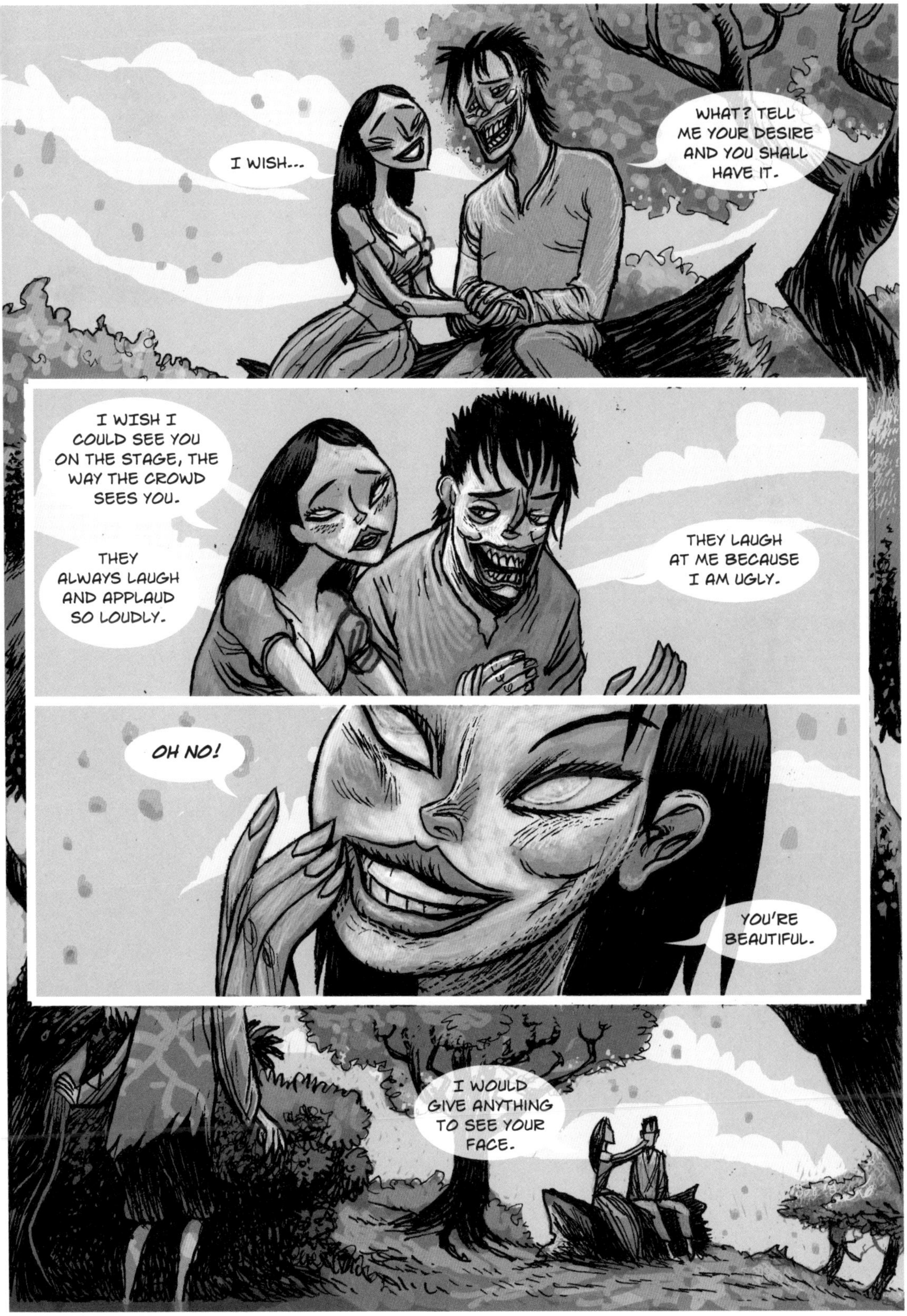
I WISH...
WHAT? TELL ME YOUR DESIRE AND YOU SHALL HAVE IT.
I WISH I COULD SEE YOU ON THE STAGE, THE WAY THE CROWD SEES YOU.
THEY ALWAYS LAUGH AND APPLAUD SO LOUDLY.
THEY LAUGH AT ME BECAUSE I AM UGLY.
OH NO!
YOU'RE BEAUTIFUL.
I WOULD GIVE ANYTHING TO SEE YOUR FACE.

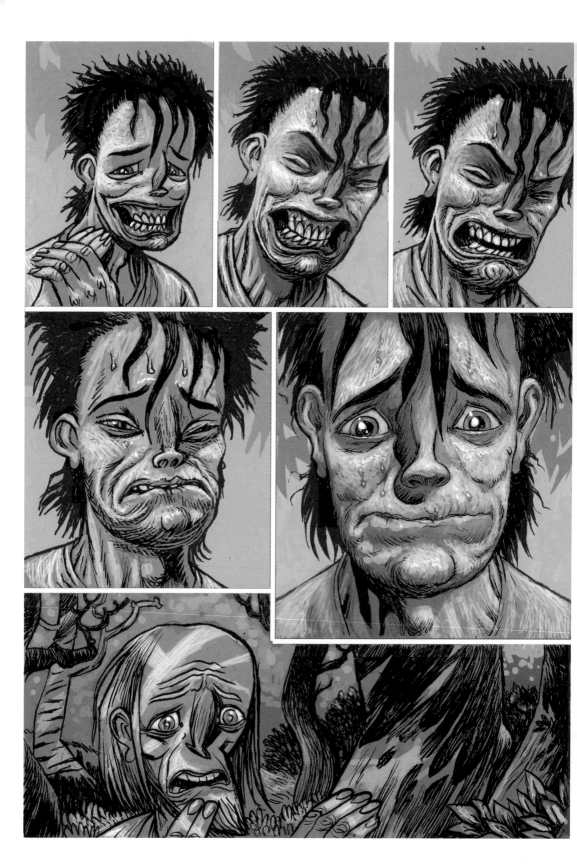

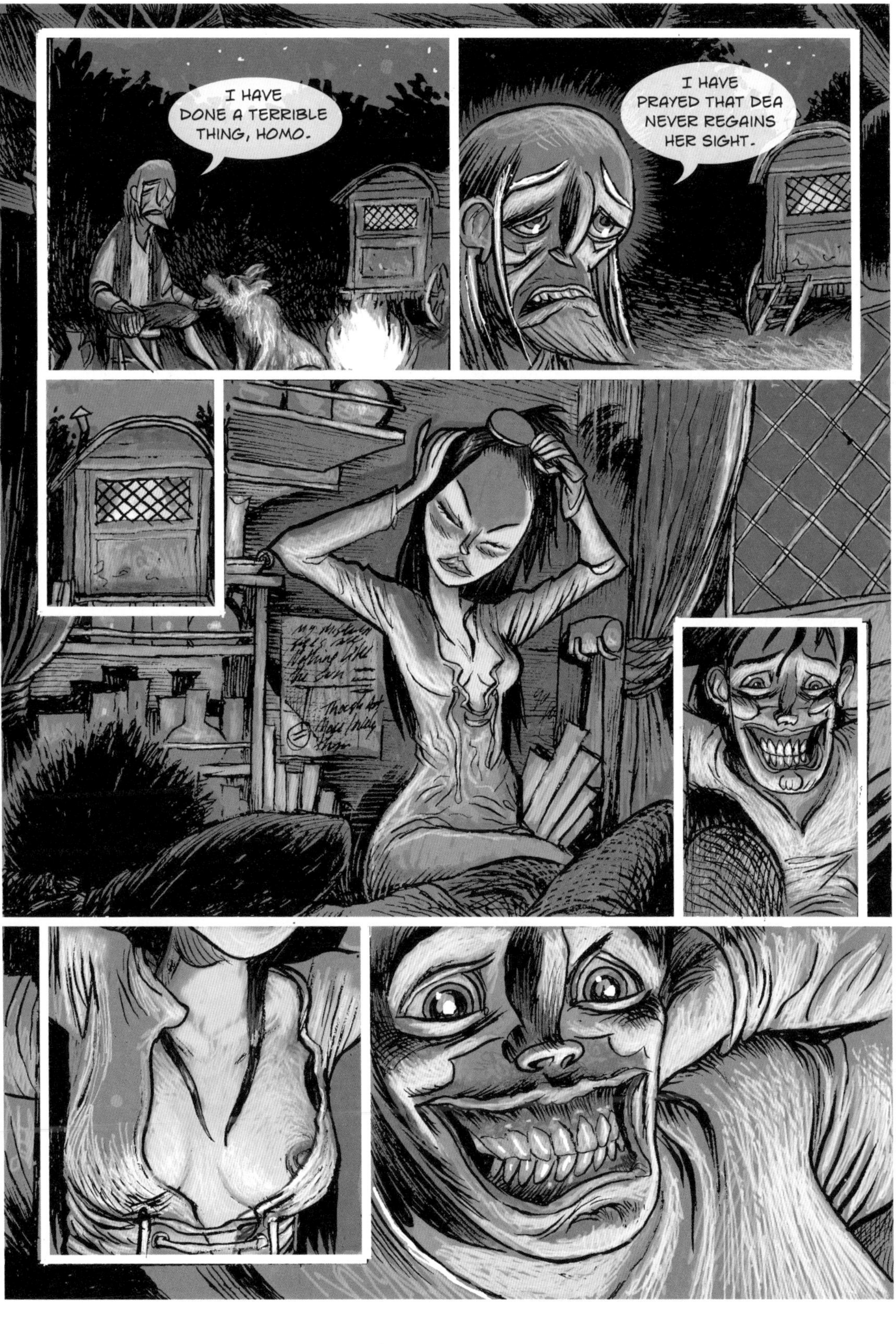
I HAVE DONE A TERRIBLE THING, HOMO.
I HAVE PRAYED THAT DEA NEVER REGAINS HER SIGHT.

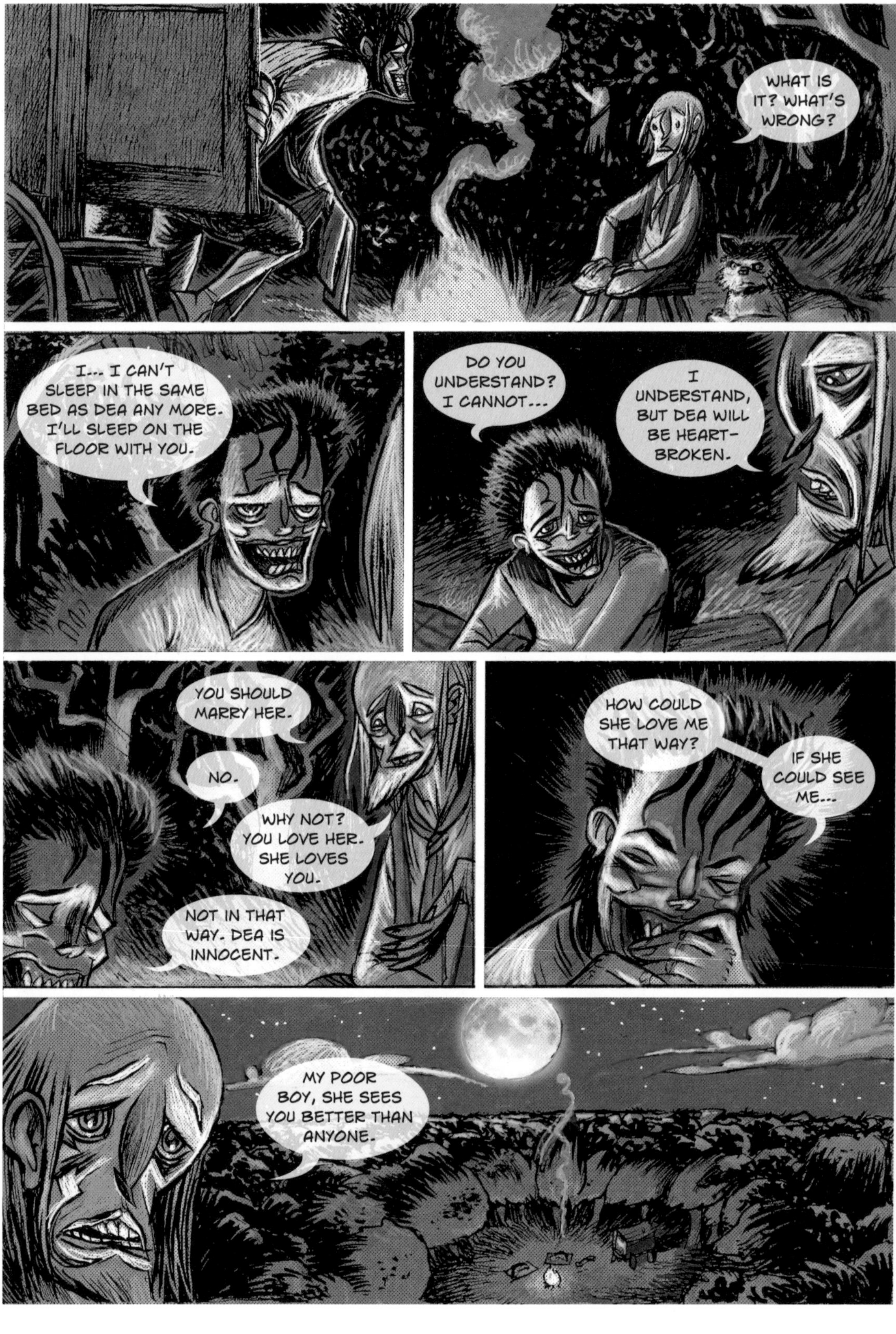
WHAT IS IT? WHAT'S WRONG?
I... I CAN'T SLEEP IN THE SAME BED AS DEA ANY MORE. I'LL SLEEP ON THE FLOOR WITH YOU.
DO YOU UNDERSTAND? I CANNOT...
I UNDERSTAND, BUT DEA WILL BE HEART-BROKEN.
YOU SHOULD MARRY HER.
NO.
WHY NOT? YOU LOVE HER. SHE LOVES YOU.
NOT IN THAT WAY. DEA IS INNOCENT.
HOW COULD SHE LOVE ME THAT WAY?
IF SHE COULD SEE ME...
MY POOR BOY, SHE SEES YOU BETTER THAN ANYONE.

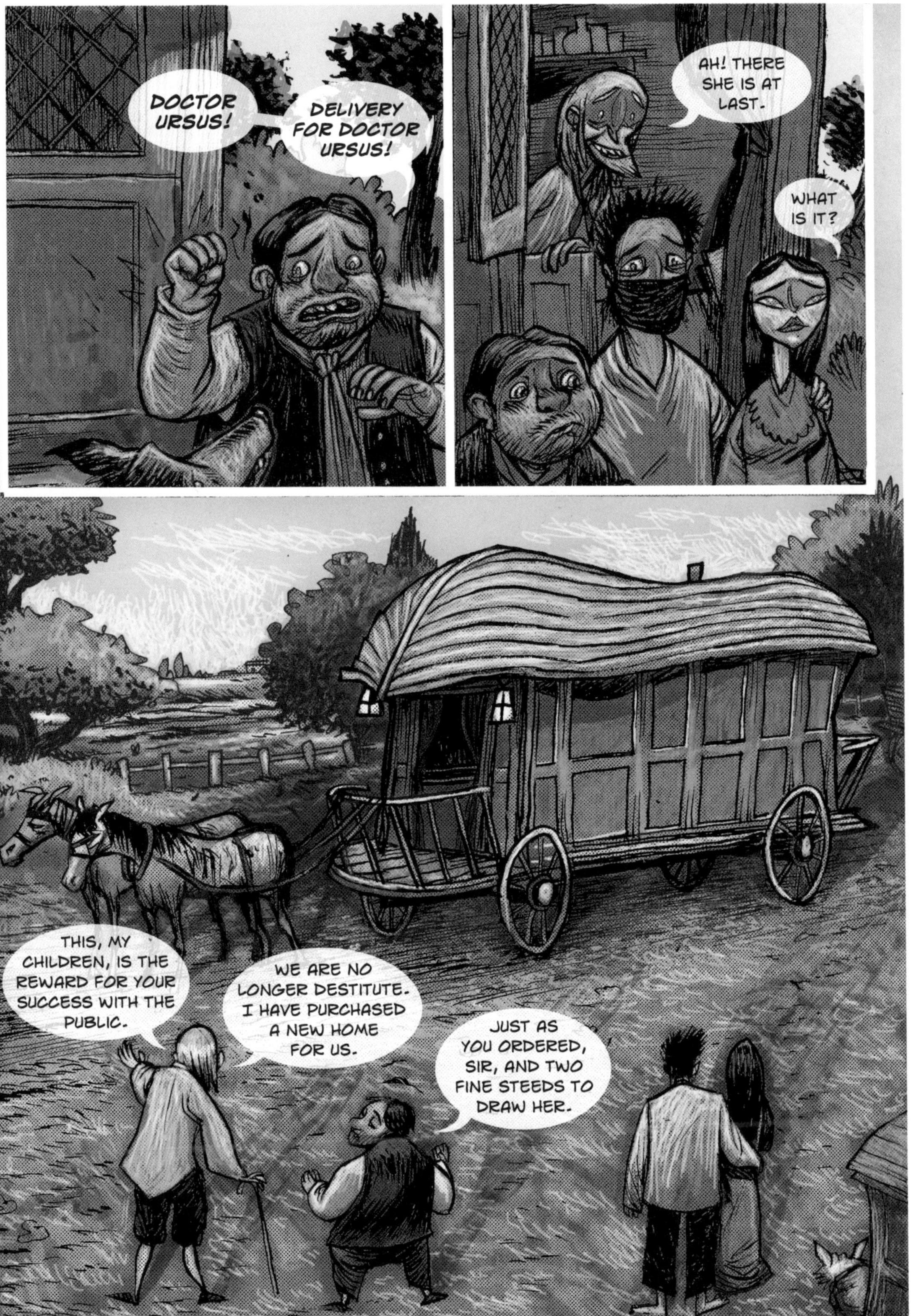
DOCTOR URSUS!
DELIVERY FOR DOCTOR URSUS!
AH! THERE SHE IS AT LAST.
WHAT IS IT?
THIS, MY CHILDREN, IS THE REWARD FOR YOUR SUCCESS WITH THE PUBLIC.
WE ARE NO LONGER DESTITUTE. I HAVE PURCHASED A NEW HOME FOR US.
JUST AS YOU ORDERED, SIR, AND TWO FINE STEEDS TO DRAW HER.

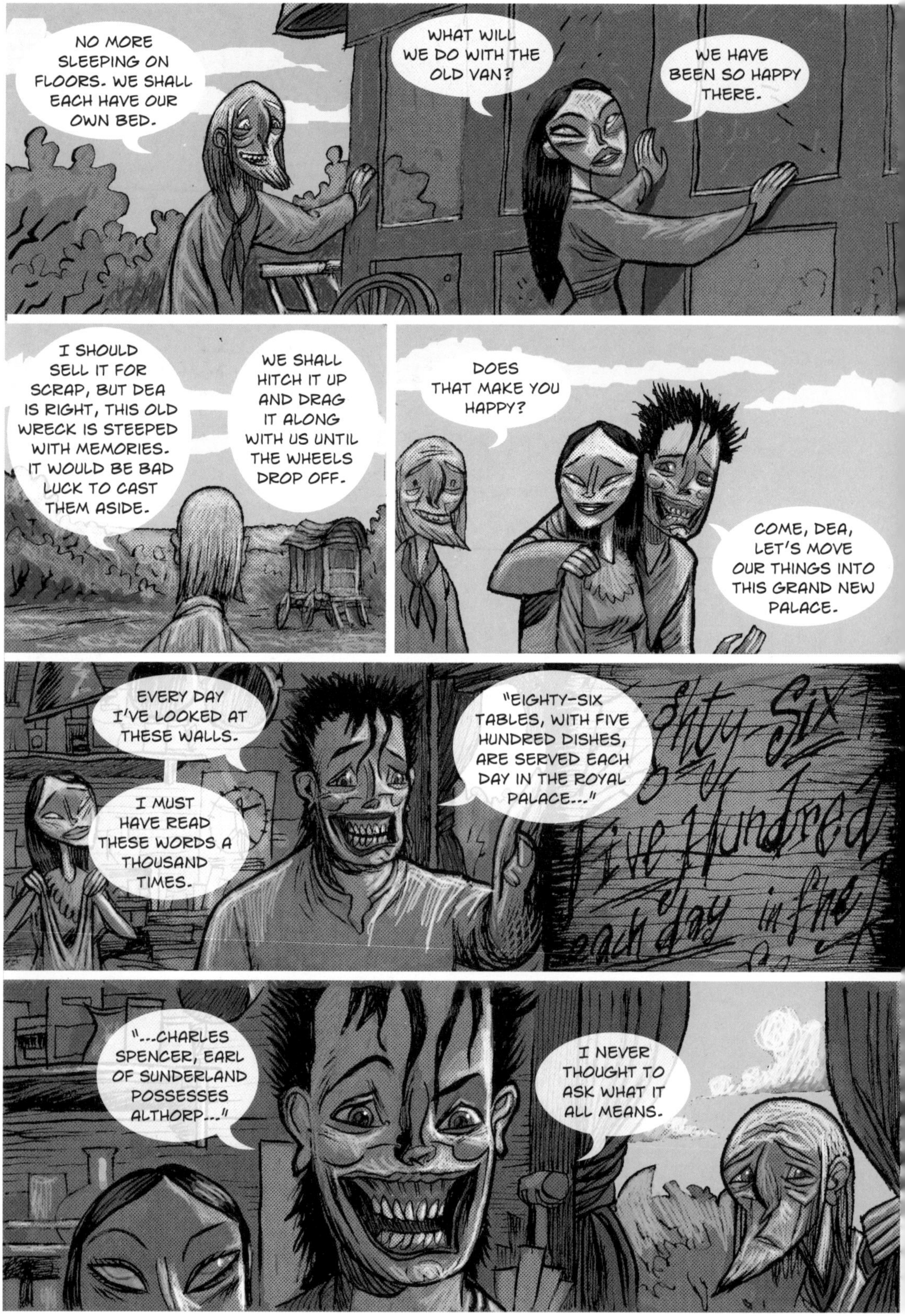
NO MORE SLEEPING ON FLOORS. WE SHALL EACH HAVE OUR OWN BED.
WHAT WILL WE DO WITH THE OLD VAN?
WE HAVE BEEN SO HAPPY THERE.
I SHOULD SELL IT FOR SCRAP, BUT DEA IS RIGHT, THIS OLD WRECK IS STEEPED WITH MEMORIES. IT WOULD BE BAD LUCK TO CAST THEM ASIDE.
WE SHALL HITCH IT UP AND DRAG IT ALONG WITH US UNTIL THE WHEELS DROP OFF.
DOES THAT MAKE YOU HAPPY?
COME, DEA, LET'S MOVE OUR THINGS INTO THIS GRAND NEW PALACE.
EVERY DAY I'VE LOOKED AT THESE WALLS.
I MUST HAVE READ THESE WORDS A THOUSAND TIMES.
"EIGHTY-SIX TABLES, WITH FIVE HUNDRED DISHES, ARE SERVED EACH DAY IN THE ROYAL PALACE..."
"...CHARLES SPENCER, EARL OF SUNDERLAND POSSESSES ALTHORP..."
I NEVER THOUGHT TO ASK WHAT IT ALL MEANS.

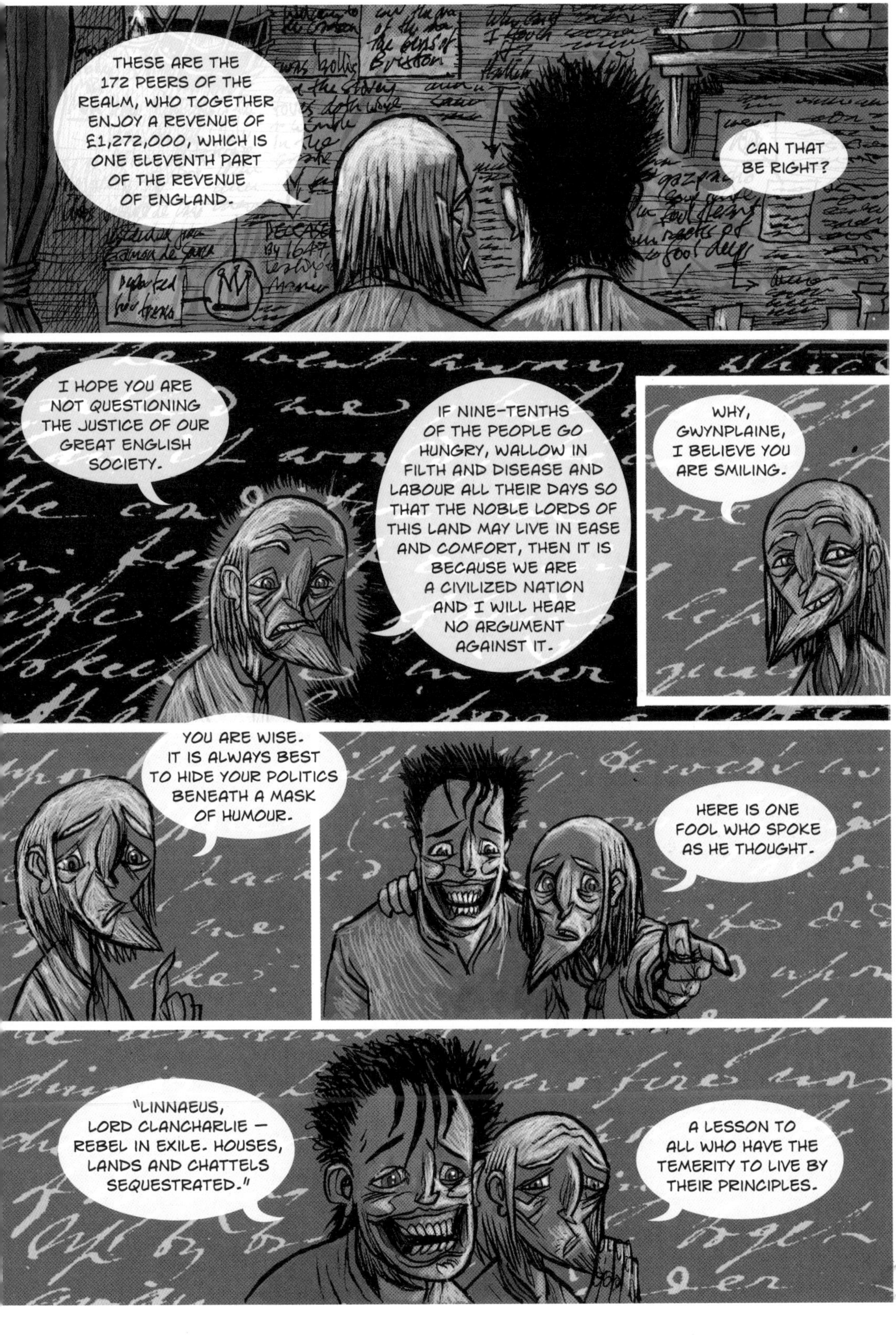
THESE ARE THE 172 PEERS OF THE REALM, WHO TOGETHER ENJOY A REVENUE OF £1,272,000, WHICH IS ONE ELEVENTH PART OF THE REVENUE OF ENGLAND.
CAN THAT BE RIGHT?
I HOPE YOU ARE NOT QUESTIONING THE JUSTICE OF OUR GREAT ENGLISH SOCIETY.
IF NINE-TENTHS OF THE PEOPLE GO HUNGRY, WALLOW IN FILTH AND DISEASE AND LABOUR ALL THEIR DAYS SO THAT THE NOBLE LORDS OF THIS LAND MAY LIVE IN EASE AND COMFORT, THEN IT IS BECAUSE WE ARE A CIVILIZED NATION AND I WILL HEAR NO ARGUMENT AGAINST IT.
WHY, GWYNPLAINE, I BELIEVE YOU ARE SMILING.
YOU ARE WISE. IT IS ALWAYS BEST TO HIDE YOUR POLITICS BENEATH A MASK OF HUMOUR.
HERE IS ONE FOOL WHO SPOKE AS HE THOUGHT.
"LINNAEUS, LORD CLANCHARLIE — REBEL IN EXILE. HOUSES, LANDS AND CHATTELS SEQUESTRATED."
A LESSON TO ALL WHO HAVE THE TEMERITY TO LIVE BY THEIR PRINCIPLES.

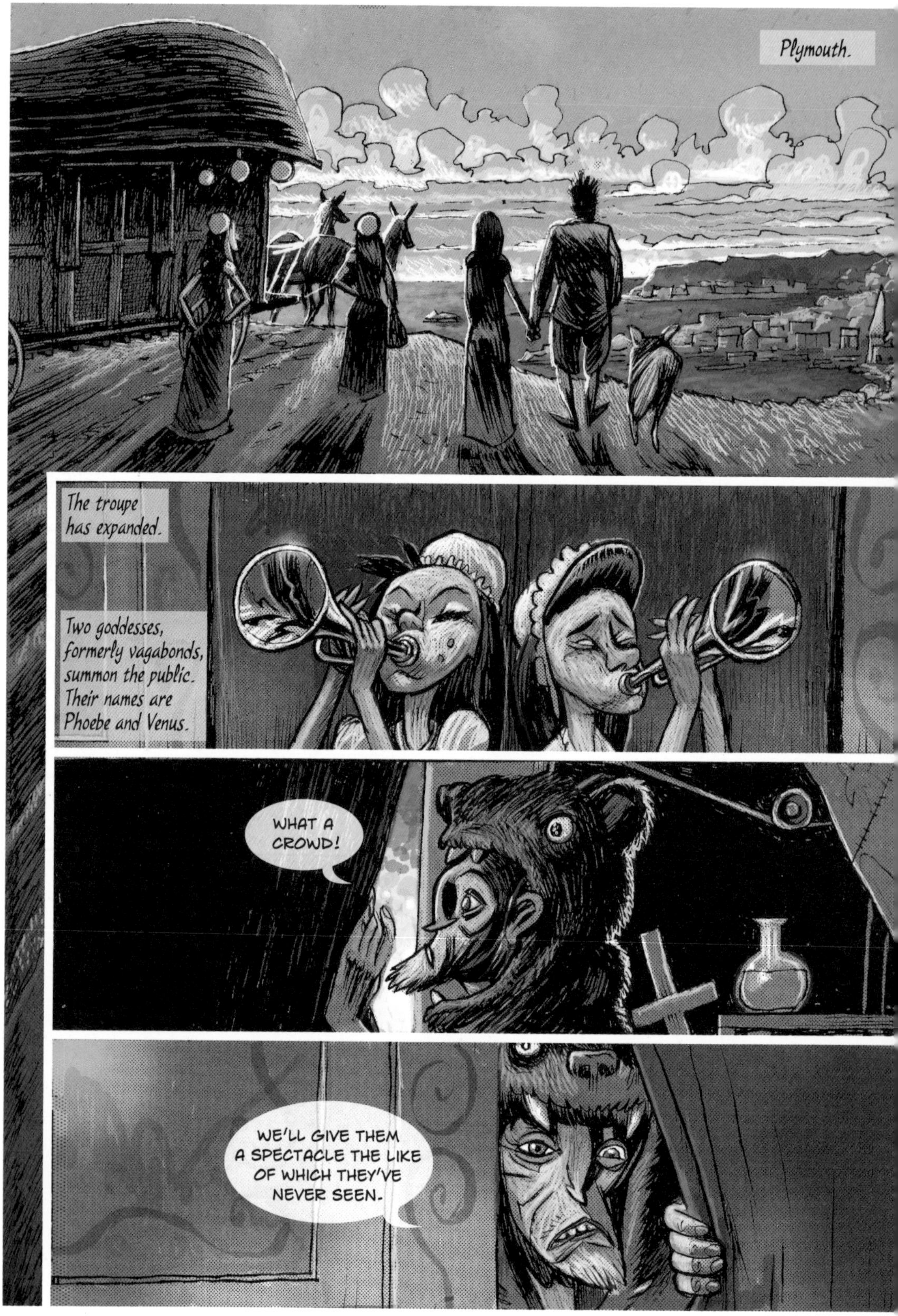
Plymouth.
The troupe has expanded.
Two goddesses, formerly vagabonds, summon the public. Their names are Phoebe and Venus.
WHAT A CROWD!
WE'LL GIVE THEM A SPECTACLE THE LIKE OF WHICH THEY'VE NEVER SEEN.

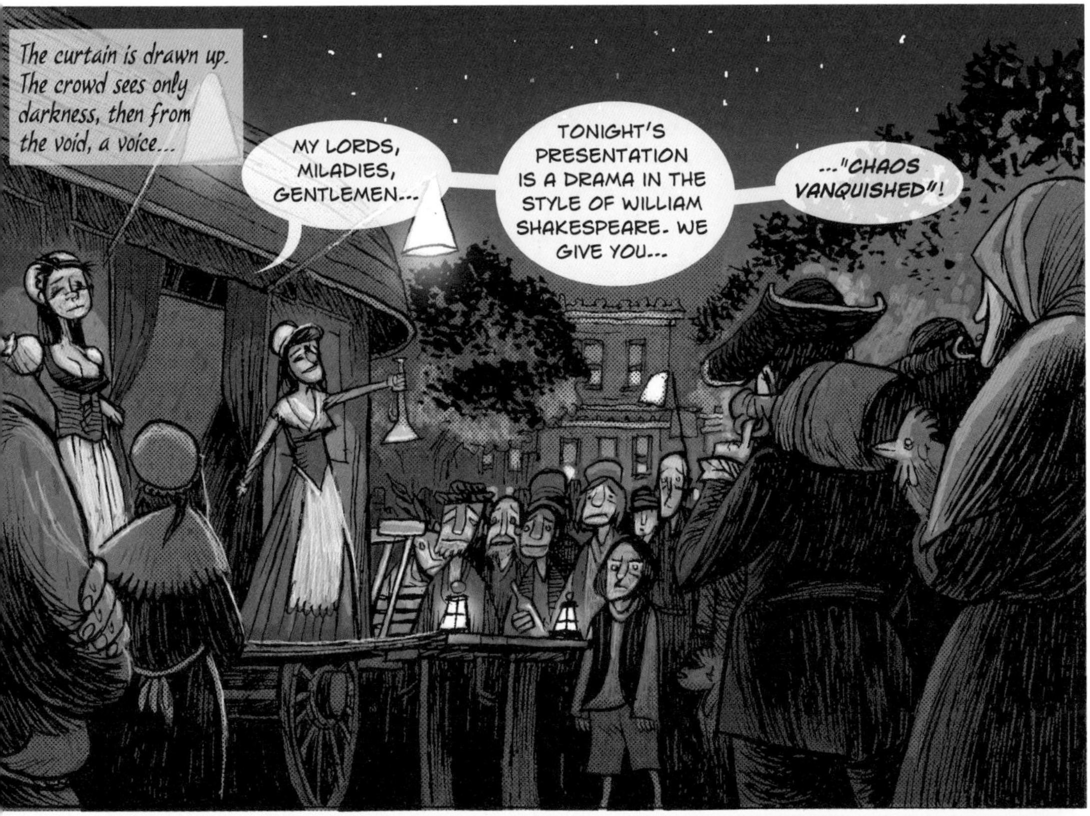
The curtain is drawn up. The crowd sees only darkness, then from the void, a voice...
MY LORDS, MILADIES, GENTLEMEN...
TONIGHT'S PRESENTATION IS A DRAMA IN THE STYLE OF WILLIAM SHAKESPEARE. WE GIVE YOU...
..."CHAOS VANQUISHED"!

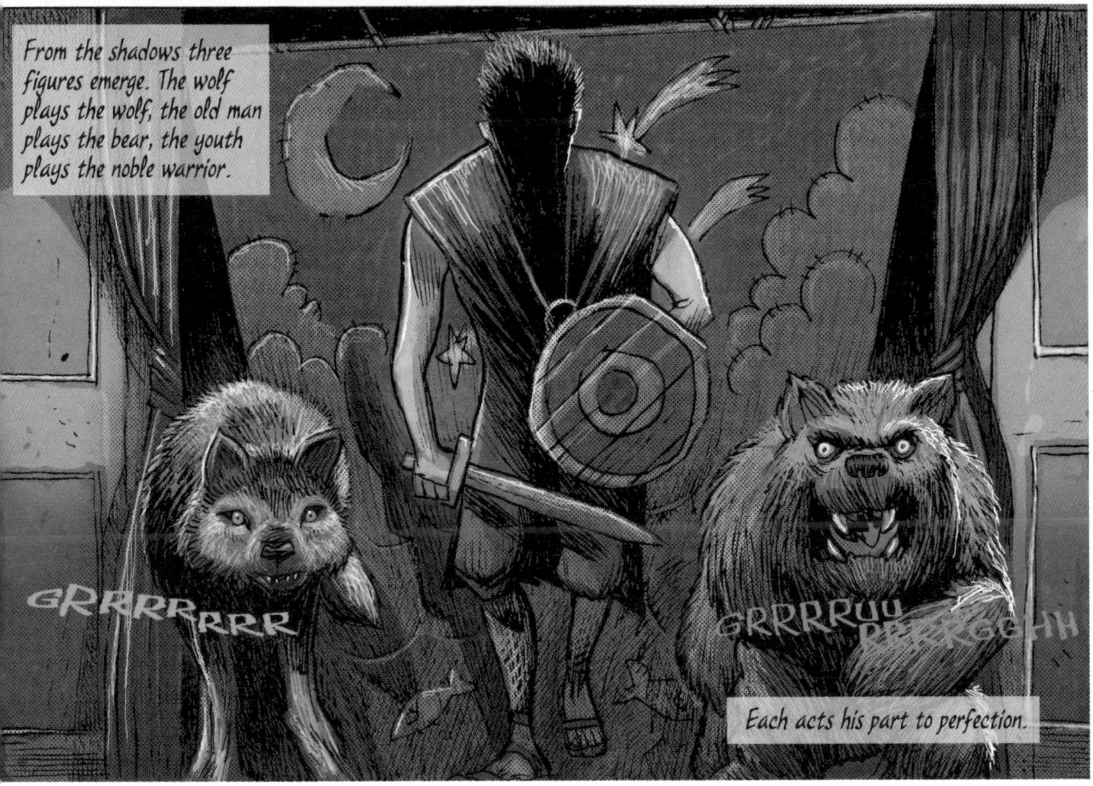
From the shadows three figures emerge. The wolf plays the wolf, the old man plays the bear, the youth plays the noble warrior.
GRRRRRRRR
GRRRRUU RRRRGGHH
Each acts his part to perfection.

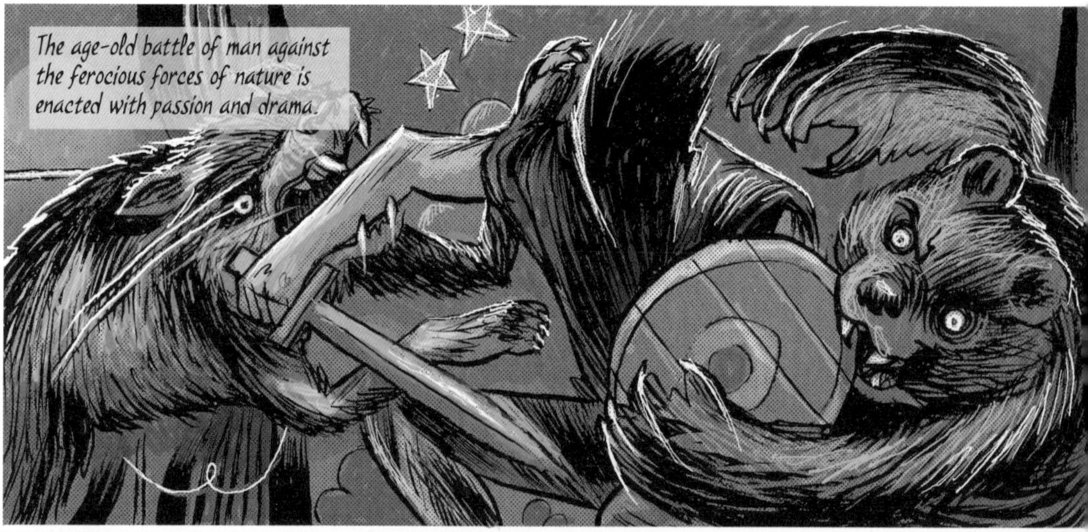
The age-old battle of man against the ferocious forces of nature is enacted with passion and drama.

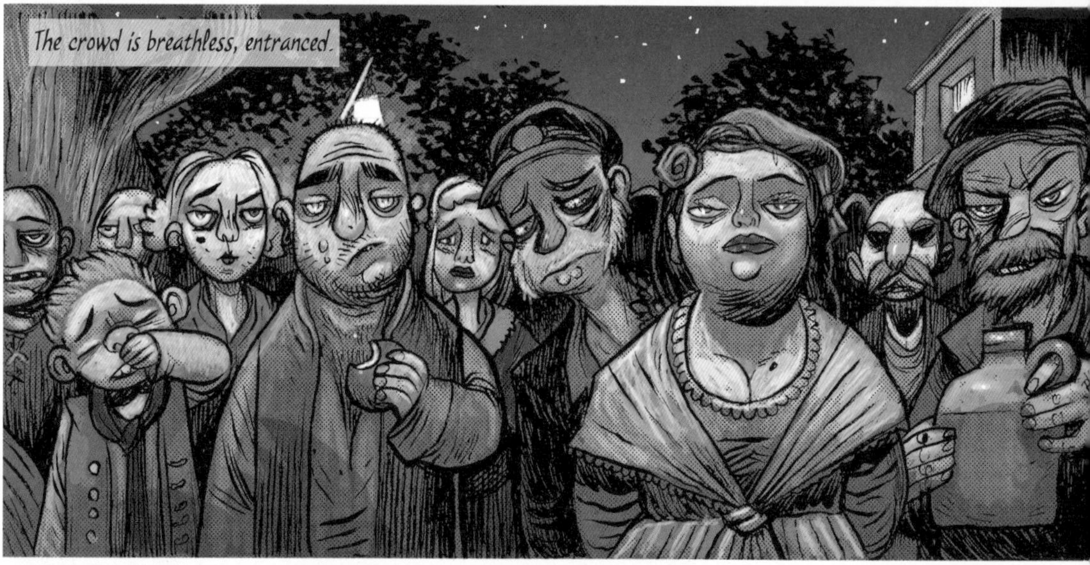
The crowd is breathless, entranced.

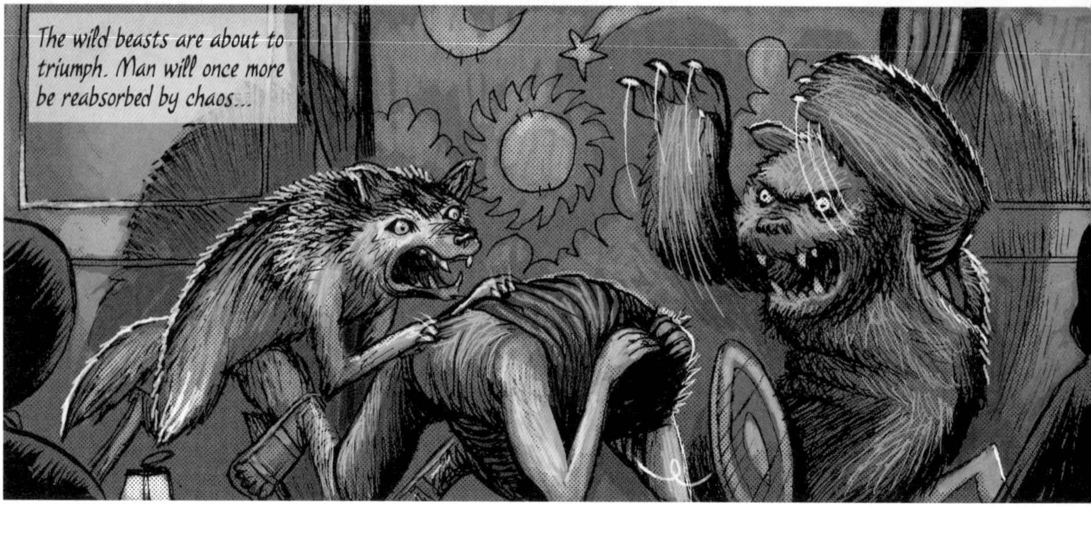
The wild beasts are about to triumph. Man will once more be reabsorbed by chaos...

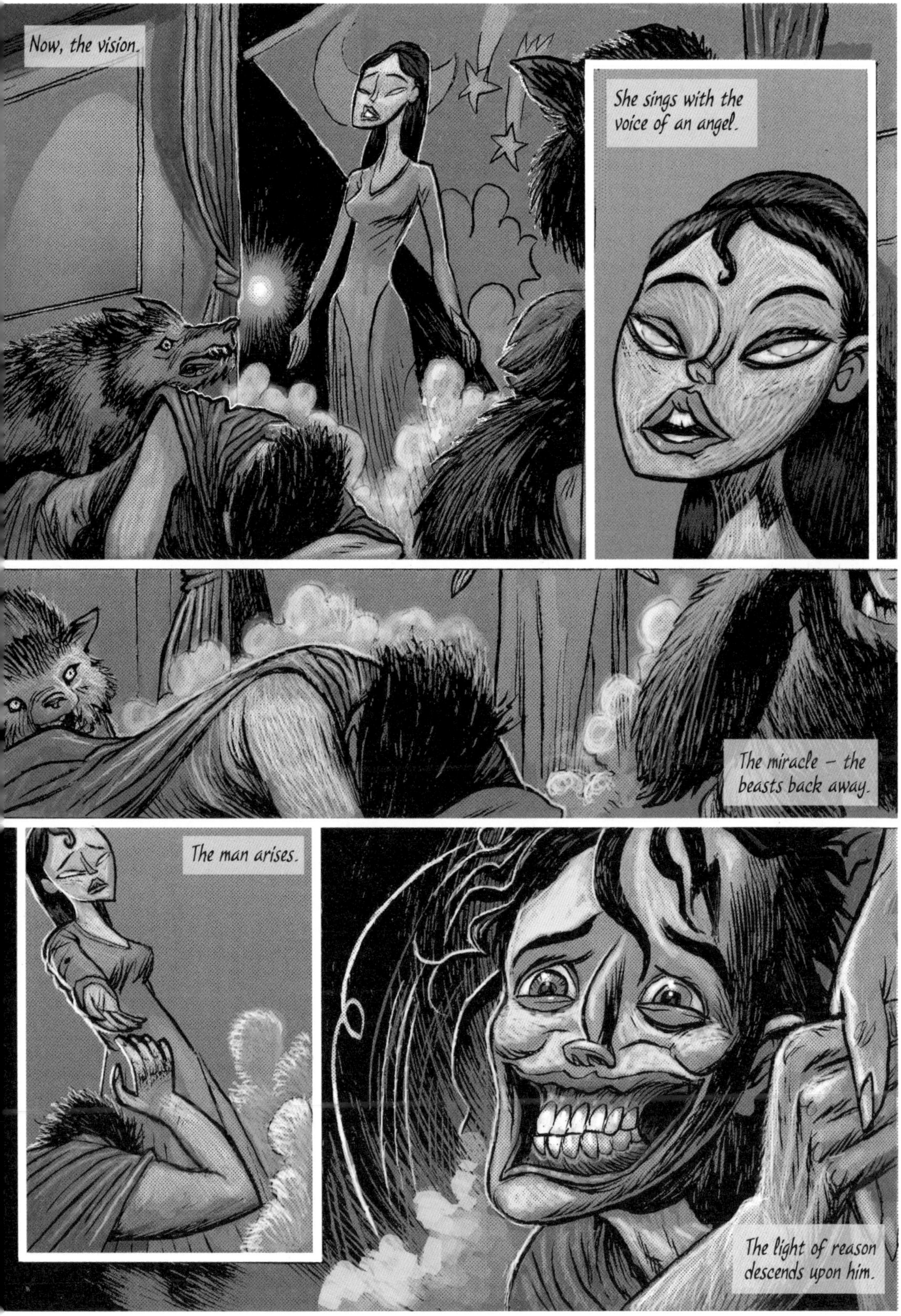
Now, the vision.
She sings with the voice of an angel.
The miracle – the beasts back away.
The man arises.
The light of reason descends upon him.

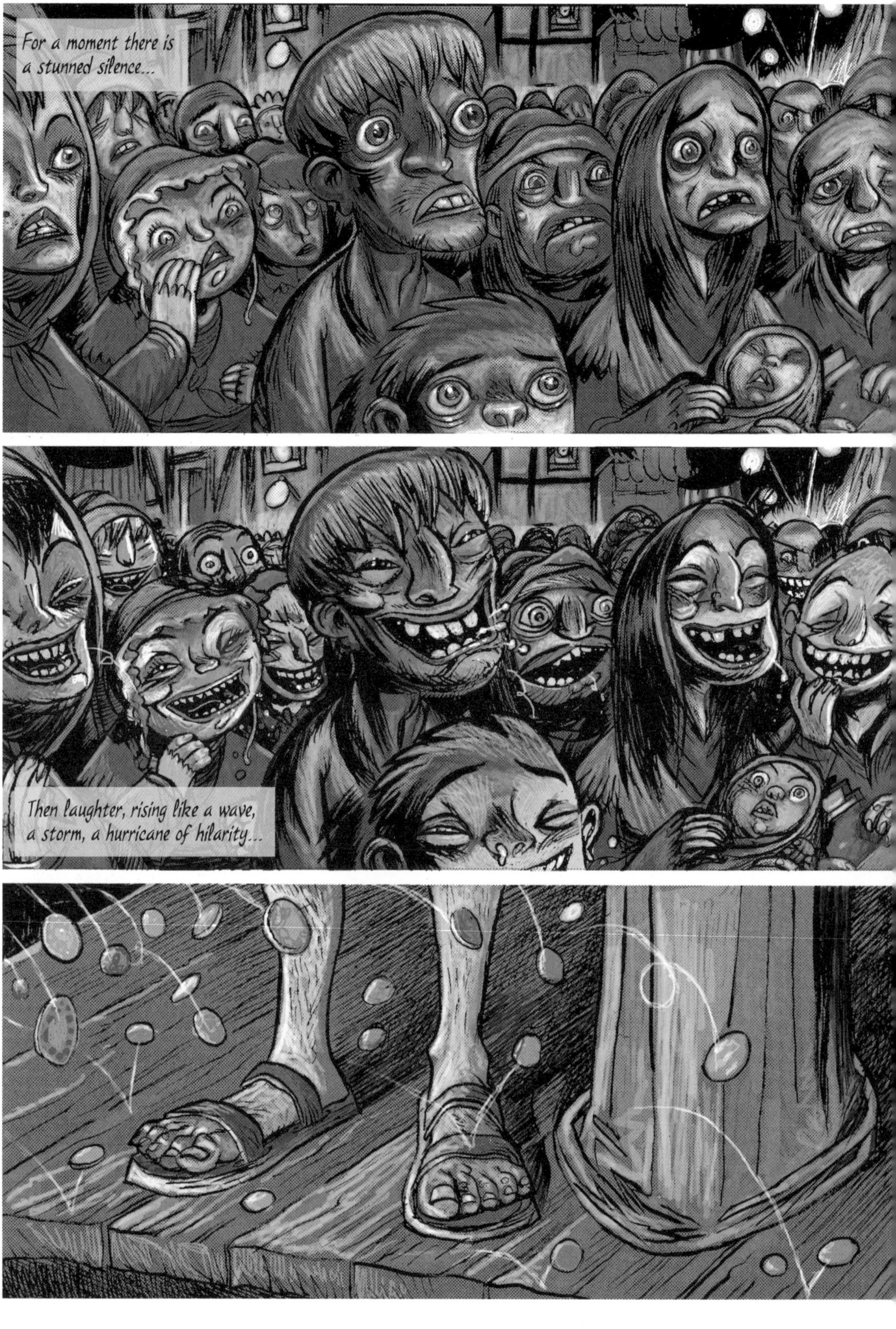
For a moment there is a stunned silence...
Then laughter, rising like a wave, a storm, a hurricane of hilarity...

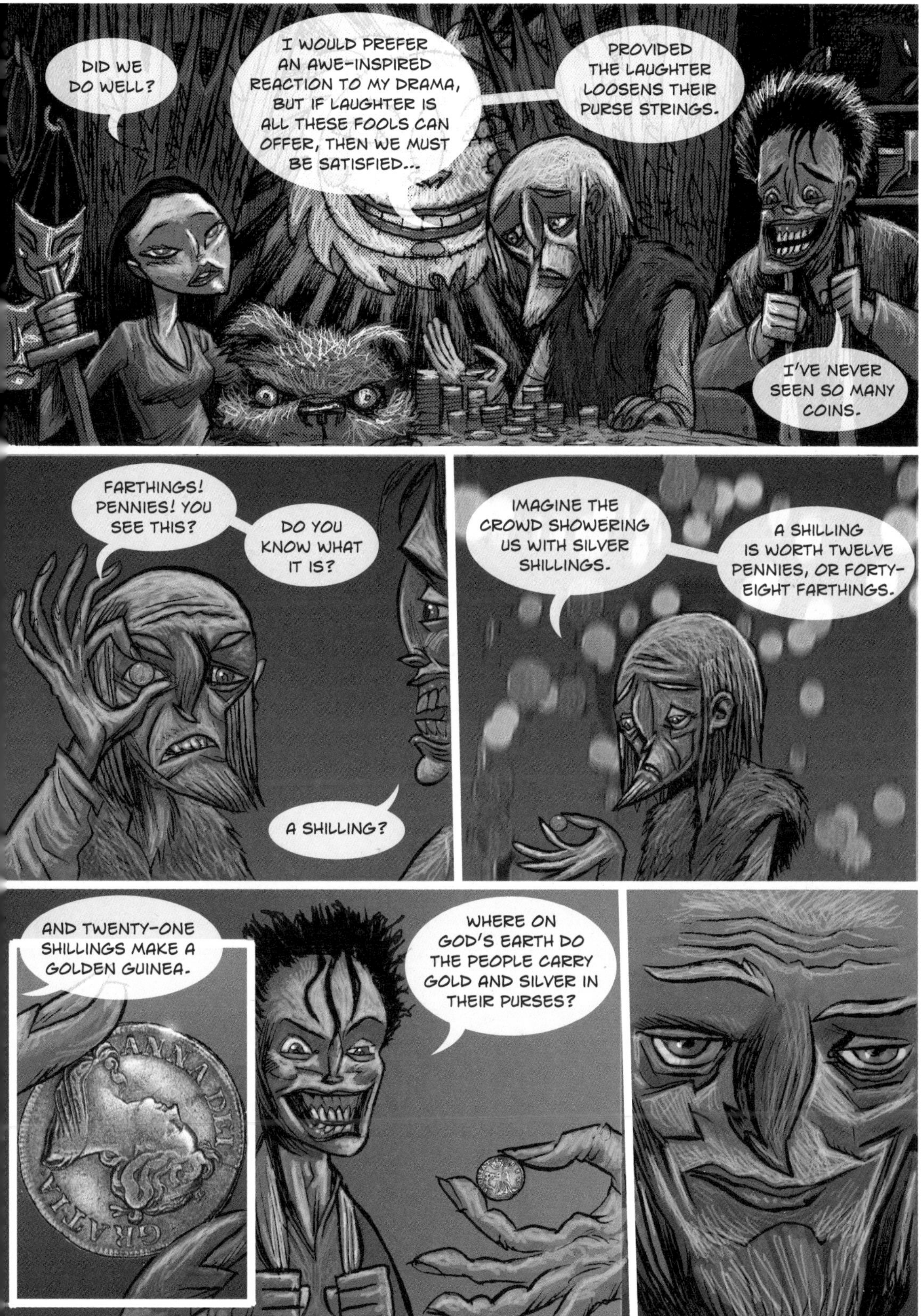
DID WE DO WELL?
I WOULD PREFER AN AWE-INSPIRED REACTION TO MY DRAMA, BUT IF LAUGHTER IS ALL THESE FOOLS CAN OFFER, THEN WE MUST BE SATISFIED...
PROVIDED THE LAUGHTER LOOSENS THEIR PURSE STRINGS.
I'VE NEVER SEEN SO MANY COINS.
FARTHINGS! PENNIES! YOU SEE THIS?
DO YOU KNOW WHAT IT IS?
A SHILLING?
IMAGINE THE CROWD SHOWERING US WITH SILVER SHILLINGS.
A SHILLING IS WORTH TWELVE PENNIES, OR FORTY-EIGHT FARTHINGS.
AND TWENTY-ONE SHILLINGS MAKE A GOLDEN GUINEA.
ANNA DEI GRATIA
WHERE ON GOD'S EARTH DO THE PEOPLE CARRY GOLD AND SILVER IN THEIR PURSES?

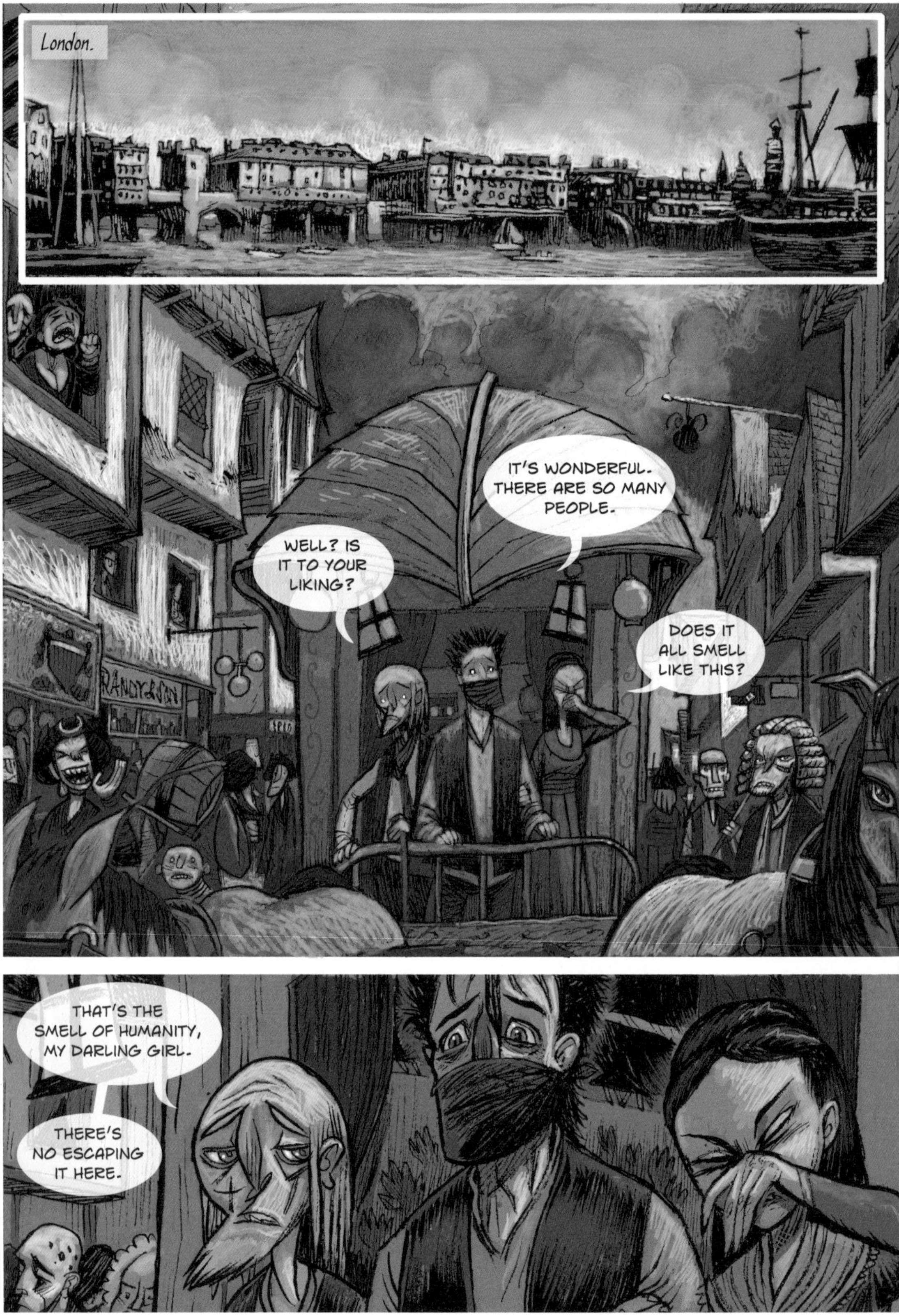
London.
WELL? IS IT TO YOUR LIKING?
IT'S WONDERFUL. THERE ARE SO MANY PEOPLE.
DOES IT ALL SMELL LIKE THIS?
THAT'S THE SMELL OF HUMANITY, MY DARLING GIRL.
THERE'S NO ESCAPING IT HERE.

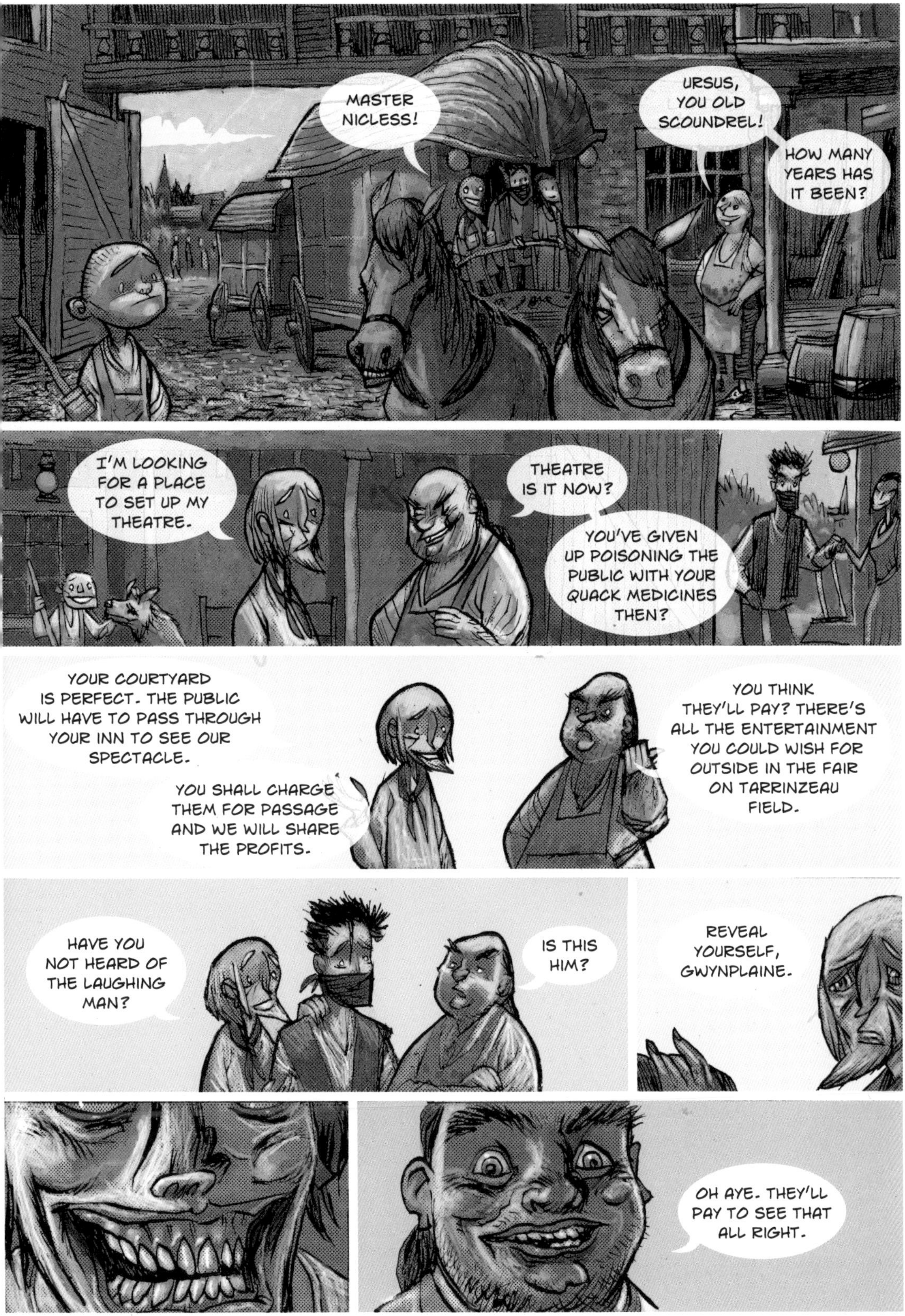
MASTER NICLESS!
URSUS, YOU OLD SCOUNDREL!
HOW MANY YEARS HAS IT BEEN?
I'M LOOKING FOR A PLACE TO SET UP MY THEATRE.
THEATRE IS IT NOW?
YOU'VE GIVEN UP POISONING THE PUBLIC WITH YOUR QUACK MEDICINES THEN?
YOUR COURTYARD IS PERFECT. THE PUBLIC WILL HAVE TO PASS THROUGH YOUR INN TO SEE OUR SPECTACLE.
YOU SHALL CHARGE THEM FOR PASSAGE AND WE WILL SHARE THE PROFITS.
YOU THINK THEY'LL PAY? THERE'S ALL THE ENTERTAINMENT YOU COULD WISH FOR OUTSIDE IN THE FAIR ON TARRINZEAU FIELD.
HAVE YOU NOT HEARD OF THE LAUGHING MAN?
IS THIS HIM?
REVEAL YOURSELF, GWYNPLAINE.
OH AYE. THEY'LL PAY TO SEE THAT ALL RIGHT.

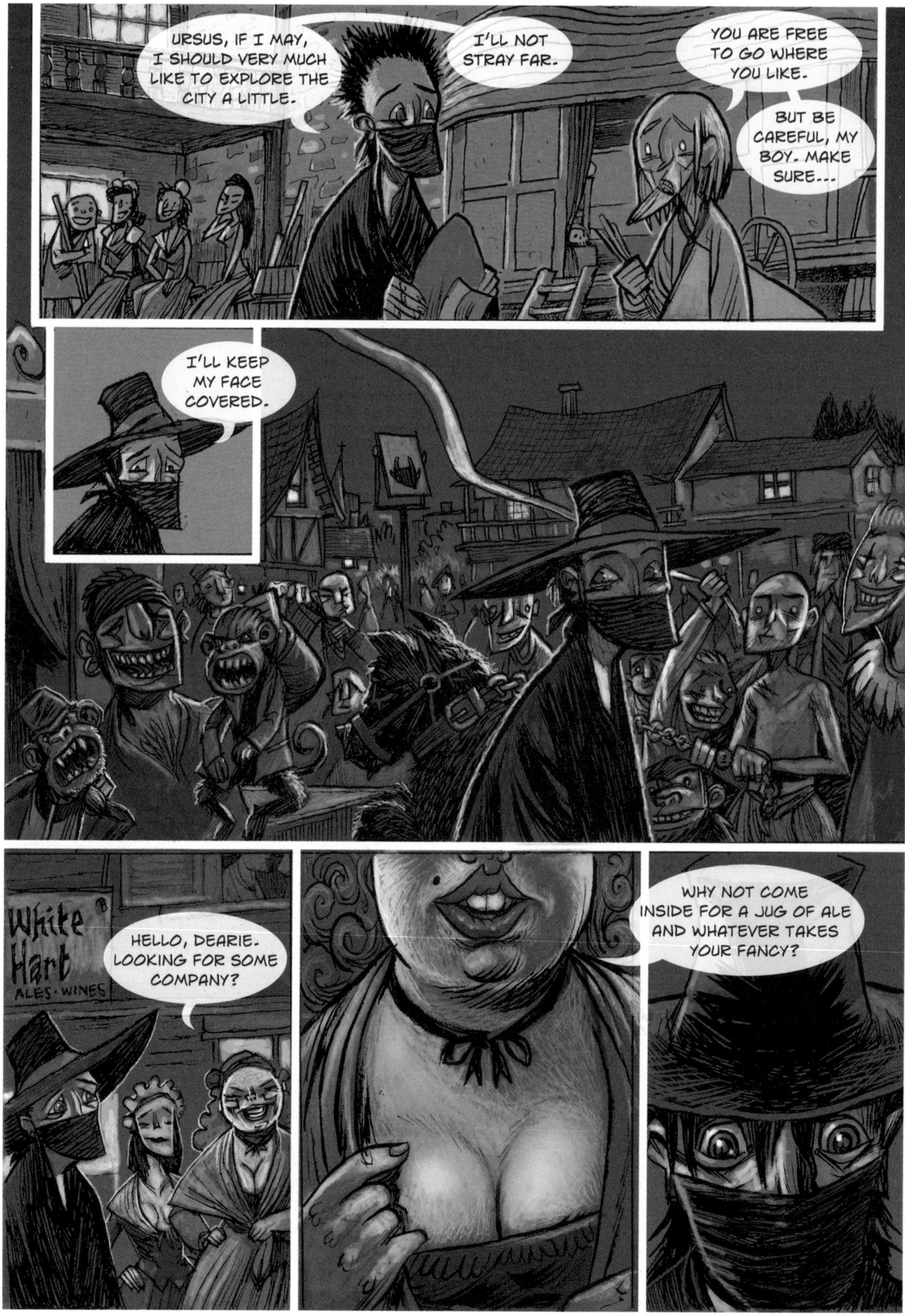
URSUS, IF I MAY, I SHOULD VERY MUCH LIKE TO EXPLORE THE CITY A LITTLE.
I'LL NOT STRAY FAR.
YOU ARE FREE TO GO WHERE YOU LIKE.
BUT BE CAREFUL, MY BOY. MAKE SURE...
I'LL KEEP MY FACE COVERED.
White Hart ALES · WINES
HELLO, DEARIE. LOOKING FOR SOME COMPANY?
WHY NOT COME INSIDE FOR A JUG OF ALE AND WHATEVER TAKES YOUR FANCY?

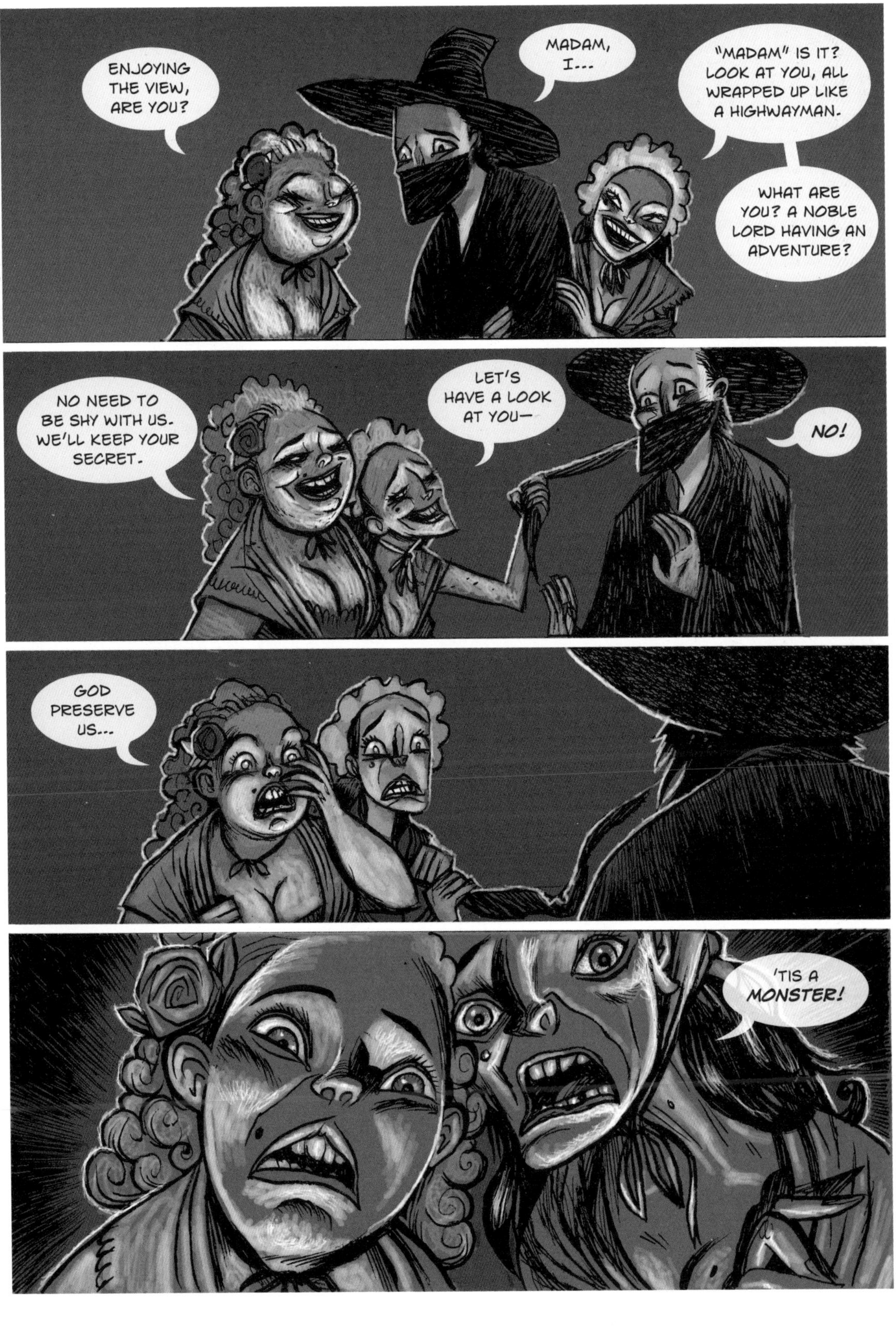
ENJOYING THE VIEW, ARE YOU?
MADAM, I...
"MADAM" IS IT? LOOK AT YOU, ALL WRAPPED UP LIKE A HIGHWAYMAN.
WHAT ARE YOU? A NOBLE LORD HAVING AN ADVENTURE?
NO NEED TO BE SHY WITH US. WE'LL KEEP YOUR SECRET.
LET'S HAVE A LOOK AT YOU—
NO!
GOD PRESERVE US...
'TIS A MONSTER!

HOW WAS YOUR WALK?

I LOST MY WAY.

THE CITY HAS NOTHING FOR ME. ALL THAT I NEED IS HERE.

I COULD HAVE TOLD YOU THAT.

NEVER MIND. SOON ALL OF LONDON WILL COME TO US.

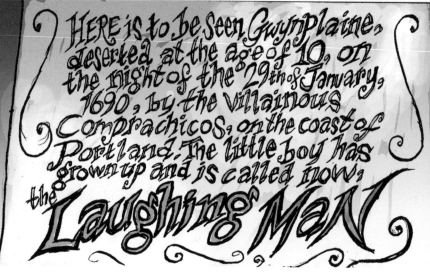

HERE is to be seen Gwynplaine, deserted at the age of 10, on the night of the 29th of January, 1690, by the villainous Comprachicos, on the coast of Portland. The little boy has grown up and is called now, the Laughing Man

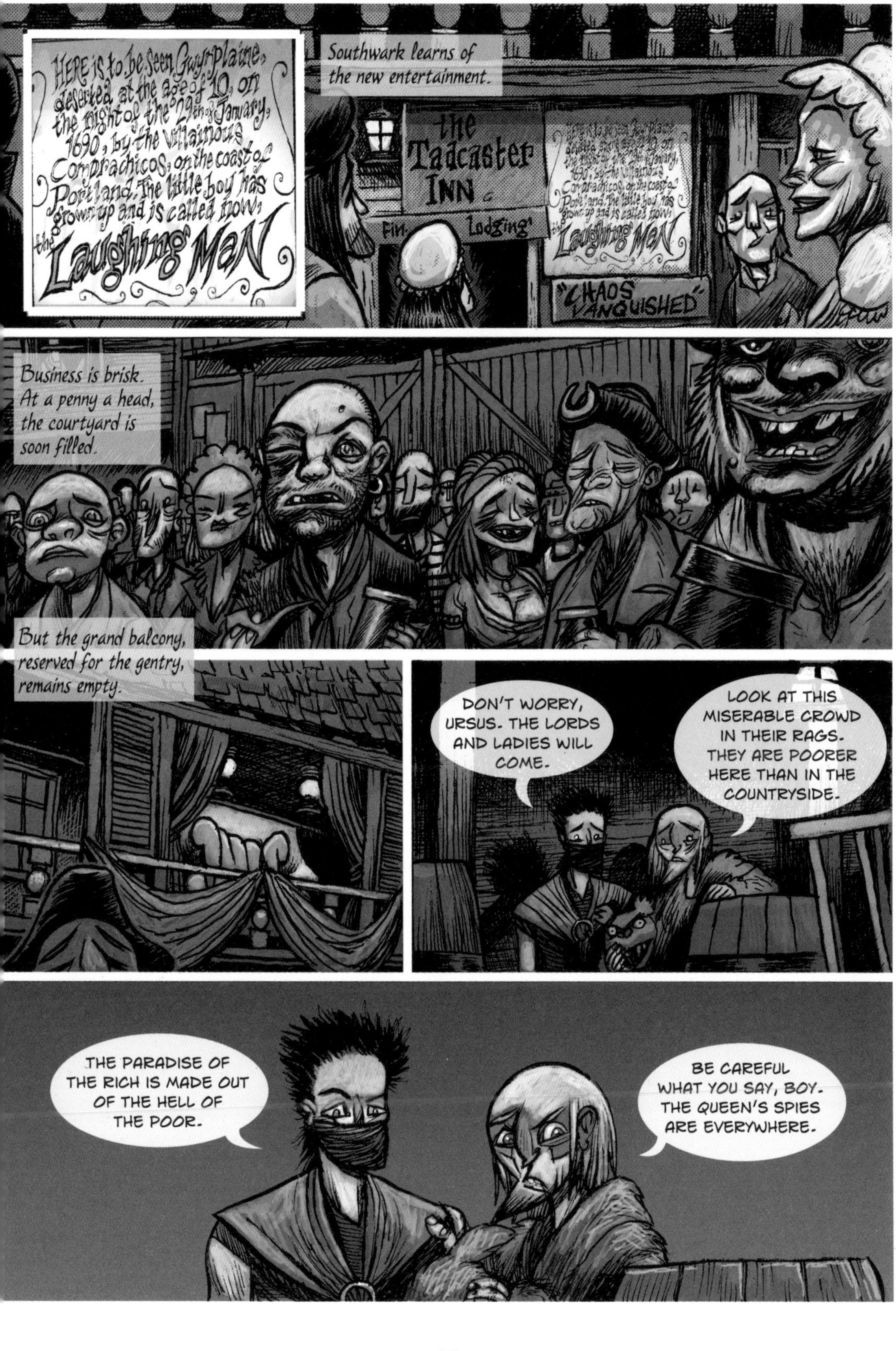
HERE is to be seen Gwynplaine, deserted at the age of 10, on the night of the 29th of January, 1690, by the villainous Comprachicos, on the coast of Portland. The little boy has grown up and is called now, the Laughing MAN
Southwark learns of the new entertainment.
the Tadcaster INN
Lodging
"CHAOS VANQUISHED"
Business is brisk. At a penny a head, the courtyard is soon filled.
But the grand balcony, reserved for the gentry, remains empty.
DON'T WORRY, URSUS. THE LORDS AND LADIES WILL COME.
LOOK AT THIS MISERABLE CROWD IN THEIR RAGS. THEY ARE POORER HERE THAN IN THE COUNTRYSIDE.
THE PARADISE OF THE RICH IS MADE OUT OF THE HELL OF THE POOR.
BE CAREFUL WHAT YOU SAY, BOY. THE QUEEN'S SPIES ARE EVERYWHERE.

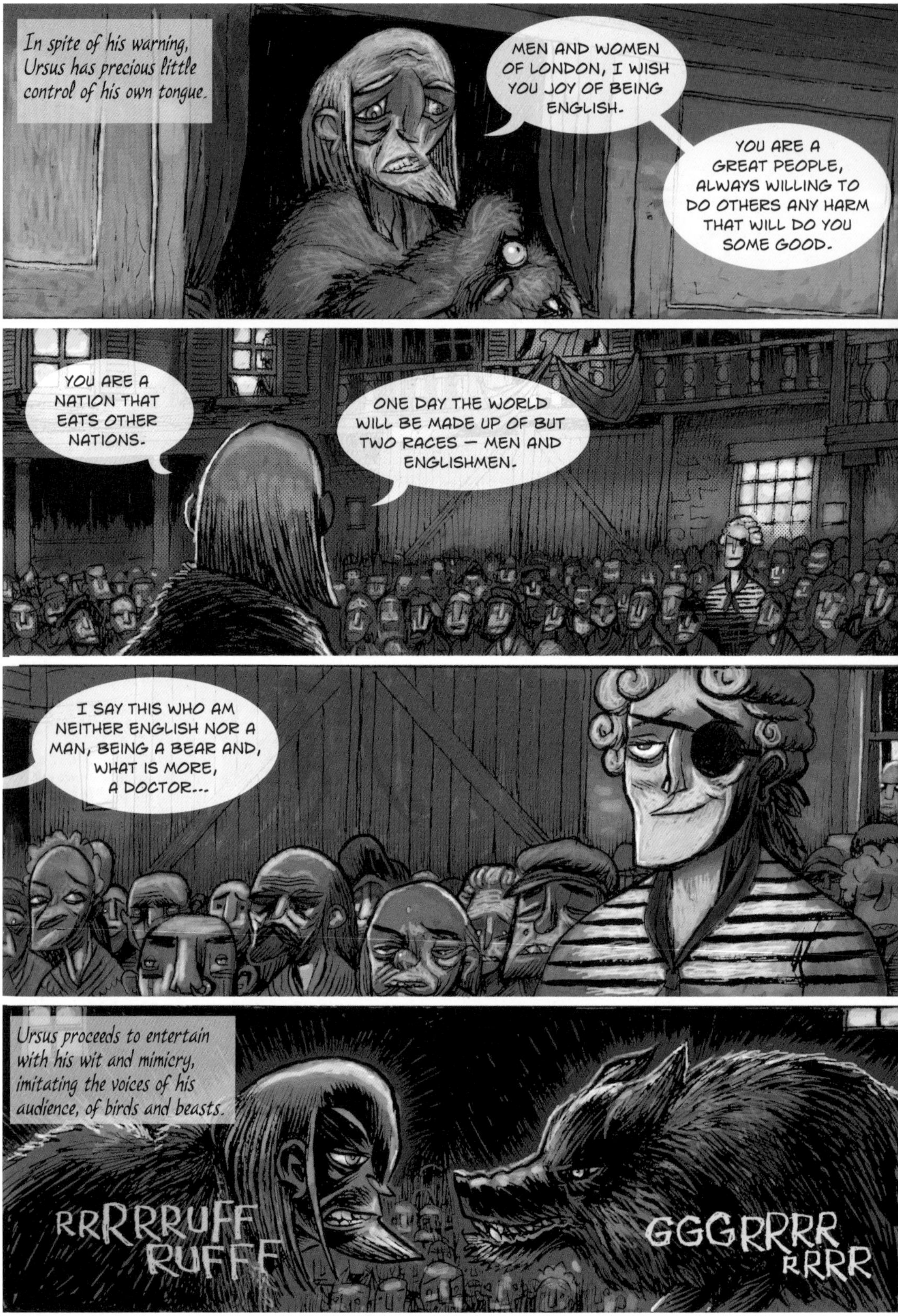
In spite of his warning, Ursus has precious little control of his own tongue.
MEN AND WOMEN OF LONDON, I WISH YOU JOY OF BEING ENGLISH.
YOU ARE A GREAT PEOPLE, ALWAYS WILLING TO DO OTHERS ANY HARM THAT WILL DO YOU SOME GOOD.
YOU ARE A NATION THAT EATS OTHER NATIONS.
ONE DAY THE WORLD WILL BE MADE UP OF BUT TWO RACES — MEN AND ENGLISHMEN.
I SAY THIS WHO AM NEITHER ENGLISH NOR A MAN, BEING A BEAR AND, WHAT IS MORE, A DOCTOR...
Ursus proceeds to entertain with his wit and mimicry, imitating the voices of his audience, of birds and beasts.
RRRRRUFF RUFFF
GGGRRRR RRRR

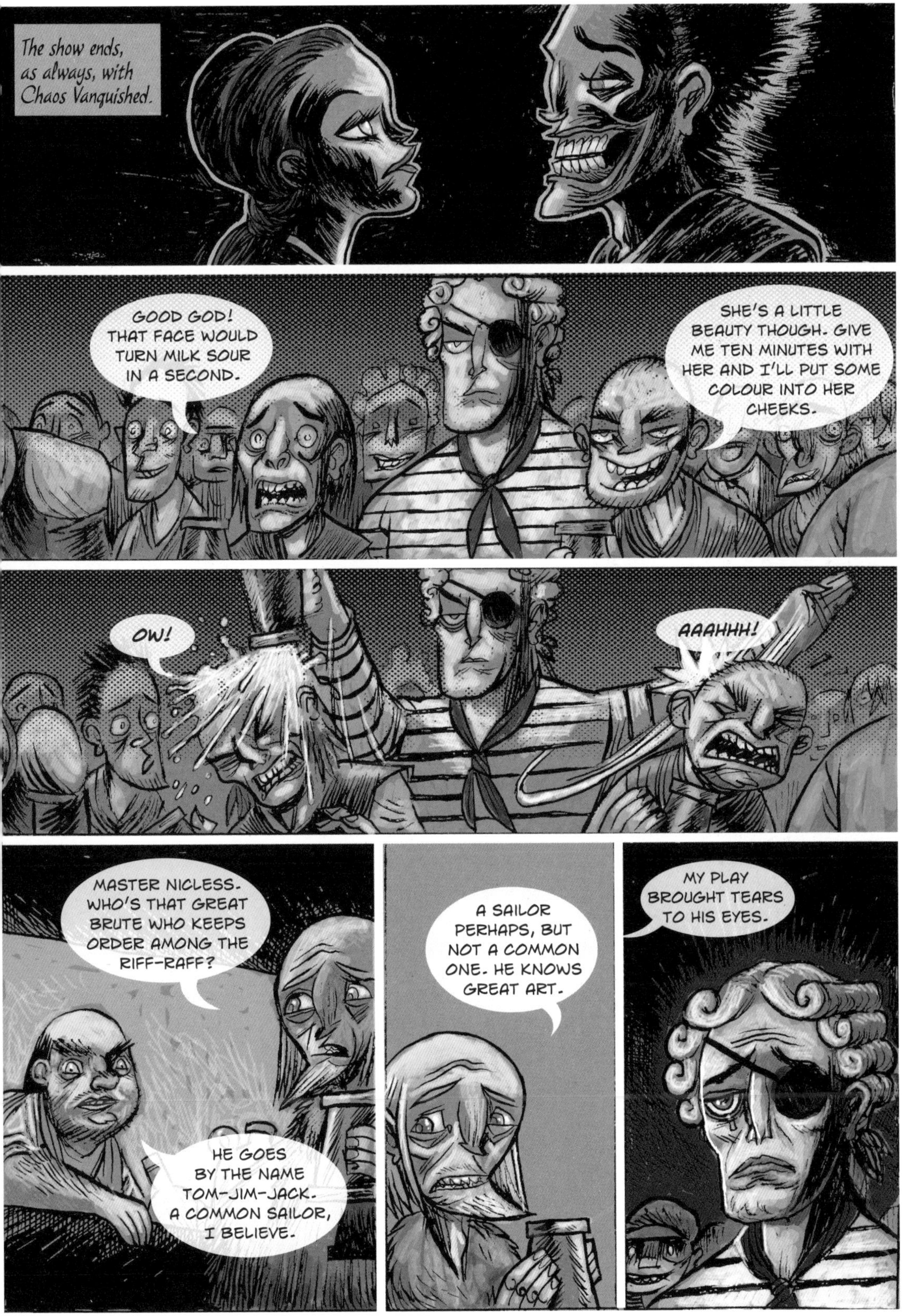
The show ends, as always, with Chaos Vanquished.
GOOD GOD! THAT FACE WOULD TURN MILK SOUR IN A SECOND.
SHE'S A LITTLE BEAUTY THOUGH. GIVE ME TEN MINUTES WITH HER AND I'LL PUT SOME COLOUR INTO HER CHEEKS.
OW!
AAAHHH!
MASTER NICLESS. WHO'S THAT GREAT BRUTE WHO KEEPS ORDER AMONG THE RIFF-RAFF?
HE GOES BY THE NAME TOM-JIM-JACK. A COMMON SAILOR, I BELIEVE.
A SAILOR PERHAPS, BUT NOT A COMMON ONE. HE KNOWS GREAT ART.
MY PLAY BROUGHT TEARS TO HIS EYES.

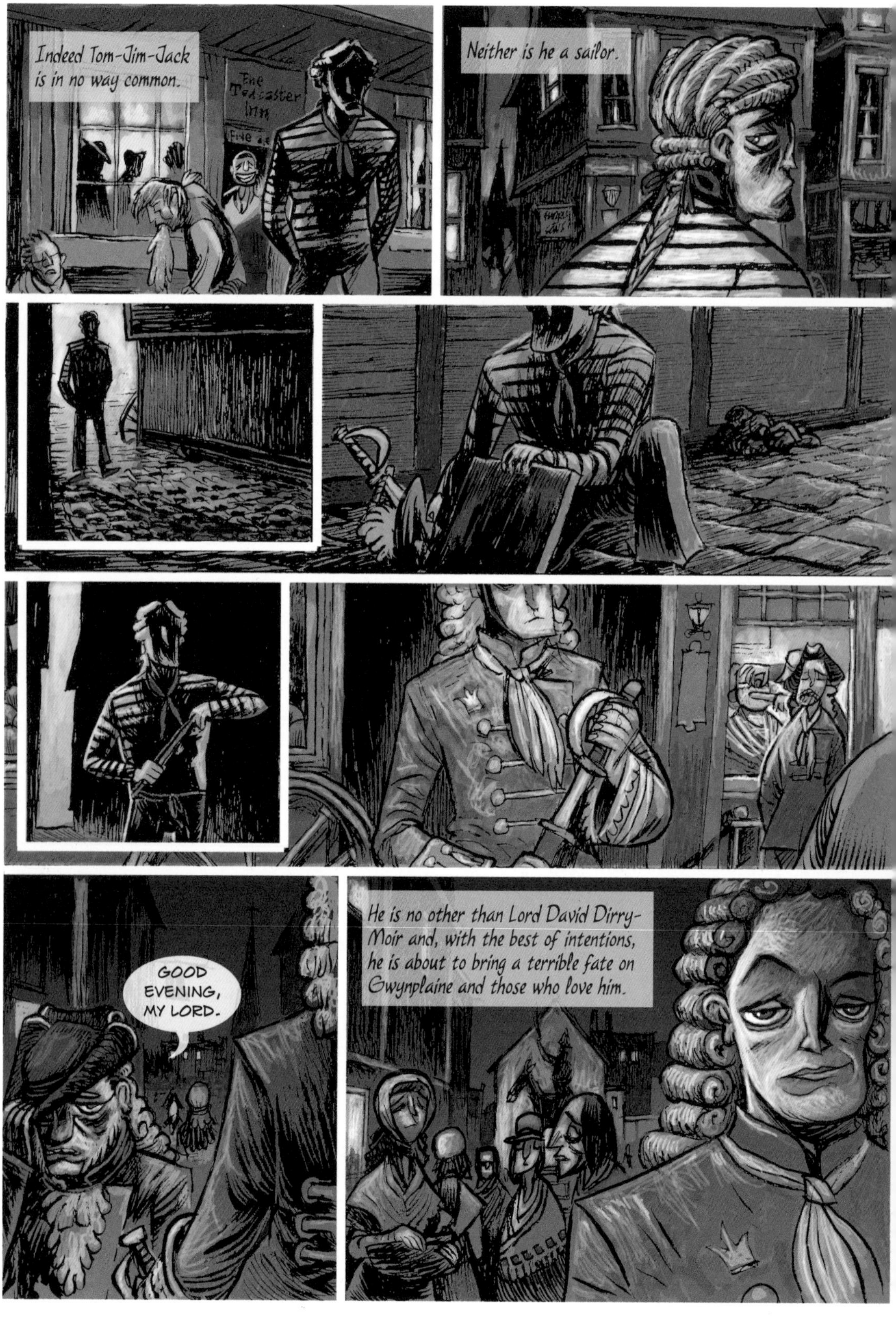
Indeed Tom-Jim-Jack is in no way common.
The Tadcaster Inn
Neither is he a sailor.
GOOD EVENING, MY LORD.
He is no other than Lord David Dirry-Moir and, with the best of intentions, he is about to bring a terrible fate on Gwynplaine and those who love him.

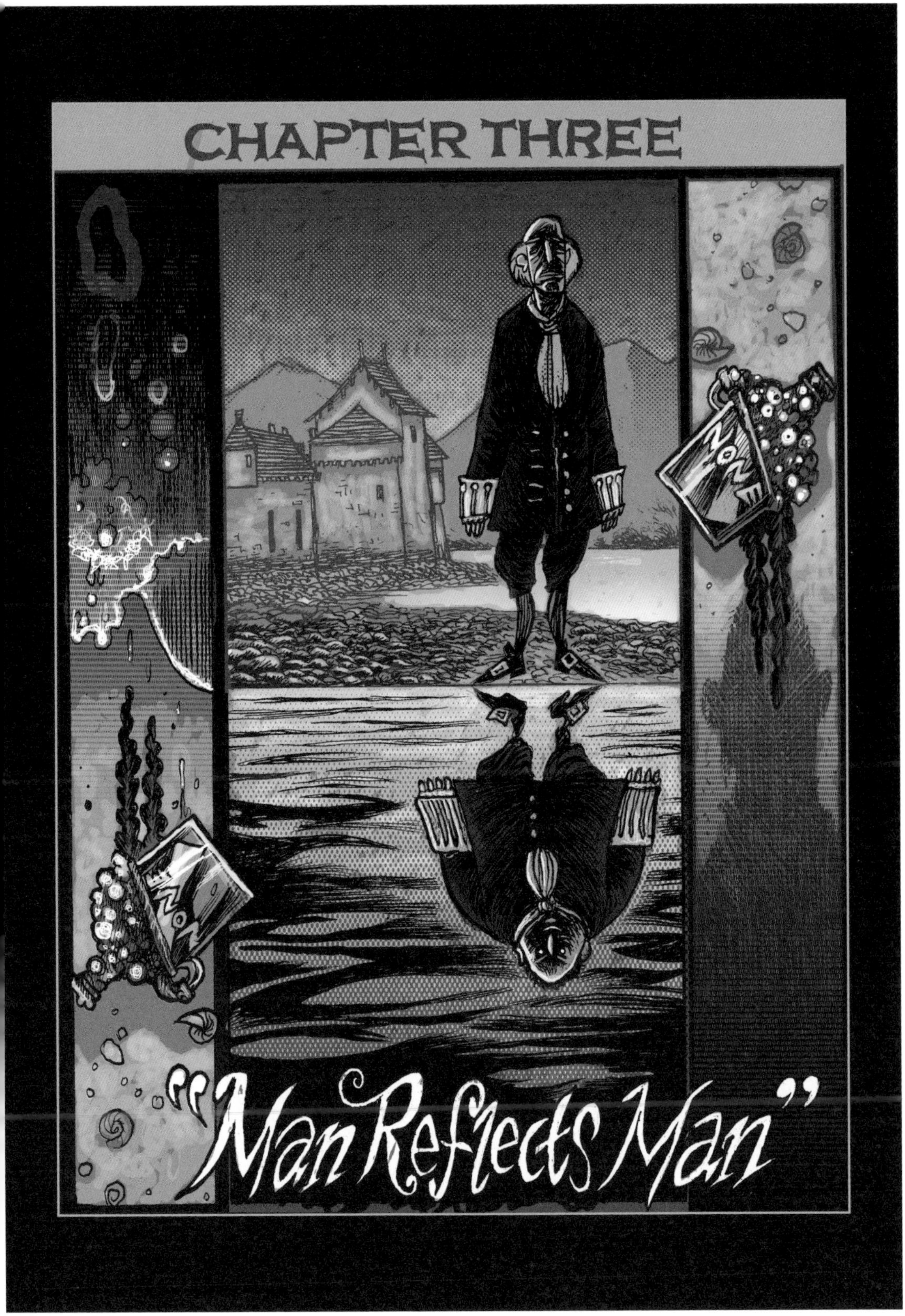
CHAPTER THREE
"Man Reflects Man"

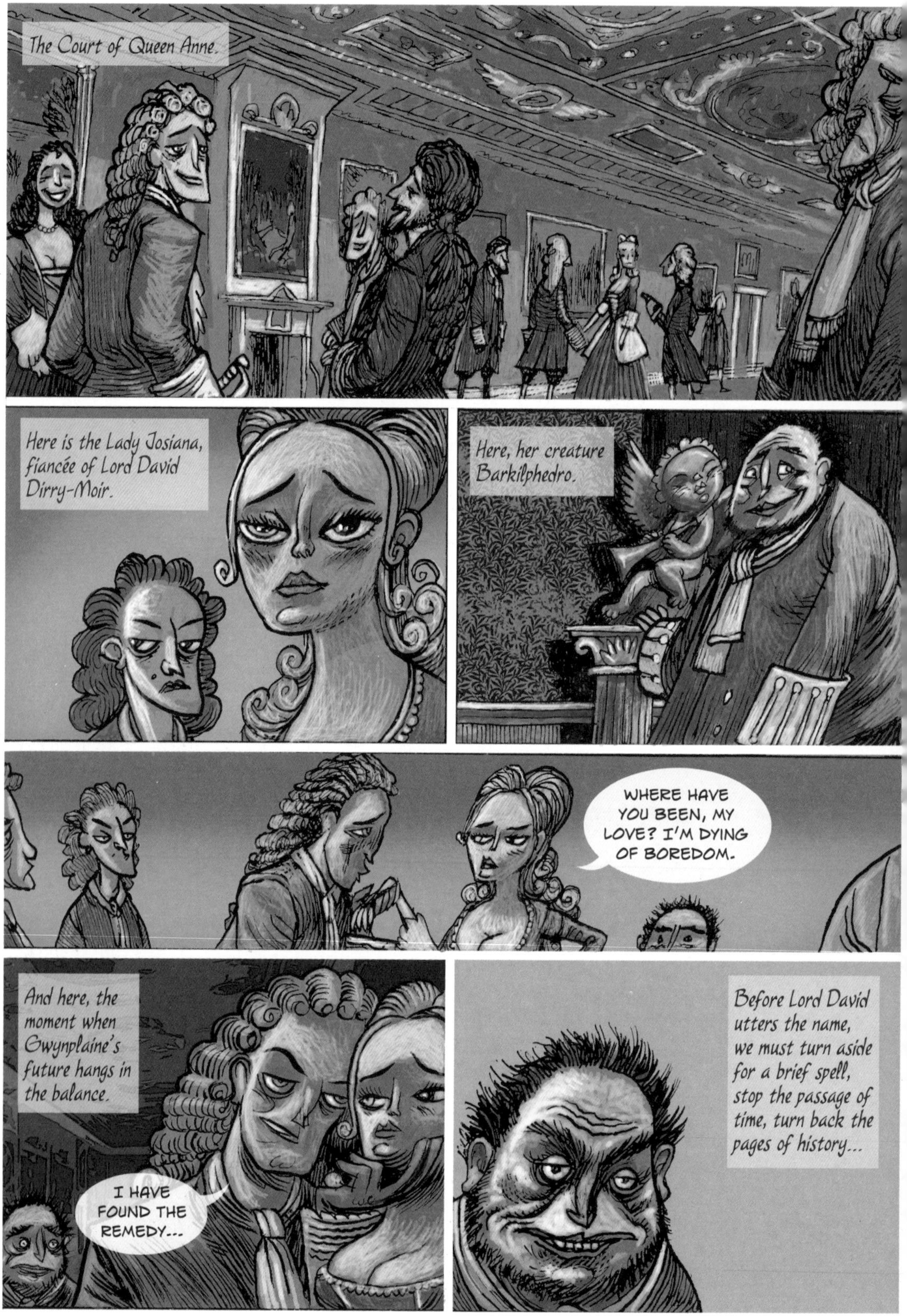
The Court of Queen Anne.
Here is the Lady Josiana, fiancée of Lord David Dirry-Moir.
Here, her creature Barkilphedro.
WHERE HAVE YOU BEEN, MY LOVE? I'M DYING OF BOREDOM.
And here, the moment when Gwynplaine's future hangs in the balance.
I HAVE FOUND THE REMEDY...
Before Lord David utters the name, we must turn aside for a brief spell, stop the passage of time, turn back the pages of history...

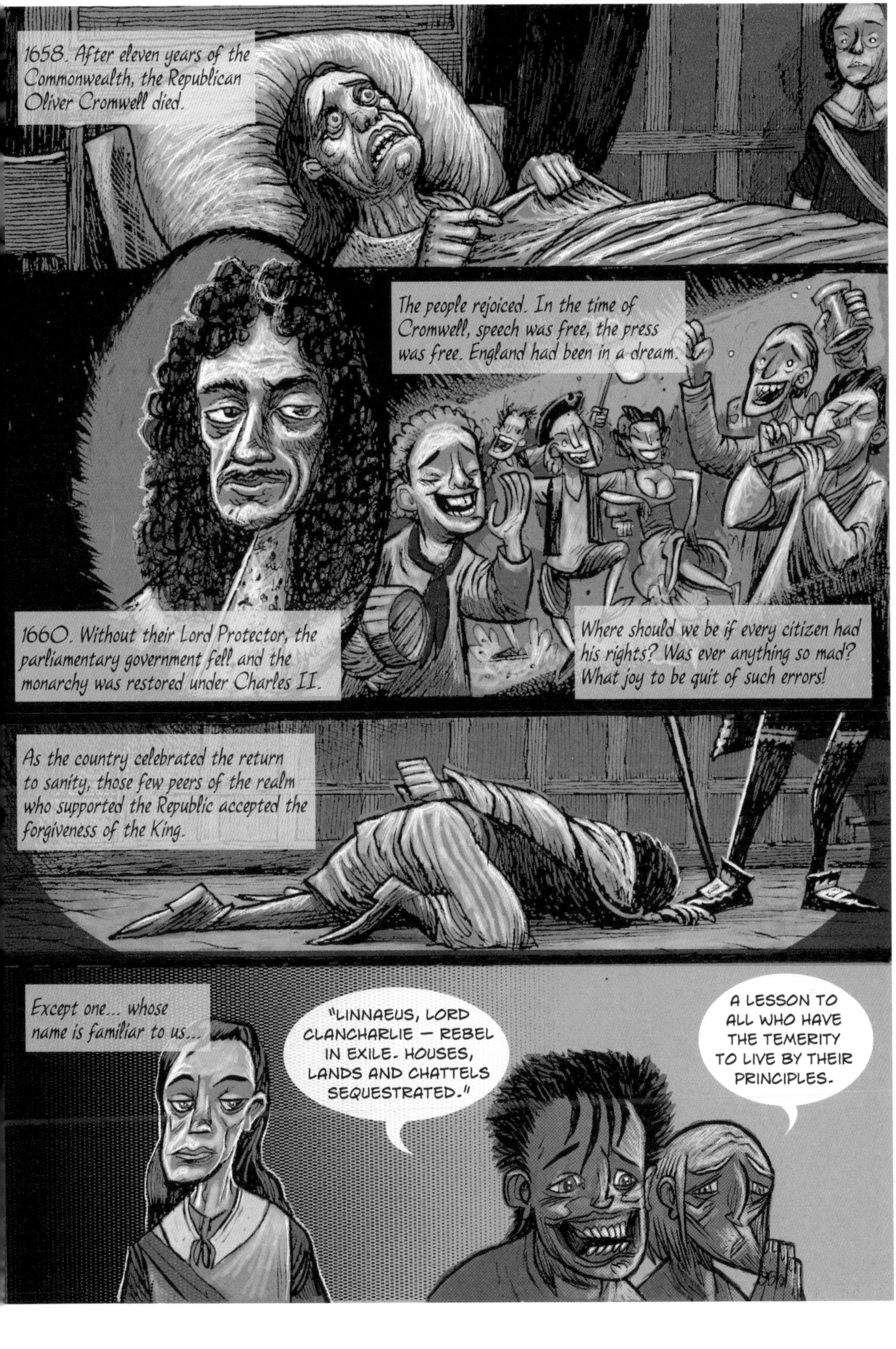

1658. After eleven years of the Commonwealth, the Republican Oliver Cromwell died.
The people rejoiced. In the time of Cromwell, speech was free, the press was free. England had been in a dream.
1660. Without their Lord Protector, the parliamentary government fell and the monarchy was restored under Charles II.
Where should we be if every citizen had his rights? Was ever anything so mad? What joy to be quit of such errors!
As the country celebrated the return to sanity, those few peers of the realm who supported the Republic accepted the forgiveness of the King.
Except one... whose name is familiar to us...
"LINNAEUS, LORD CLANCHARLIE — REBEL IN EXILE. HOUSES, LANDS AND CHATTELS SEQUESTRATED."
A LESSON TO ALL WHO HAVE THE TEMERITY TO LIVE BY THEIR PRINCIPLES.

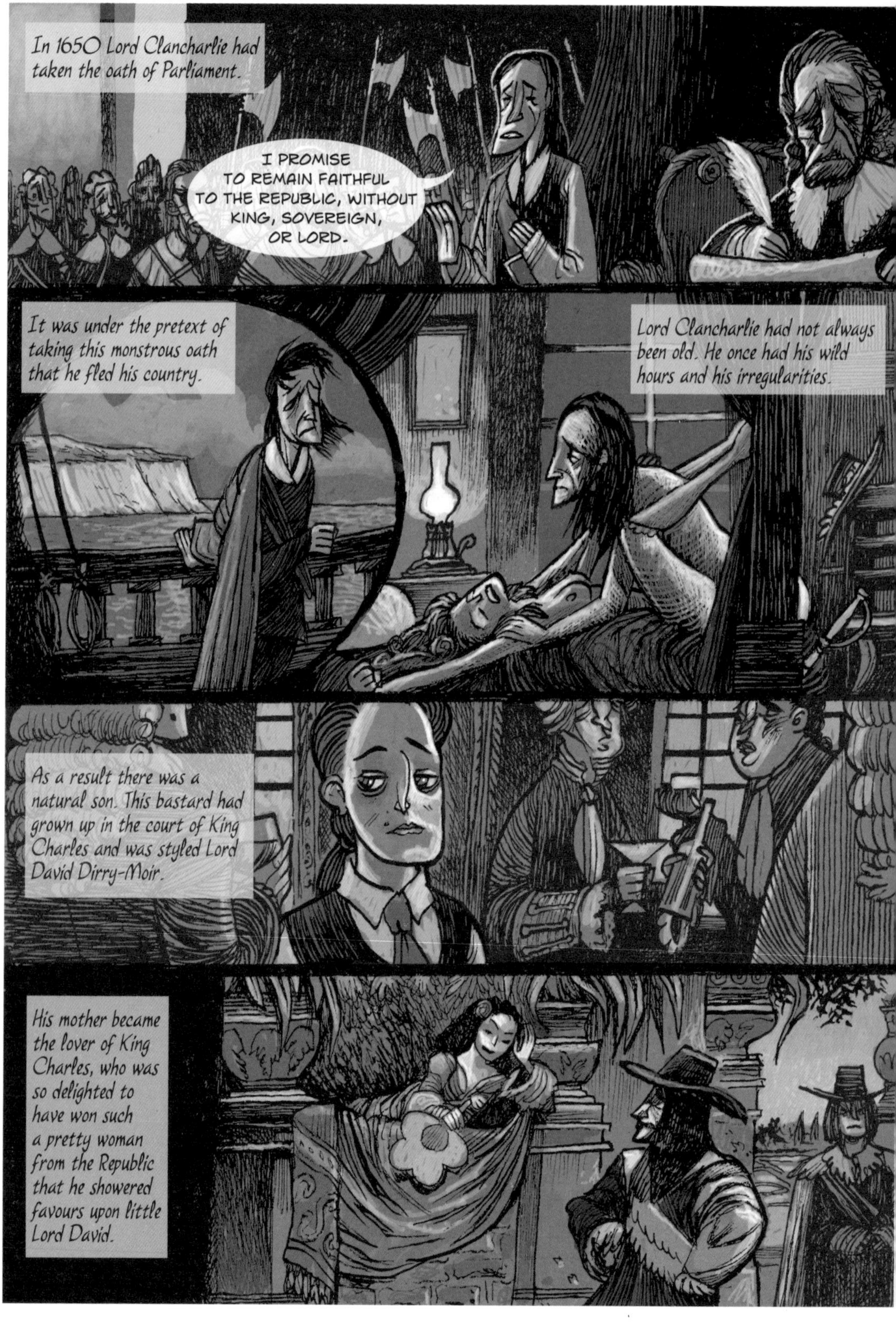
In 1650 Lord Clancharlie had taken the oath of Parliament.
I PROMISE TO REMAIN FAITHFUL TO THE REPUBLIC, WITHOUT KING, SOVEREIGN, OR LORD.
It was under the pretext of taking this monstrous oath that he fled his country.
Lord Clancharlie had not always been old. He once had his wild hours and his irregularities.
As a result there was a natural son. This bastard had grown up in the court of King Charles and was styled Lord David Dirry-Moir.
His mother became the lover of King Charles, who was so delighted to have won such a pretty woman from the Republic that he showered favours upon little Lord David.

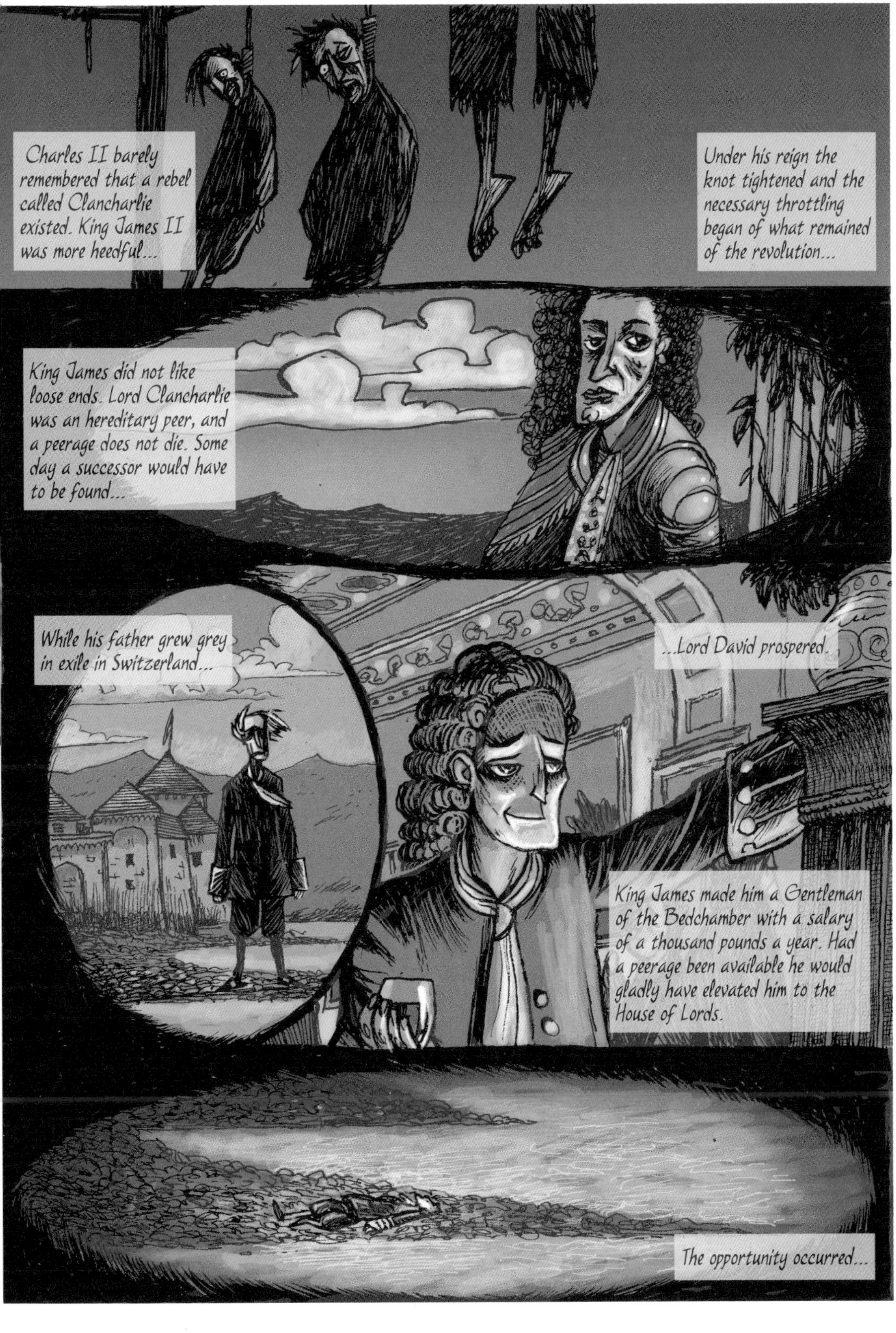
Charles II barely remembered that a rebel called Clancharlie existed. King James II was more heedful...
Under his reign the knot tightened and the necessary throttling began of what remained of the revolution...
King James did not like loose ends. Lord Clancharlie was an hereditary peer, and a peerage does not die. Some day a successor would have to be found...
While his father grew grey in exile in Switzerland...
...Lord David prospered.
King James made him a Gentleman of the Bedchamber with a salary of a thousand pounds a year. Had a peerage been available he would gladly have elevated him to the House of Lords.
The opportunity occurred...

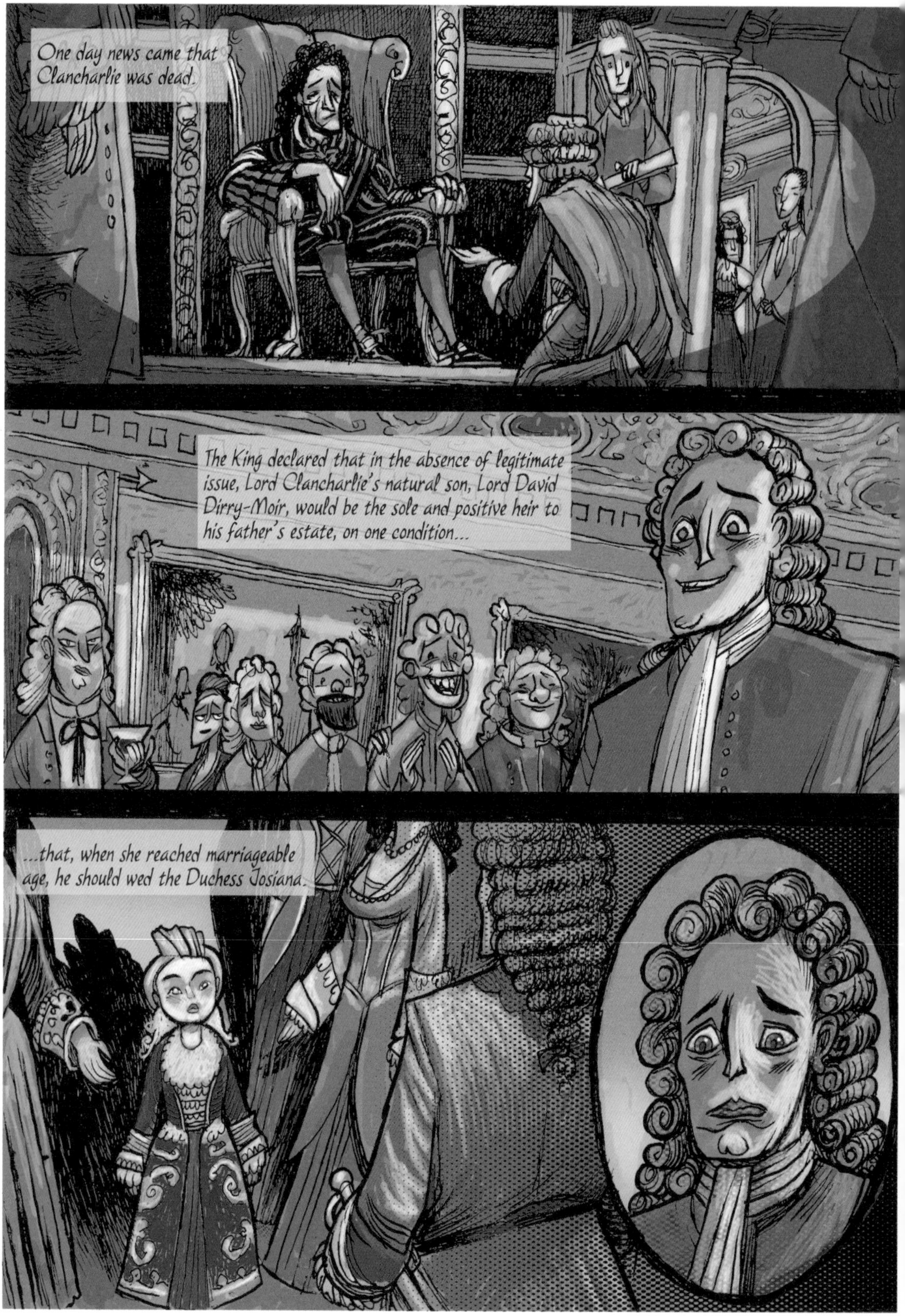
One day news came that Clancharlie was dead.
The King declared that in the absence of legitimate issue, Lord Clancharlie's natural son, Lord David Dirry-Moir, would be the sole and positive heir to his father's estate, on one condition...
...that, when she reached marriageable age, he should wed the Duchess Josiana.

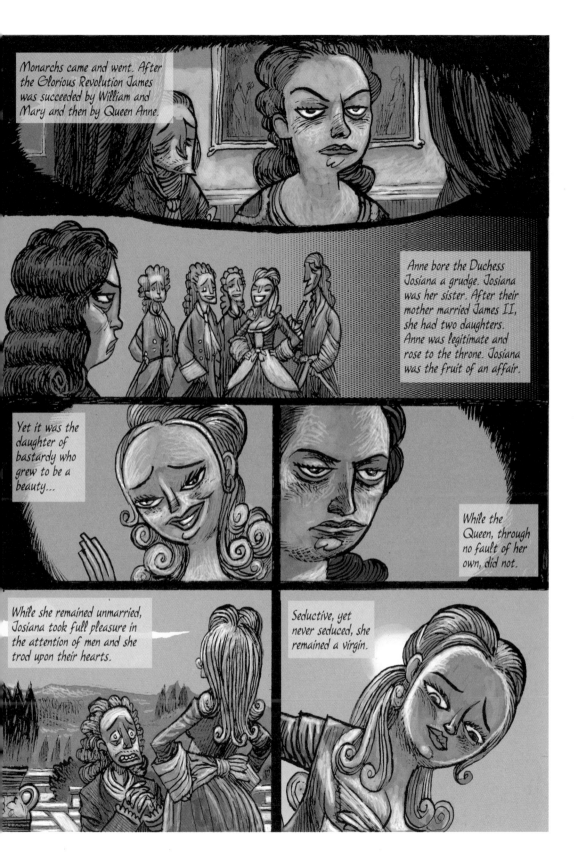

Monarchs came and went. After the Glorious Revolution James was succeeded by William and Mary and then by Queen Anne.

Anne bore the Duchess Josiana a grudge. Josiana was her sister. After their mother married James II, she had two daughters. Anne was legitimate and rose to the throne. Josiana was the fruit of an affair.

Yet it was the daughter of bastardy who grew to be a beauty...

While the Queen, through no fault of her own, did not.

While she remained unmarried, Josiana took full pleasure in the attention of men and she trod upon their hearts.

Seductive, yet never seduced, she remained a virgin.

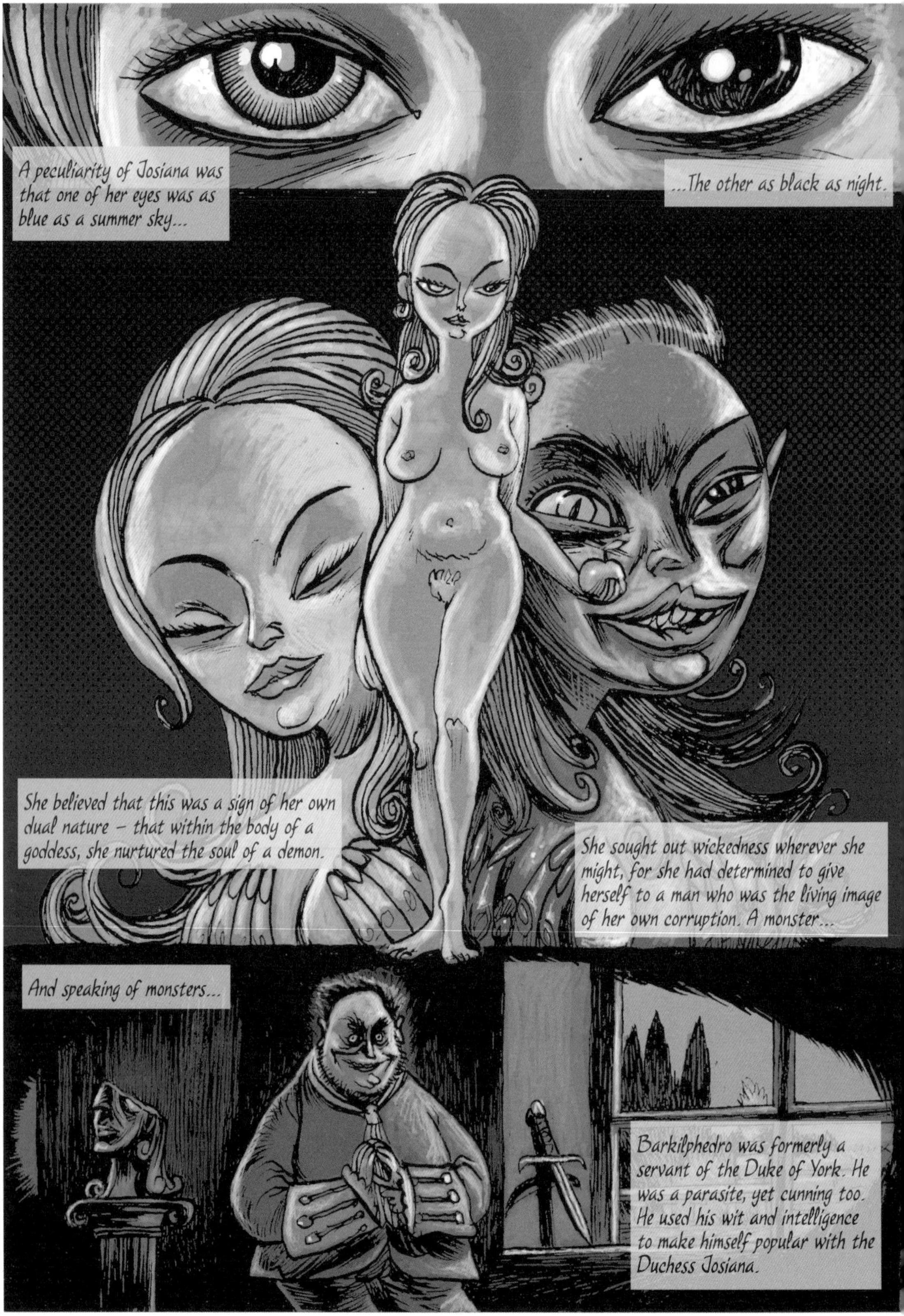
A peculiarity of Josiana was that one of her eyes was as blue as a summer sky...
...The other as black as night.
She believed that this was a sign of her own dual nature – that within the body of a goddess, she nurtured the soul of a demon.
She sought out wickedness wherever she might, for she had determined to give herself to a man who was the living image of her own corruption. A monster...
And speaking of monsters...
Barkilphedro was formerly a servant of the Duke of York. He was a parasite, yet cunning too. He used his wit and intelligence to make himself popular with the Duchess Josiana.

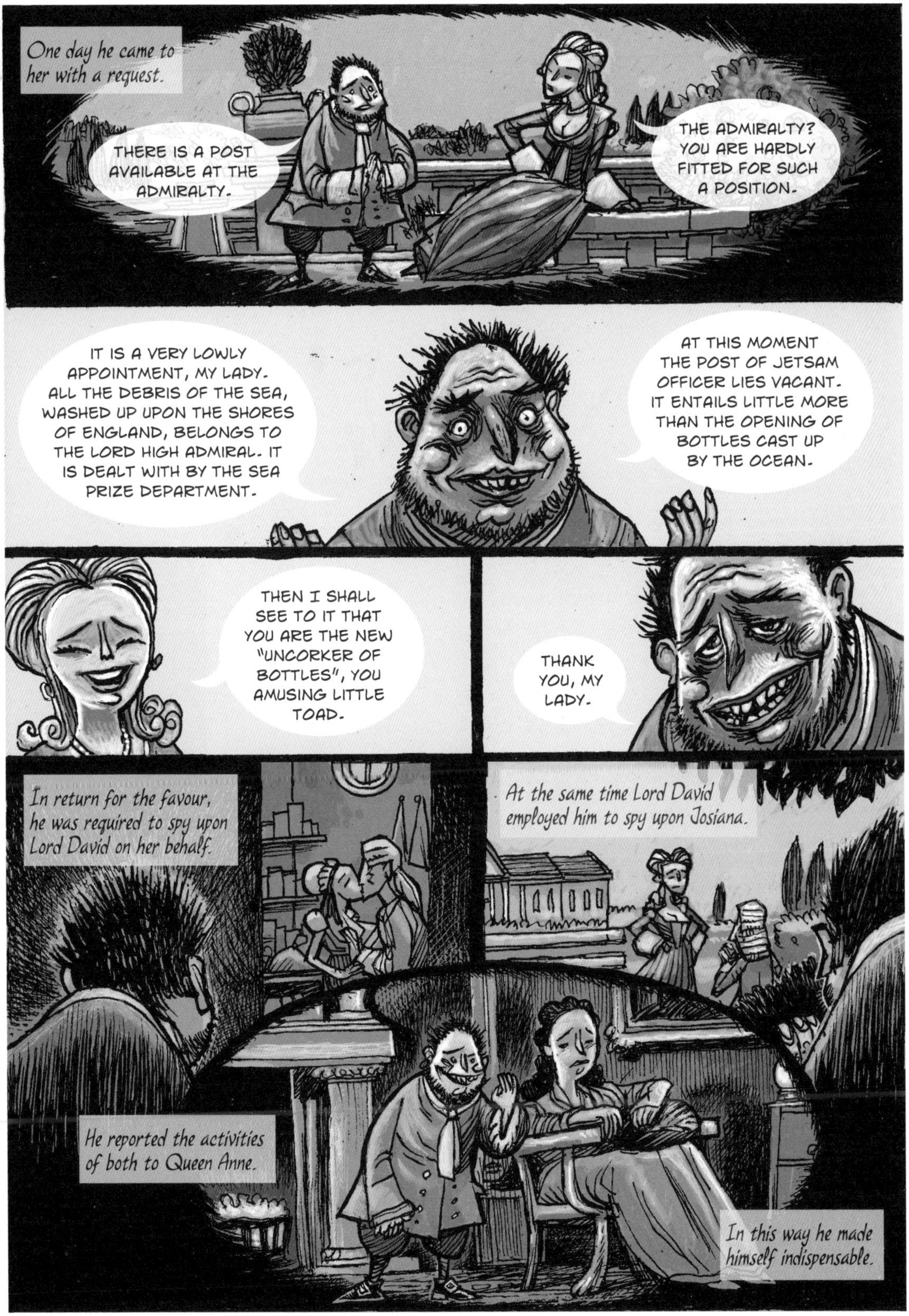

One day he came to her with a request.
THERE IS A POST AVAILABLE AT THE ADMIRALTY.
THE ADMIRALTY? YOU ARE HARDLY FITTED FOR SUCH A POSITION.
IT IS A VERY LOWLY APPOINTMENT, MY LADY. ALL THE DEBRIS OF THE SEA, WASHED UP UPON THE SHORES OF ENGLAND, BELONGS TO THE LORD HIGH ADMIRAL. IT IS DEALT WITH BY THE SEA PRIZE DEPARTMENT.
AT THIS MOMENT THE POST OF JETSAM OFFICER LIES VACANT. IT ENTAILS LITTLE MORE THAN THE OPENING OF BOTTLES CAST UP BY THE OCEAN.
THEN I SHALL SEE TO IT THAT YOU ARE THE NEW "UNCORKER OF BOTTLES", YOU AMUSING LITTLE TOAD.
THANK YOU, MY LADY.
In return for the favour, he was required to spy upon Lord David on her behalf.
At the same time Lord David employed him to spy upon Josiana.
He reported the activities of both to Queen Anne.
In this way he made himself indispensable.

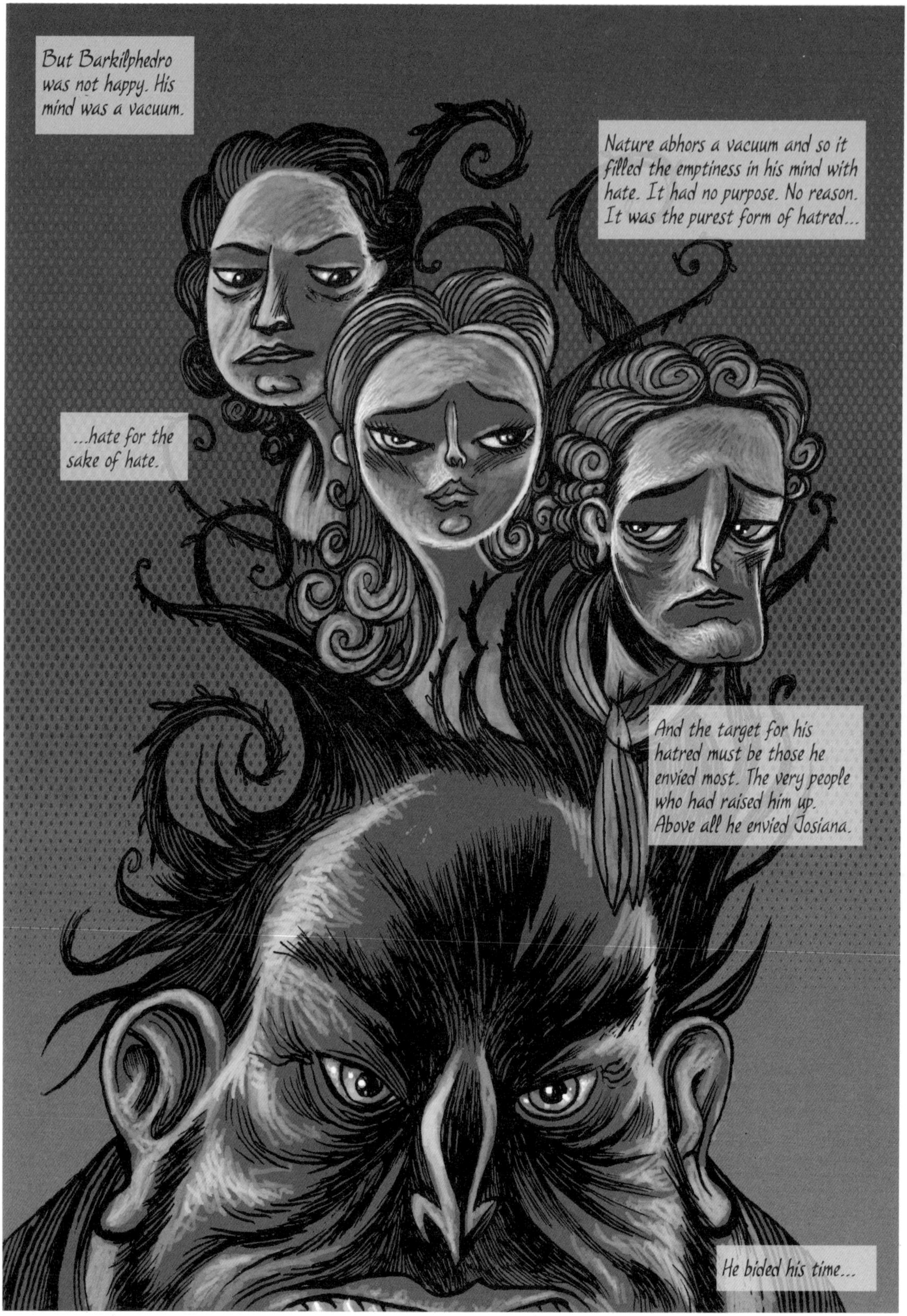
But Barkilphedro was not happy. His mind was a vacuum.
Nature abhors a vacuum and so it filled the emptiness in his mind with hate. It had no purpose. No reason. It was the purest form of hatred...
...hate for the sake of hate.
And the target for his hatred must be those he envied most. The very people who had raised him up. Above all he envied Josiana.
He bided his time...

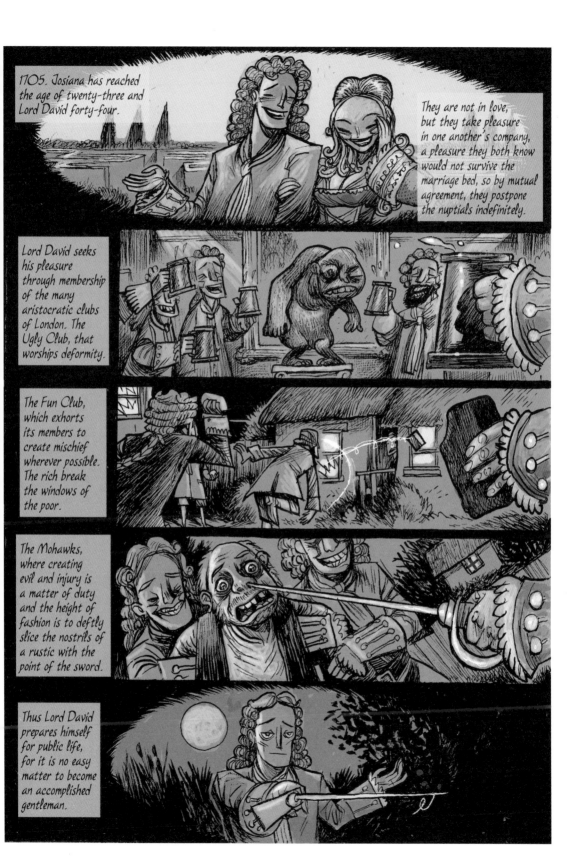

1705. Josiana has reached the age of twenty-three and Lord David forty-four.

They are not in love, but they take pleasure in one another's company, a pleasure they both know would not survive the marriage bed, so by mutual agreement, they postpone the nuptials indefinitely.

Lord David seeks his pleasure through membership of the many aristocratic clubs of London. The Ugly Club, that worships deformity.

The Fun Club, which exhorts its members to create mischief wherever possible. The rich break the windows of the poor.

The Mohawks, where creating evil and injury is a matter of duty and the height of fashion is to deftly slice the nostrils of a rustic with the point of the sword.

Thus Lord David prepares himself for public life, for it is no easy matter to become an accomplished gentleman.

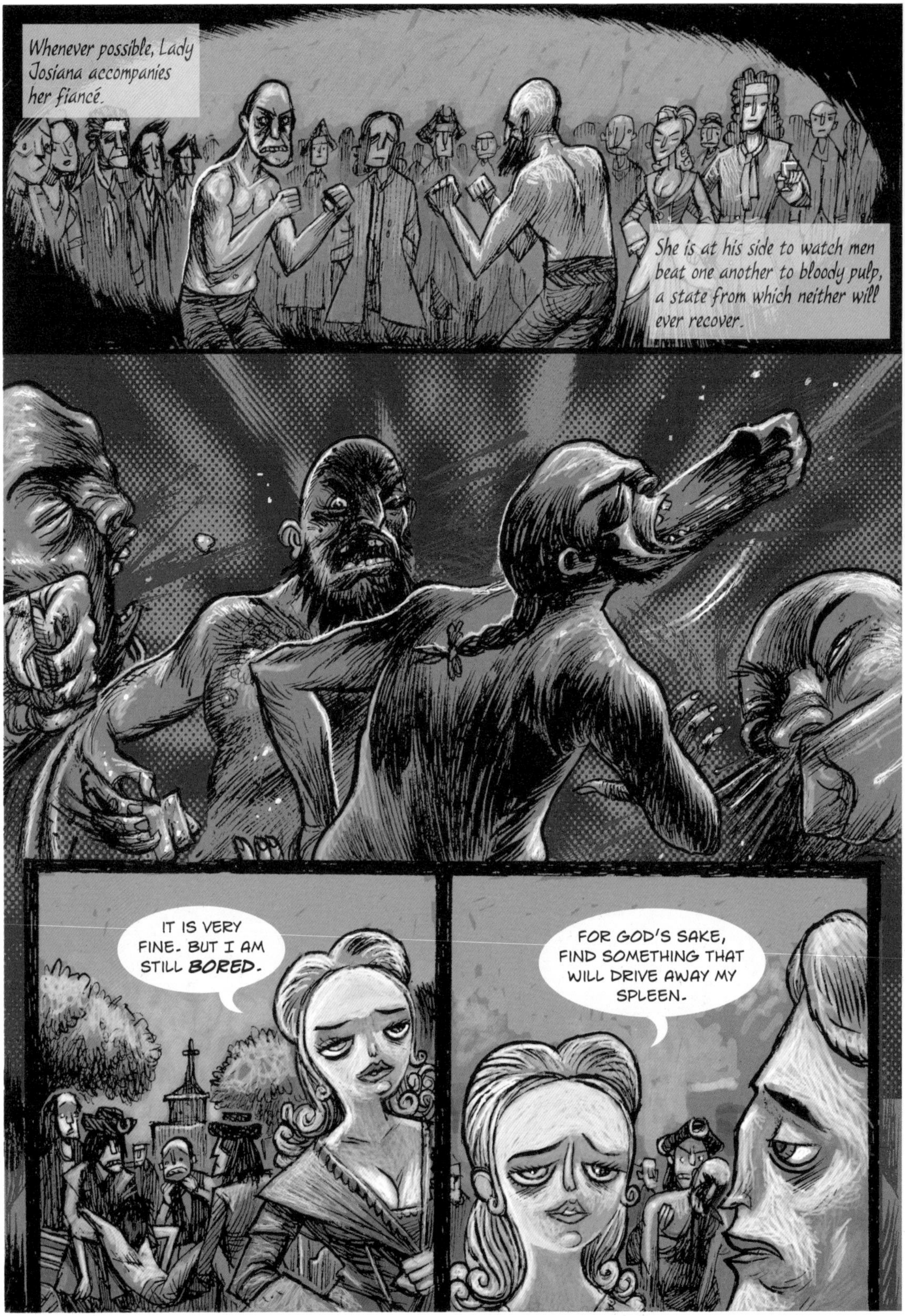
Whenever possible, Lady Josiana accompanies her fiancé.
She is at his side to watch men beat one another to bloody pulp, a state from which neither will ever recover.
IT IS VERY FINE. BUT I AM STILL **BORED**.
FOR GOD'S SAKE, FIND SOMETHING THAT WILL DRIVE AWAY MY SPLEEN.

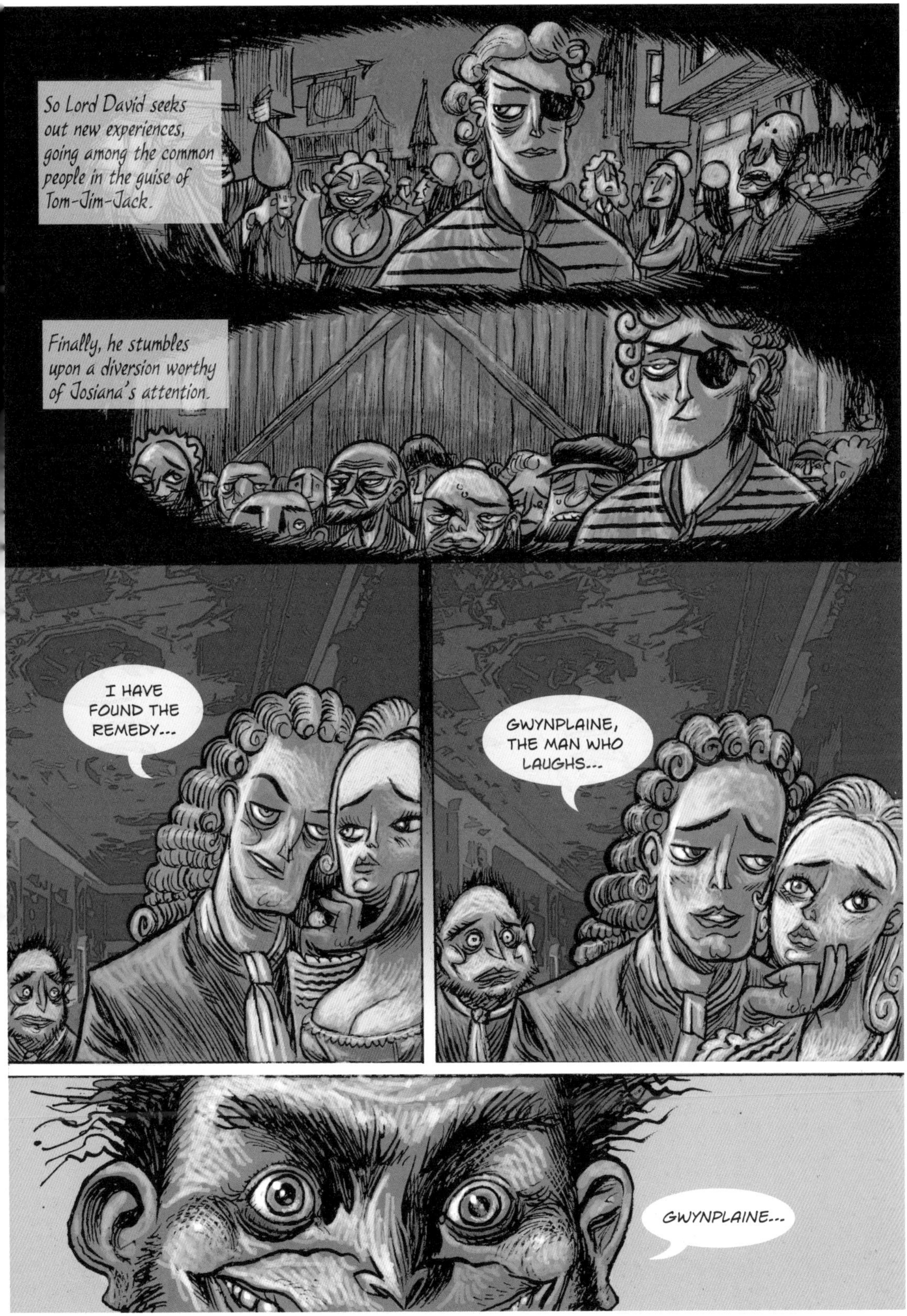
So Lord David seeks out new experiences, going among the common people in the guise of Tom-Jim-Jack.
Finally, he stumbles upon a diversion worthy of Josiana's attention.
I HAVE FOUND THE REMEDY...
GWYNPLAINE, THE MAN WHO LAUGHS...
GWYNPLAINE...

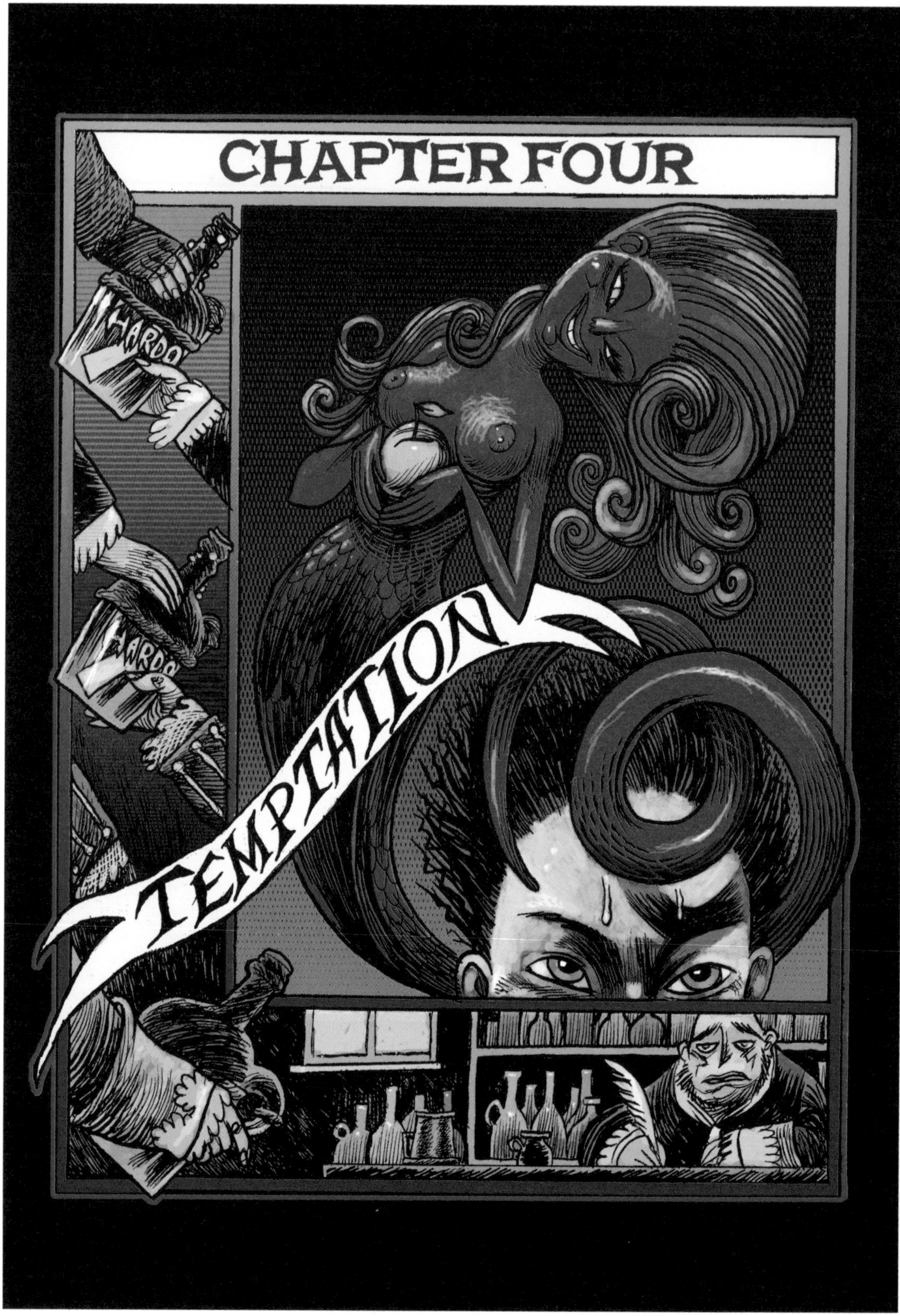
CHAPTER FOUR
TEMPTATION

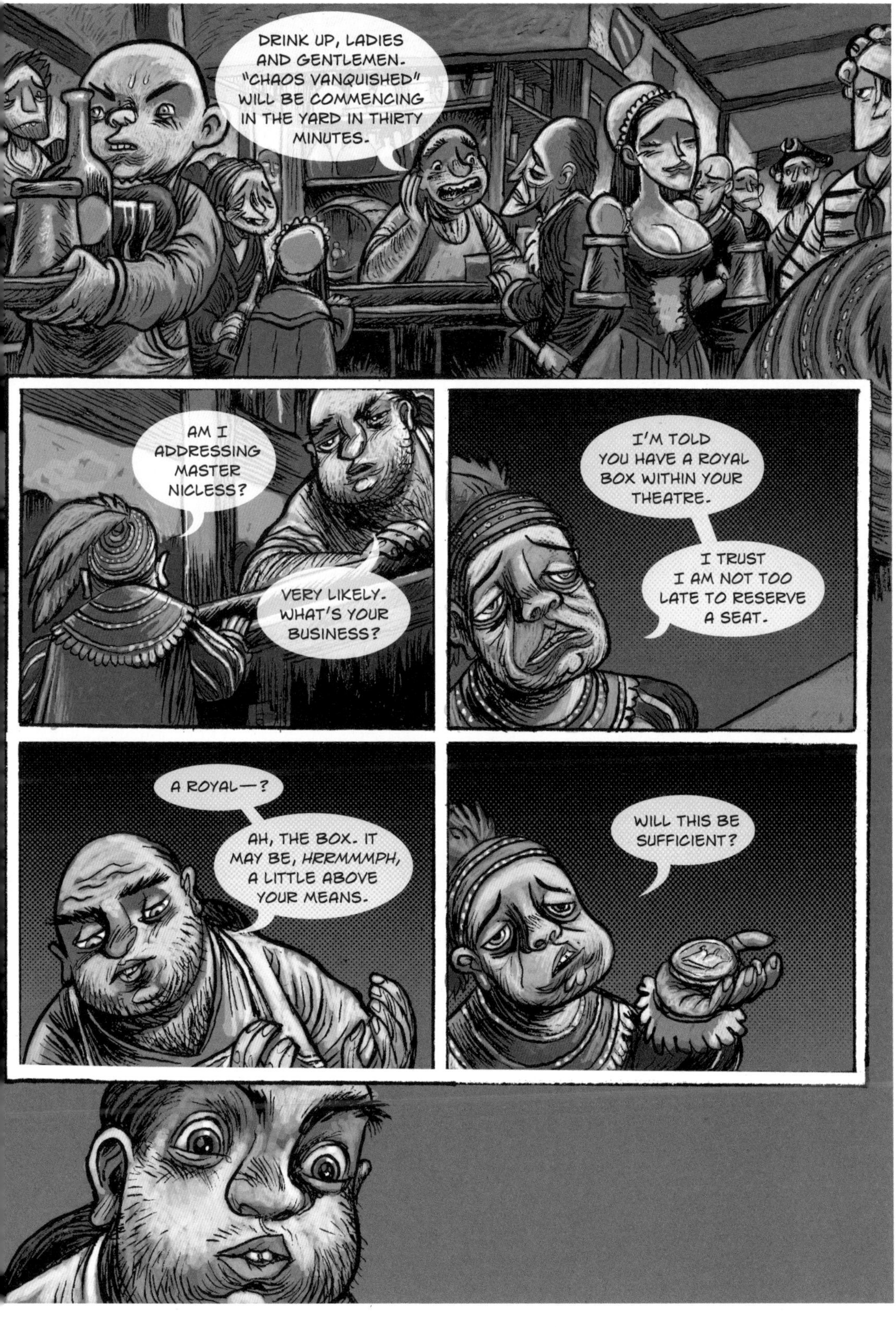
DRINK UP, LADIES AND GENTLEMEN. "CHAOS VANQUISHED" WILL BE COMMENCING IN THE YARD IN THIRTY MINUTES.
AM I ADDRESSING MASTER NICLESS?
VERY LIKELY. WHAT'S YOUR BUSINESS?
I'M TOLD YOU HAVE A ROYAL BOX WITHIN YOUR THEATRE.
I TRUST I AM NOT TOO LATE TO RESERVE A SEAT.
A ROYAL—?
AH, THE BOX. IT MAY BE, HRRMMMPH, A LITTLE ABOVE YOUR MEANS.
WILL THIS BE SUFFICIENT?

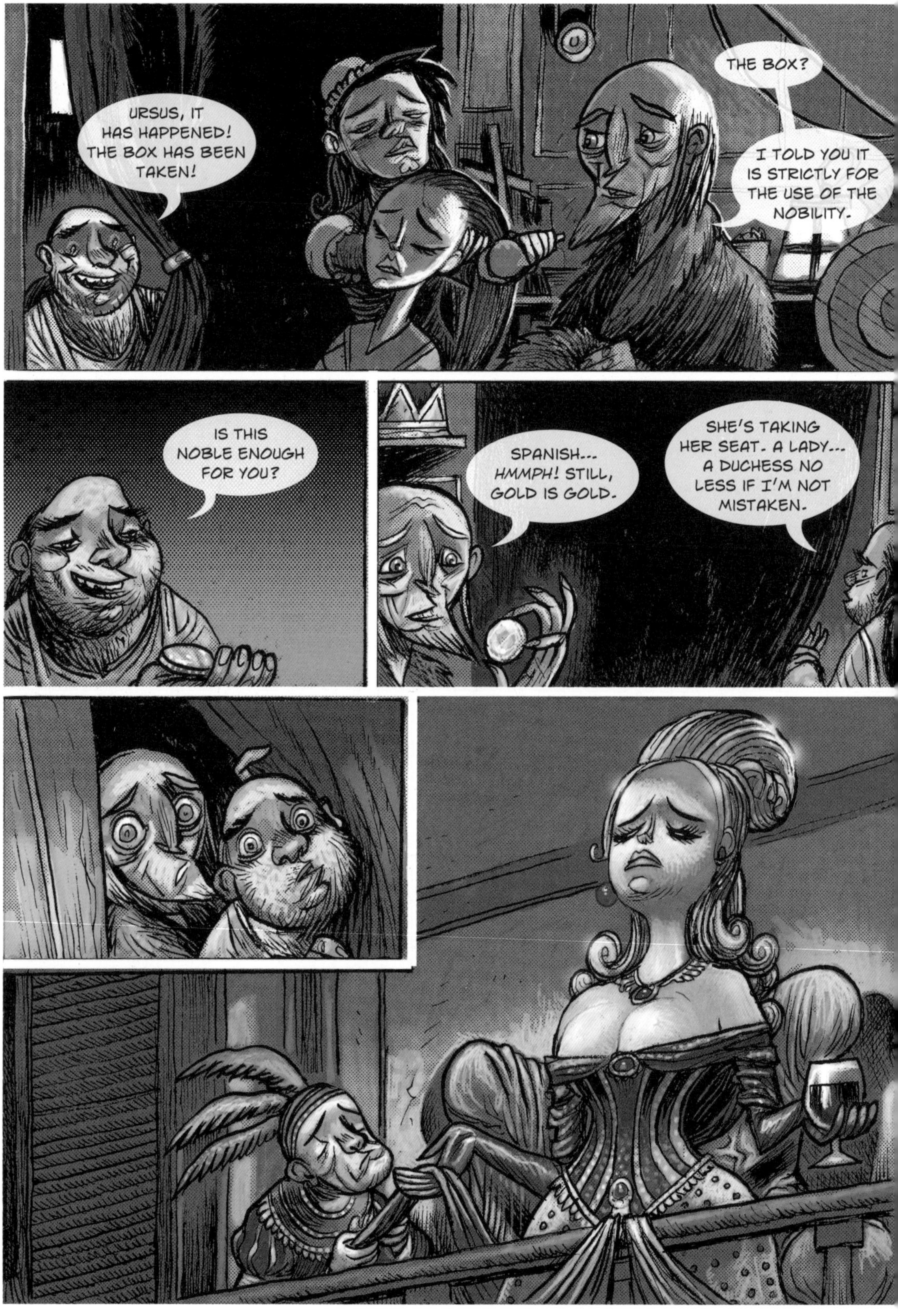
URSUS, IT HAS HAPPENED! THE BOX HAS BEEN TAKEN!
THE BOX?
I TOLD YOU IT IS STRICTLY FOR THE USE OF THE NOBILITY.
IS THIS NOBLE ENOUGH FOR YOU?
SPANISH... HMMPH! STILL, GOLD IS GOLD.
SHE'S TAKING HER SEAT. A LADY... A DUCHESS NO LESS IF I'M NOT MISTAKEN.

The play begins...

There is an atmosphere tonight, an air of expectation that draws out the very finest performance from Gwynplaine.

The Lady Josiana occupies the shadows.

As he reveals his face, Gwynplaine is blinded by the stage lights.

He does not see the effect his features have on her.

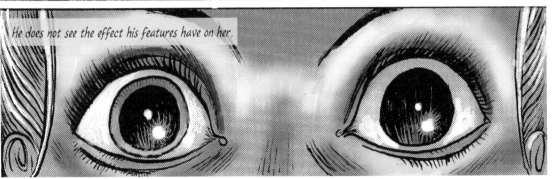

It is only when the lights dim and she rises to leave, that he sees her clearly for the first time...

WHAT IS SHE LIKE, THIS DUCHESS?

SHE...

SHE IS BEAUTIFUL... SHE SHINES LIKE THE SUN... SHE IS A *GODDESS*!

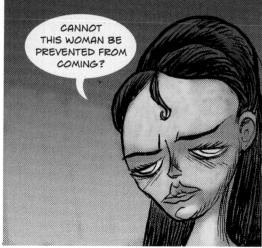

CANNOT THIS WOMAN BE PREVENTED FROM COMING?

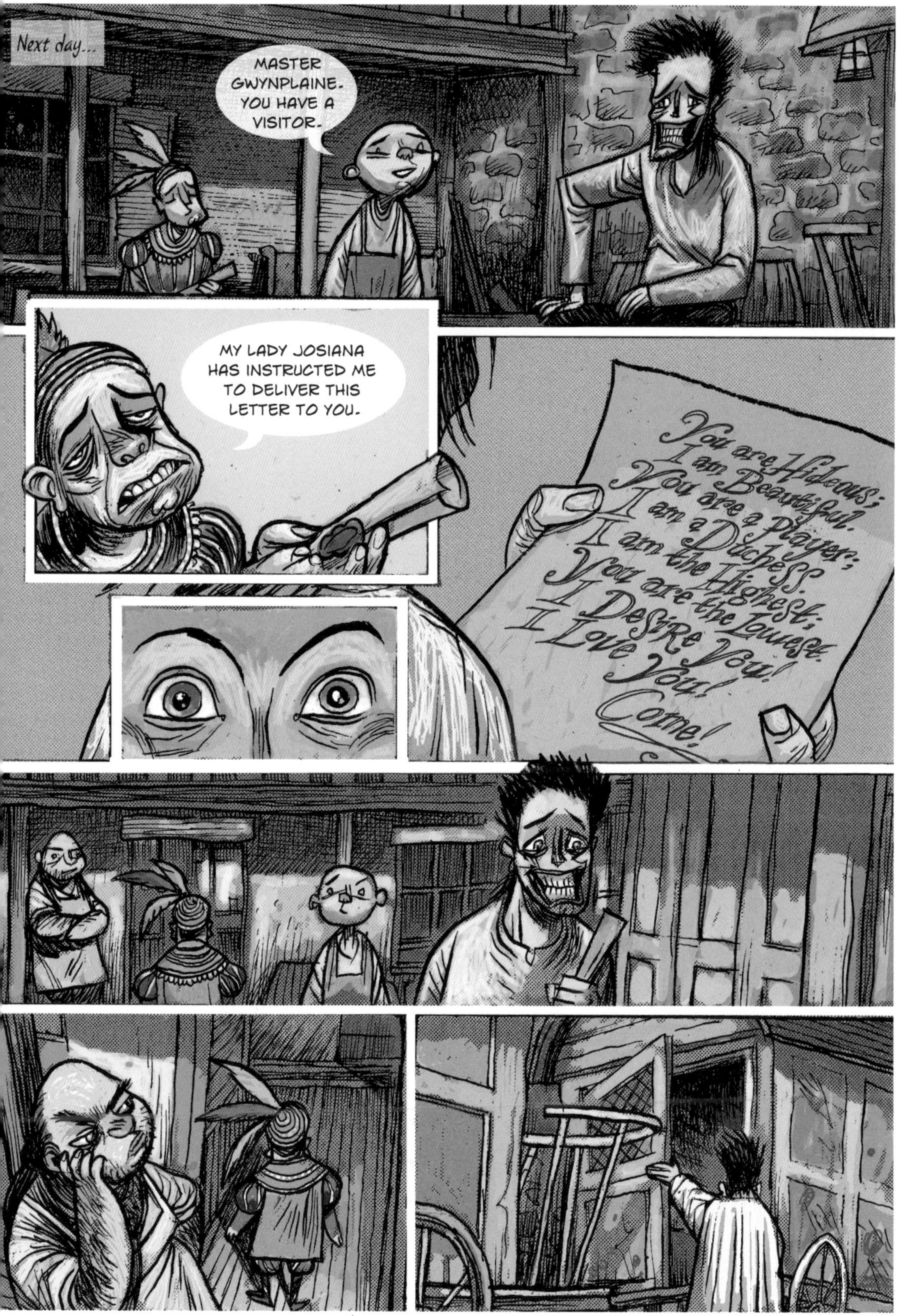
Next day...
MASTER GWYNPLAINE. YOU HAVE A VISITOR.
MY LADY JOSIANA HAS INSTRUCTED ME TO DELIVER THIS LETTER TO YOU.
You are Hideous; I am Beautiful. You are a Player; I am a Duchess. I am the Highest; You are the Lowest. I Desire You! I Love You! Come!

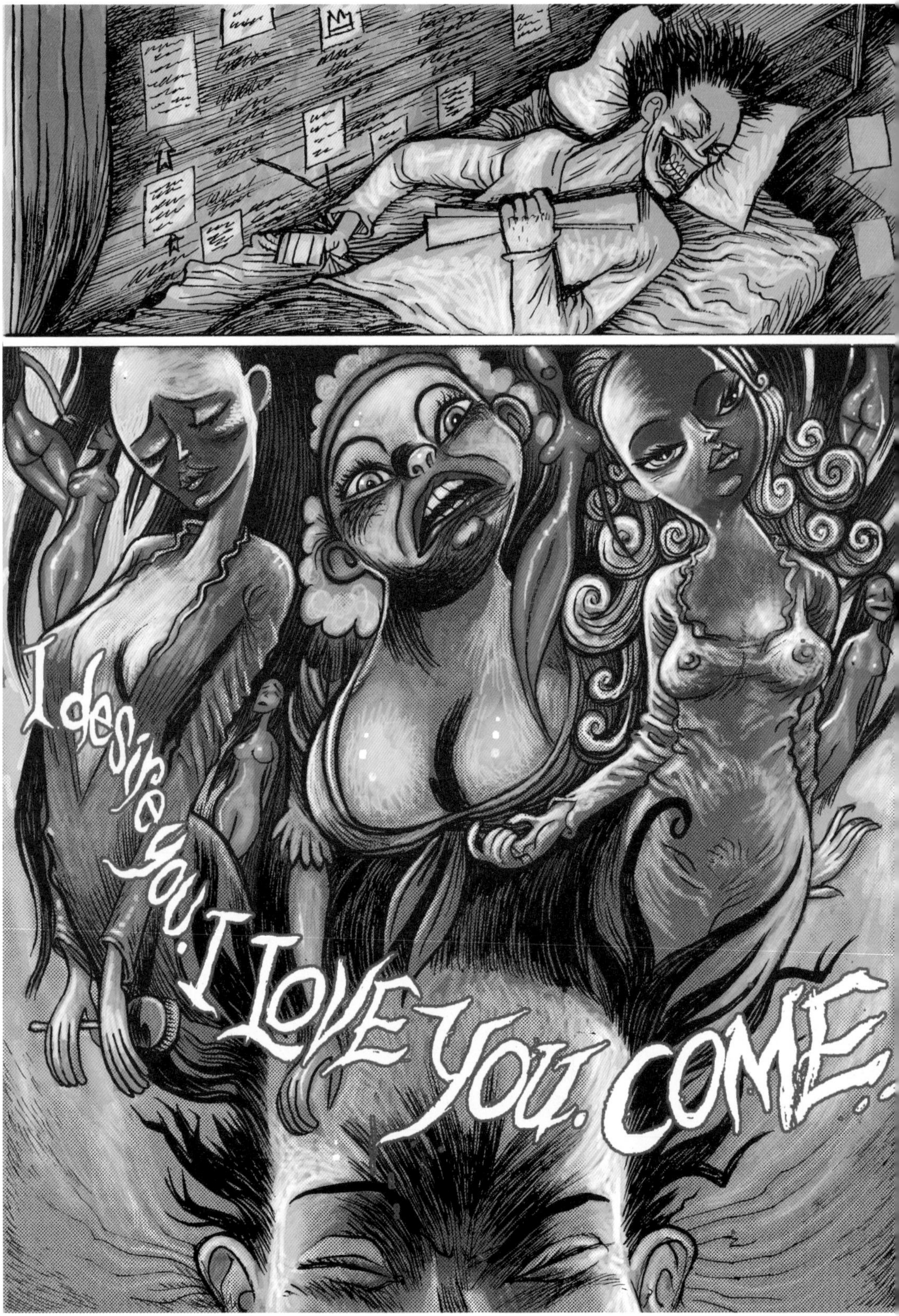
I desire you. I LOVE YOU. COME...

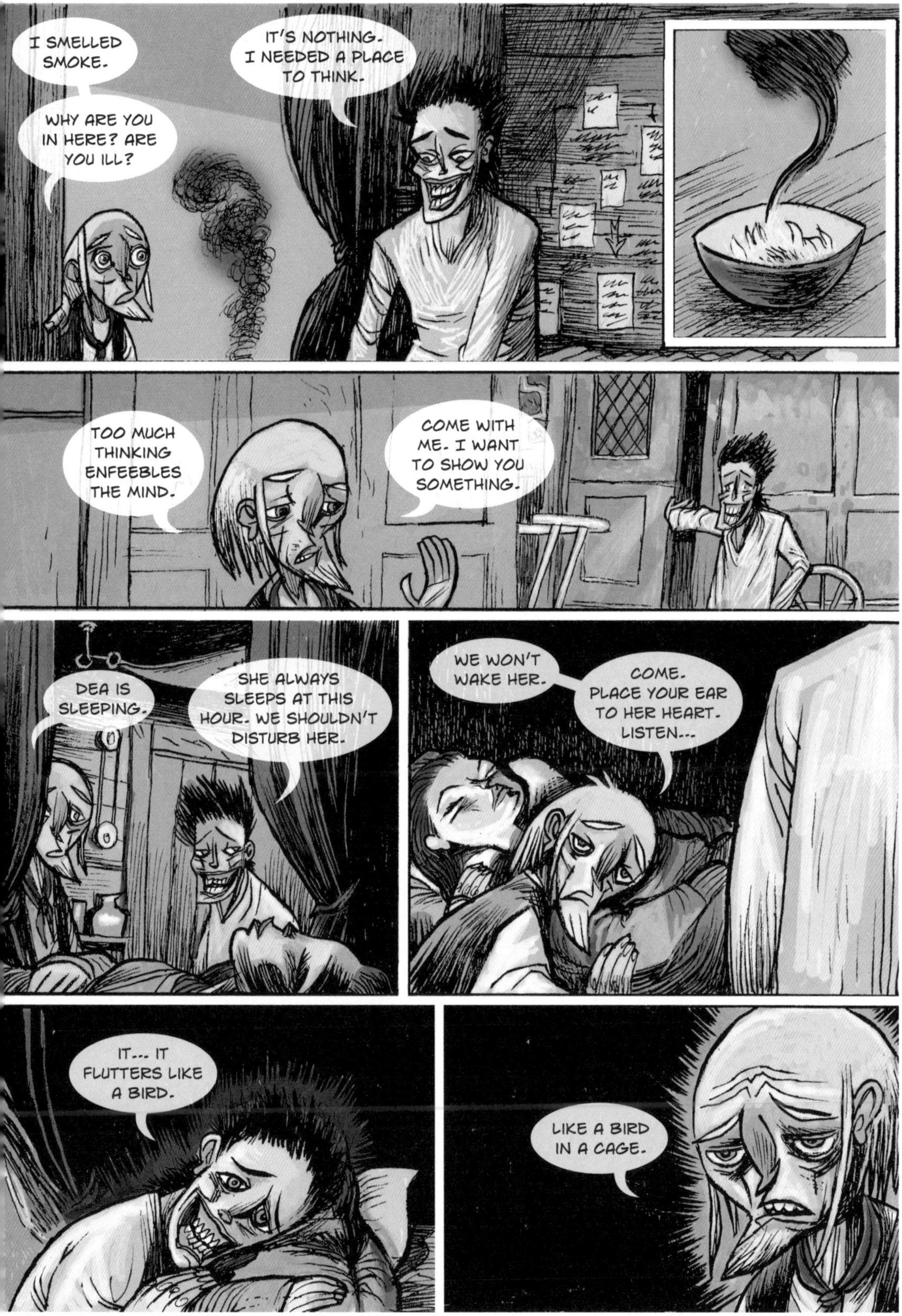
I SMELLED SMOKE.
WHY ARE YOU IN HERE? ARE YOU ILL?
IT'S NOTHING. I NEEDED A PLACE TO THINK.
TOO MUCH THINKING ENFEEBLES THE MIND.
COME WITH ME. I WANT TO SHOW YOU SOMETHING.
DEA IS SLEEPING.
SHE ALWAYS SLEEPS AT THIS HOUR. WE SHOULDN'T DISTURB HER.
WE WON'T WAKE HER.
COME. PLACE YOUR EAR TO HER HEART. LISTEN...
IT... IT FLUTTERS LIKE A BIRD.
LIKE A BIRD IN A CAGE.

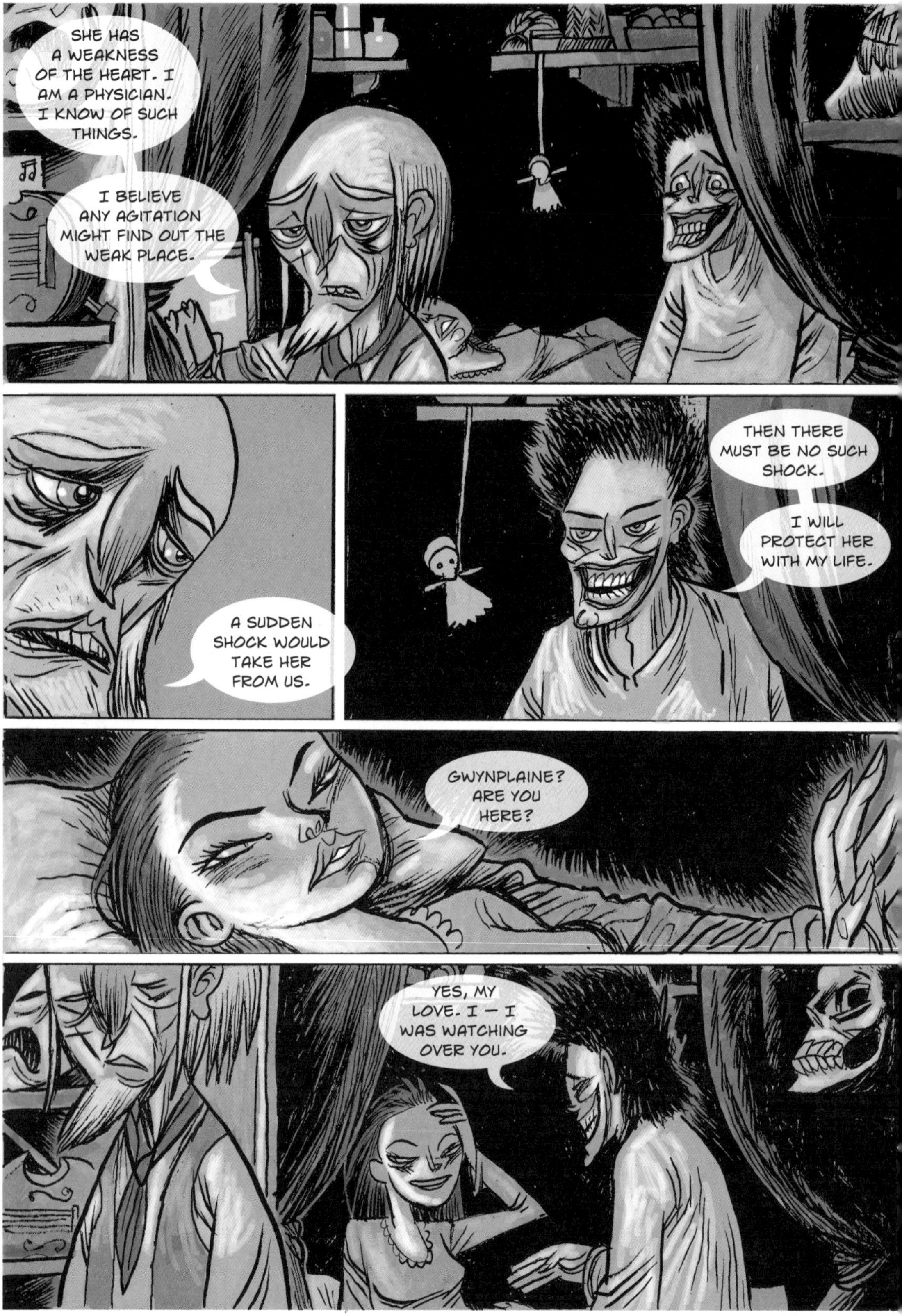
SHE HAS A WEAKNESS OF THE HEART. I AM A PHYSICIAN. I KNOW OF SUCH THINGS.
I BELIEVE ANY AGITATION MIGHT FIND OUT THE WEAK PLACE.
A SUDDEN SHOCK WOULD TAKE HER FROM US.
THEN THERE MUST BE NO SUCH SHOCK.
I WILL PROTECT HER WITH MY LIFE.
GWYNPLAINE? ARE YOU HERE?
YES, MY LOVE. I — I WAS WATCHING OVER YOU.

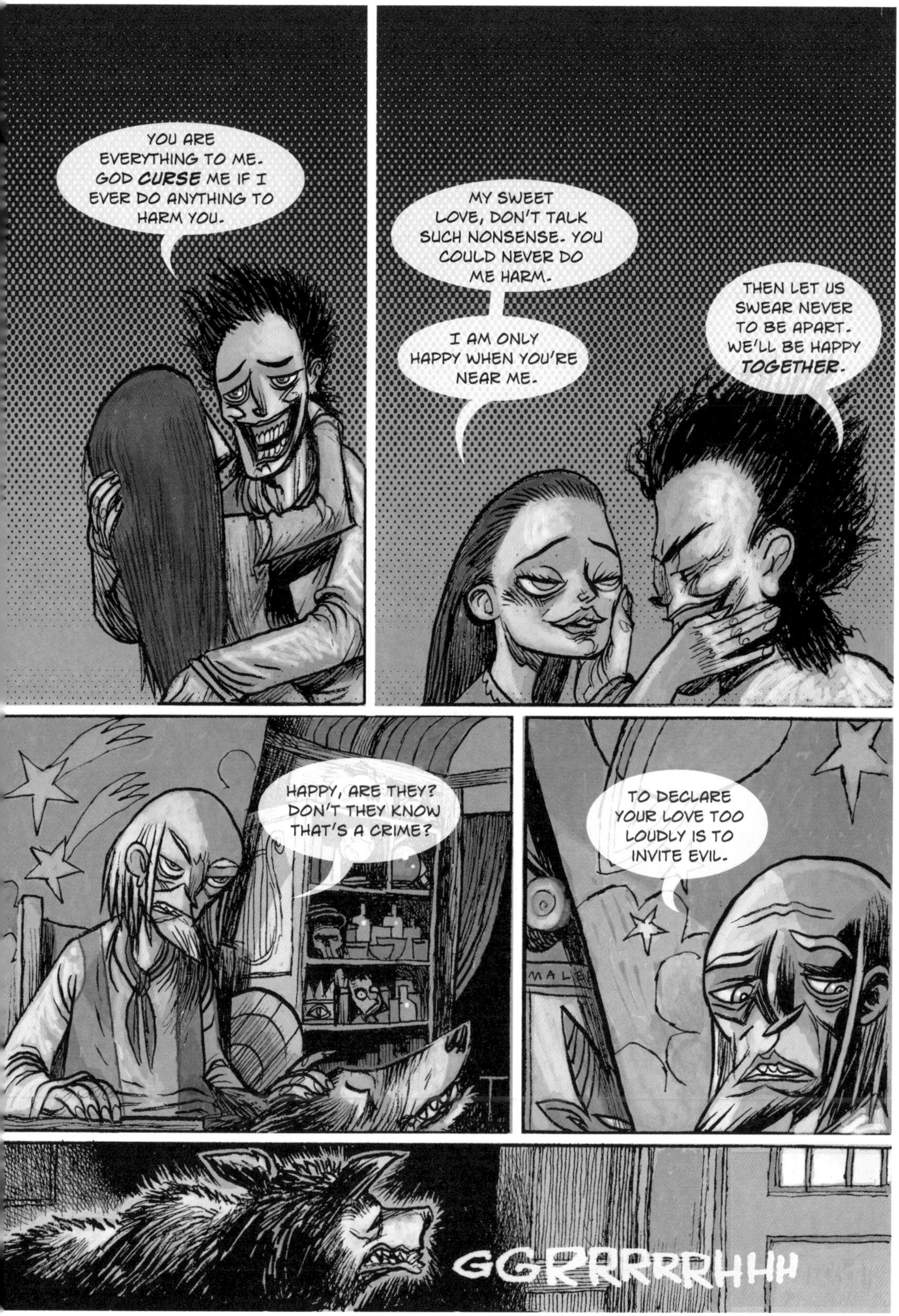
YOU ARE EVERYTHING TO ME. GOD CURSE ME IF I EVER DO ANYTHING TO HARM YOU.
MY SWEET LOVE, DON'T TALK SUCH NONSENSE. YOU COULD NEVER DO ME HARM.
I AM ONLY HAPPY WHEN YOU'RE NEAR ME.
THEN LET US SWEAR NEVER TO BE APART. WE'LL BE HAPPY TOGETHER.
HAPPY, ARE THEY? DON'T THEY KNOW THAT'S A CRIME?
TO DECLARE YOUR LOVE TOO LOUDLY IS TO INVITE EVIL.
GGRRRRRRHHH

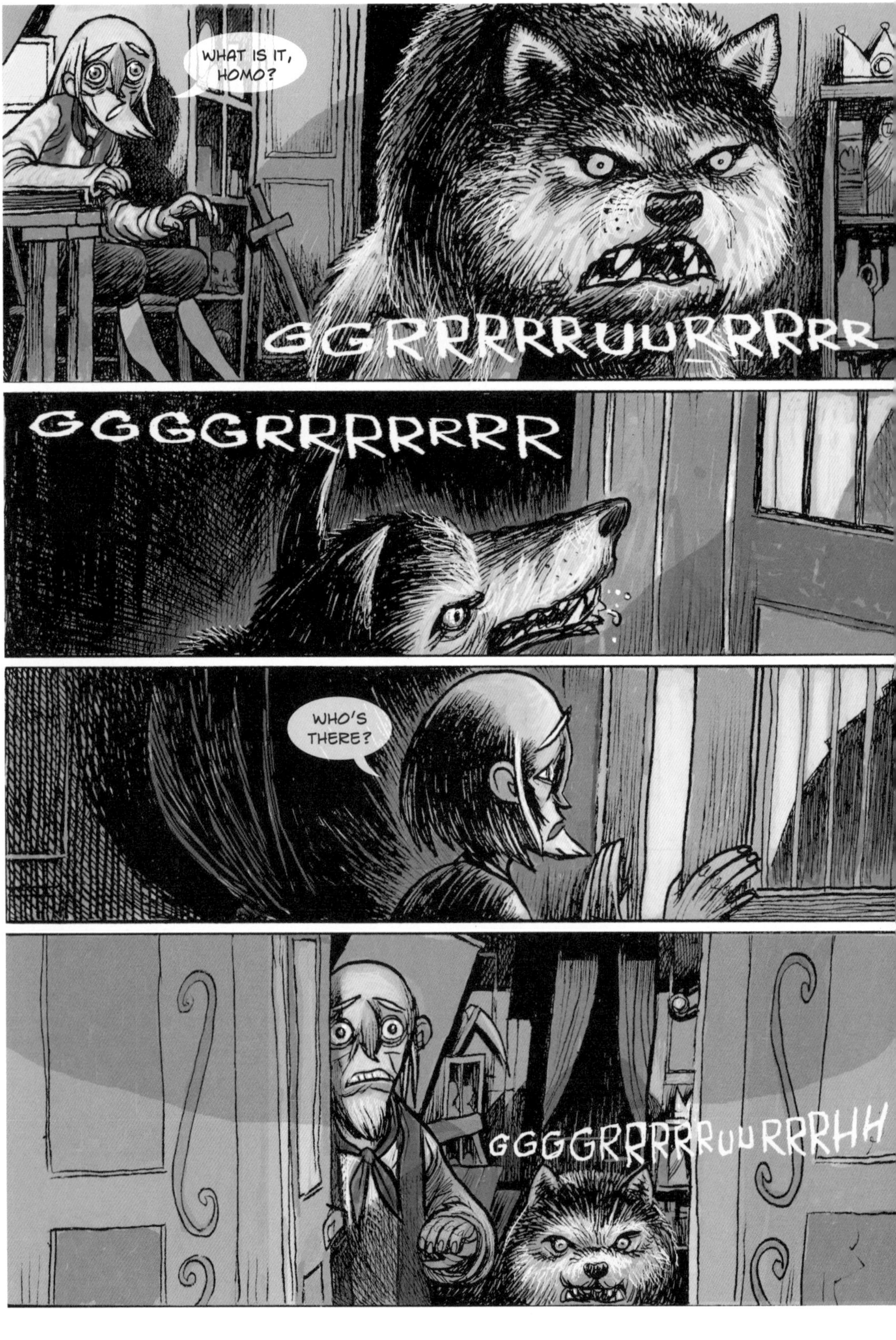
WHAT IS IT, HOMO?
GGRRRRRRUURRRRR
GGGGRRRRRRRR
WHO'S THERE?
GGGGRRRRRUURRRHH

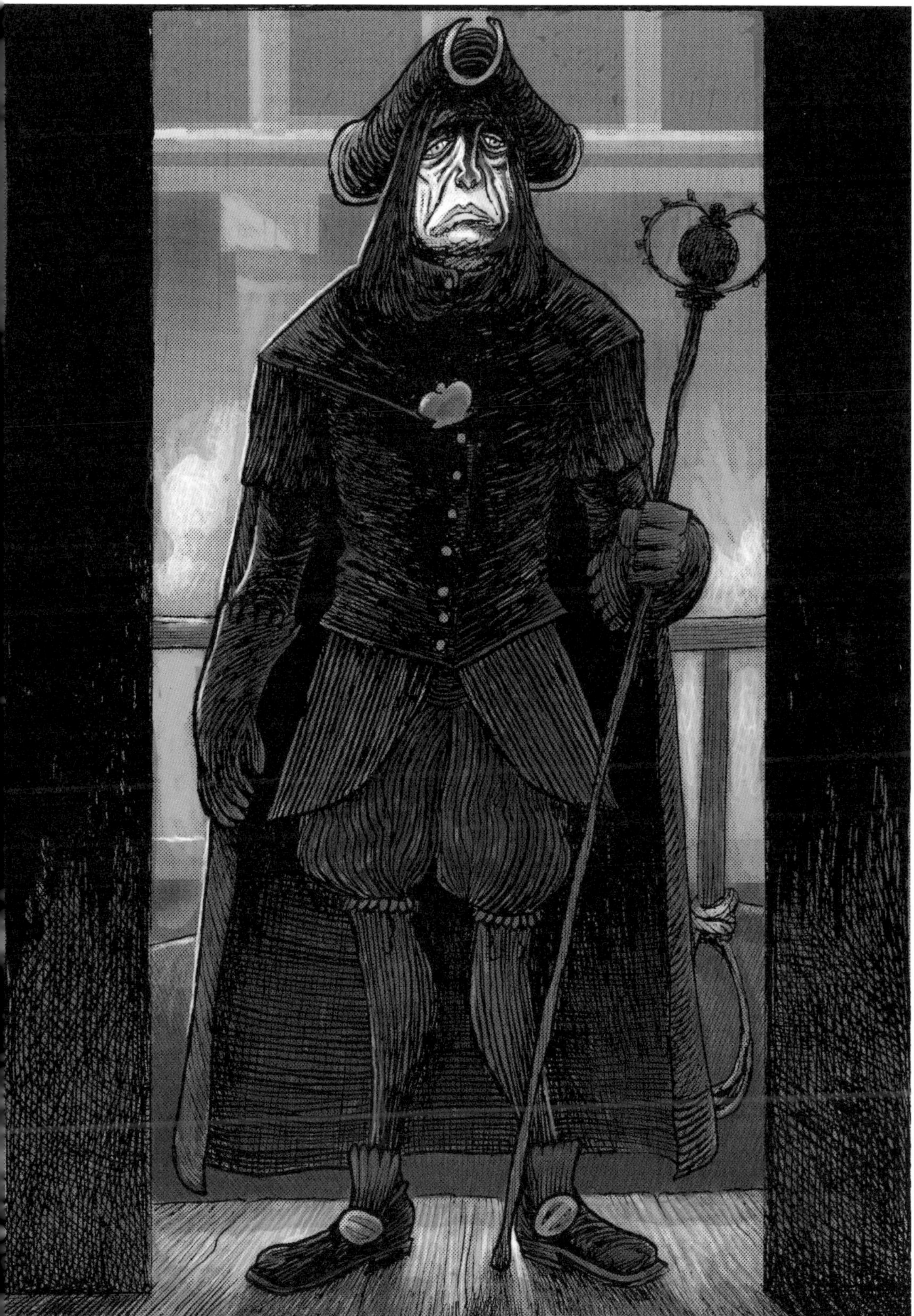

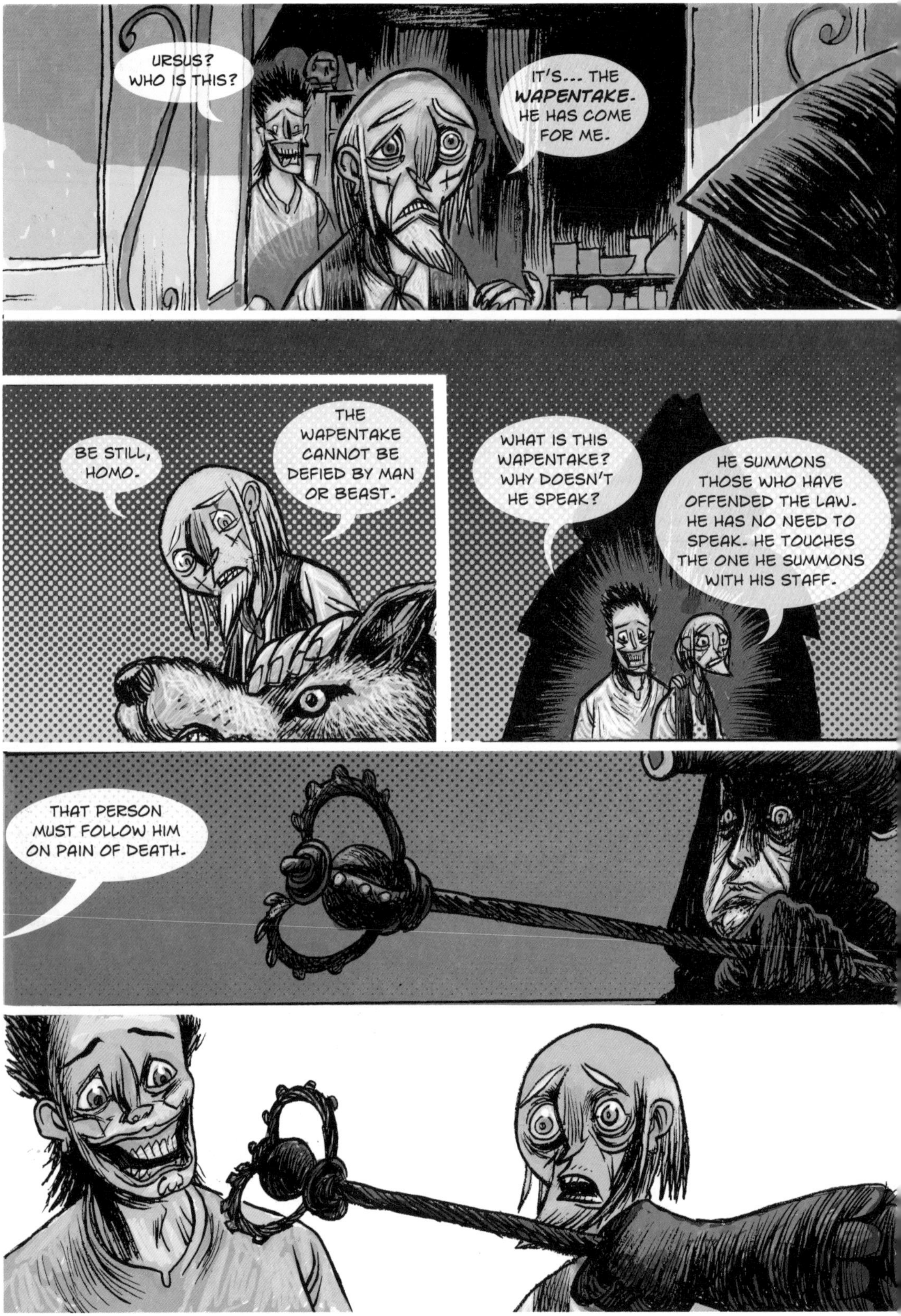
URSUS? WHO IS THIS?
IT'S... THE WAPENTAKE. HE HAS COME FOR ME.
BE STILL, HOMO.
THE WAPENTAKE CANNOT BE DEFIED BY MAN OR BEAST.
WHAT IS THIS WAPENTAKE? WHY DOESN'T HE SPEAK?
HE SUMMONS THOSE WHO HAVE OFFENDED THE LAW. HE HAS NO NEED TO SPEAK. HE TOUCHES THE ONE HE SUMMONS WITH HIS STAFF.
THAT PERSON MUST FOLLOW HIM ON PAIN OF DEATH.

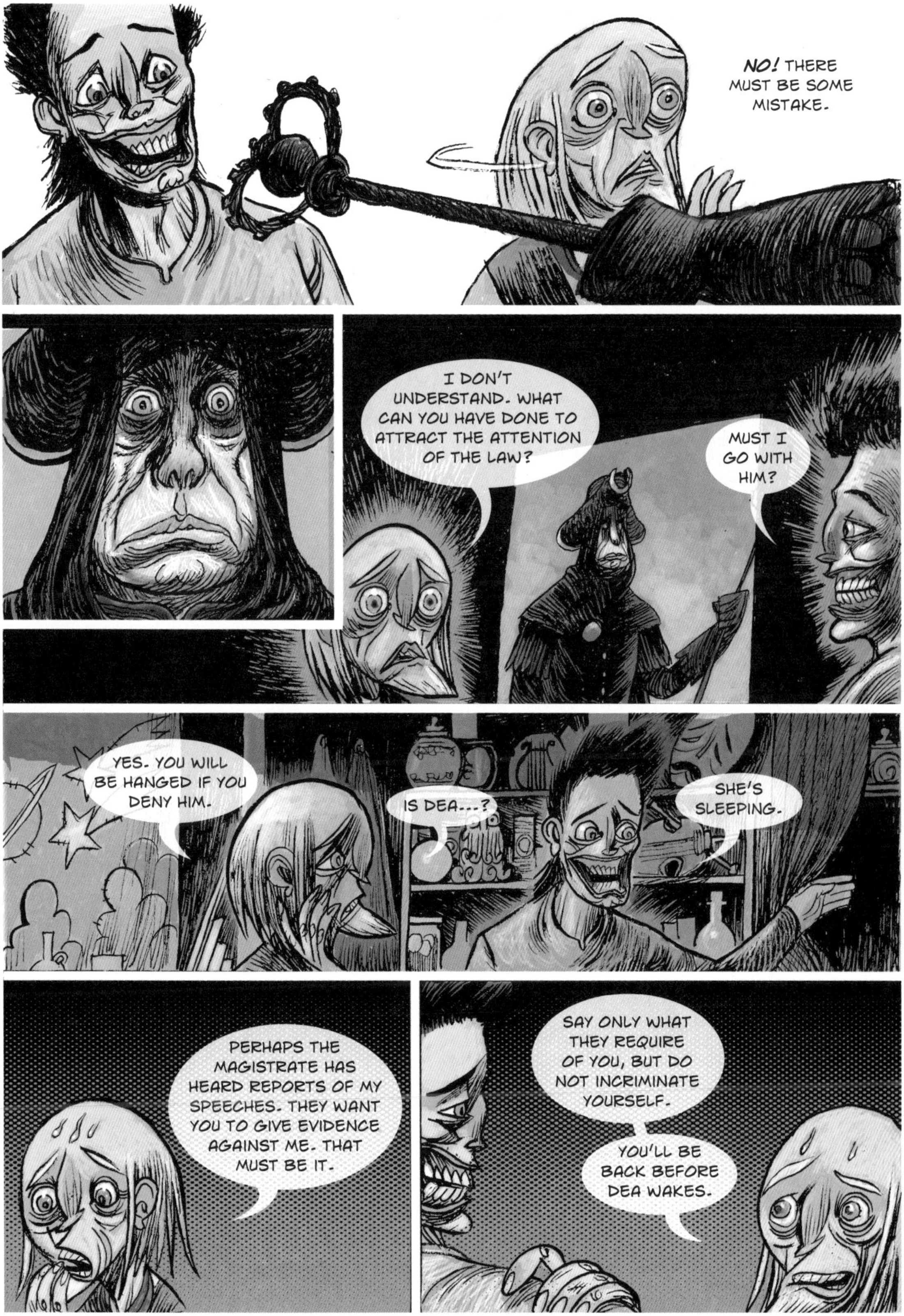
NO! THERE MUST BE SOME MISTAKE.
I DON'T UNDERSTAND. WHAT CAN YOU HAVE DONE TO ATTRACT THE ATTENTION OF THE LAW?
MUST I GO WITH HIM?
YES. YOU WILL BE HANGED IF YOU DENY HIM.
IS DEA...?
SHE'S SLEEPING.
PERHAPS THE MAGISTRATE HAS HEARD REPORTS OF MY SPEECHES. THEY WANT YOU TO GIVE EVIDENCE AGAINST ME. THAT MUST BE IT.
SAY ONLY WHAT THEY REQUIRE OF YOU, BUT DO NOT INCRIMINATE YOURSELF.
YOU'LL BE BACK BEFORE DEA WAKES.

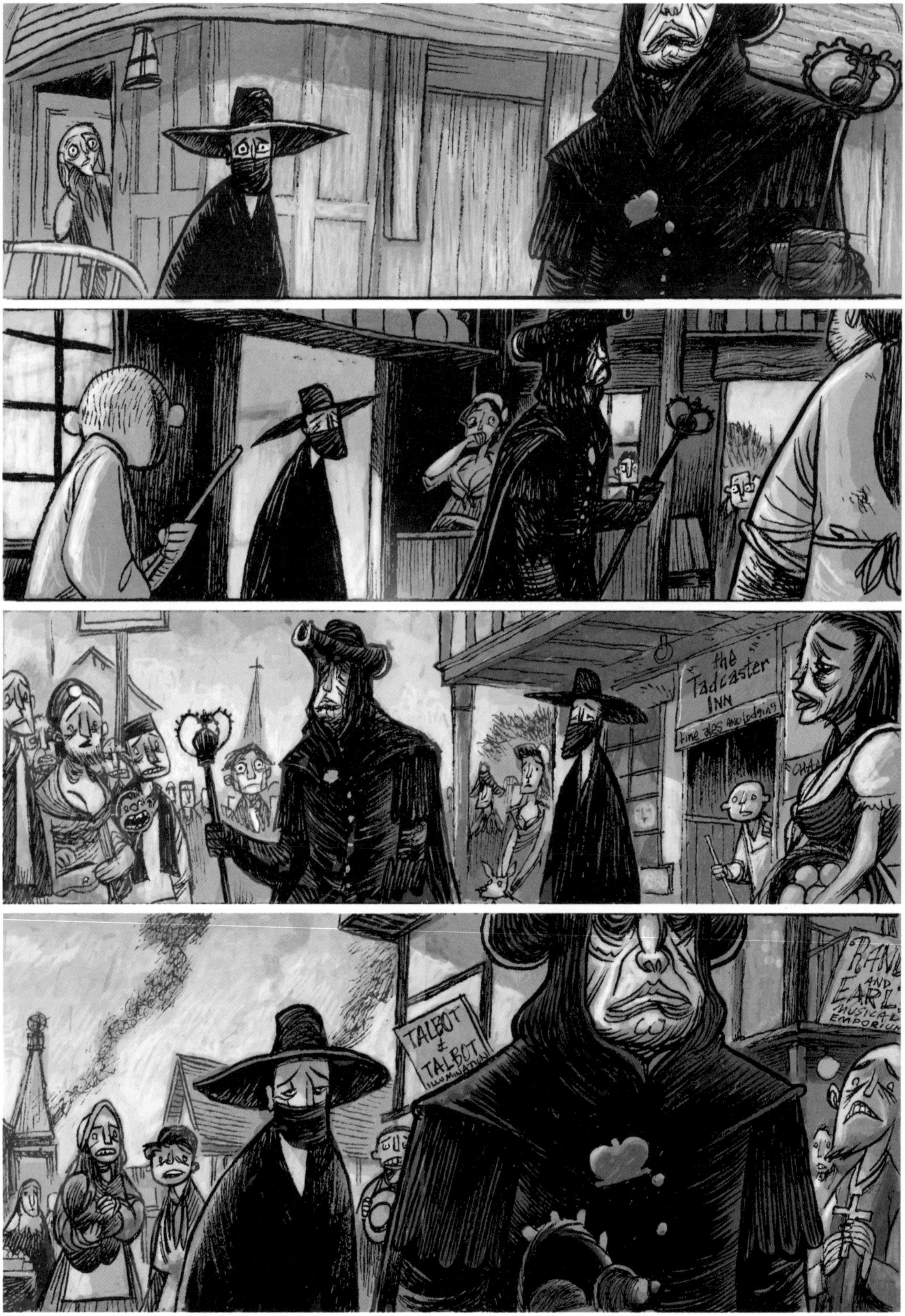
the Tadcaster INN
Fine ales and lodging
TALBOT & TALBOT
AND
MUSICAL
EMPORIUM

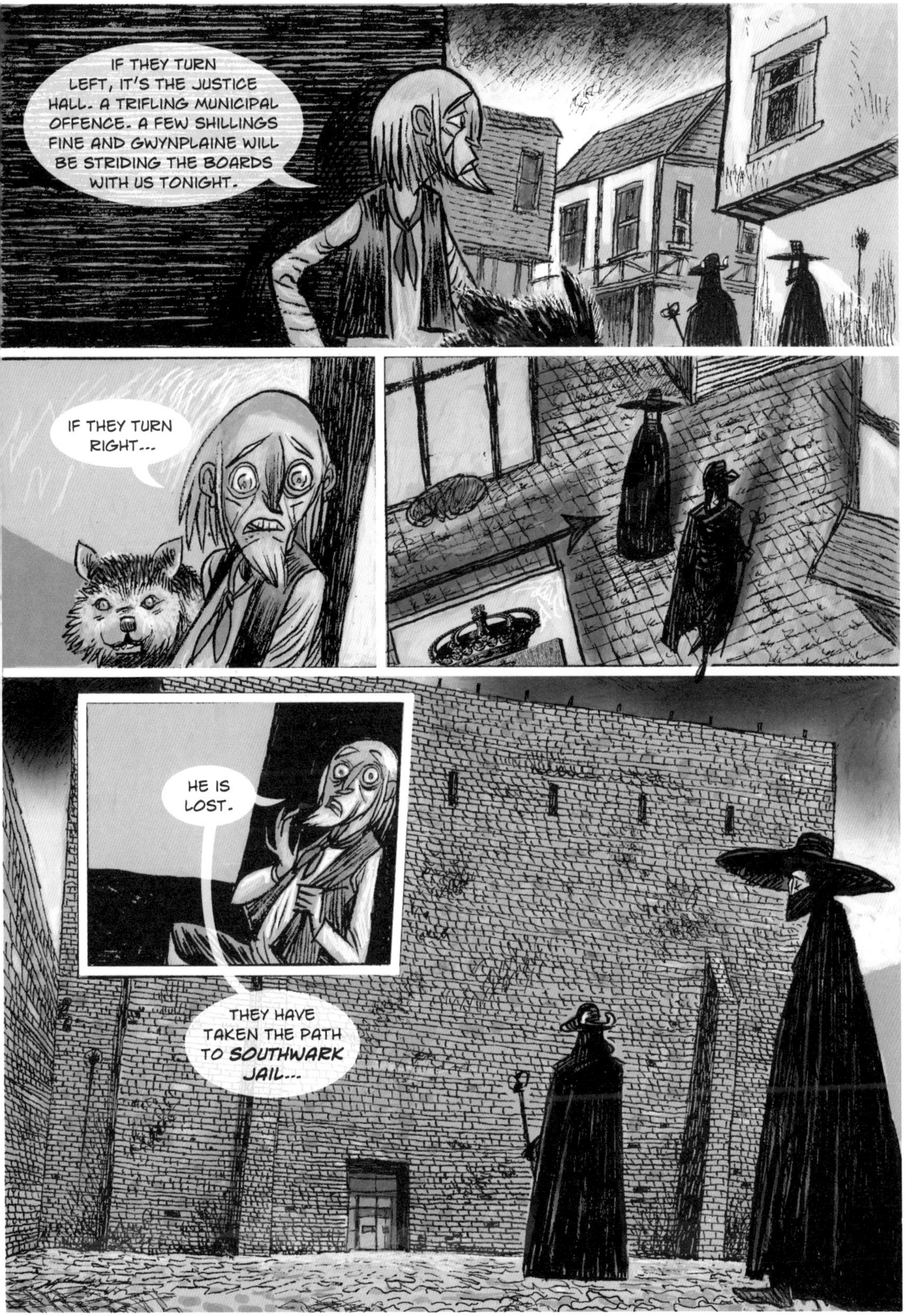
IF THEY TURN LEFT, IT'S THE JUSTICE HALL. A TRIFLING MUNICIPAL OFFENCE. A FEW SHILLINGS FINE AND GWYNPLAINE WILL BE STRIDING THE BOARDS WITH US TONIGHT.
IF THEY TURN RIGHT...
HE IS LOST.
THEY HAVE TAKEN THE PATH TO **SOUTHWARK JAIL**...

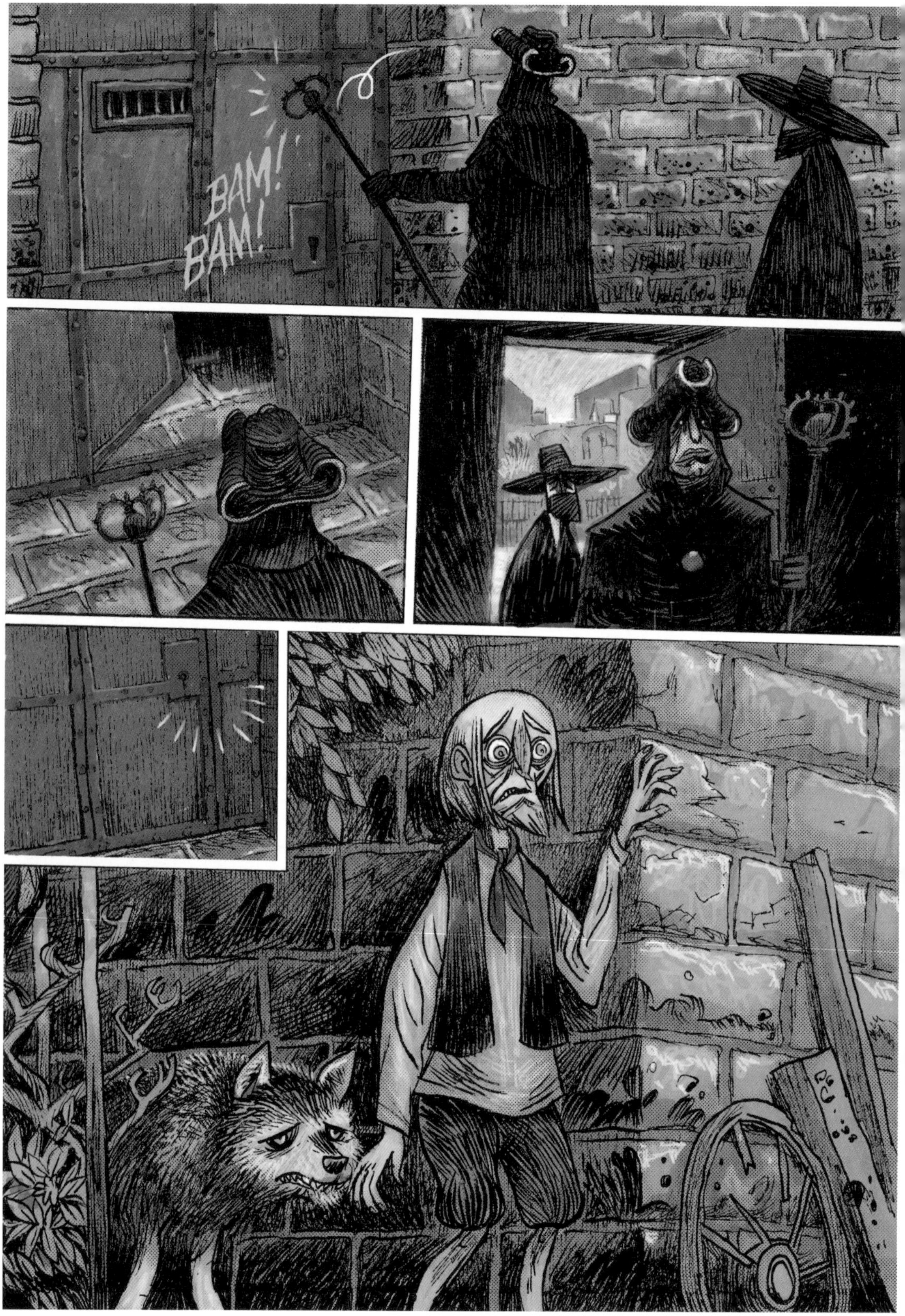
BAM!
BAM!

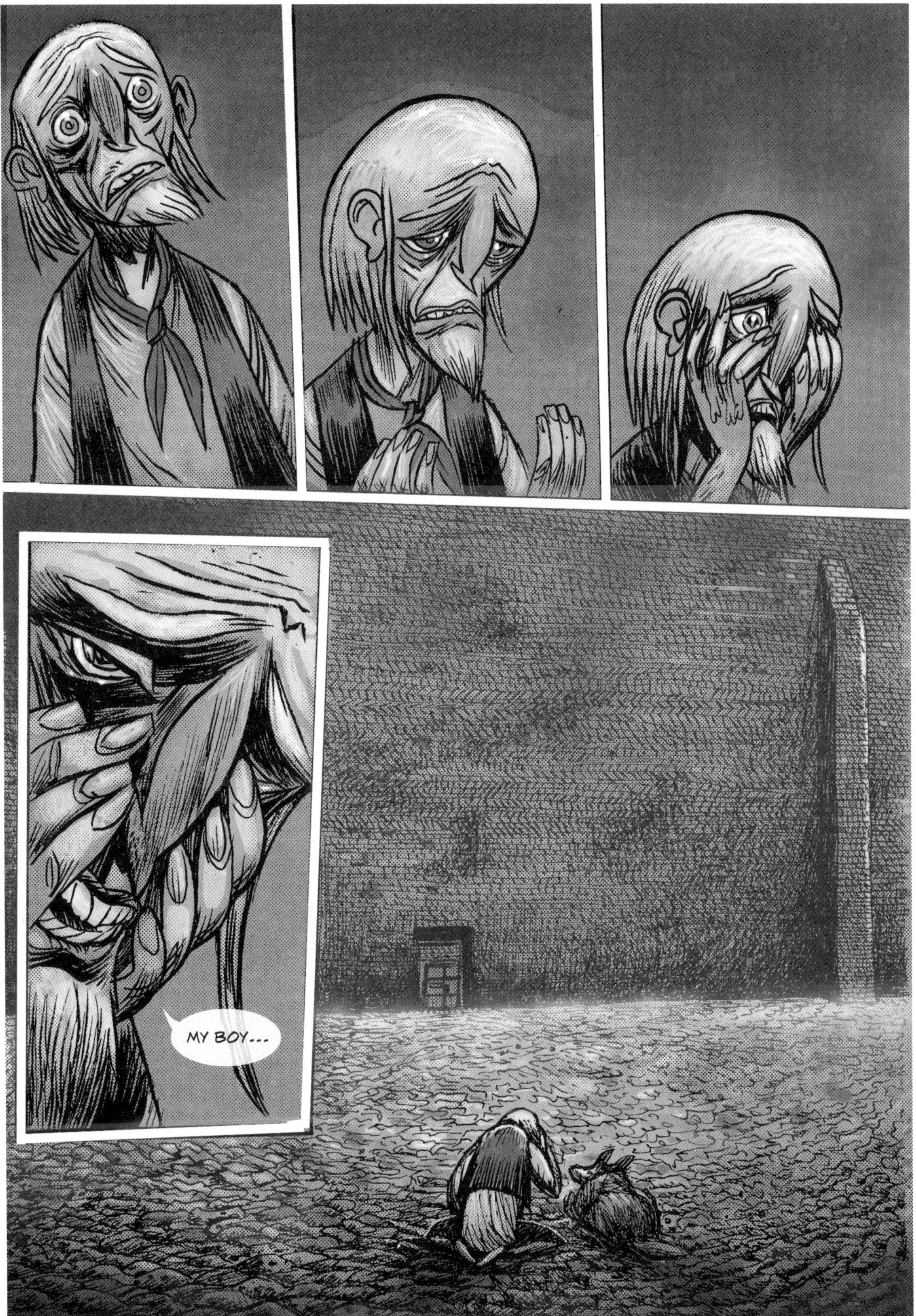
MY BOY...

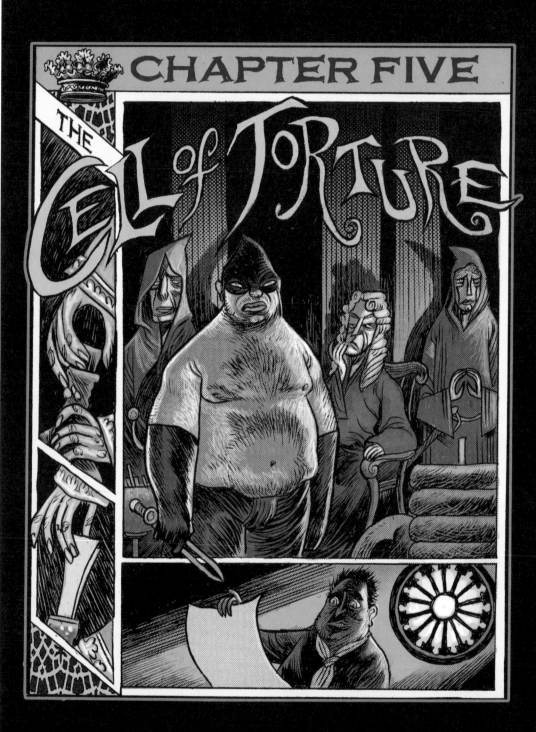

CHAPTER FIVE

THE CELL of TORTURE

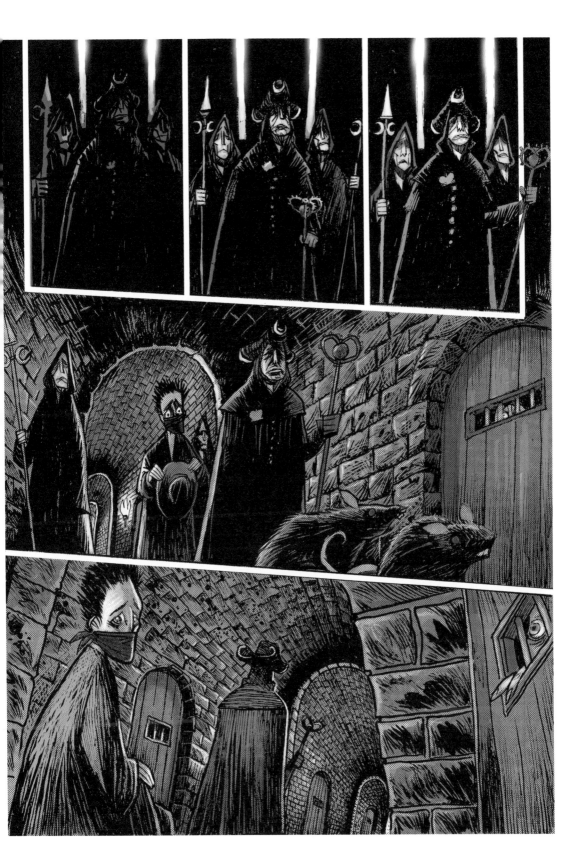

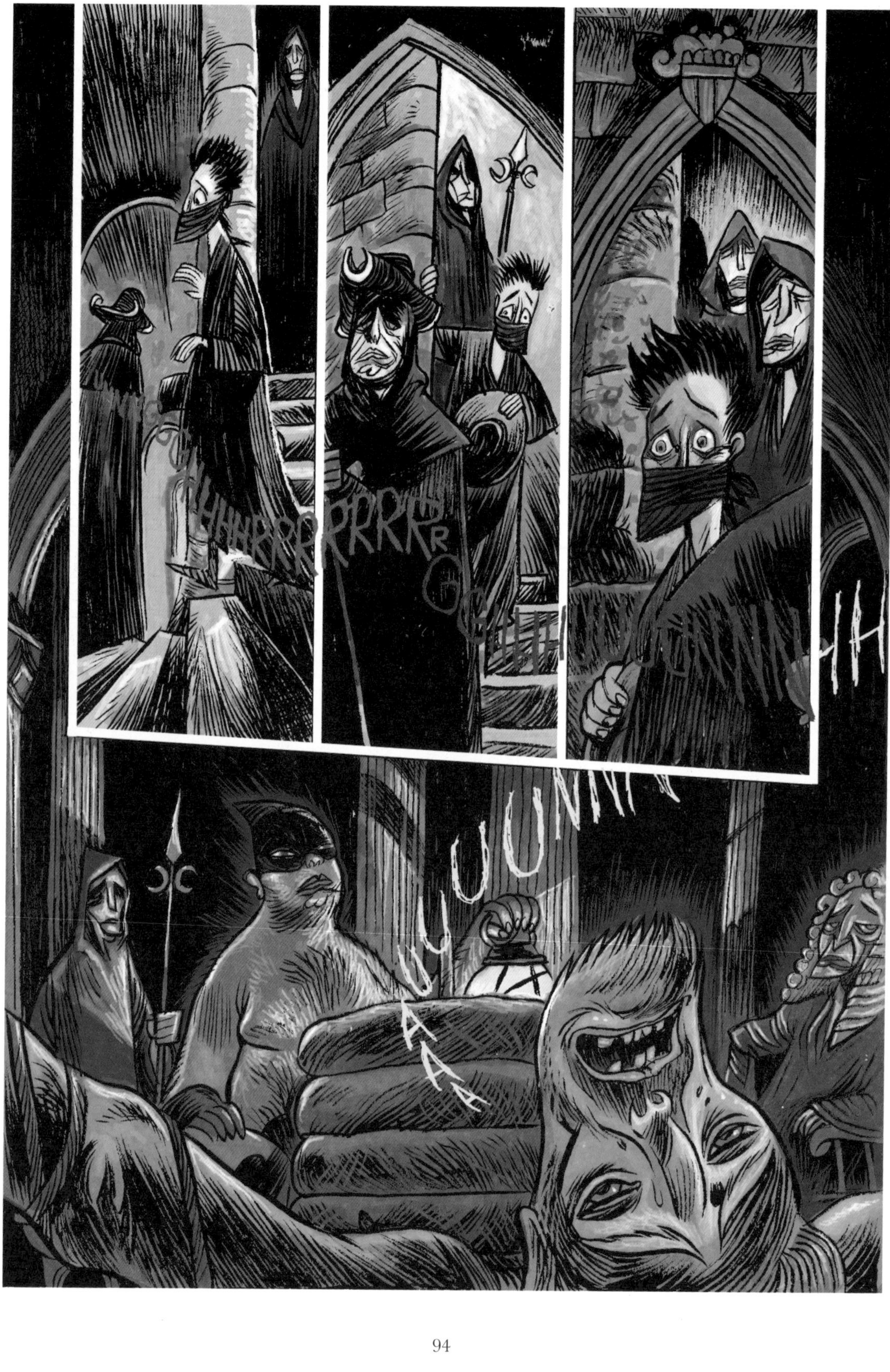
HHHHRRRRRRRRRr
UUUNN
AAAA

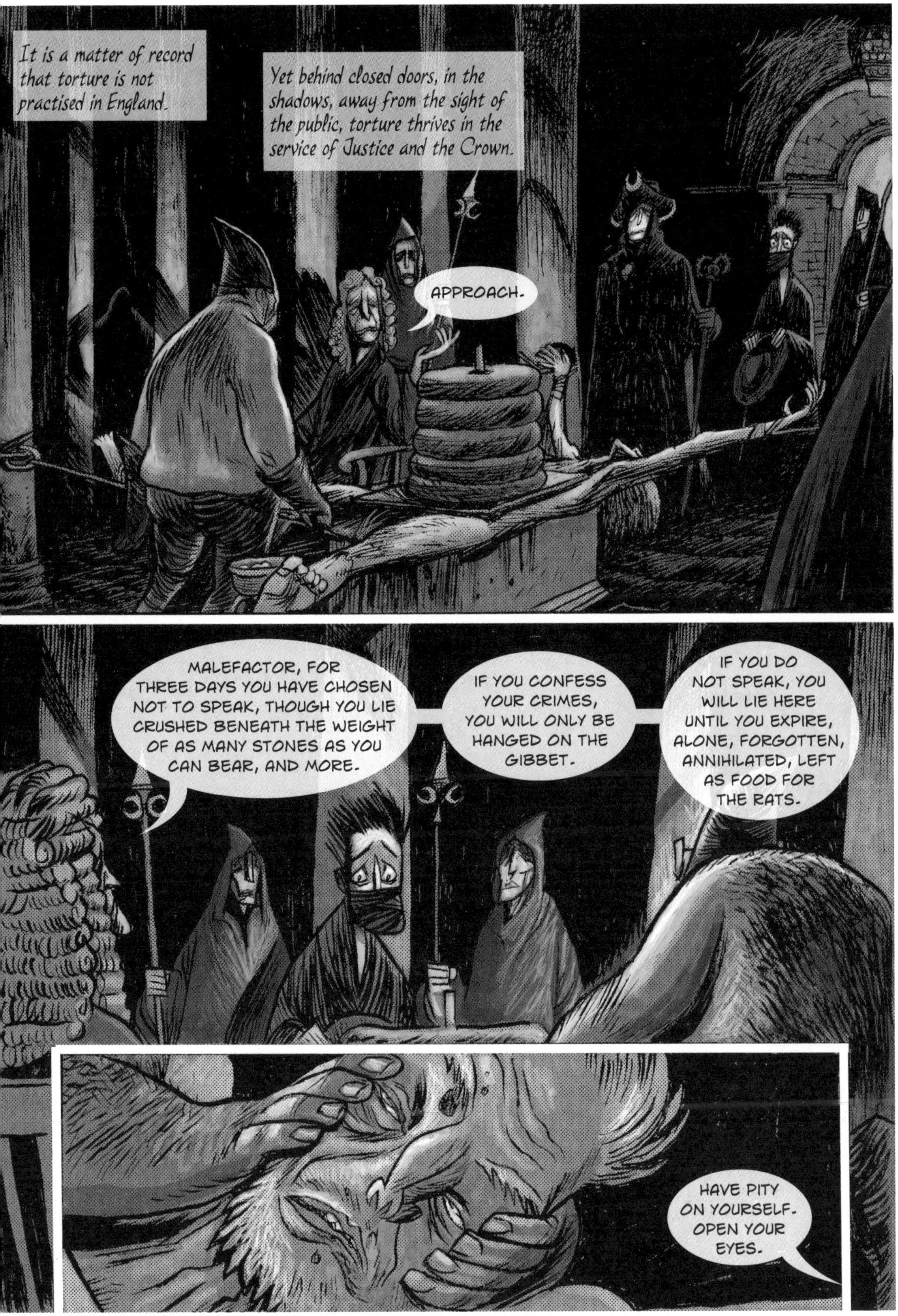
It is a matter of record that torture is not practised in England.
Yet behind closed doors, in the shadows, away from the sight of the public, torture thrives in the service of Justice and the Crown.
APPROACH.
MALEFACTOR, FOR THREE DAYS YOU HAVE CHOSEN NOT TO SPEAK, THOUGH YOU LIE CRUSHED BENEATH THE WEIGHT OF AS MANY STONES AS YOU CAN BEAR, AND MORE.
IF YOU CONFESS YOUR CRIMES, YOU WILL ONLY BE HANGED ON THE GIBBET.
IF YOU DO NOT SPEAK, YOU WILL LIE HERE UNTIL YOU EXPIRE, ALONE, FORGOTTEN, ANNIHILATED, LEFT AS FOOD FOR THE RATS.
HAVE PITY ON YOURSELF. OPEN YOUR EYES.

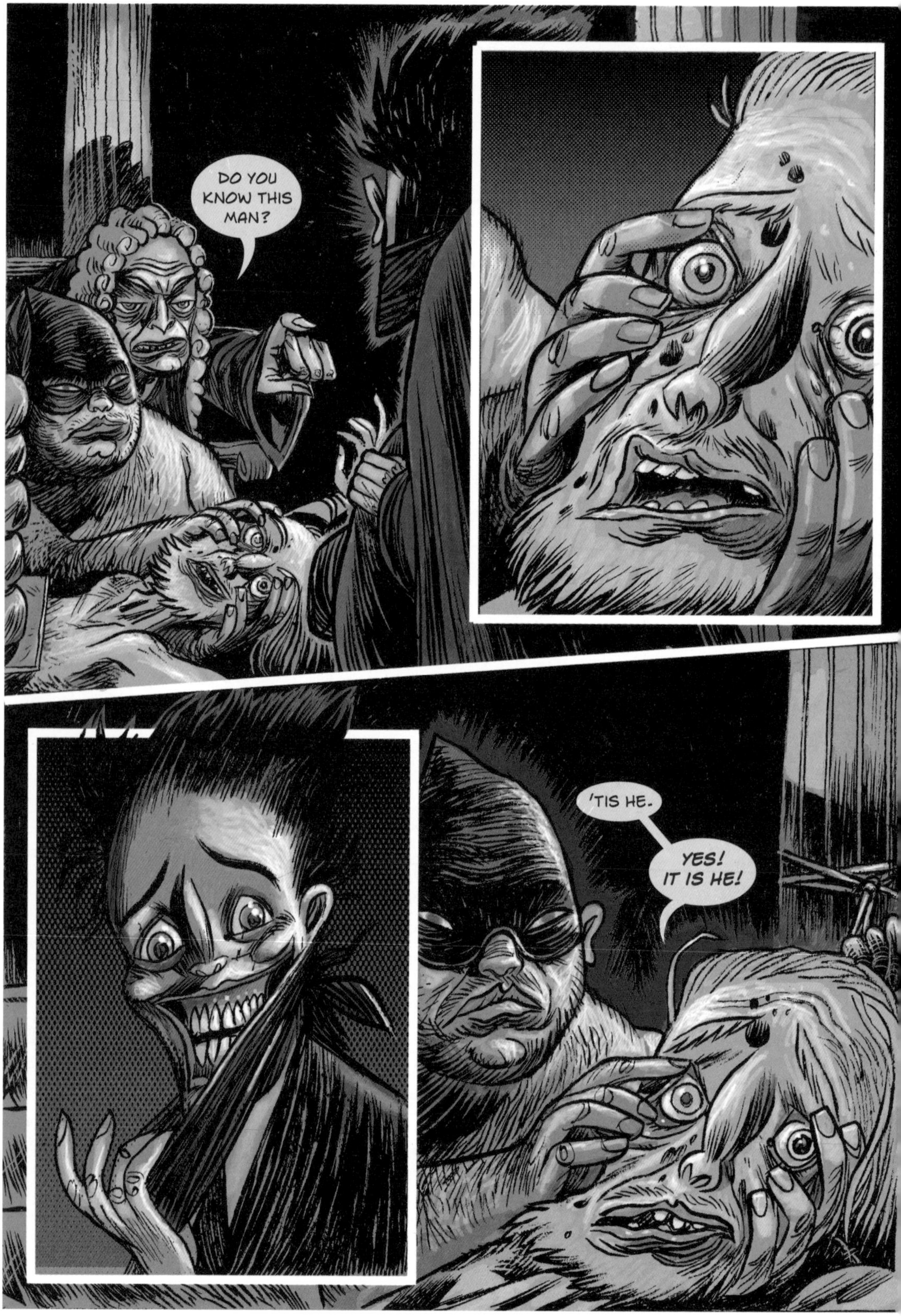
DO YOU KNOW THIS MAN?
'TIS HE.
YES! IT IS HE!

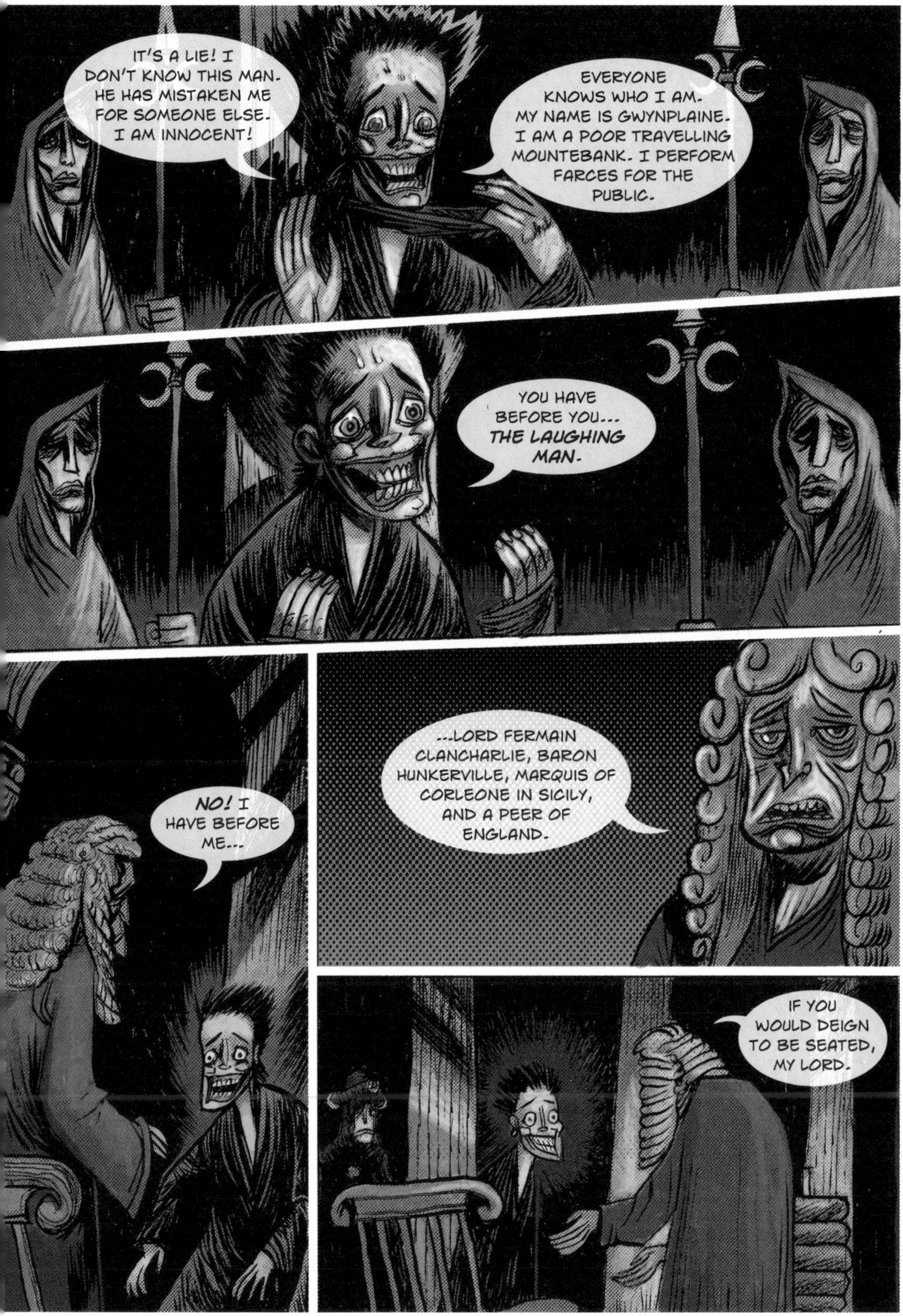
IT'S A LIE! I DON'T KNOW THIS MAN. HE HAS MISTAKEN ME FOR SOMEONE ELSE. I AM INNOCENT!
EVERYONE KNOWS WHO I AM. MY NAME IS GWYNPLAINE. I AM A POOR TRAVELLING MOUNTEBANK. I PERFORM FARCES FOR THE PUBLIC.
YOU HAVE BEFORE YOU... THE LAUGHING MAN.
NO! I HAVE BEFORE ME...
...LORD FERMAIN CLANCHARLIE, BARON HUNKERVILLE, MARQUIS OF CORLEONE IN SICILY, AND A PEER OF ENGLAND.
IF YOU WOULD DEIGN TO BE SEATED, MY LORD.

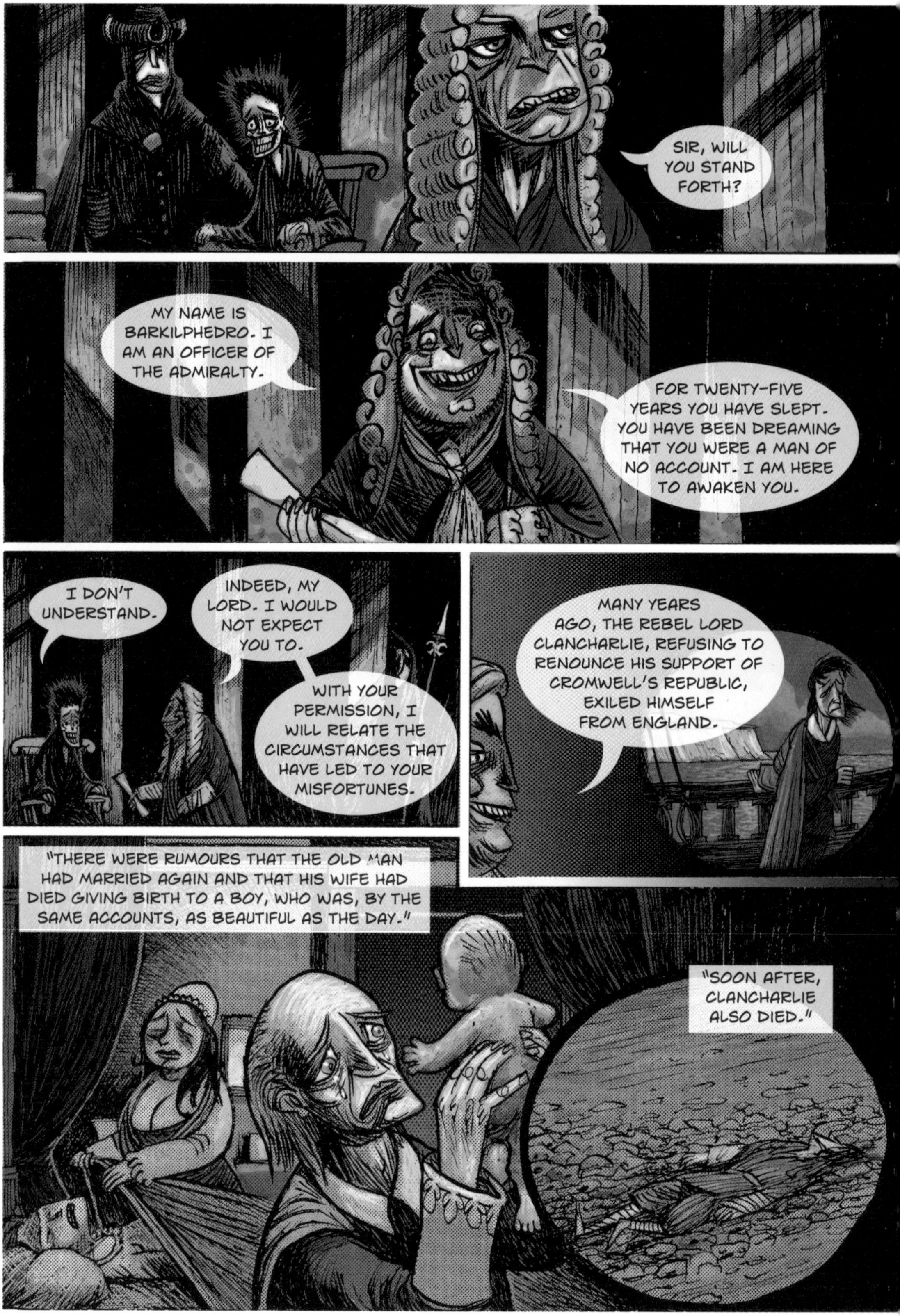
SIR, WILL YOU STAND FORTH?
MY NAME IS BARKILPHEDRO. I AM AN OFFICER OF THE ADMIRALTY.
FOR TWENTY-FIVE YEARS YOU HAVE SLEPT. YOU HAVE BEEN DREAMING THAT YOU WERE A MAN OF NO ACCOUNT. I AM HERE TO AWAKEN YOU.
I DON'T UNDERSTAND.
INDEED, MY LORD. I WOULD NOT EXPECT YOU TO.
WITH YOUR PERMISSION, I WILL RELATE THE CIRCUMSTANCES THAT HAVE LED TO YOUR MISFORTUNES.
MANY YEARS AGO, THE REBEL LORD CLANCHARLIE, REFUSING TO RENOUNCE HIS SUPPORT OF CROMWELL'S REPUBLIC, EXILED HIMSELF FROM ENGLAND.
"THERE WERE RUMOURS THAT THE OLD MAN HAD MARRIED AGAIN AND THAT HIS WIFE HAD DIED GIVING BIRTH TO A BOY, WHO WAS, BY THE SAME ACCOUNTS, AS BEAUTIFUL AS THE DAY."
"SOON AFTER, CLANCHARLIE ALSO DIED."

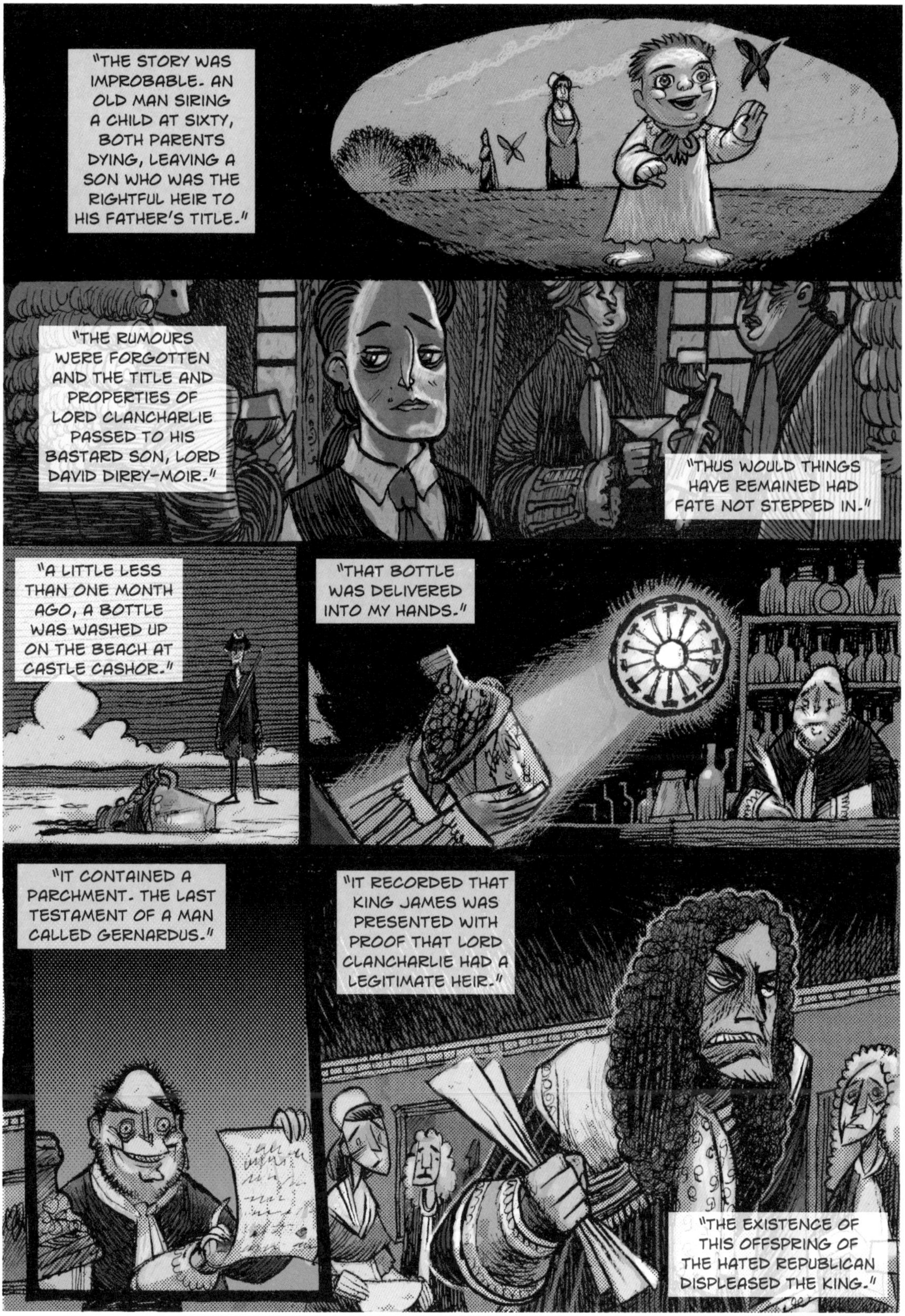
"THE STORY WAS IMPROBABLE. AN OLD MAN SIRING A CHILD AT SIXTY, BOTH PARENTS DYING, LEAVING A SON WHO WAS THE RIGHTFUL HEIR TO HIS FATHER'S TITLE."
"THE RUMOURS WERE FORGOTTEN AND THE TITLE AND PROPERTIES OF LORD CLANCHARLIE PASSED TO HIS BASTARD SON, LORD DAVID DIRRY-MOIR."
"THUS WOULD THINGS HAVE REMAINED HAD FATE NOT STEPPED IN."
"A LITTLE LESS THAN ONE MONTH AGO, A BOTTLE WAS WASHED UP ON THE BEACH AT CASTLE CASHOR."
"THAT BOTTLE WAS DELIVERED INTO MY HANDS."
"IT CONTAINED A PARCHMENT. THE LAST TESTAMENT OF A MAN CALLED GERNARDUS."
"IT RECORDED THAT KING JAMES WAS PRESENTED WITH PROOF THAT LORD CLANCHARLIE HAD A LEGITIMATE HEIR."
"THE EXISTENCE OF THIS OFFSPRING OF THE HATED REPUBLICAN DISPLEASED THE KING."

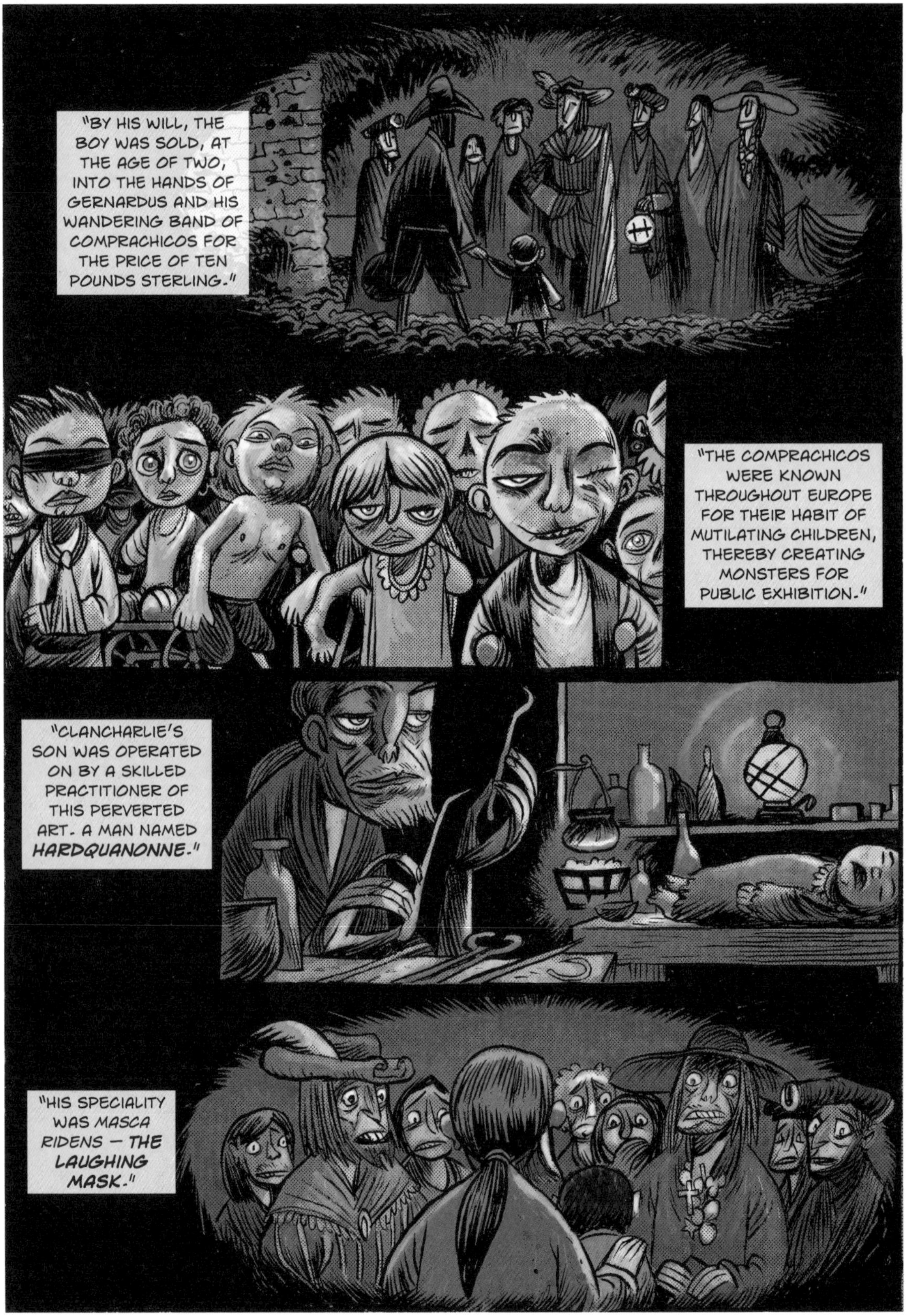
"BY HIS WILL, THE BOY WAS SOLD, AT THE AGE OF TWO, INTO THE HANDS OF GERNARDUS AND HIS WANDERING BAND OF COMPRACHICOS FOR THE PRICE OF TEN POUNDS STERLING."
"THE COMPRACHICOS WERE KNOWN THROUGHOUT EUROPE FOR THEIR HABIT OF MUTILATING CHILDREN, THEREBY CREATING MONSTERS FOR PUBLIC EXHIBITION."
"CLANCHARLIE'S SON WAS OPERATED ON BY A SKILLED PRACTITIONER OF THIS PERVERTED ART. A MAN NAMED HARDQUANONNE."
"HIS SPECIALITY WAS MASCA RIDENS — THE LAUGHING MASK."

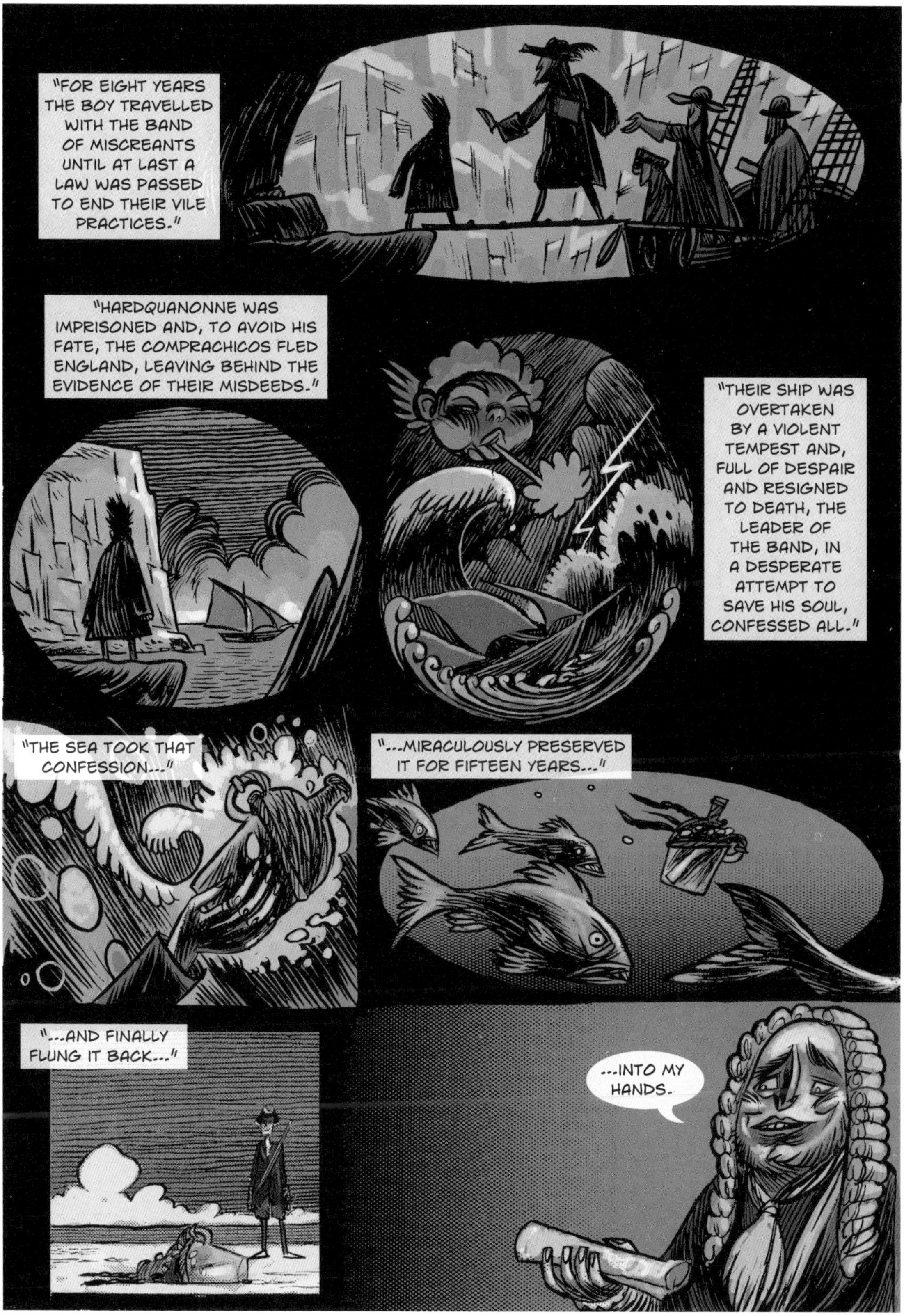
"FOR EIGHT YEARS THE BOY TRAVELLED WITH THE BAND OF MISCREANTS UNTIL AT LAST A LAW WAS PASSED TO END THEIR VILE PRACTICES."
"HARDQUANONNE WAS IMPRISONED AND, TO AVOID HIS FATE, THE COMPRACHICOS FLED ENGLAND, LEAVING BEHIND THE EVIDENCE OF THEIR MISDEEDS."
"THEIR SHIP WAS OVERTAKEN BY A VIOLENT TEMPEST AND, FULL OF DESPAIR AND RESIGNED TO DEATH, THE LEADER OF THE BAND, IN A DESPERATE ATTEMPT TO SAVE HIS SOUL, CONFESSED ALL."
"THE SEA TOOK THAT CONFESSION..."
"...MIRACULOUSLY PRESERVED IT FOR FIFTEEN YEARS..."
"...AND FINALLY FLUNG IT BACK..."
...INTO MY HANDS.

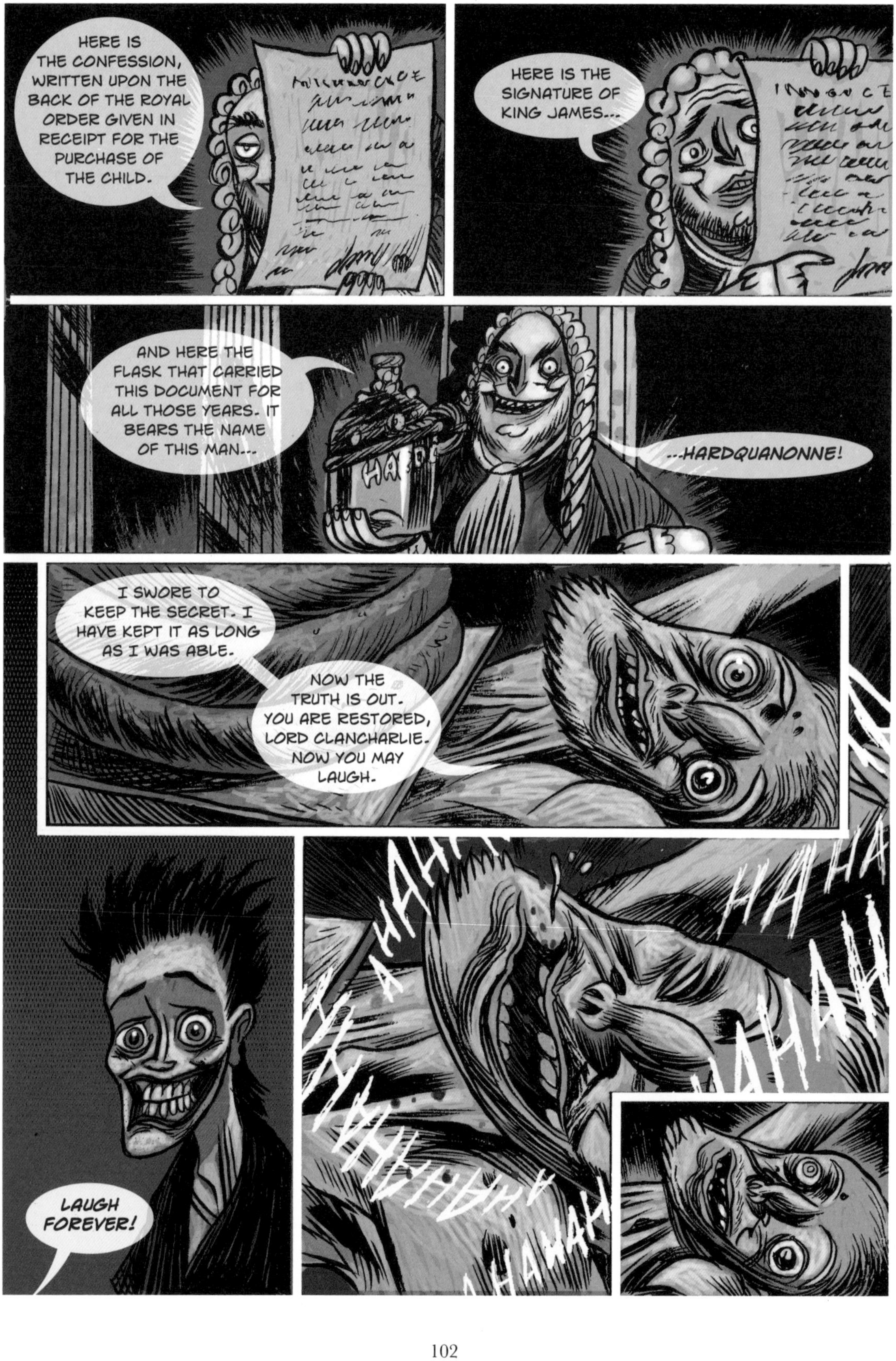
HERE IS THE CONFESSION, WRITTEN UPON THE BACK OF THE ROYAL ORDER GIVEN IN RECEIPT FOR THE PURCHASE OF THE CHILD.
HERE IS THE SIGNATURE OF KING JAMES...
AND HERE THE FLASK THAT CARRIED THIS DOCUMENT FOR ALL THOSE YEARS. IT BEARS THE NAME OF THIS MAN...
...HARDQUANONNE!
I SWORE TO KEEP THE SECRET. I HAVE KEPT IT AS LONG AS I WAS ABLE.
NOW THE TRUTH IS OUT. YOU ARE RESTORED, LORD CLANCHARLIE. NOW YOU MAY LAUGH.
LAUGH FOREVER!

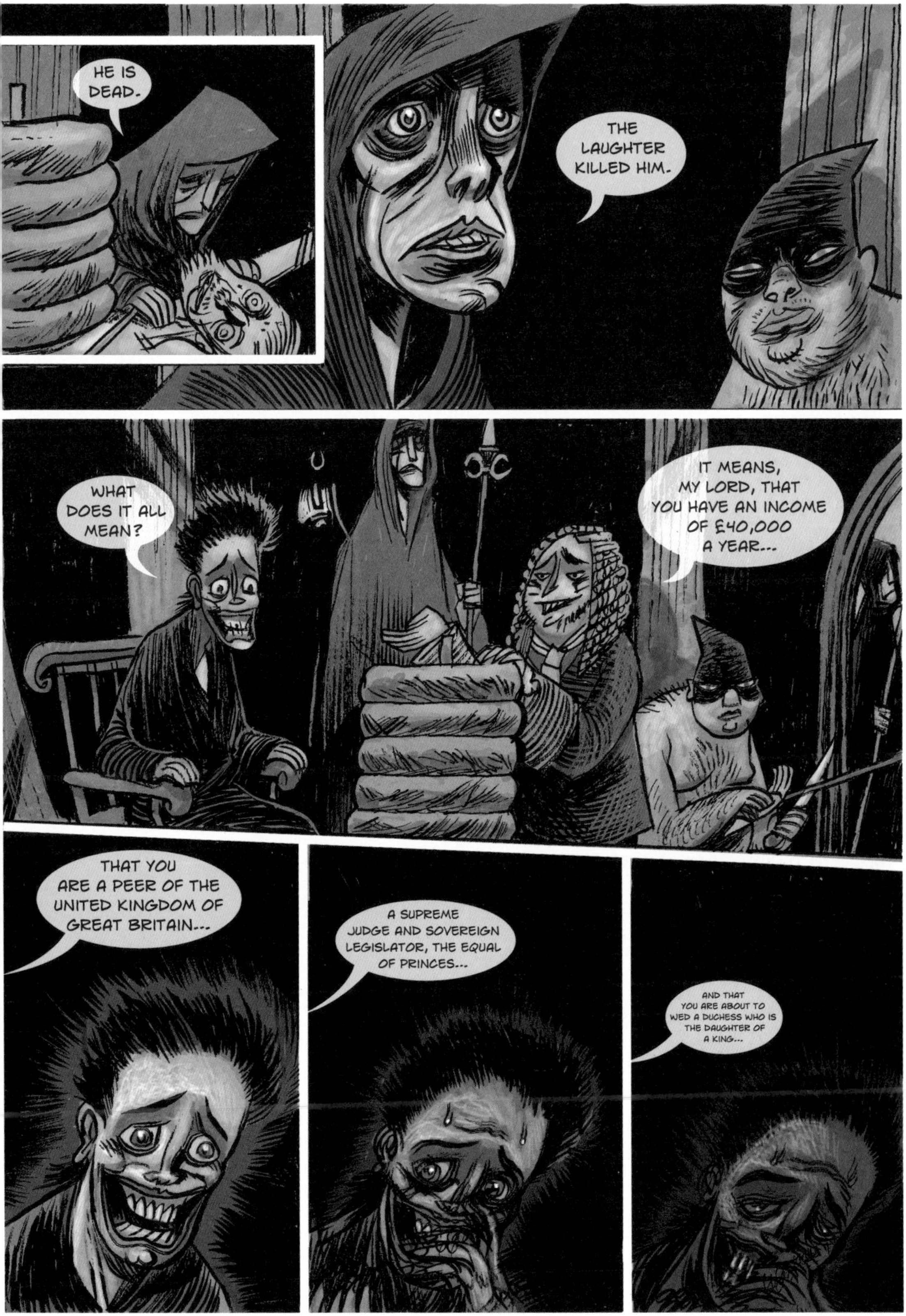
HE IS DEAD.
THE LAUGHTER KILLED HIM.
WHAT DOES IT ALL MEAN?
IT MEANS, MY LORD, THAT YOU HAVE AN INCOME OF £40,000 A YEAR...
THAT YOU ARE A PEER OF THE UNITED KINGDOM OF GREAT BRITAIN...
A SUPREME JUDGE AND SOVEREIGN LEGISLATOR, THE EQUAL OF PRINCES...
AND THAT YOU ARE ABOUT TO WED A DUCHESS WHO IS THE DAUGHTER OF A KING...

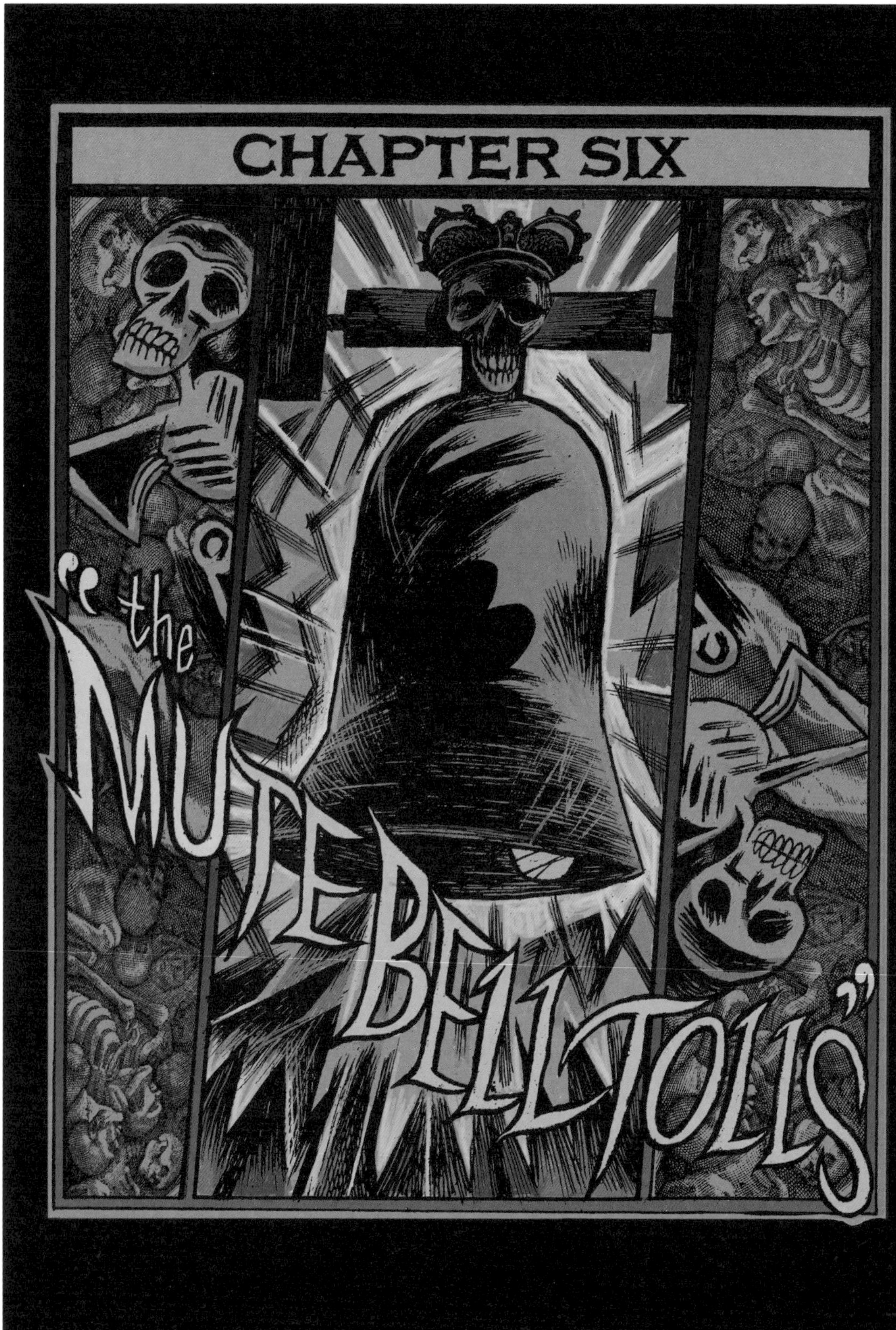
CHAPTER SIX
"the MUTE BELL TOLLS"

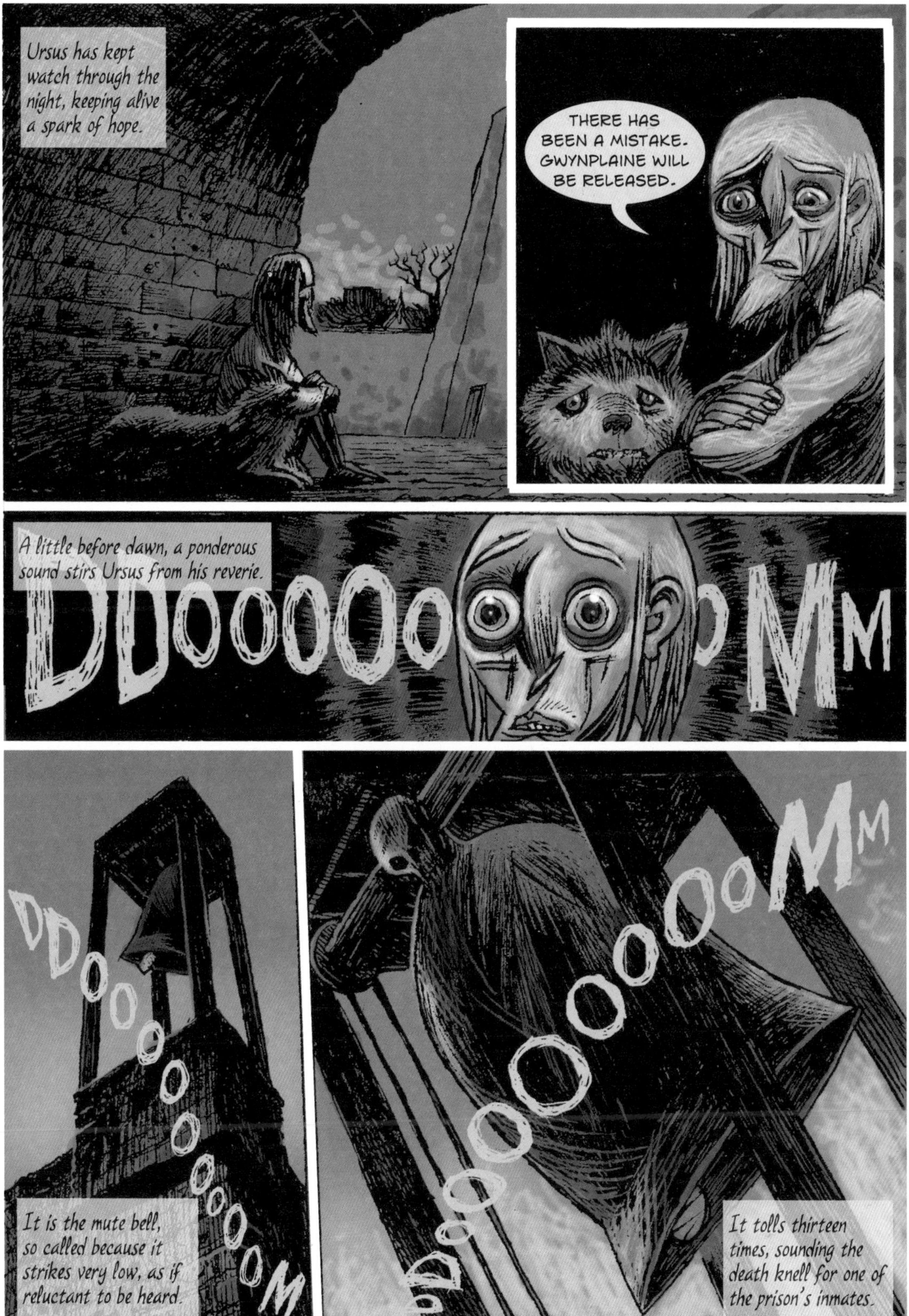

Ursus has kept watch through the night, keeping alive a spark of hope.
THERE HAS BEEN A MISTAKE. GWYNPLAINE WILL BE RELEASED.
A little before dawn, a ponderous sound stirs Ursus from his reverie.
DDOOOOOOOOMM
DDOOOOOOOOOOOM
It is the mute bell, so called because it strikes very low, as if reluctant to be heard.
DDOOOOOOOOOOOMM
It tolls thirteen times, sounding the death knell for one of the prison's inmates.

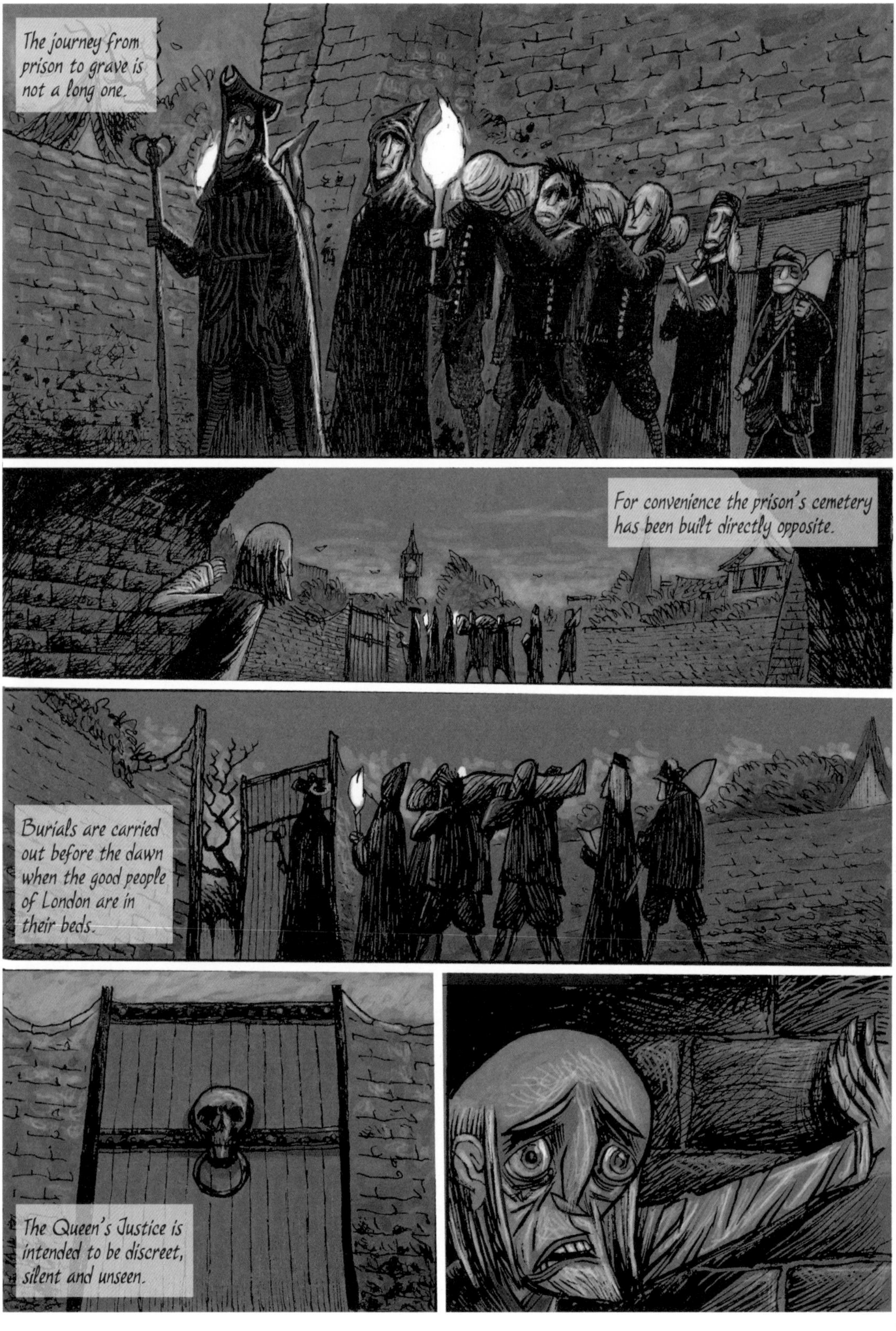
The journey from prison to grave is not a long one.
For convenience the prison's cemetery has been built directly opposite.
Burials are carried out before the dawn when the good people of London are in their beds.
The Queen's Justice is intended to be discreet, silent and unseen.

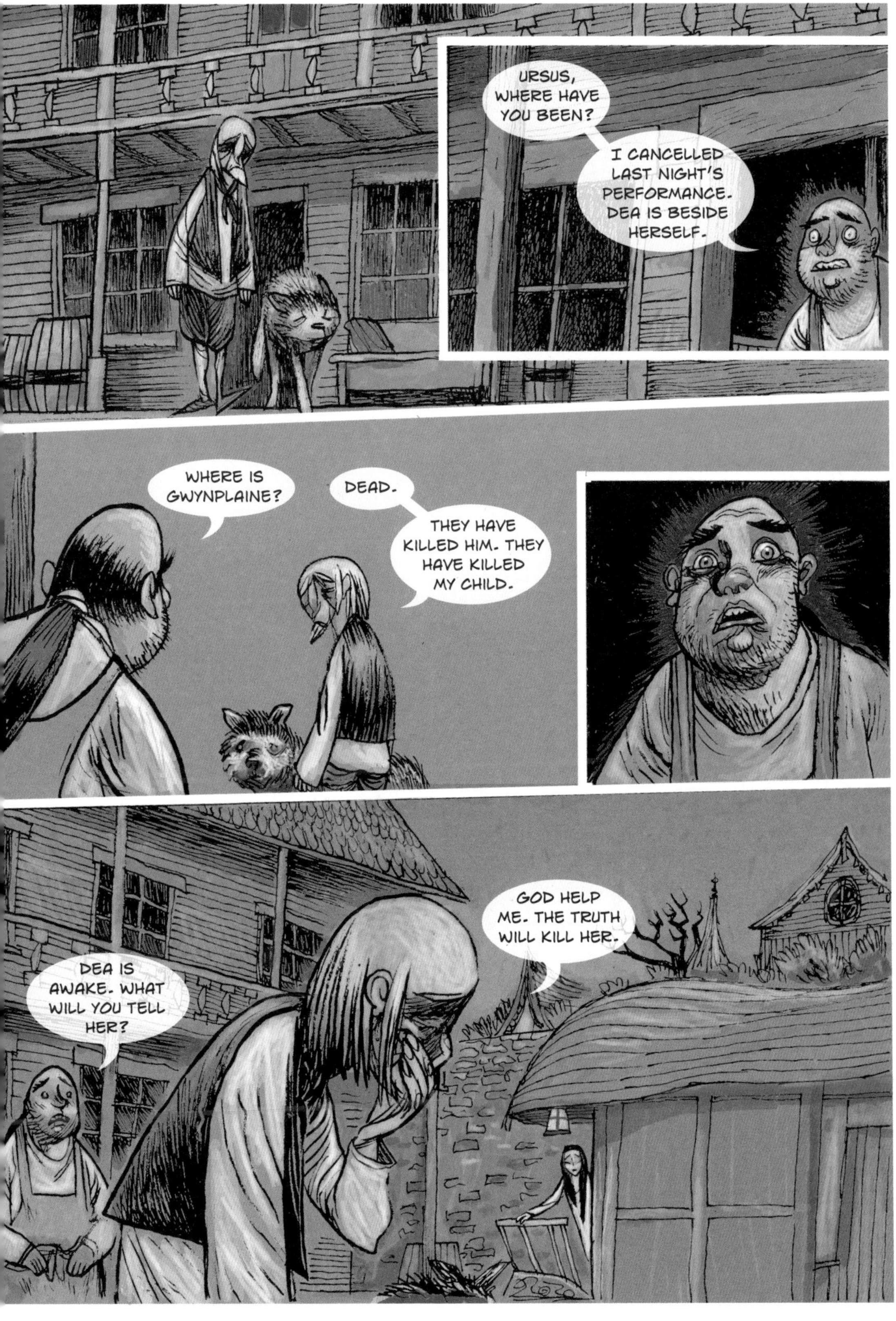
URSUS, WHERE HAVE YOU BEEN?
I CANCELLED LAST NIGHT'S PERFORMANCE. DEA IS BESIDE HERSELF.
WHERE IS GWYNPLAINE?
DEAD.
THEY HAVE KILLED HIM. THEY HAVE KILLED MY CHILD.
DEA IS AWAKE. WHAT WILL YOU TELL HER?
GOD HELP ME. THE TRUTH WILL KILL HER.

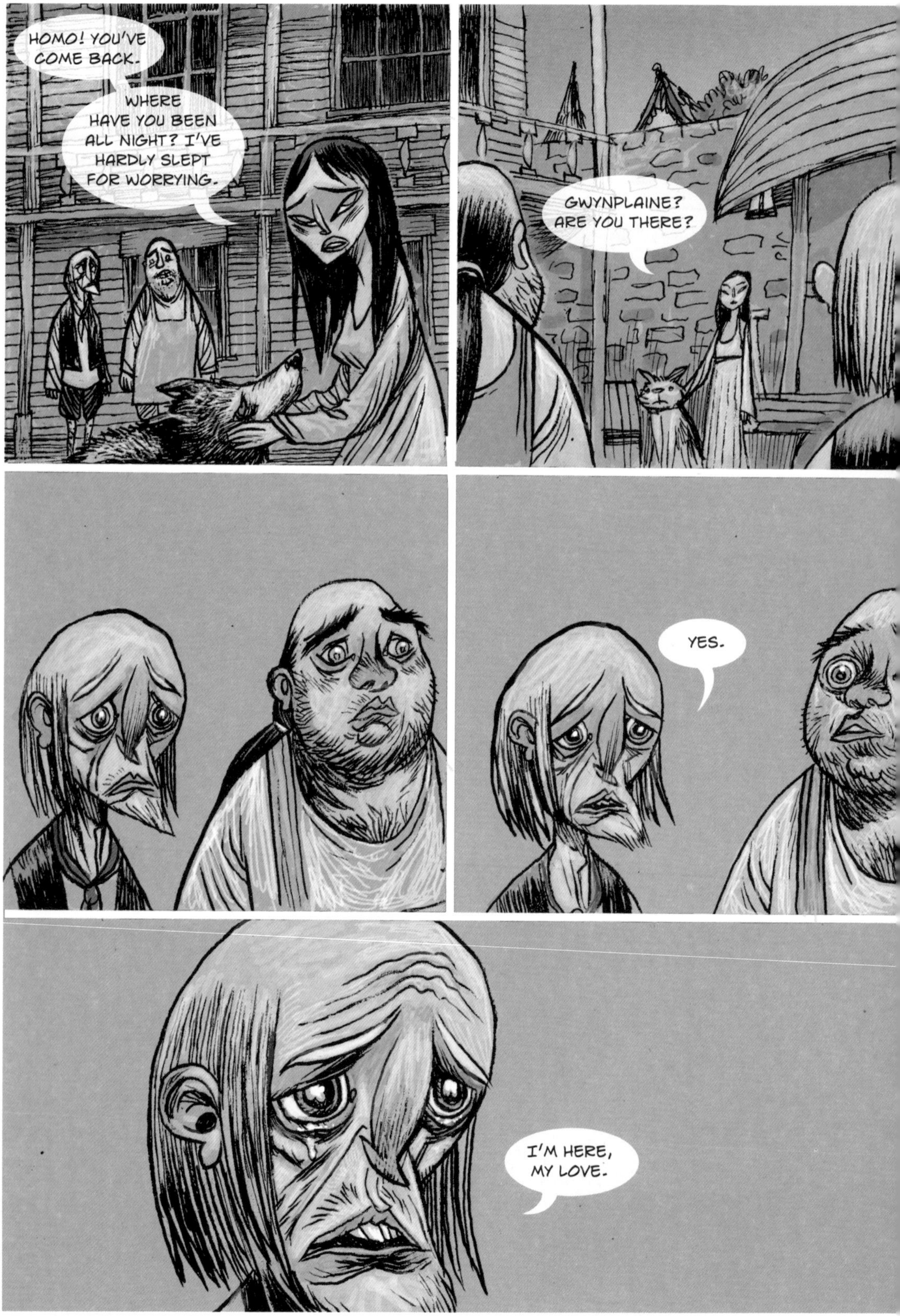
HOMO! YOU'VE COME BACK.
WHERE HAVE YOU BEEN ALL NIGHT? I'VE HARDLY SLEPT FOR WORRYING.
GWYNPLAINE? ARE YOU THERE?
YES.
I'M HERE, MY LOVE.

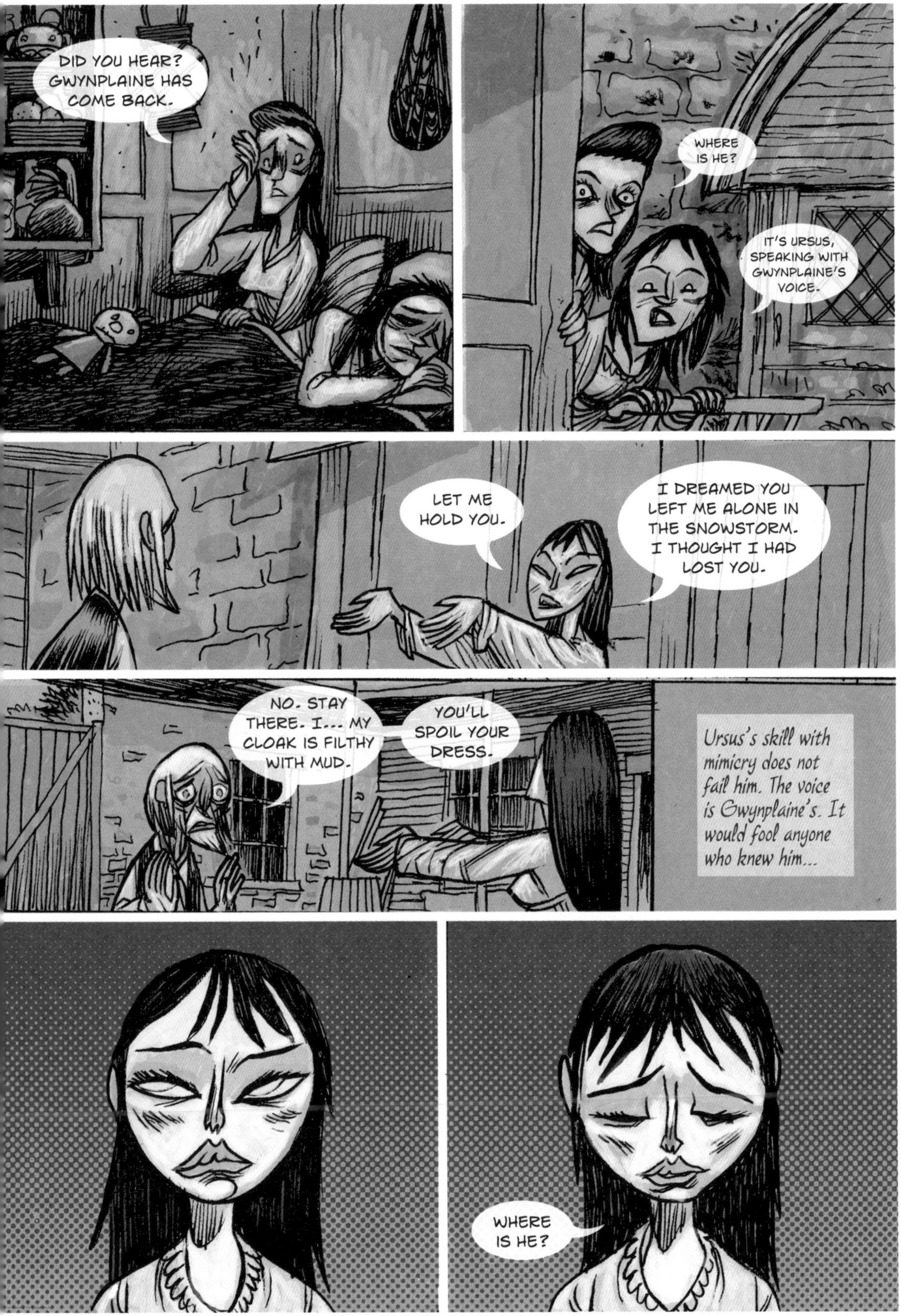
DID YOU HEAR? GWYNPLAINE HAS COME BACK.
WHERE IS HE?
IT'S URSUS, SPEAKING WITH GWYNPLAINE'S VOICE.
LET ME HOLD YOU.
I DREAMED YOU LEFT ME ALONE IN THE SNOWSTORM. I THOUGHT I HAD LOST YOU.
NO. STAY THERE. I... MY CLOAK IS FILTHY WITH MUD.
YOU'LL SPOIL YOUR DRESS.
Ursus's skill with mimicry does not fail him. The voice is Gwynplaine's. It would fool anyone who knew him...
WHERE IS HE?

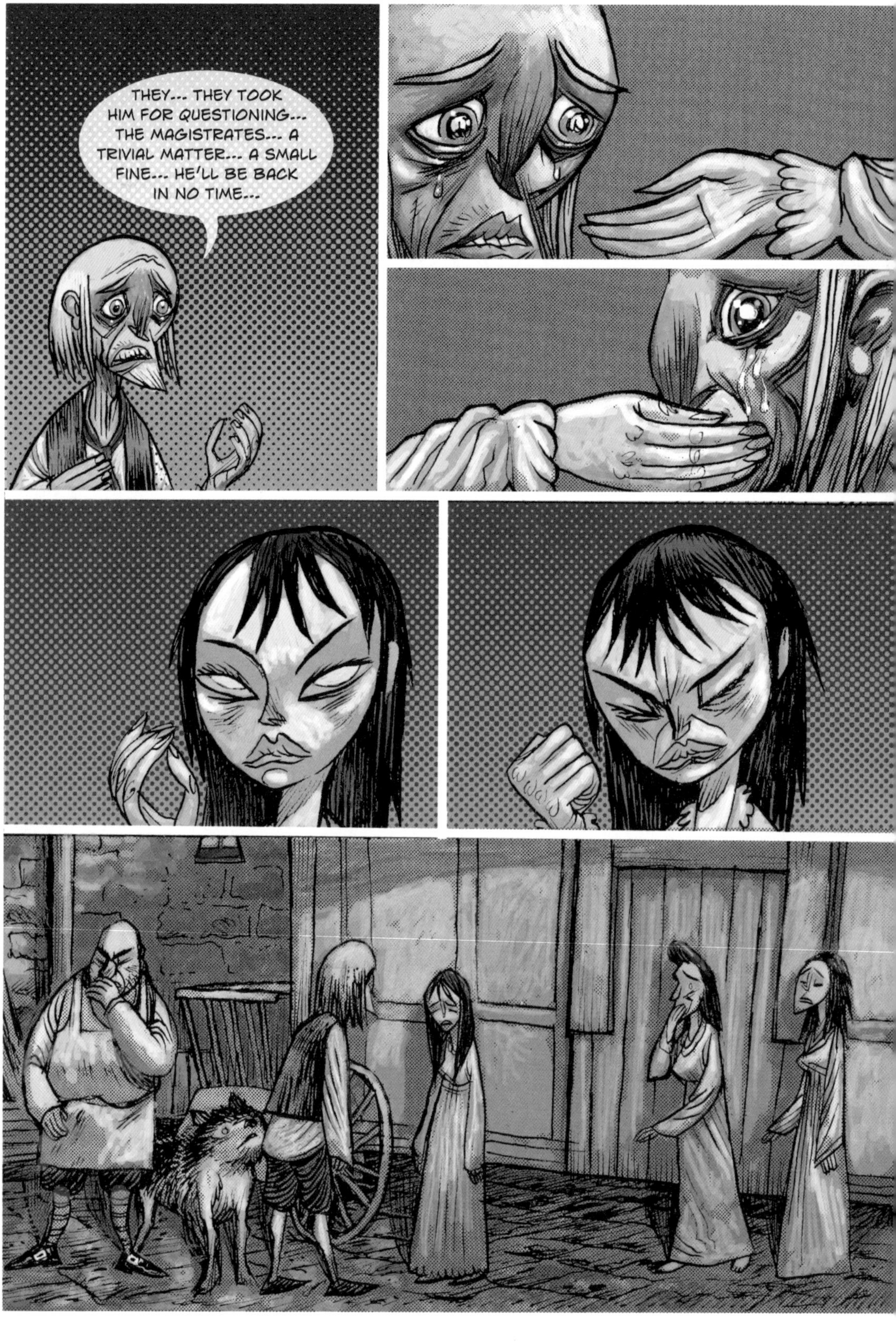
THEY... THEY TOOK HIM FOR QUESTIONING... THE MAGISTRATES... A TRIVIAL MATTER... A SMALL FINE... HE'LL BE BACK IN NO TIME...

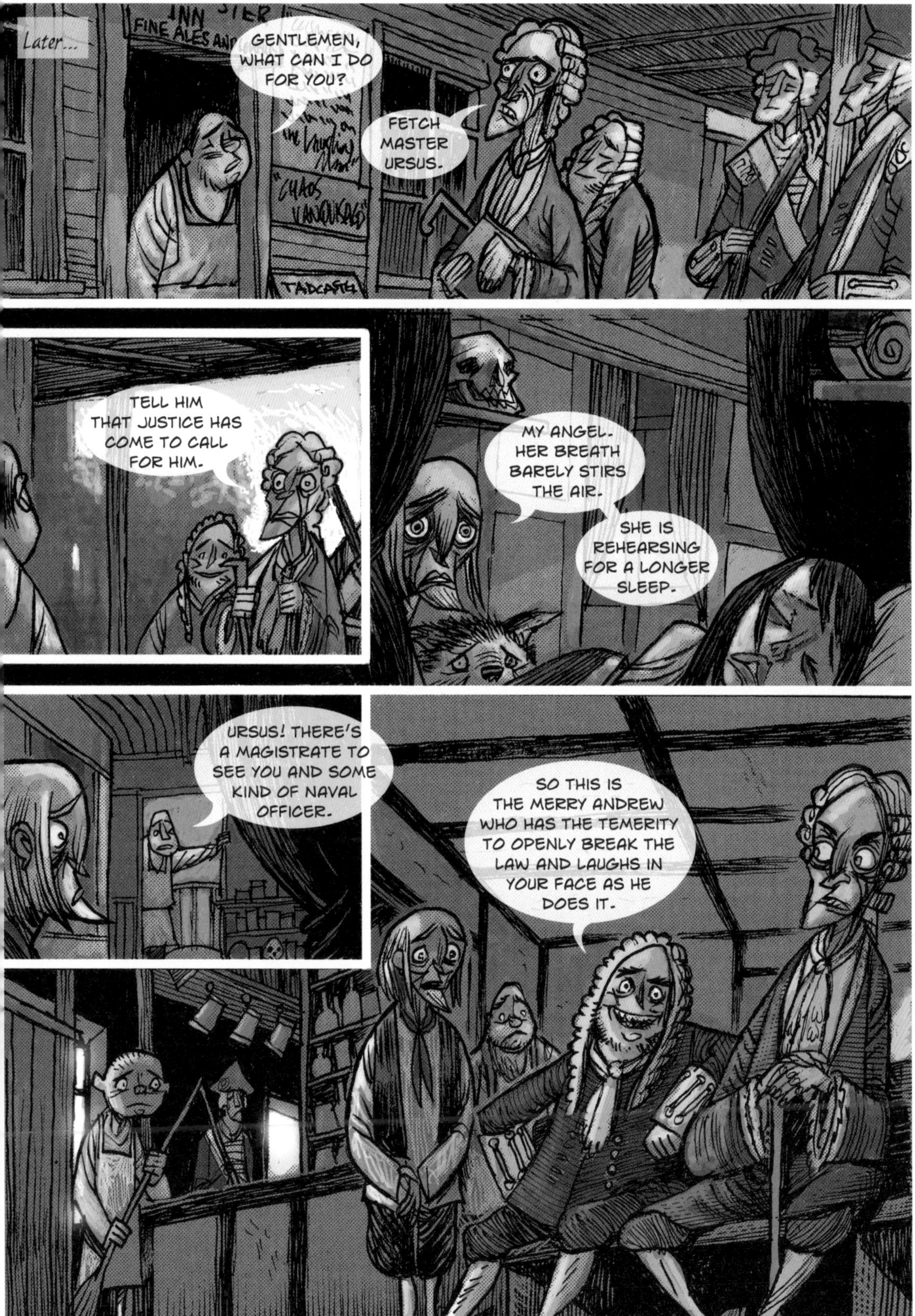
Later...
INN
FINE ALES AND
GENTLEMEN, WHAT CAN I DO FOR YOU?
FETCH MASTER URSUS.
"CHAOS VANQUISHED"
TADCASTER
TELL HIM THAT JUSTICE HAS COME TO CALL FOR HIM.
MY ANGEL. HER BREATH BARELY STIRS THE AIR.
SHE IS REHEARSING FOR A LONGER SLEEP.
URSUS! THERE'S A MAGISTRATE TO SEE YOU AND SOME KIND OF NAVAL OFFICER.
SO THIS IS THE MERRY ANDREW WHO HAS THE TEMERITY TO OPENLY BREAK THE LAW AND LAUGHS IN YOUR FACE AS HE DOES IT.

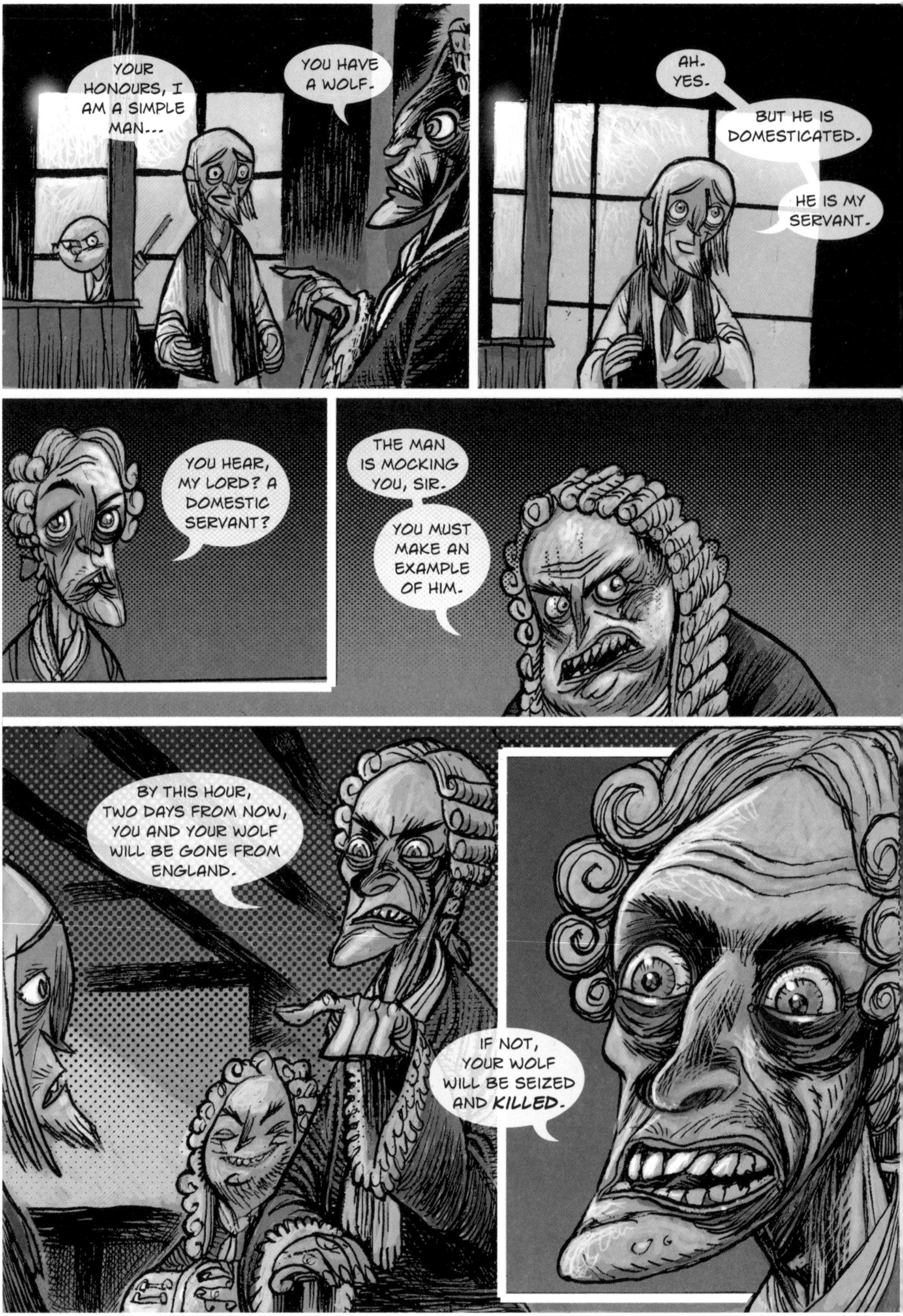
YOUR HONOURS, I AM A SIMPLE MAN...
YOU HAVE A WOLF.
AH. YES.
BUT HE IS DOMESTICATED.
HE IS MY SERVANT.
YOU HEAR, MY LORD? A DOMESTIC SERVANT?
THE MAN IS MOCKING YOU, SIR.
YOU MUST MAKE AN EXAMPLE OF HIM.
BY THIS HOUR, TWO DAYS FROM NOW, YOU AND YOUR WOLF WILL BE GONE FROM ENGLAND.
IF NOT, YOUR WOLF WILL BE SEIZED AND **KILLED**.

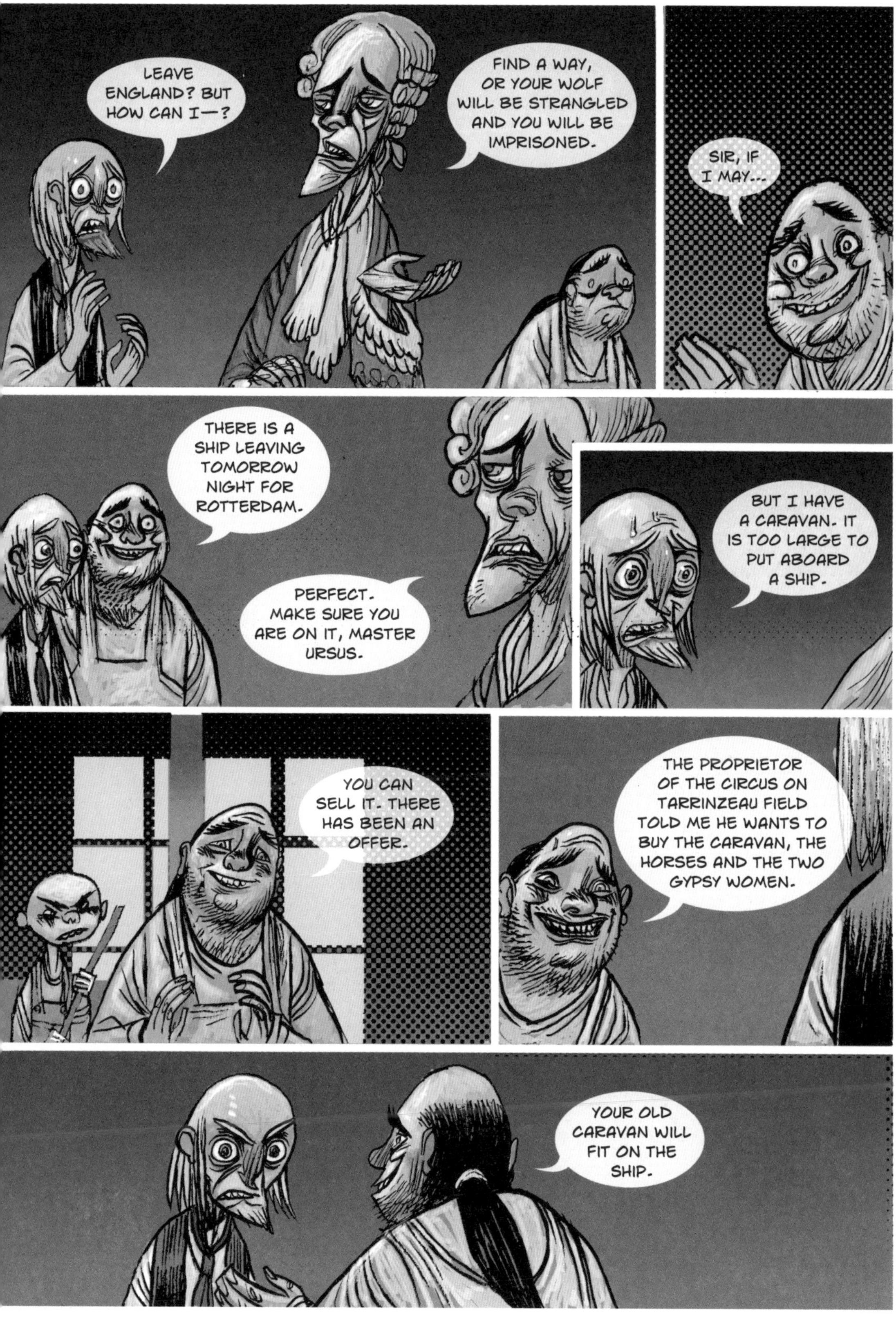
LEAVE ENGLAND? BUT HOW CAN I—?
FIND A WAY, OR YOUR WOLF WILL BE STRANGLED AND YOU WILL BE IMPRISONED.
SIR, IF I MAY...
THERE IS A SHIP LEAVING TOMORROW NIGHT FOR ROTTERDAM.
PERFECT. MAKE SURE YOU ARE ON IT, MASTER URSUS.
BUT I HAVE A CARAVAN. IT IS TOO LARGE TO PUT ABOARD A SHIP.
YOU CAN SELL IT. THERE HAS BEEN AN OFFER.
THE PROPRIETOR OF THE CIRCUS ON TARRINZEAU FIELD TOLD ME HE WANTS TO BUY THE CARAVAN, THE HORSES AND THE TWO GYPSY WOMEN.
YOUR OLD CARAVAN WILL FIT ON THE SHIP.

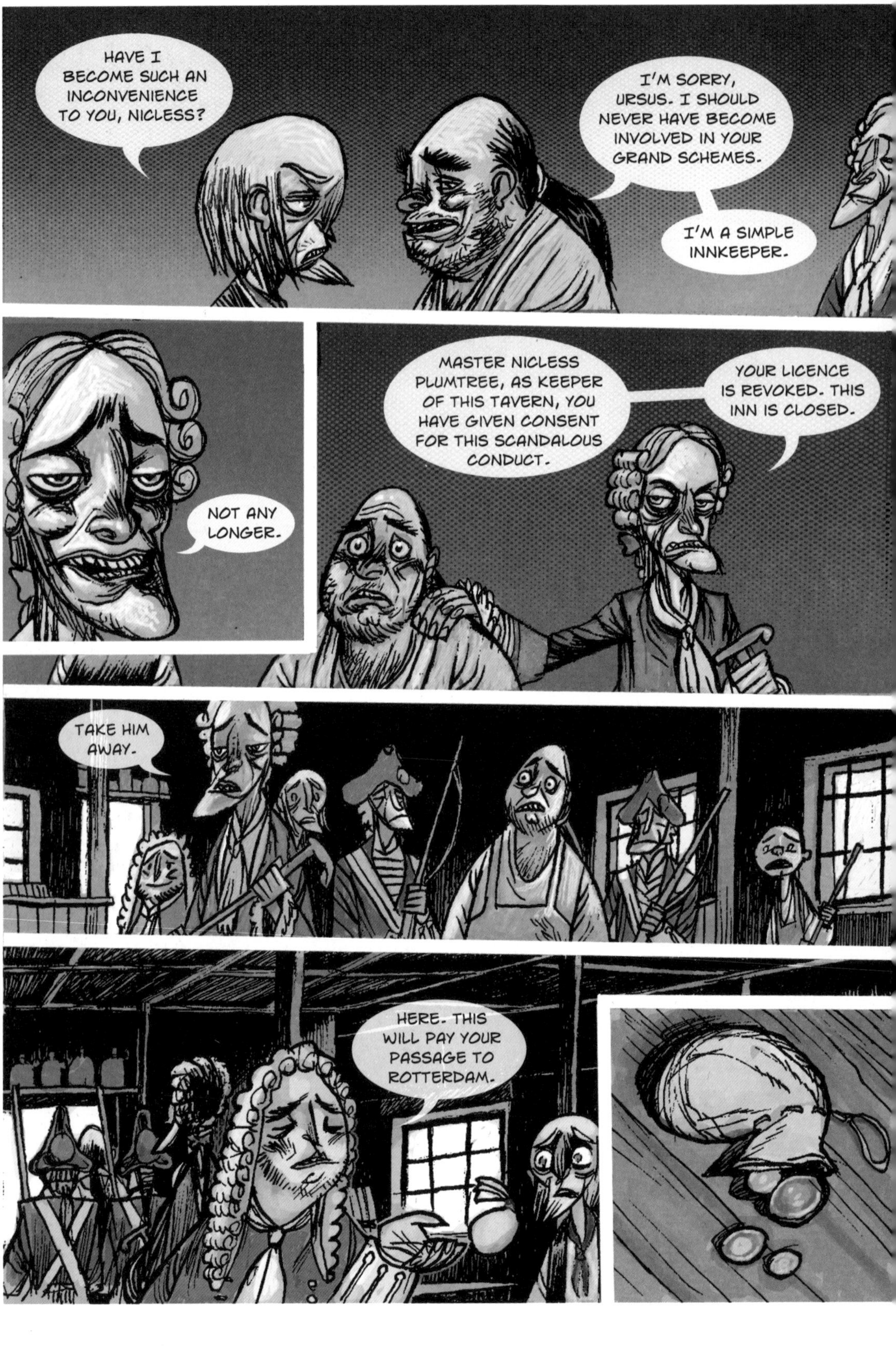
HAVE I BECOME SUCH AN INCONVENIENCE TO YOU, NICLESS?
I'M SORRY, URSUS. I SHOULD NEVER HAVE BECOME INVOLVED IN YOUR GRAND SCHEMES.
I'M A SIMPLE INNKEEPER.
NOT ANY LONGER.
MASTER NICLESS PLUMTREE, AS KEEPER OF THIS TAVERN, YOU HAVE GIVEN CONSENT FOR THIS SCANDALOUS CONDUCT.
YOUR LICENCE IS REVOKED. THIS INN IS CLOSED.
TAKE HIM AWAY.
HERE. THIS WILL PAY YOUR PASSAGE TO ROTTERDAM.

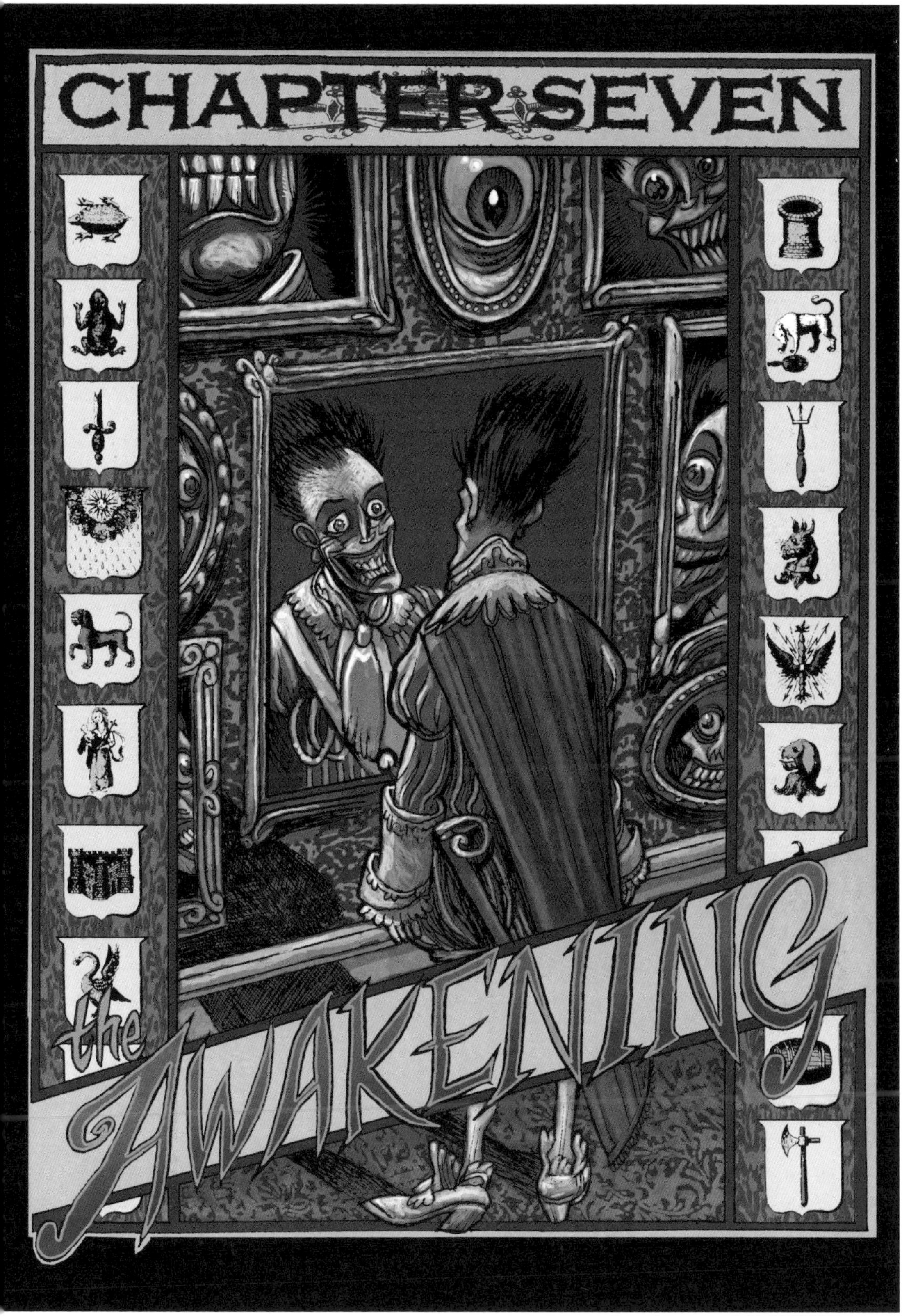
CHAPTER SEVEN
the AWAKENING

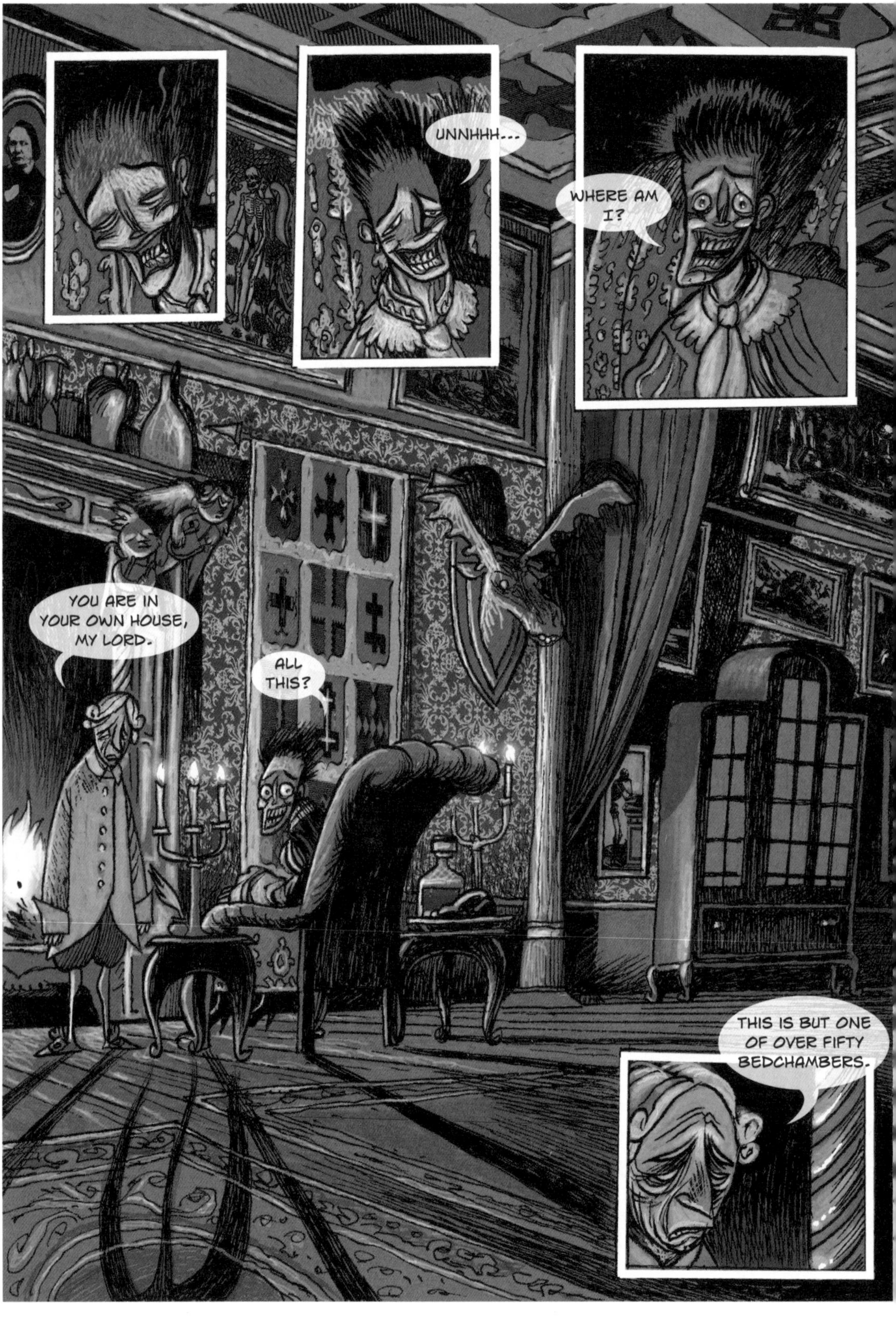
UNNHHH...
WHERE AM I?
YOU ARE IN YOUR OWN HOUSE, MY LORD.
ALL THIS?
THIS IS BUT ONE OF OVER FIFTY BEDCHAMBERS.

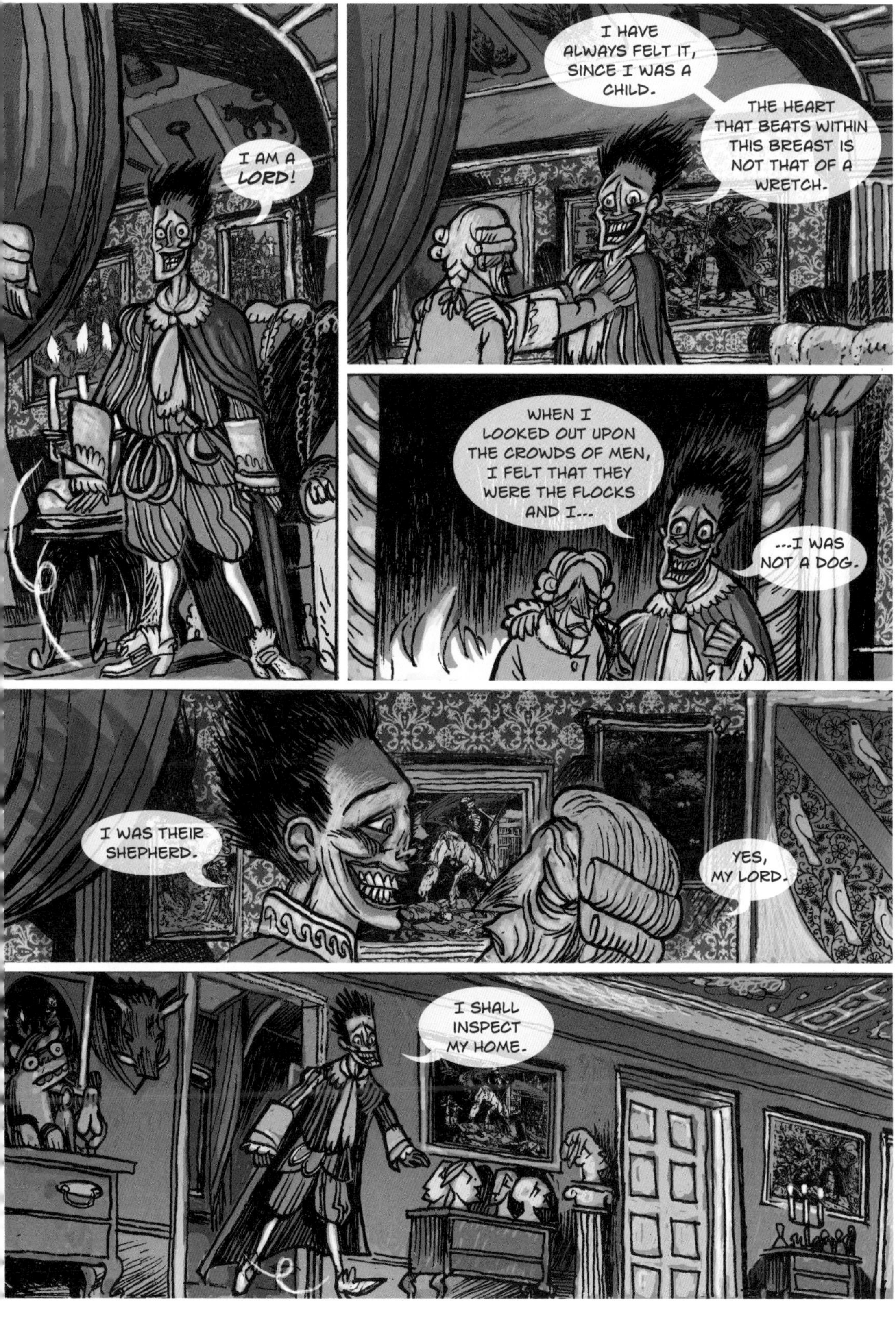
I AM A LORD!
I HAVE ALWAYS FELT IT, SINCE I WAS A CHILD.
THE HEART THAT BEATS WITHIN THIS BREAST IS NOT THAT OF A WRETCH.
WHEN I LOOKED OUT UPON THE CROWDS OF MEN, I FELT THAT THEY WERE THE FLOCKS AND I...
...I WAS NOT A DOG.
I WAS THEIR SHEPHERD.
YES, MY LORD.
I SHALL INSPECT MY HOME.

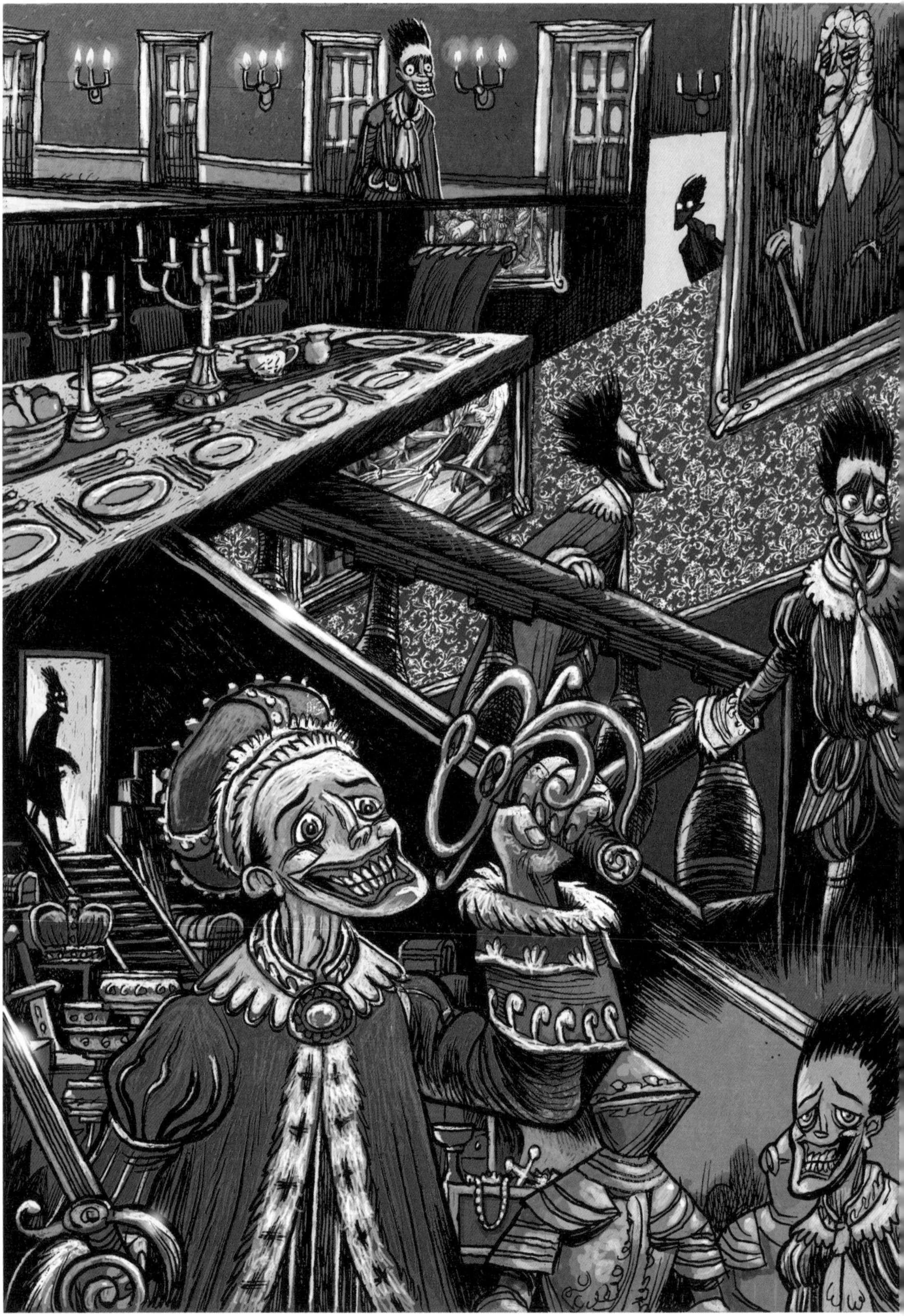

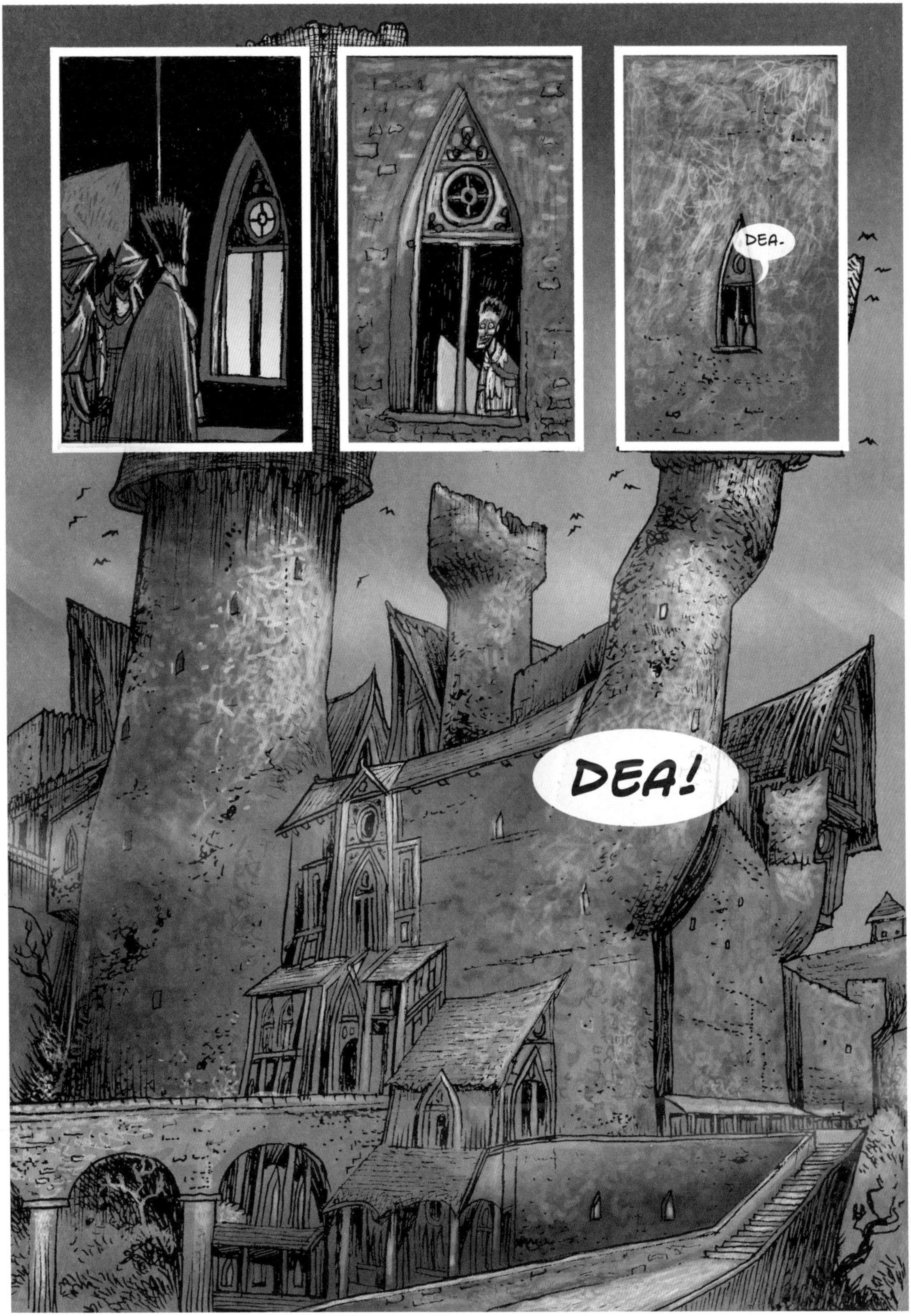
DEA.
DEA!

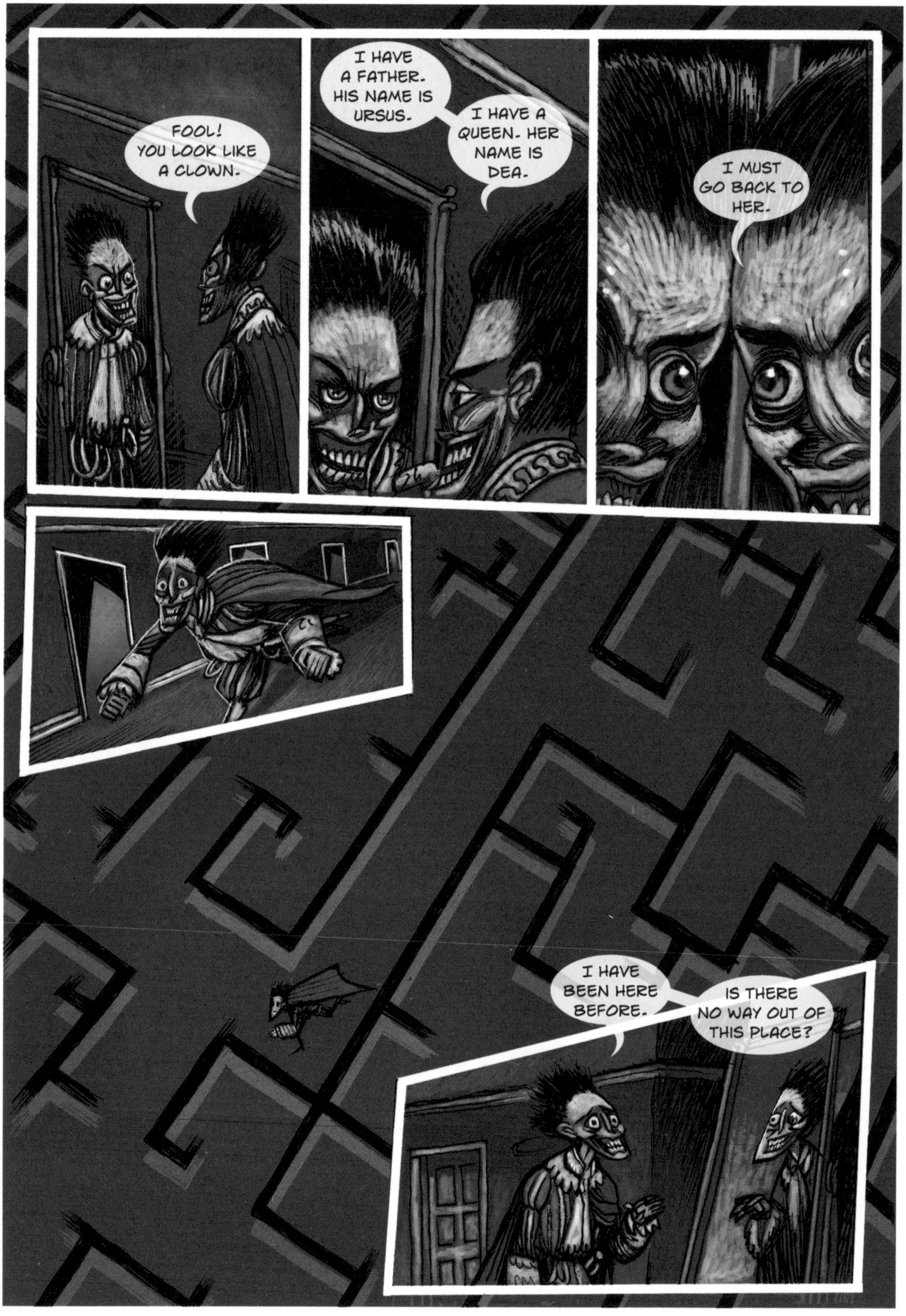
FOOL! YOU LOOK LIKE A CLOWN.
I HAVE A FATHER. HIS NAME IS URSUS.
I HAVE A QUEEN. HER NAME IS DEA.
I MUST GO BACK TO HER.
I HAVE BEEN HERE BEFORE.
IS THERE NO WAY OUT OF THIS PLACE?

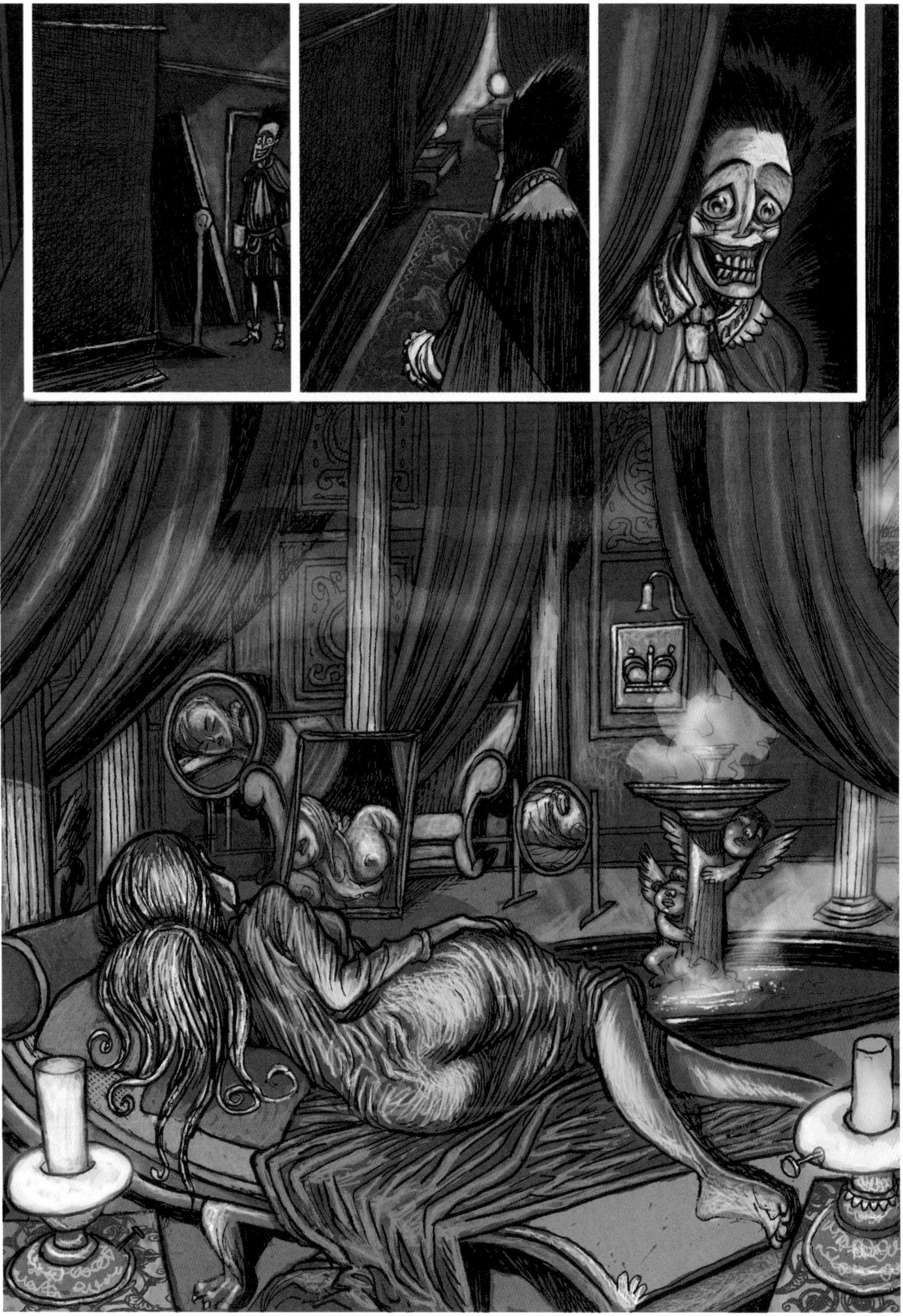

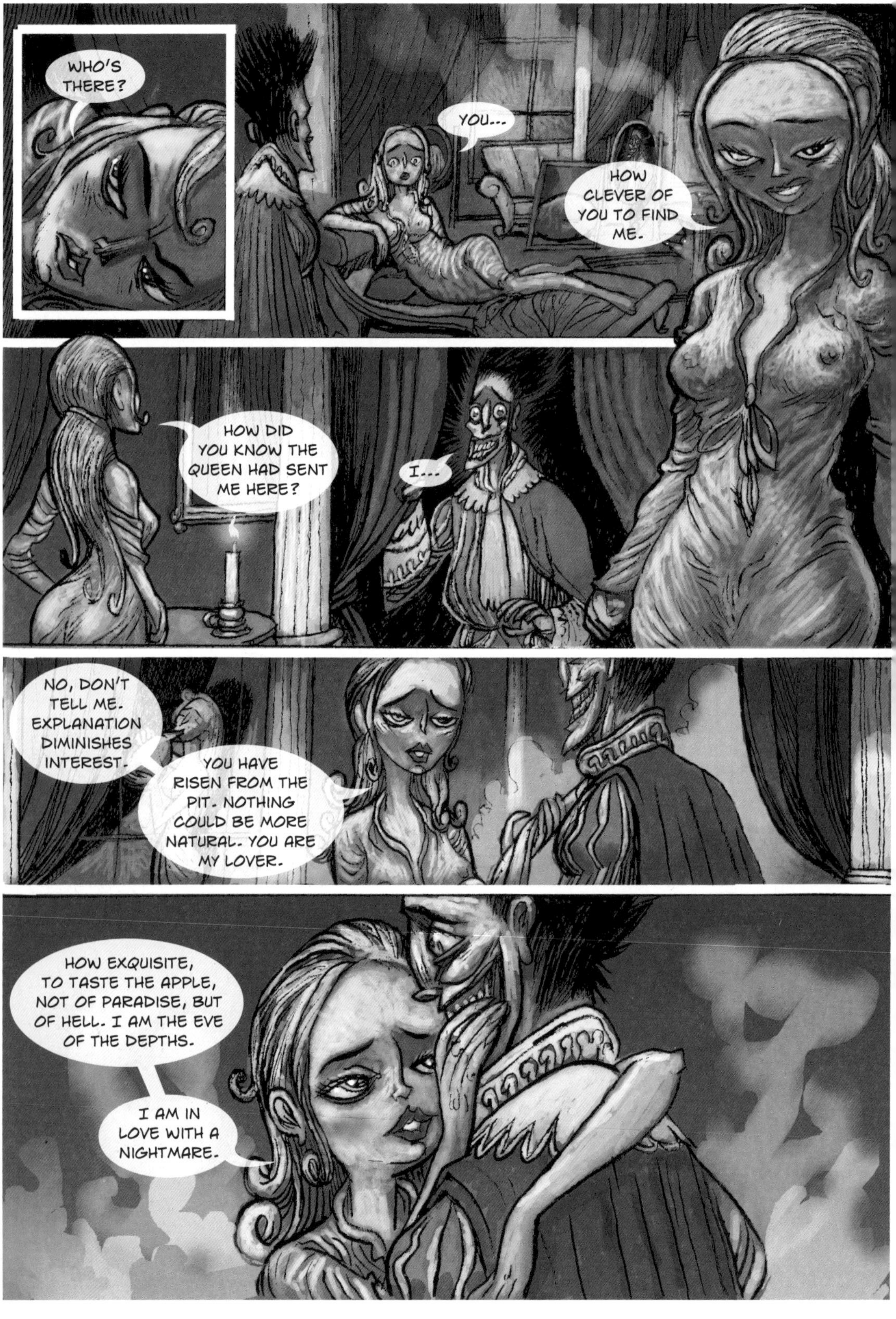
WHO'S THERE?
YOU...
HOW CLEVER OF YOU TO FIND ME.
HOW DID YOU KNOW THE QUEEN HAD SENT ME HERE?
I...
NO, DON'T TELL ME. EXPLANATION DIMINISHES INTEREST.
YOU HAVE RISEN FROM THE PIT. NOTHING COULD BE MORE NATURAL. YOU ARE MY LOVER.
HOW EXQUISITE, TO TASTE THE APPLE, NOT OF PARADISE, BUT OF HELL. I AM THE EVE OF THE DEPTHS.
I AM IN LOVE WITH A NIGHTMARE.

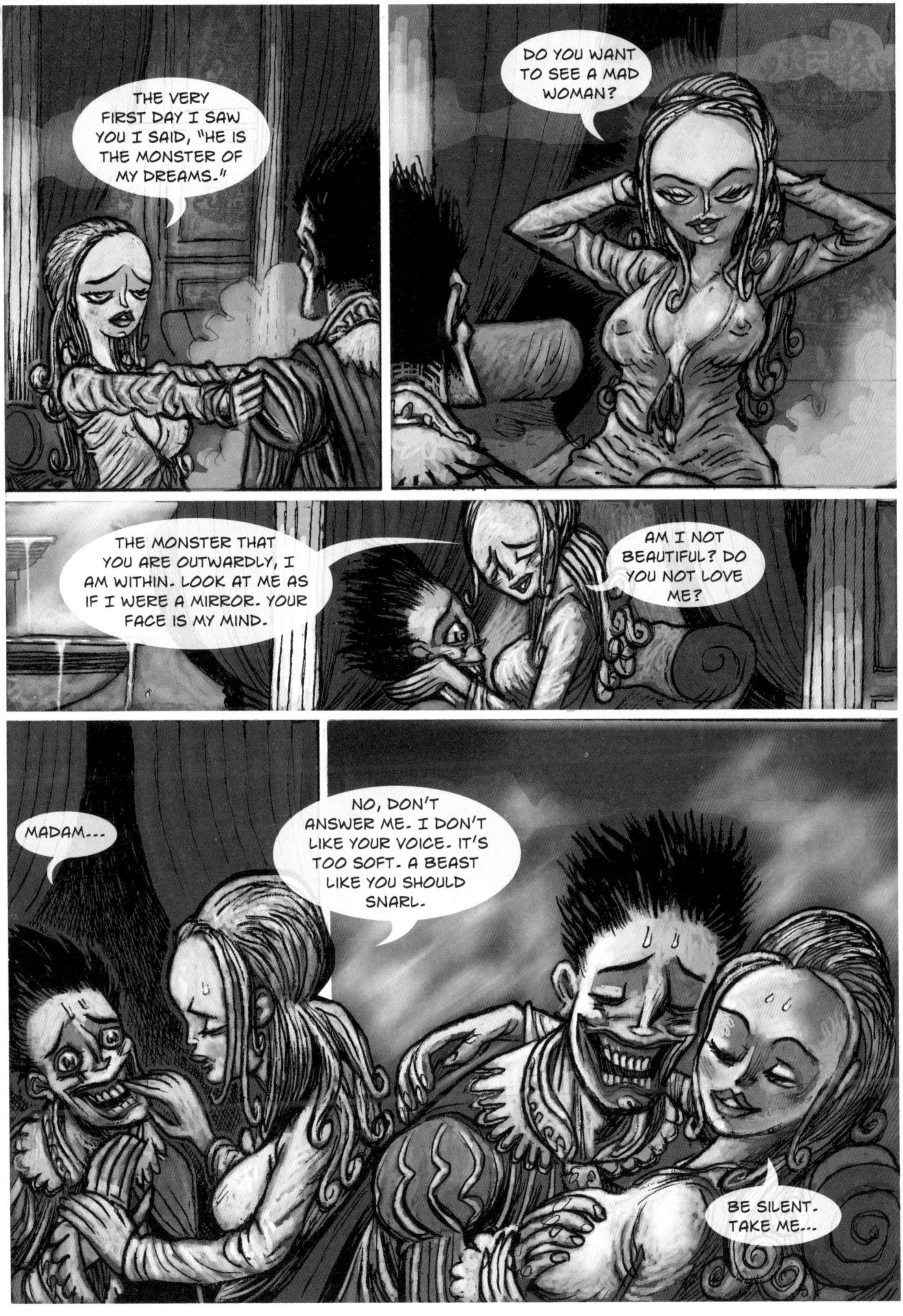
THE VERY FIRST DAY I SAW YOU I SAID, "HE IS THE MONSTER OF MY DREAMS."
DO YOU WANT TO SEE A MAD WOMAN?
THE MONSTER THAT YOU ARE OUTWARDLY, I AM WITHIN. LOOK AT ME AS IF I WERE A MIRROR. YOUR FACE IS MY MIND.
AM I NOT BEAUTIFUL? DO YOU NOT LOVE ME?
MADAM...
NO, DON'T ANSWER ME. I DON'T LIKE YOUR VOICE. IT'S TOO SOFT. A BEAST LIKE YOU SHOULD SNARL.
BE SILENT. TAKE ME...

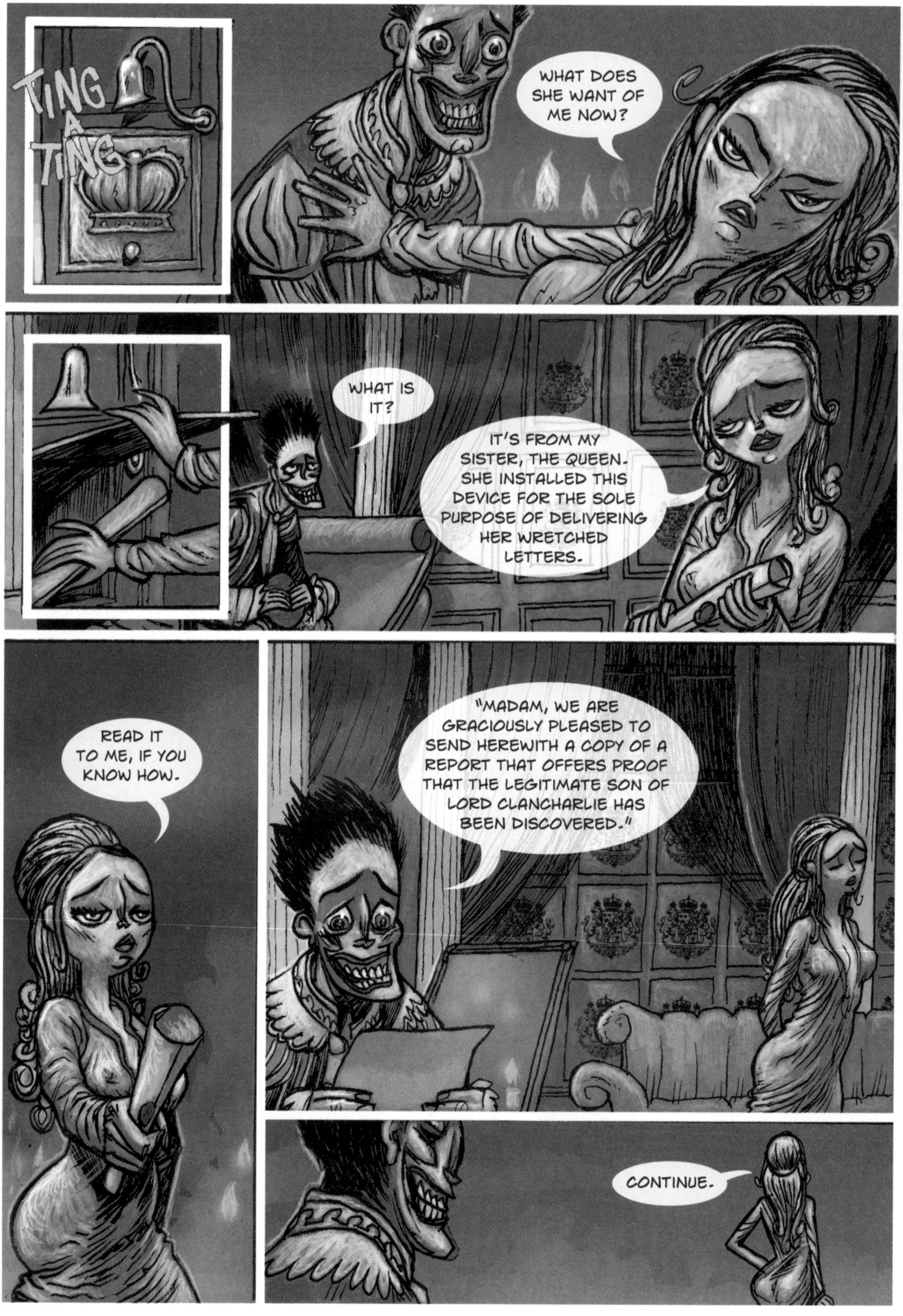
TING A TING
WHAT DOES SHE WANT OF ME NOW?
WHAT IS IT?
IT'S FROM MY SISTER, THE QUEEN. SHE INSTALLED THIS DEVICE FOR THE SOLE PURPOSE OF DELIVERING HER WRETCHED LETTERS.
READ IT TO ME, IF YOU KNOW HOW.
"MADAM, WE ARE GRACIOUSLY PLEASED TO SEND HEREWITH A COPY OF A REPORT THAT OFFERS PROOF THAT THE LEGITIMATE SON OF LORD CLANCHARLIE HAS BEEN DISCOVERED."
CONTINUE.

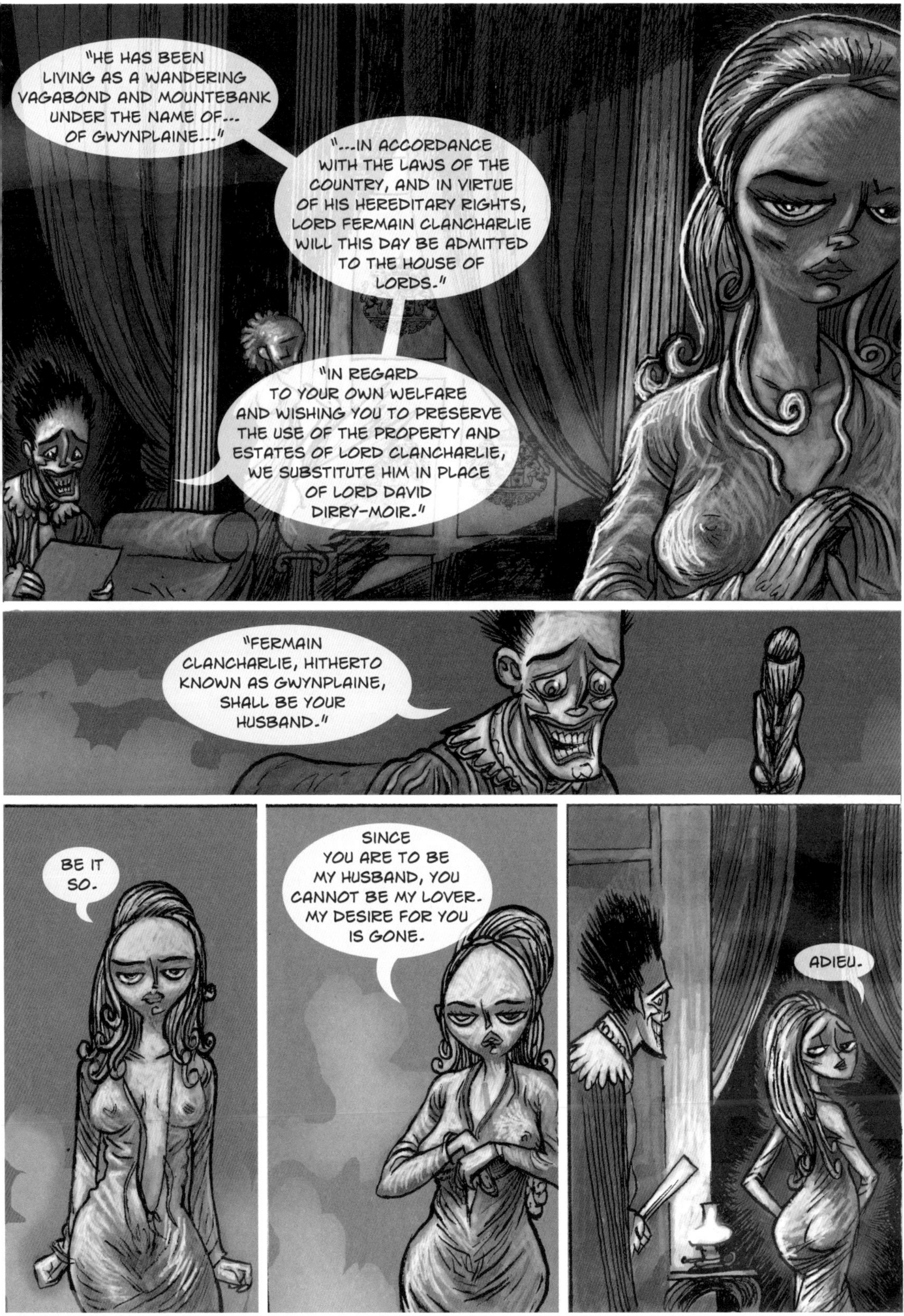
"HE HAS BEEN LIVING AS A WANDERING VAGABOND AND MOUNTEBANK UNDER THE NAME OF... OF GWYNPLAINE..."
"...IN ACCORDANCE WITH THE LAWS OF THE COUNTRY, AND IN VIRTUE OF HIS HEREDITARY RIGHTS, LORD FERMAIN CLANCHARLIE WILL THIS DAY BE ADMITTED TO THE HOUSE OF LORDS."
"IN REGARD TO YOUR OWN WELFARE AND WISHING YOU TO PRESERVE THE USE OF THE PROPERTY AND ESTATES OF LORD CLANCHARLIE, WE SUBSTITUTE HIM IN PLACE OF LORD DAVID DIRRY-MOIR."
"FERMAIN CLANCHARLIE, HITHERTO KNOWN AS GWYNPLAINE, SHALL BE YOUR HUSBAND."
BE IT SO.
SINCE YOU ARE TO BE MY HUSBAND, YOU CANNOT BE MY LOVER. MY DESIRE FOR YOU IS GONE.
ADIEU.

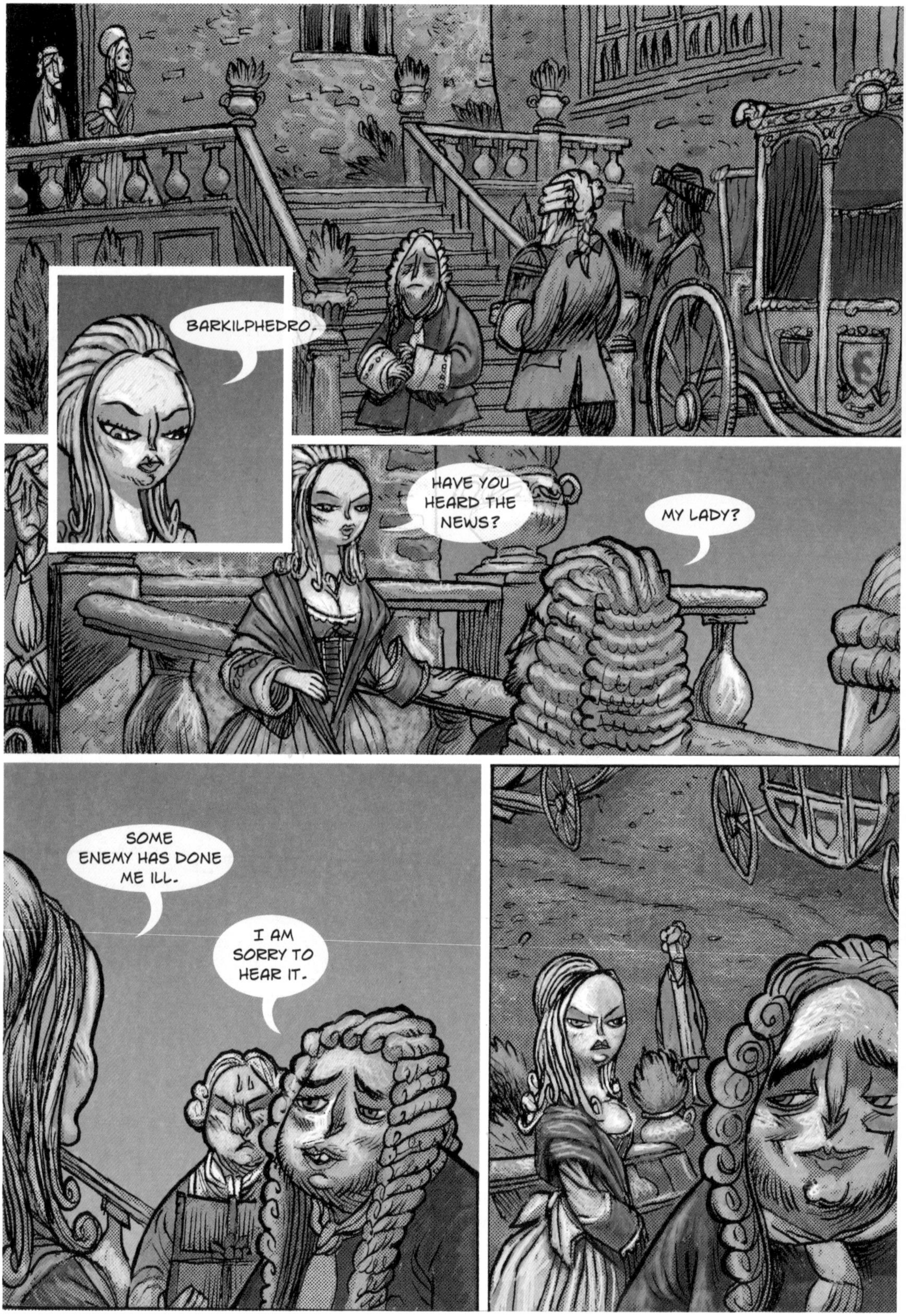
BARKILPHEDRO.
HAVE YOU HEARD THE NEWS?
MY LADY?
SOME ENEMY HAS DONE ME ILL.
I AM SORRY TO HEAR IT.

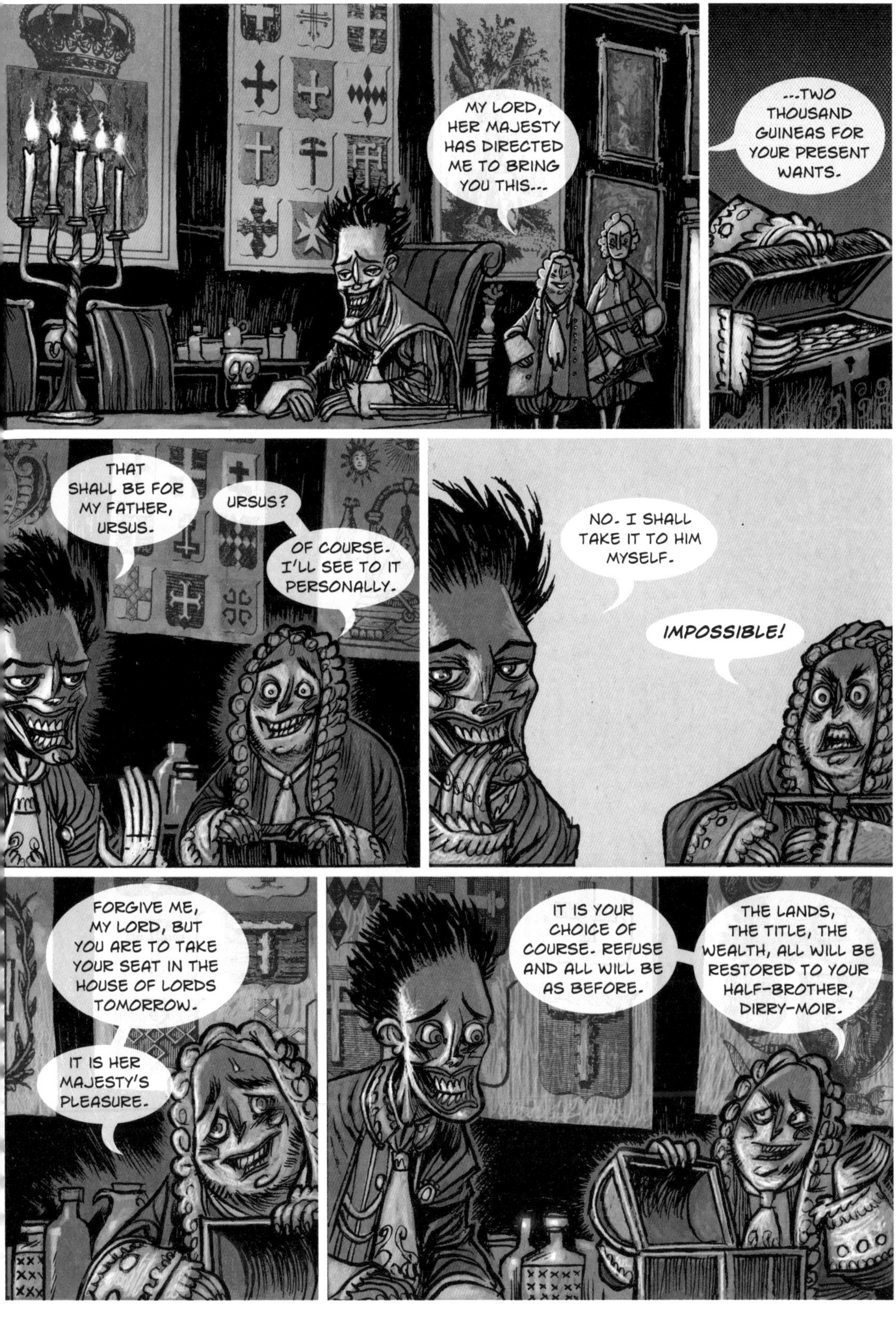
MY LORD, HER MAJESTY HAS DIRECTED ME TO BRING YOU THIS...
...TWO THOUSAND GUINEAS FOR YOUR PRESENT WANTS.
THAT SHALL BE FOR MY FATHER, URSUS.
URSUS?
OF COURSE. I'LL SEE TO IT PERSONALLY.
NO. I SHALL TAKE IT TO HIM MYSELF.
IMPOSSIBLE!
FORGIVE ME, MY LORD, BUT YOU ARE TO TAKE YOUR SEAT IN THE HOUSE OF LORDS TOMORROW.
IT IS HER MAJESTY'S PLEASURE.
IT IS YOUR CHOICE OF COURSE. REFUSE AND ALL WILL BE AS BEFORE.
THE LANDS, THE TITLE, THE WEALTH, ALL WILL BE RESTORED TO YOUR HALF-BROTHER, DIRRY-MOIR.

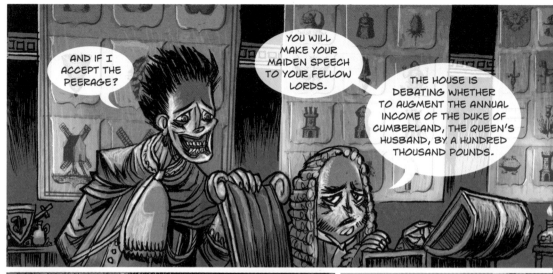

AND IF I ACCEPT THE PEERAGE?

YOU WILL MAKE YOUR MAIDEN SPEECH TO YOUR FELLOW LORDS.

THE HOUSE IS DEBATING WHETHER TO AUGMENT THE ANNUAL INCOME OF THE DUKE OF CUMBERLAND, THE QUEEN'S HUSBAND, BY A HUNDRED THOUSAND POUNDS.

WILL I HAVE THE RIGHT TO SPEAK FREELY? THE LORDS WILL LISTEN TO ME?

AS AN EQUAL.

THEN I SHALL ACCEPT.

YOU MUST INFORM URSUS AND... HIS HOUSEHOLD... OF MY GOOD FORTUNE WHEN YOU DELIVER THIS MONEY.

OF COURSE, MY LORD.

IT WILL BE MY PLEASURE.

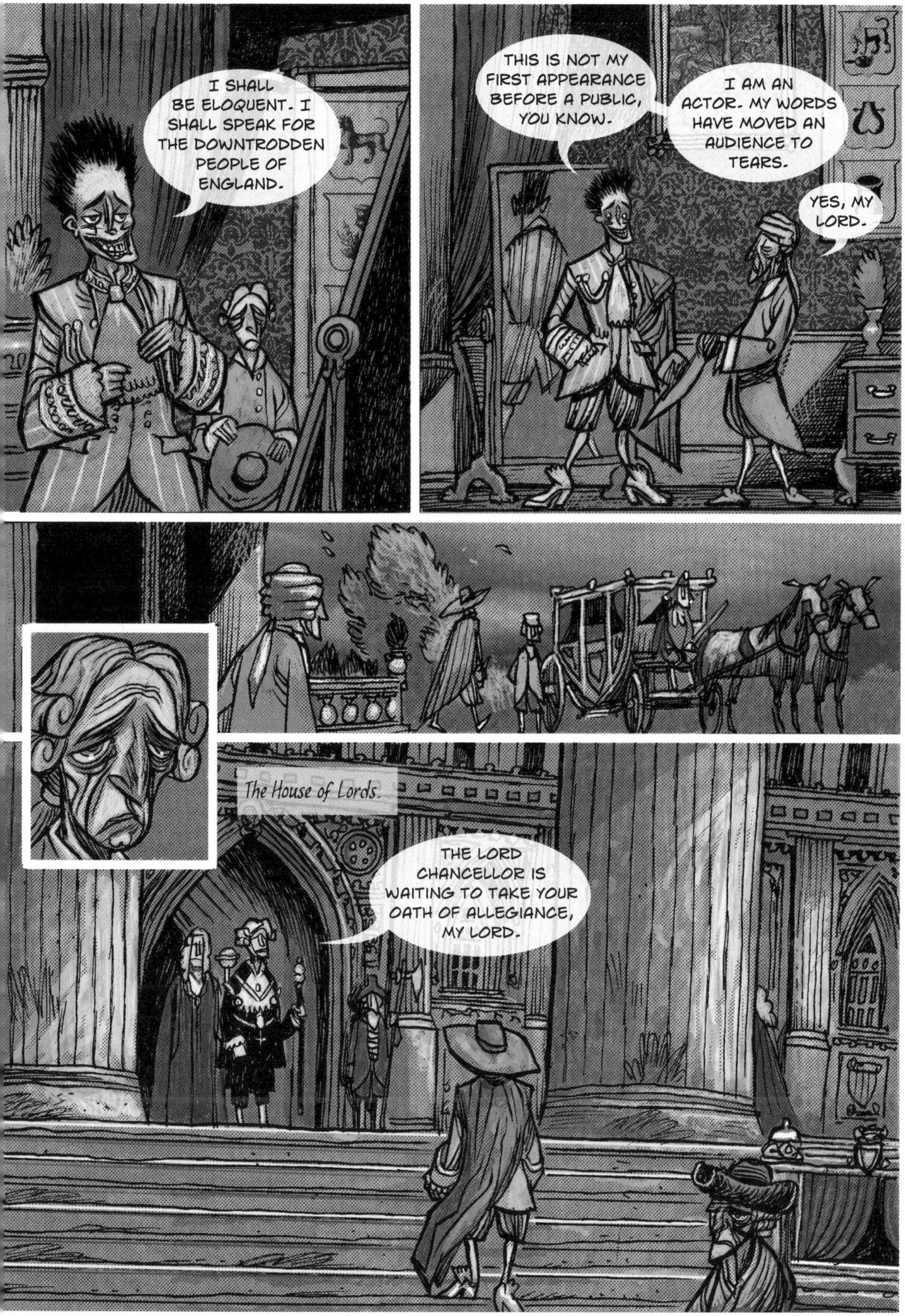
I SHALL BE ELOQUENT. I SHALL SPEAK FOR THE DOWNTRODDEN PEOPLE OF ENGLAND.
THIS IS NOT MY FIRST APPEARANCE BEFORE A PUBLIC, YOU KNOW.
I AM AN ACTOR. MY WORDS HAVE MOVED AN AUDIENCE TO TEARS.
YES, MY LORD.
The House of Lords.
THE LORD CHANCELLOR IS WAITING TO TAKE YOUR OATH OF ALLEGIANCE, MY LORD.

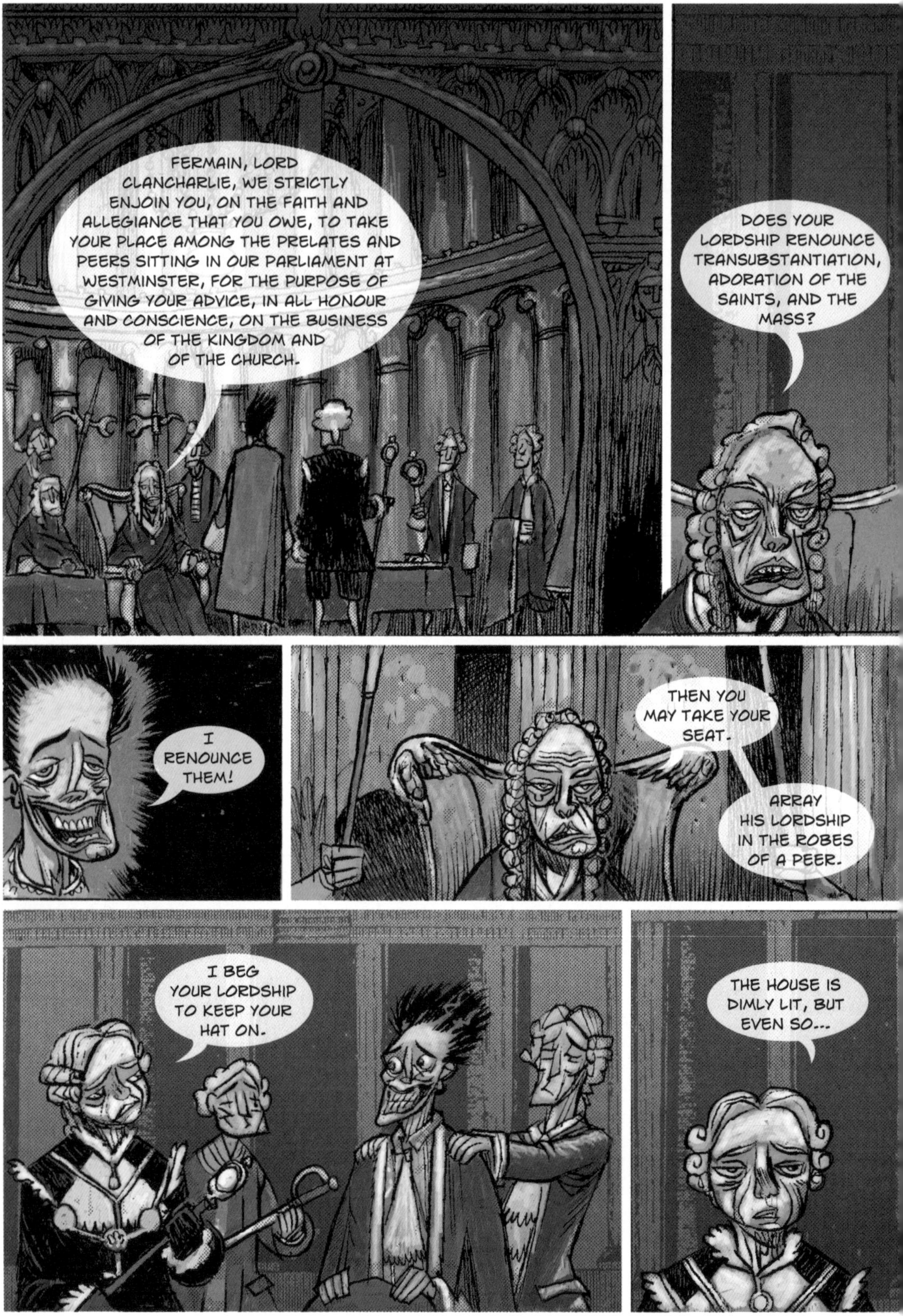
FERMAIN, LORD CLANCHARLIE, WE STRICTLY ENJOIN YOU, ON THE FAITH AND ALLEGIANCE THAT YOU OWE, TO TAKE YOUR PLACE AMONG THE PRELATES AND PEERS SITTING IN OUR PARLIAMENT AT WESTMINSTER, FOR THE PURPOSE OF GIVING YOUR ADVICE, IN ALL HONOUR AND CONSCIENCE, ON THE BUSINESS OF THE KINGDOM AND OF THE CHURCH.
DOES YOUR LORDSHIP RENOUNCE TRANSUBSTANTIATION, ADORATION OF THE SAINTS, AND THE MASS?
I RENOUNCE THEM!
THEN YOU MAY TAKE YOUR SEAT.
ARRAY HIS LORDSHIP IN THE ROBES OF A PEER.
I BEG YOUR LORDSHIP TO KEEP YOUR HAT ON.
THE HOUSE IS DIMLY LIT, BUT EVEN SO...

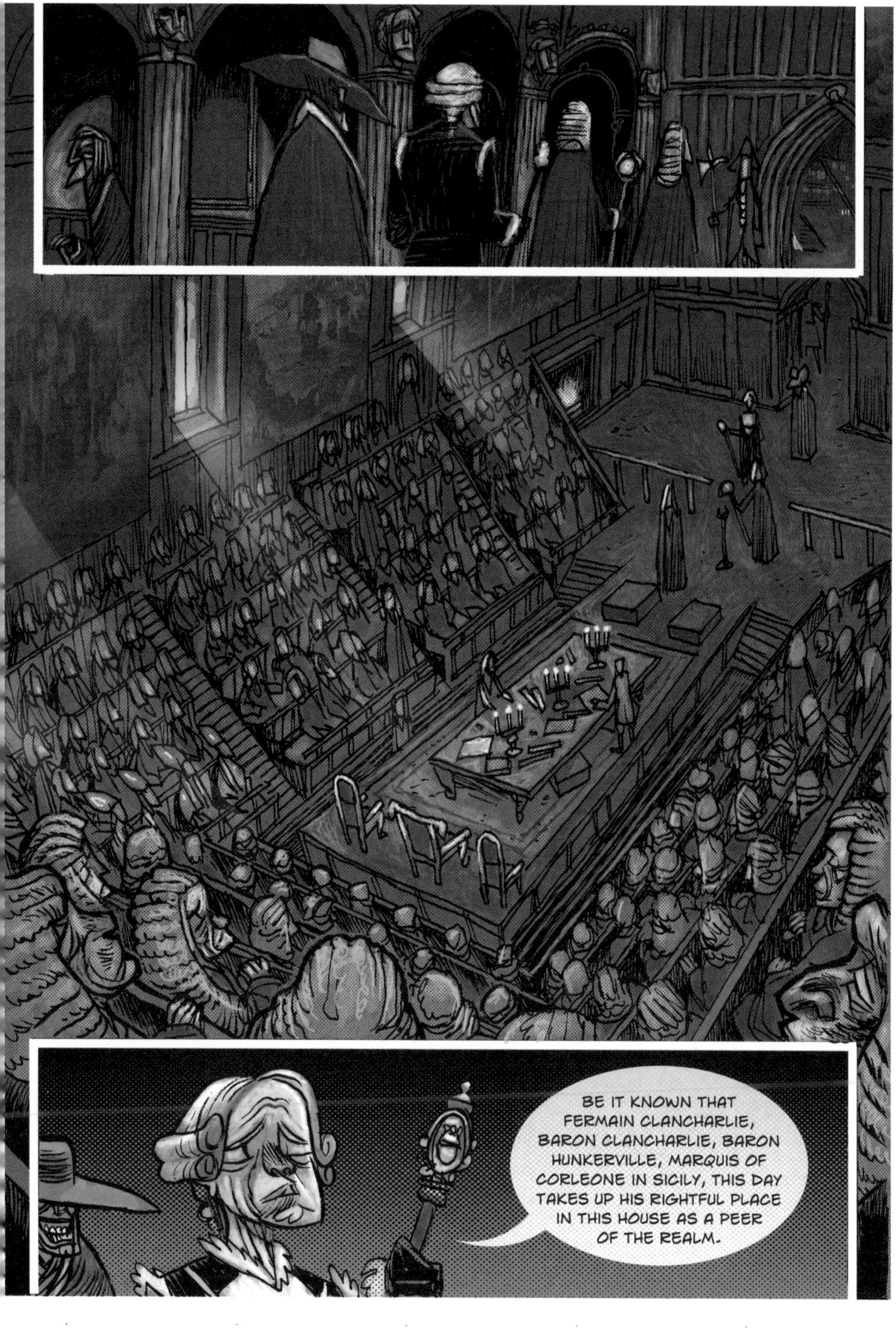
BE IT KNOWN THAT FERMAIN CLANCHARLIE, BARON CLANCHARLIE, BARON HUNKERVILLE, MARQUIS OF CORLEONE IN SICILY, THIS DAY TAKES UP HIS RIGHTFUL PLACE IN THIS HOUSE AS A PEER OF THE REALM.

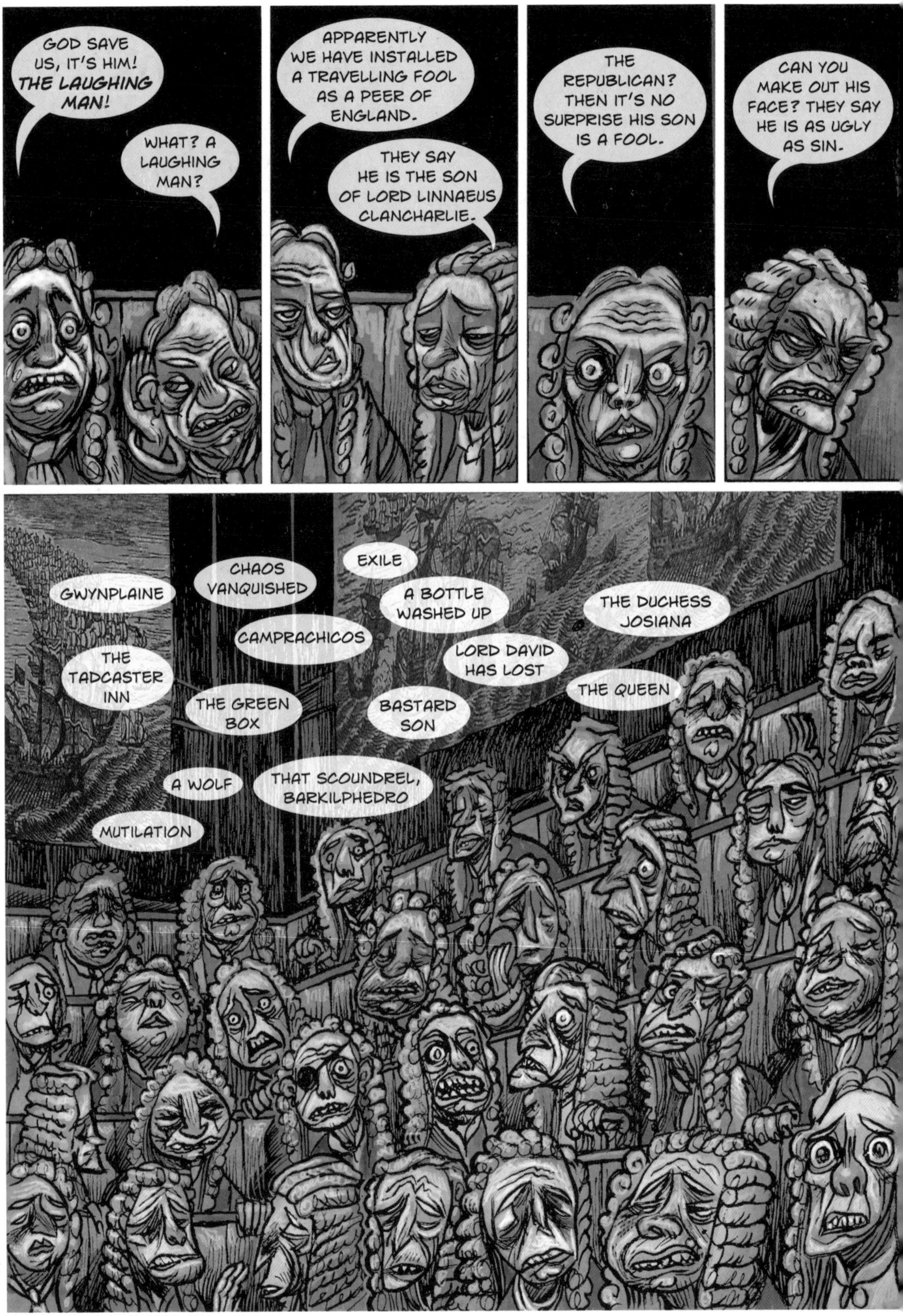
GOD SAVE US, IT'S HIM! THE LAUGHING MAN!
WHAT? A LAUGHING MAN?
APPARENTLY WE HAVE INSTALLED A TRAVELLING FOOL AS A PEER OF ENGLAND.
THEY SAY HE IS THE SON OF LORD LINNAEUS CLANCHARLIE.
THE REPUBLICAN? THEN IT'S NO SURPRISE HIS SON IS A FOOL.
CAN YOU MAKE OUT HIS FACE? THEY SAY HE IS AS UGLY AS SIN.
GWYNPLAINE
CHAOS VANQUISHED
EXILE
A BOTTLE WASHED UP
THE DUCHESS JOSIANA
CAMPRACHICOS
LORD DAVID HAS LOST
THE TADCASTER INN
THE QUEEN
THE GREEN BOX
BASTARD SON
A WOLF
THAT SCOUNDREL, BARKILPHEDRO
MUTILATION

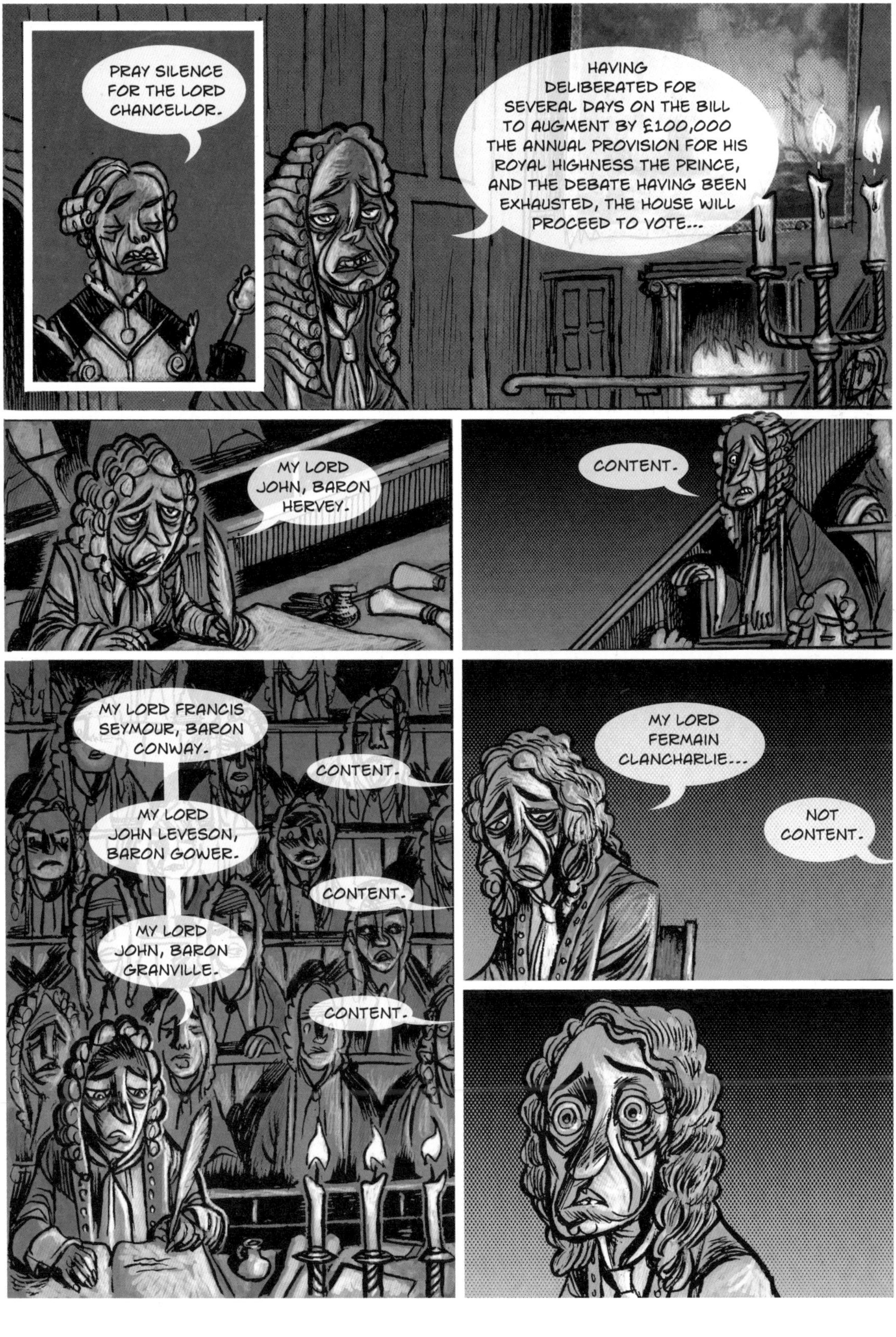
PRAY SILENCE FOR THE LORD CHANCELLOR.
HAVING DELIBERATED FOR SEVERAL DAYS ON THE BILL TO AUGMENT BY £100,000 THE ANNUAL PROVISION FOR HIS ROYAL HIGHNESS THE PRINCE, AND THE DEBATE HAVING BEEN EXHAUSTED, THE HOUSE WILL PROCEED TO VOTE...
MY LORD JOHN, BARON HERVEY.
CONTENT.
MY LORD FRANCIS SEYMOUR, BARON CONWAY.
CONTENT.
MY LORD JOHN LEVESON, BARON GOWER.
CONTENT.
MY LORD JOHN, BARON GRANVILLE.
CONTENT.
MY LORD FERMAIN CLANCHARLIE...
NOT CONTENT.

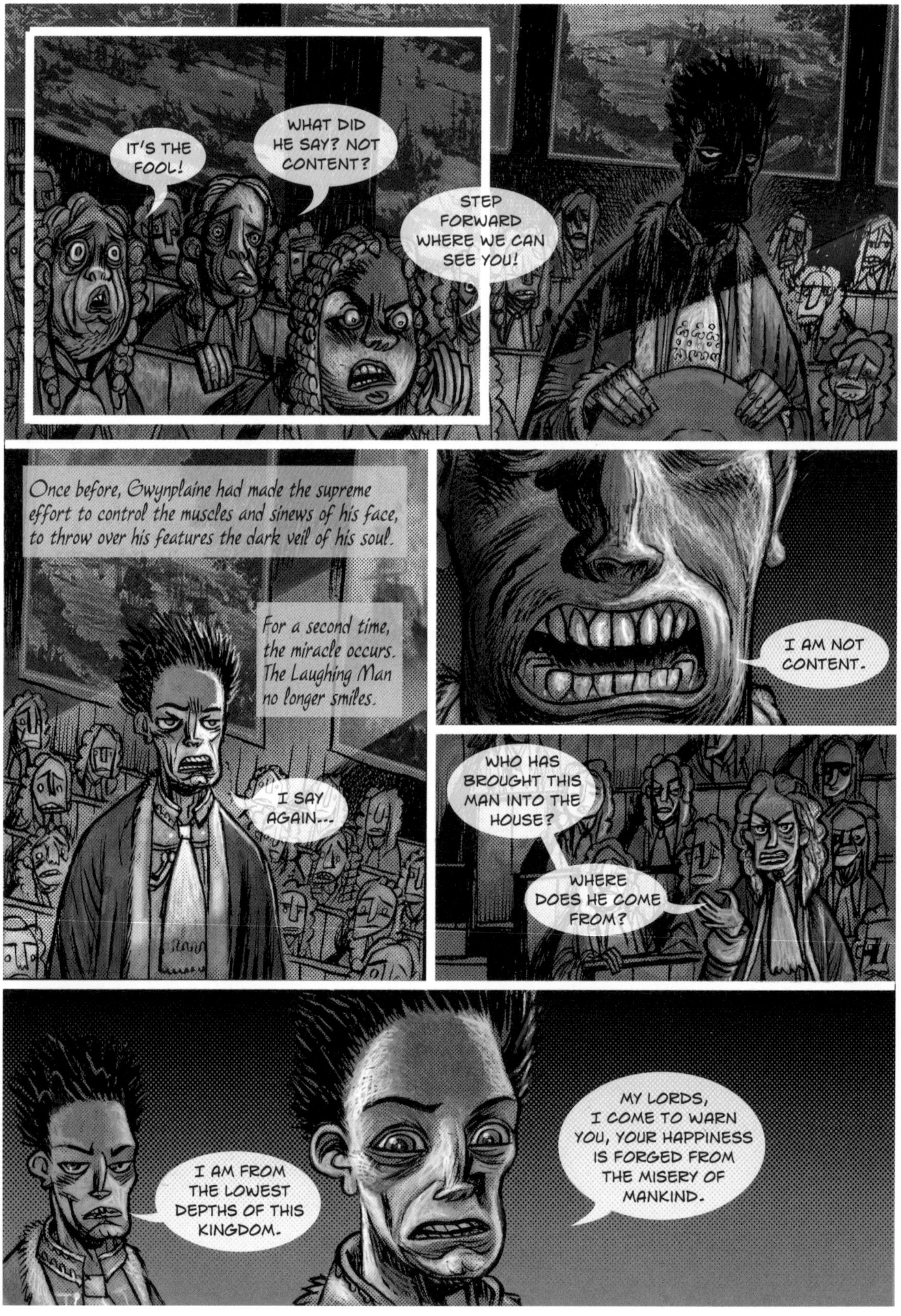
IT'S THE FOOL!
WHAT DID HE SAY? NOT CONTENT?
STEP FORWARD WHERE WE CAN SEE YOU!
Once before, Gwynplaine had made the supreme effort to control the muscles and sinews of his face, to throw over his features the dark veil of his soul.
For a second time, the miracle occurs. The Laughing Man no longer smiles.
I SAY AGAIN...
I AM NOT CONTENT.
WHO HAS BROUGHT THIS MAN INTO THE HOUSE?
WHERE DOES HE COME FROM?
I AM FROM THE LOWEST DEPTHS OF THIS KINGDOM.
MY LORDS, I COME TO WARN YOU, YOUR HAPPINESS IS FORGED FROM THE MISERY OF MANKIND.

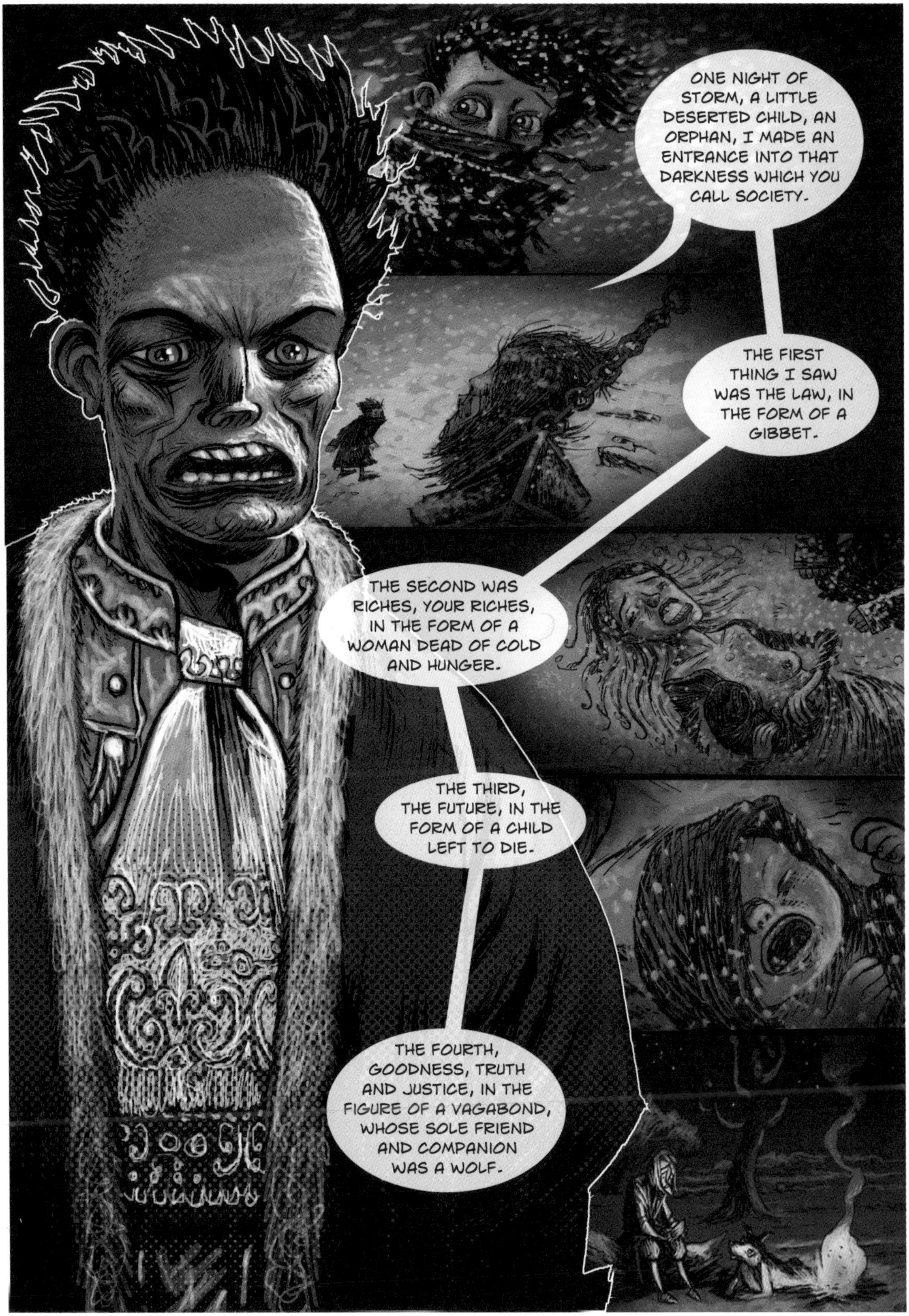
ONE NIGHT OF STORM, A LITTLE DESERTED CHILD, AN ORPHAN, I MADE AN ENTRANCE INTO THAT DARKNESS WHICH YOU CALL SOCIETY.
THE FIRST THING I SAW WAS THE LAW, IN THE FORM OF A GIBBET.
THE SECOND WAS RICHES, YOUR RICHES, IN THE FORM OF A WOMAN DEAD OF COLD AND HUNGER.
THE THIRD, THE FUTURE, IN THE FORM OF A CHILD LEFT TO DIE.
THE FOURTH, GOODNESS, TRUTH AND JUSTICE, IN THE FIGURE OF A VAGABOND, WHOSE SOLE FRIEND AND COMPANION WAS A WOLF.

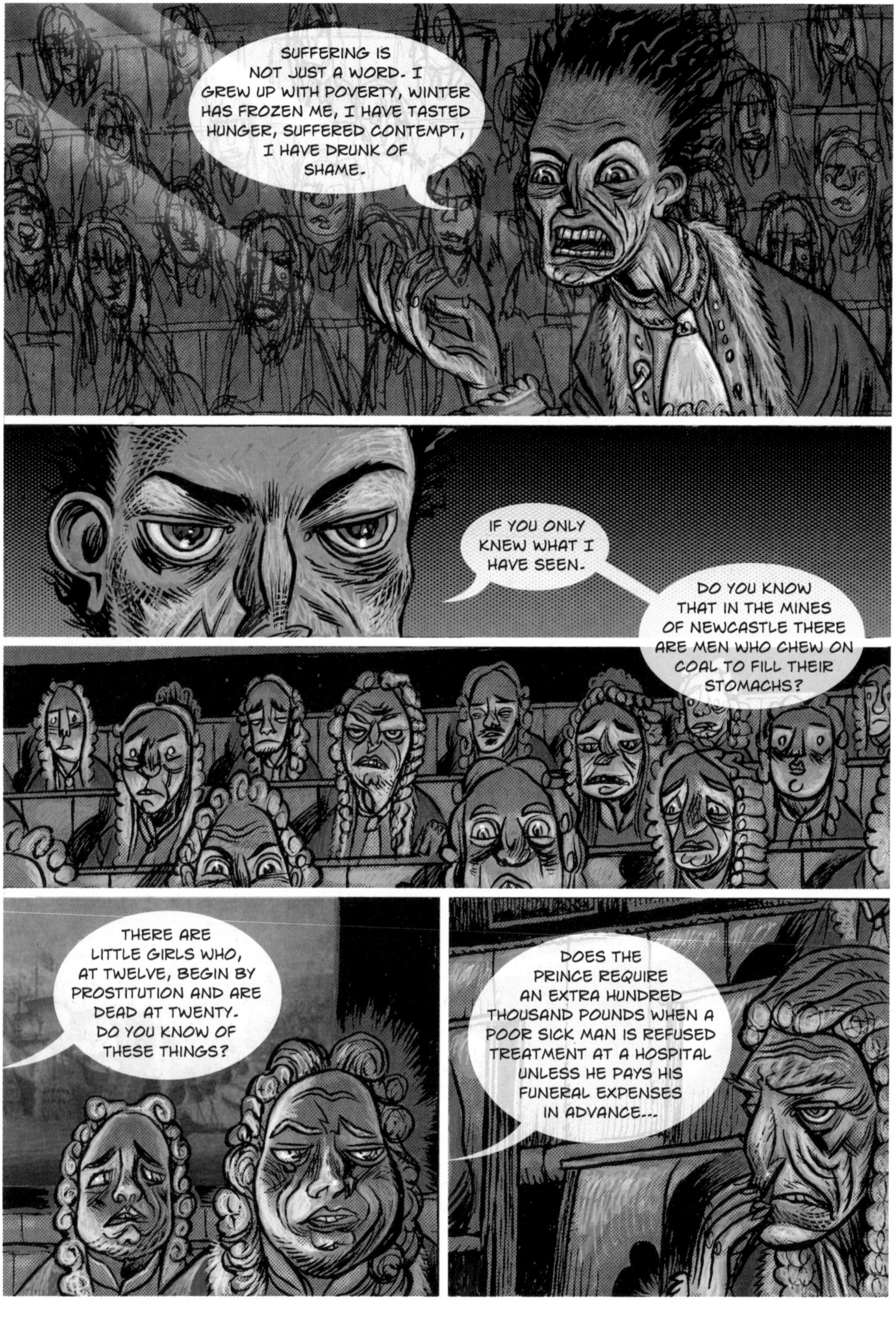
SUFFERING IS NOT JUST A WORD. I GREW UP WITH POVERTY, WINTER HAS FROZEN ME, I HAVE TASTED HUNGER, SUFFERED CONTEMPT, I HAVE DRUNK OF SHAME.
IF YOU ONLY KNEW WHAT I HAVE SEEN.
DO YOU KNOW THAT IN THE MINES OF NEWCASTLE THERE ARE MEN WHO CHEW ON COAL TO FILL THEIR STOMACHS?
THERE ARE LITTLE GIRLS WHO, AT TWELVE, BEGIN BY PROSTITUTION AND ARE DEAD AT TWENTY. DO YOU KNOW OF THESE THINGS?
DOES THE PRINCE REQUIRE AN EXTRA HUNDRED THOUSAND POUNDS WHEN A POOR SICK MAN IS REFUSED TREATMENT AT A HOSPITAL UNLESS HE PAYS HIS FUNERAL EXPENSES IN ADVANCE...

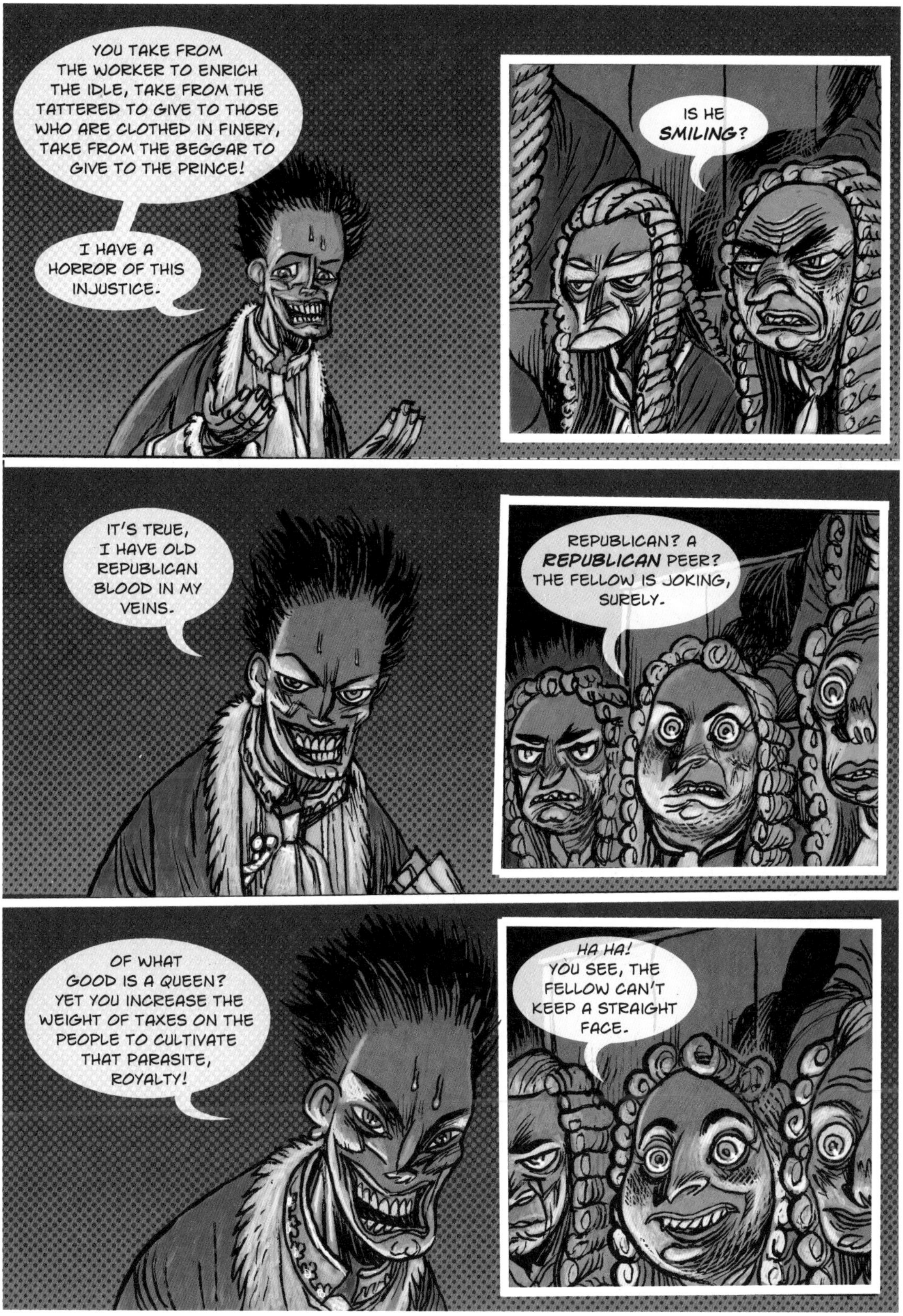
YOU TAKE FROM THE WORKER TO ENRICH THE IDLE, TAKE FROM THE TATTERED TO GIVE TO THOSE WHO ARE CLOTHED IN FINERY, TAKE FROM THE BEGGAR TO GIVE TO THE PRINCE!
I HAVE A HORROR OF THIS INJUSTICE.
IS HE SMILING?
IT'S TRUE, I HAVE OLD REPUBLICAN BLOOD IN MY VEINS.
REPUBLICAN? A REPUBLICAN PEER? THE FELLOW IS JOKING, SURELY.
OF WHAT GOOD IS A QUEEN? YET YOU INCREASE THE WEIGHT OF TAXES ON THE PEOPLE TO CULTIVATE THAT PARASITE, ROYALTY!
HA HA! YOU SEE, THE FELLOW CAN'T KEEP A STRAIGHT FACE.

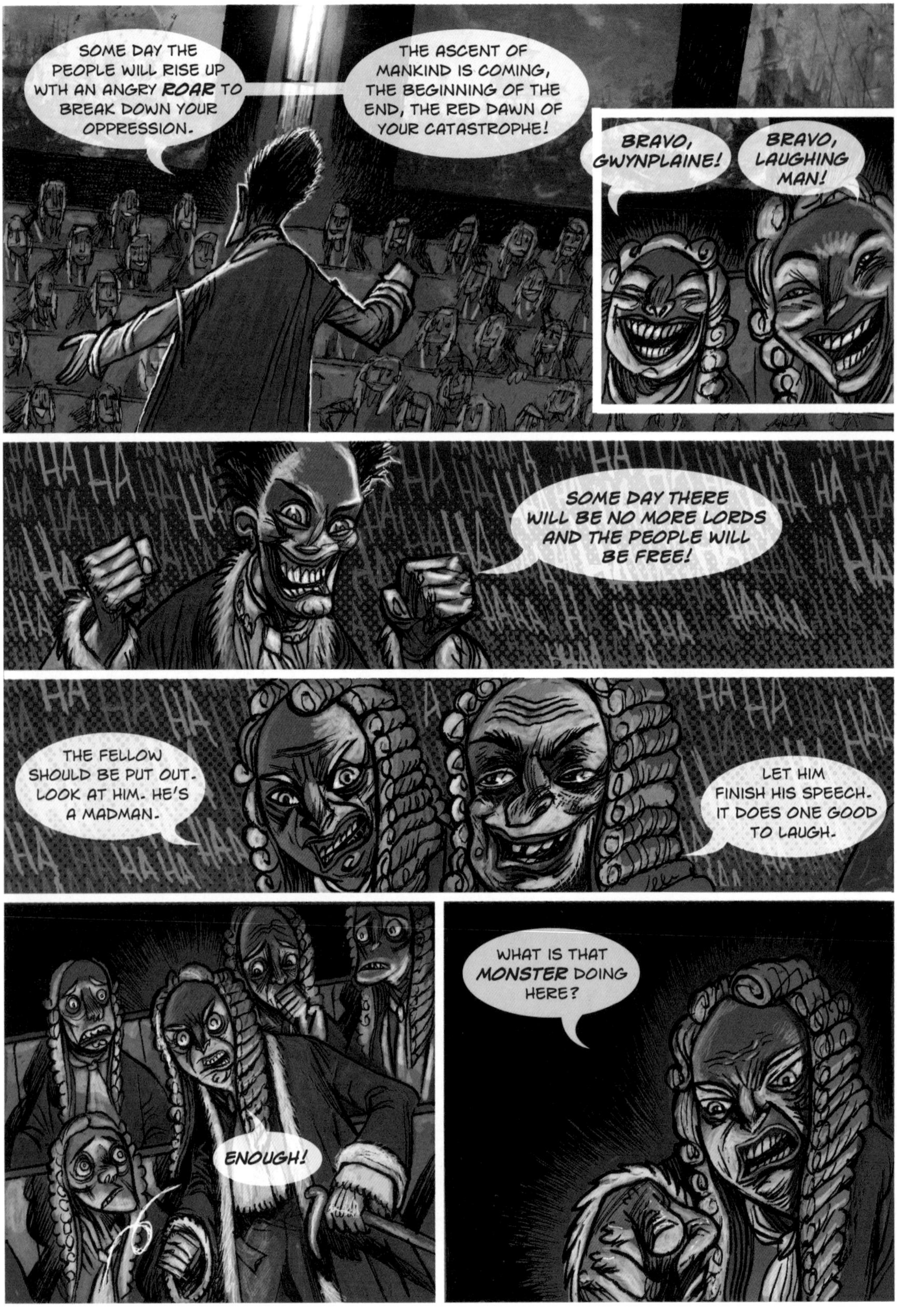
SOME DAY THE PEOPLE WILL RISE UP WTH AN ANGRY ROAR TO BREAK DOWN YOUR OPPRESSION.
THE ASCENT OF MANKIND IS COMING, THE BEGINNING OF THE END, THE RED DAWN OF YOUR CATASTROPHE!
BRAVO, GWYNPLAINE!
BRAVO, LAUGHING MAN!
SOME DAY THERE WILL BE NO MORE LORDS AND THE PEOPLE WILL BE FREE!
THE FELLOW SHOULD BE PUT OUT. LOOK AT HIM. HE'S A MADMAN.
LET HIM FINISH HIS SPEECH. IT DOES ONE GOOD TO LAUGH.
ENOUGH!
WHAT IS THAT MONSTER DOING HERE?

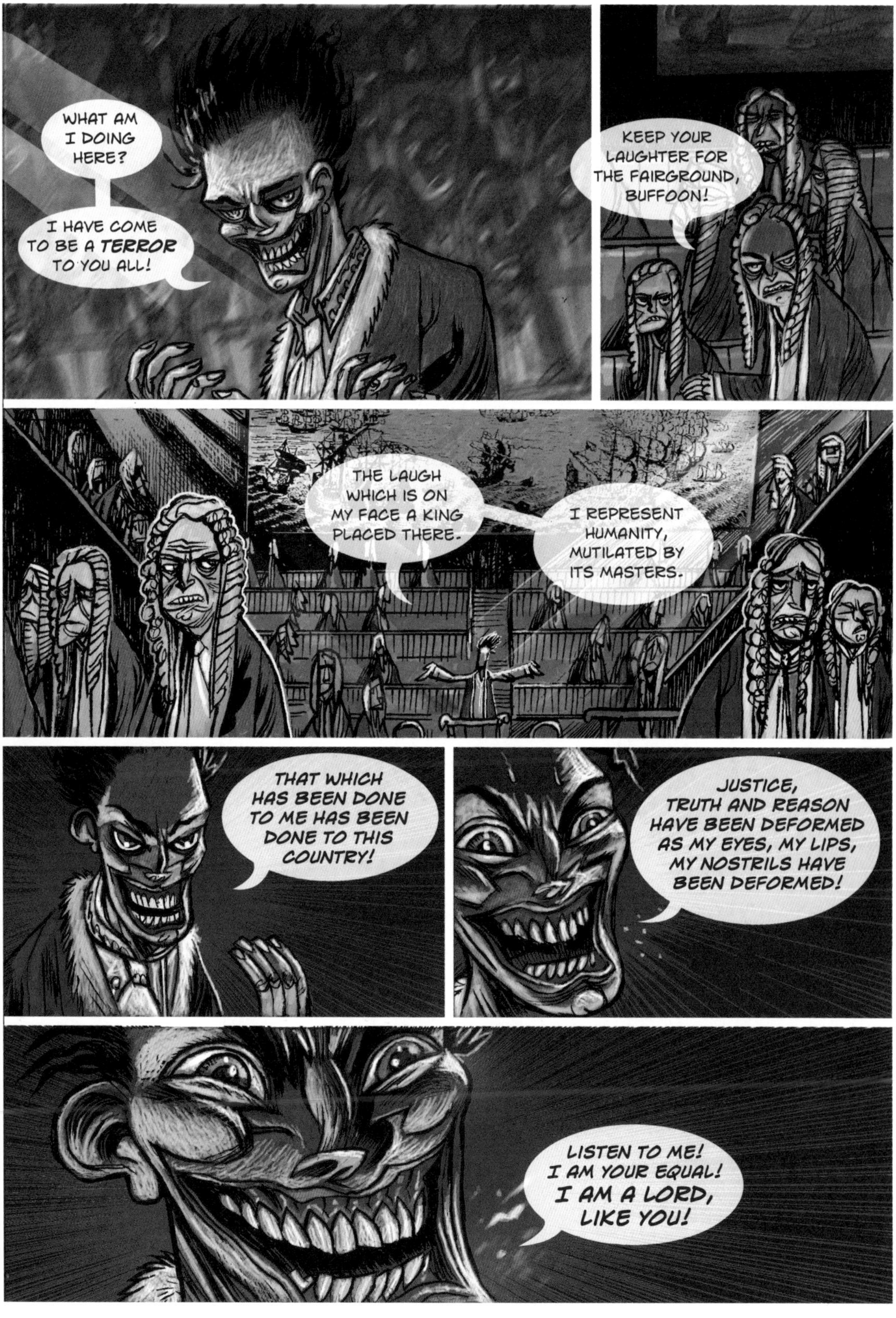
WHAT AM I DOING HERE?
I HAVE COME TO BE A TERROR TO YOU ALL!
KEEP YOUR LAUGHTER FOR THE FAIRGROUND, BUFFOON!
THE LAUGH WHICH IS ON MY FACE A KING PLACED THERE.
I REPRESENT HUMANITY, MUTILATED BY ITS MASTERS.
THAT WHICH HAS BEEN DONE TO ME HAS BEEN DONE TO THIS COUNTRY!
JUSTICE, TRUTH AND REASON HAVE BEEN DEFORMED AS MY EYES, MY LIPS, MY NOSTRILS HAVE BEEN DEFORMED!
LISTEN TO ME! I AM YOUR EQUAL! I AM A LORD, LIKE YOU!

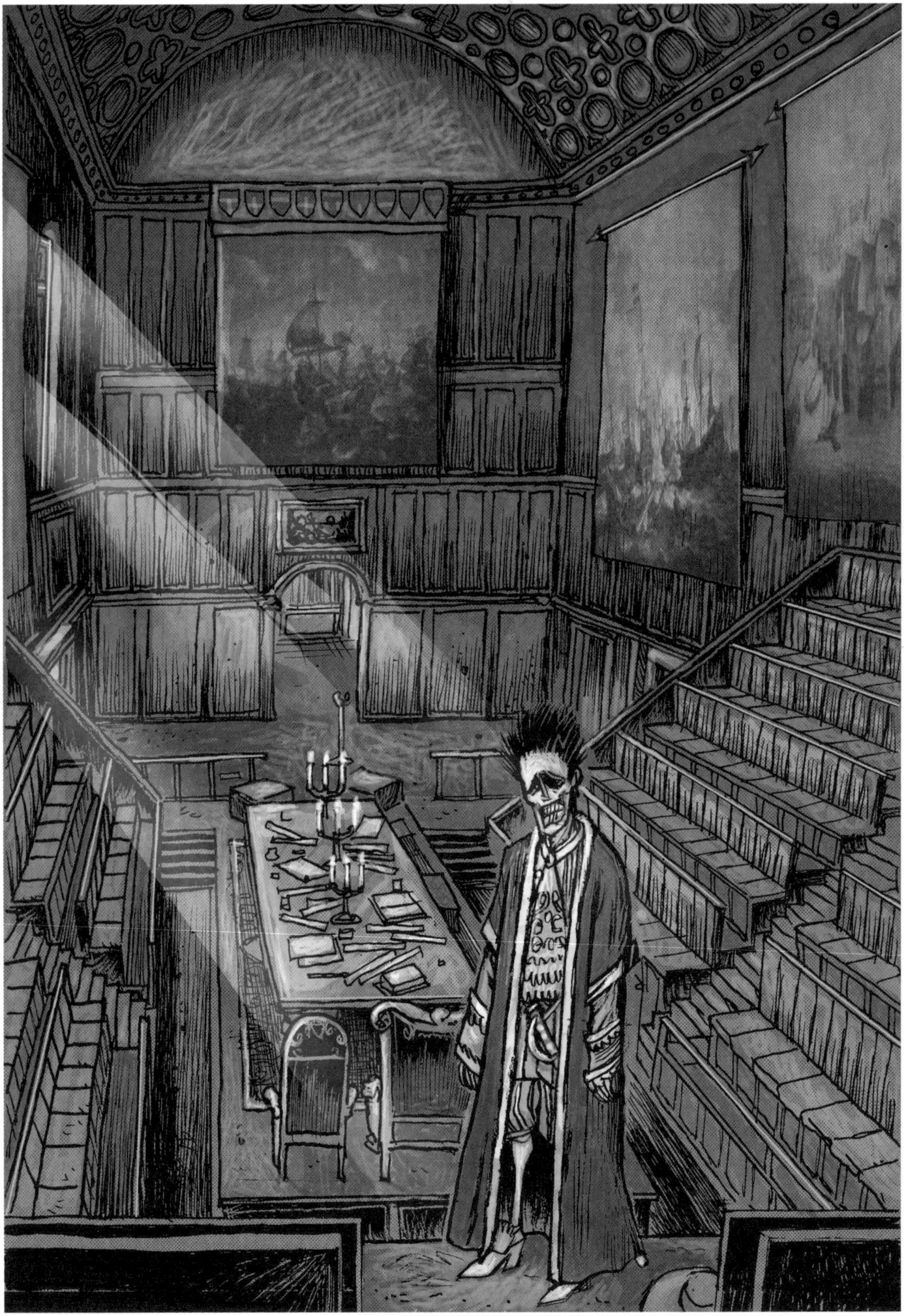

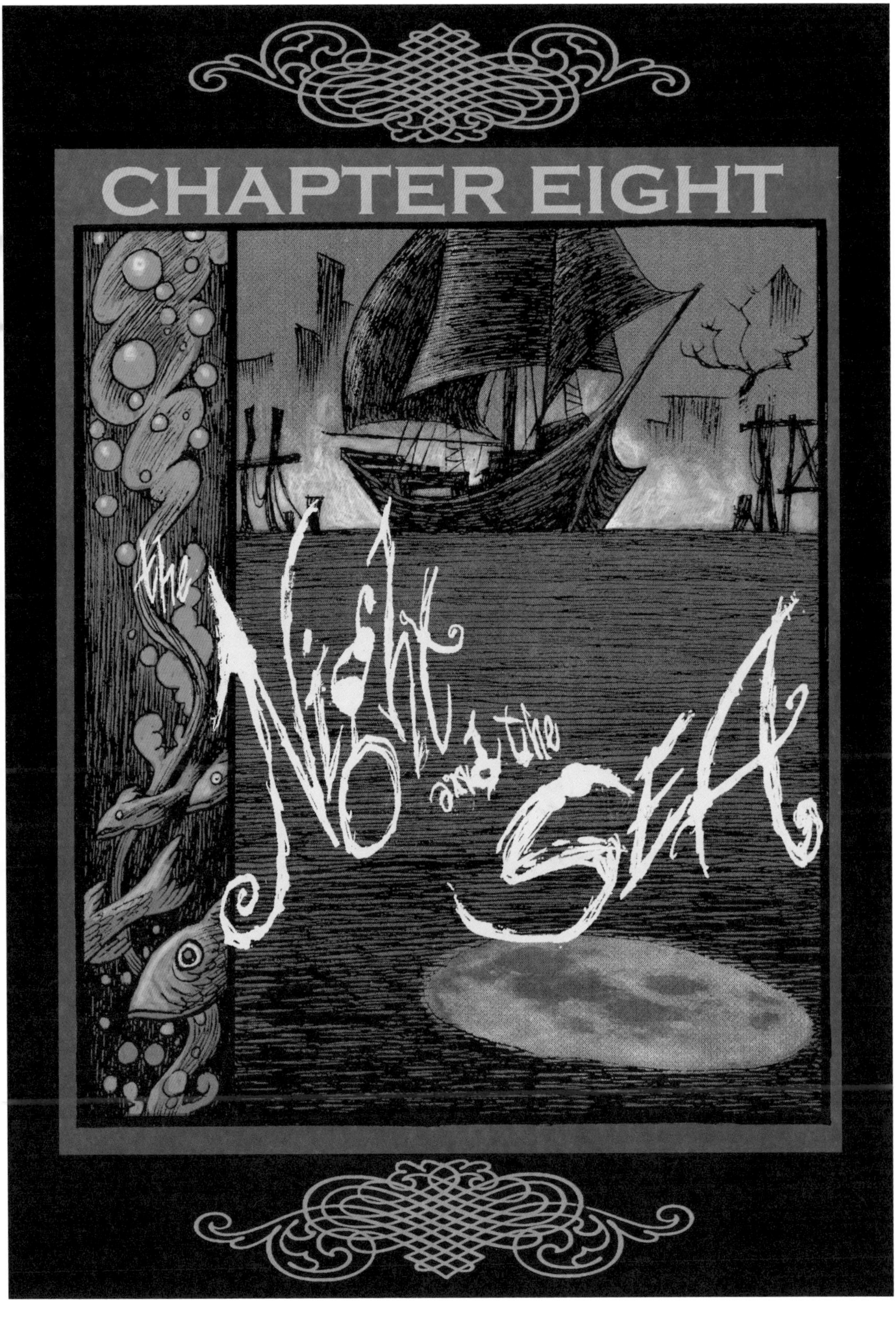
CHAPTER EIGHT
The Night and the Sea

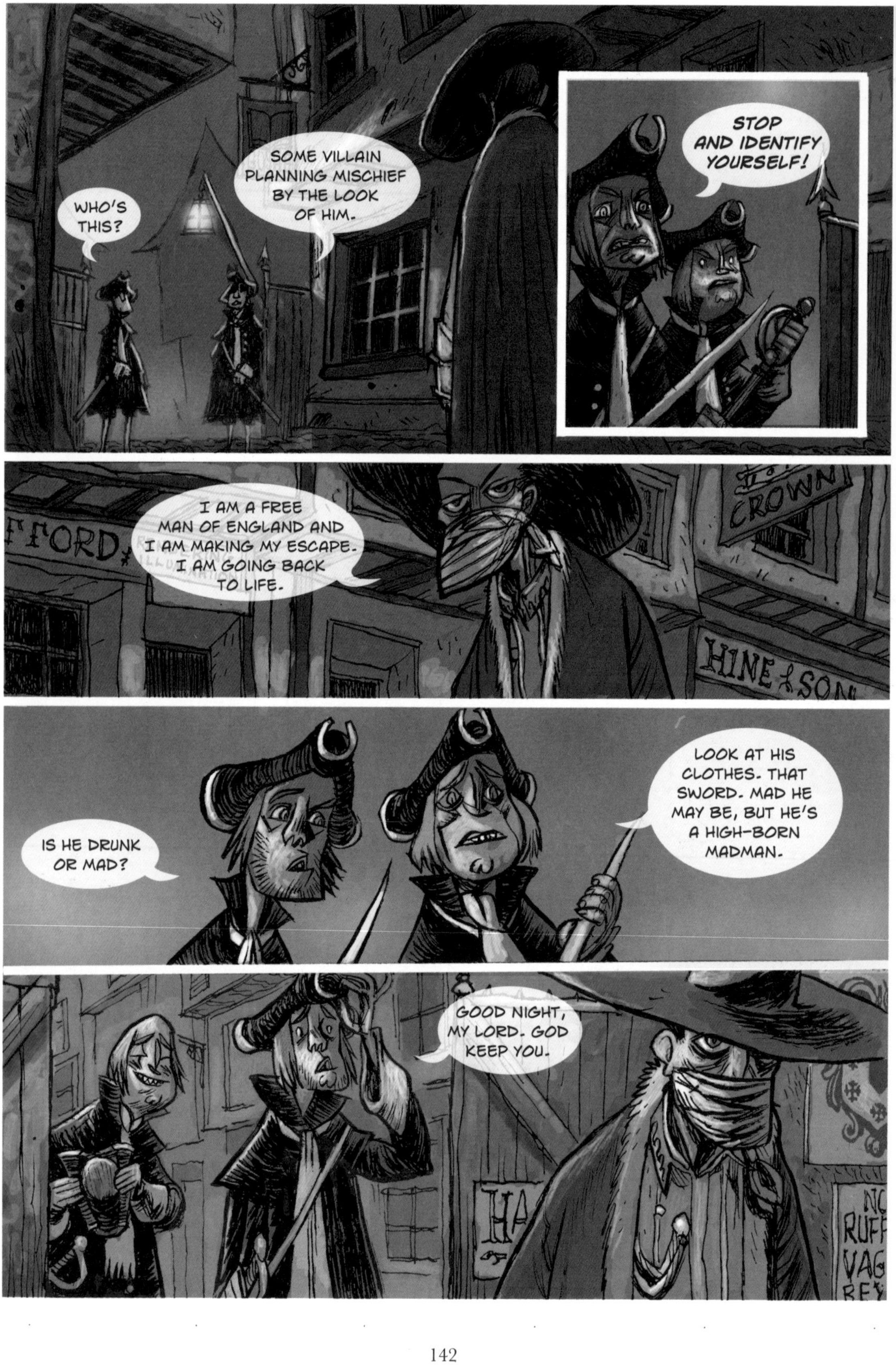
WHO'S THIS?
SOME VILLAIN PLANNING MISCHIEF BY THE LOOK OF HIM.
STOP AND IDENTIFY YOURSELF!
I AM A FREE MAN OF ENGLAND AND I AM MAKING MY ESCAPE. I AM GOING BACK TO LIFE.
CROWN
HINE & SON
IS HE DRUNK OR MAD?
LOOK AT HIS CLOTHES. THAT SWORD. MAD HE MAY BE, BUT HE'S A HIGH-BORN MADMAN.
GOOD NIGHT, MY LORD. GOD KEEP YOU.

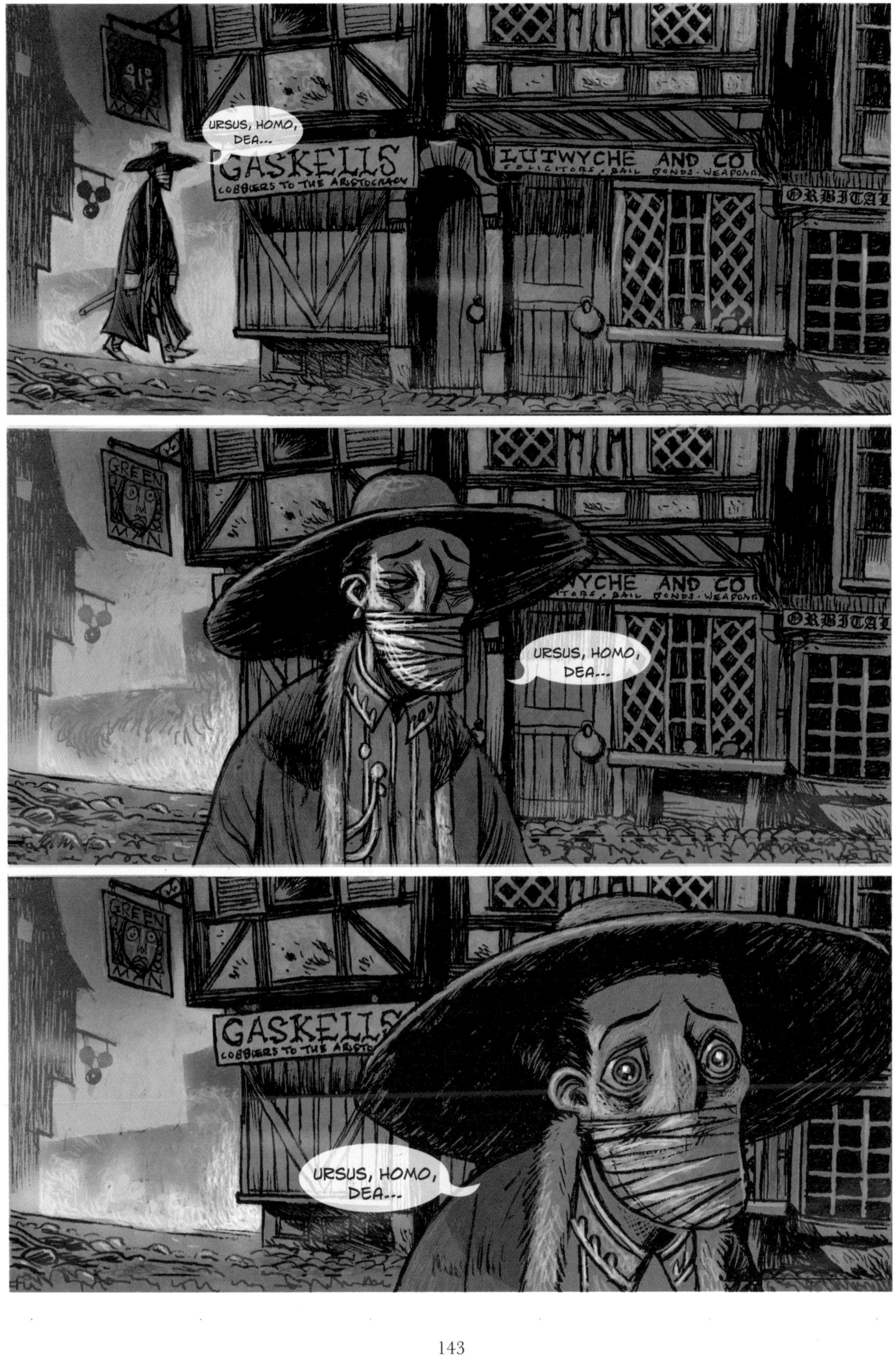
URSUS, HOMO, DEA...
GASKELLS
COBBLERS TO THE ARISTOCRACY
LUTWYCHE AND CO
SOLICITORS, BAIL BONDS, WEAPONRY
ORBITAL
GREEN MAN
URSUS, HOMO, DEA...
URSUS, HOMO, DEA...

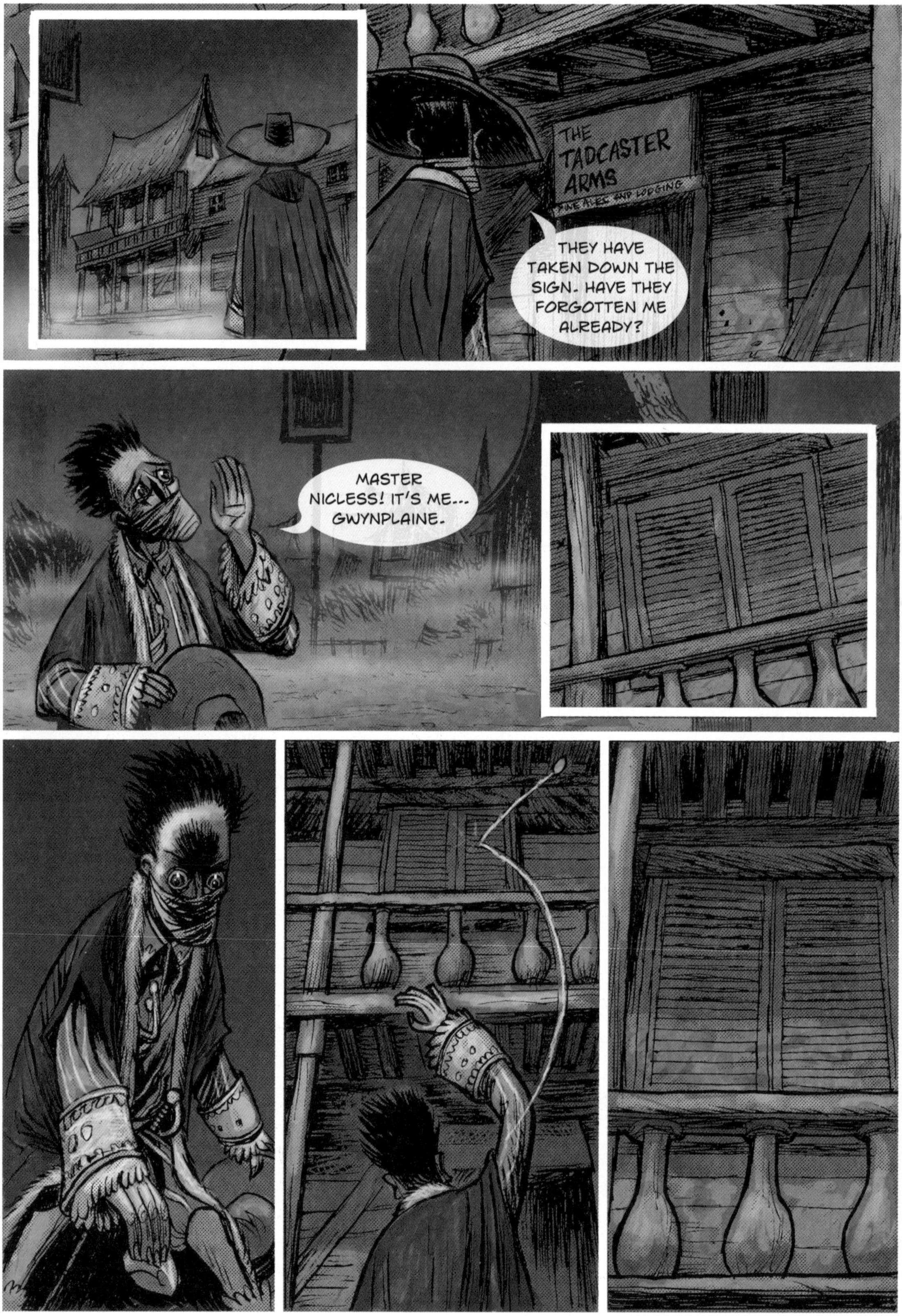
THE TADCASTER ARMS
FINE ALES AND LODGING
THEY HAVE TAKEN DOWN THE SIGN. HAVE THEY FORGOTTEN ME ALREADY?
MASTER NICLESS! IT'S ME... GWYNPLAINE.

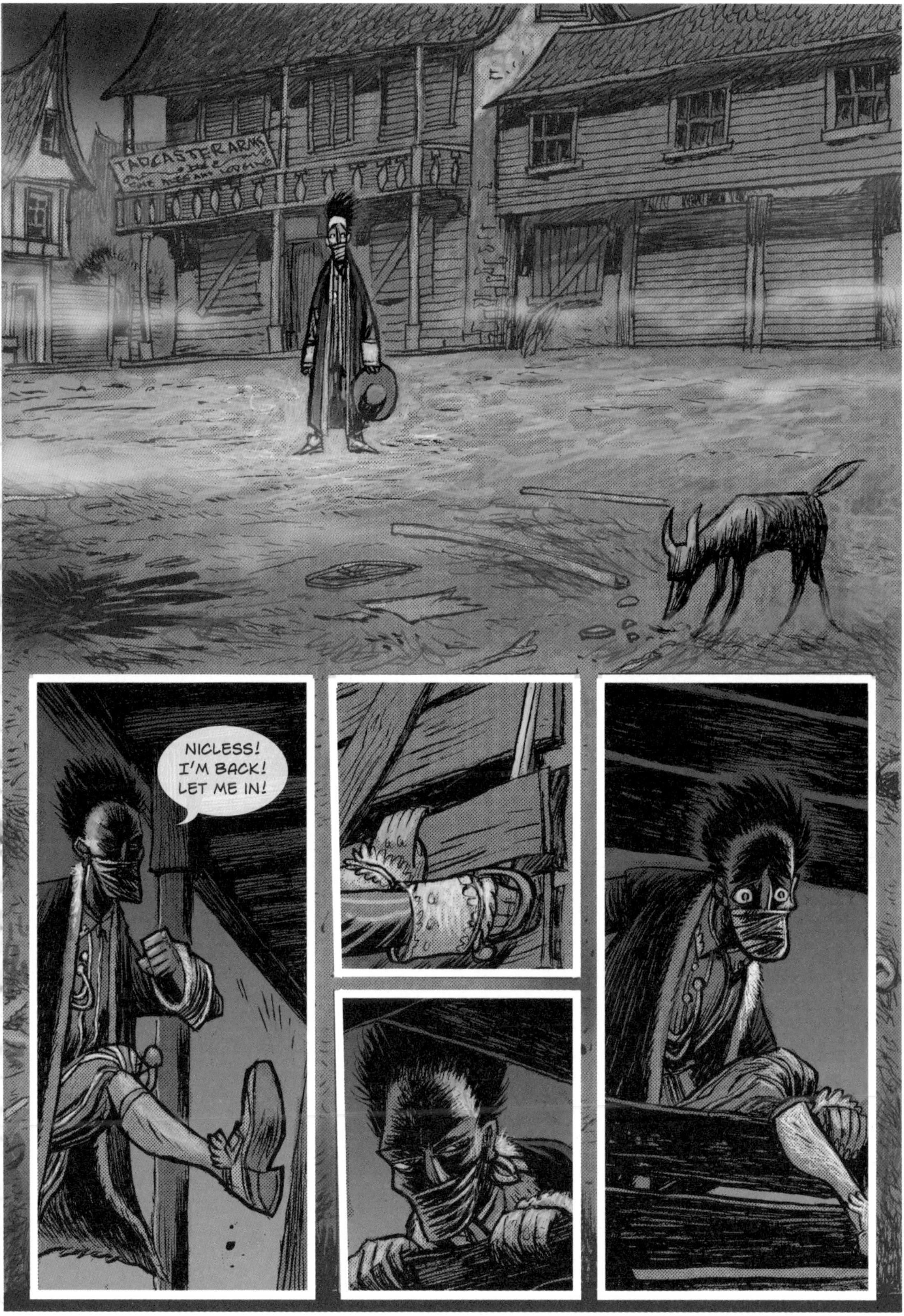
TADCASTER ARMS
NICLESS! I'M BACK! LET ME IN!

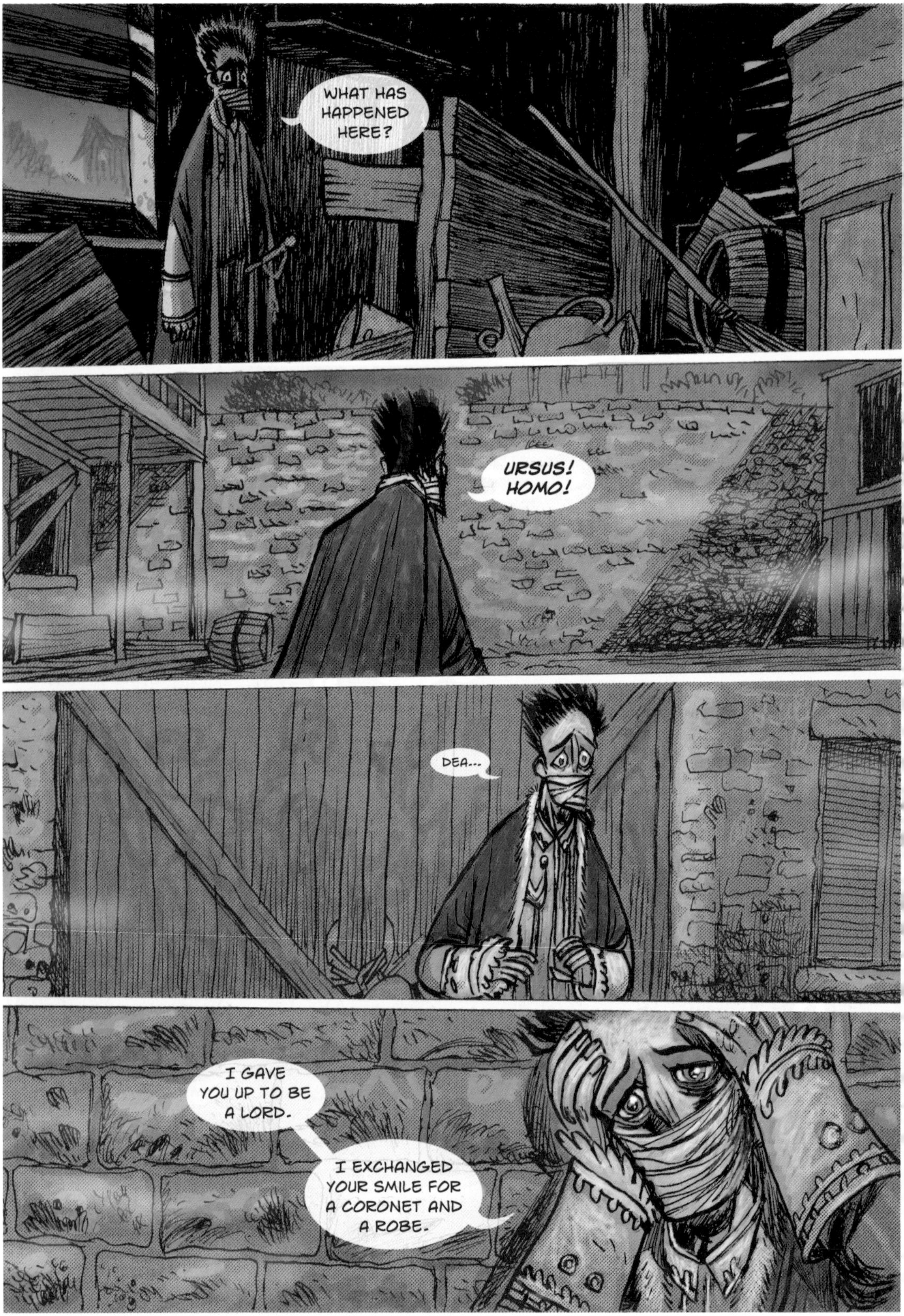
WHAT HAS HAPPENED HERE?
URSUS! HOMO!
DEA...
I GAVE YOU UP TO BE A LORD.
I EXCHANGED YOUR SMILE FOR A CORONET AND A ROBE.

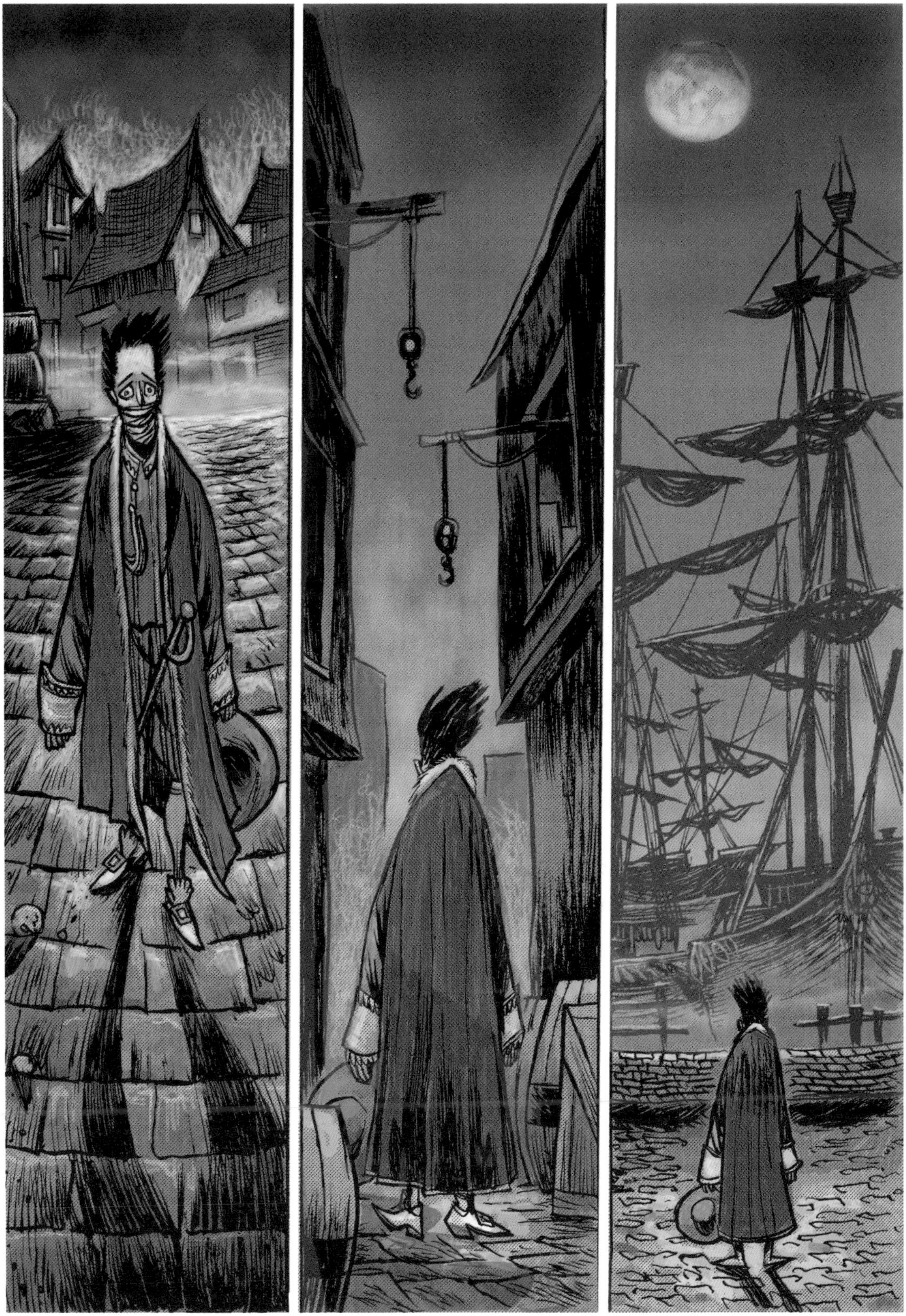

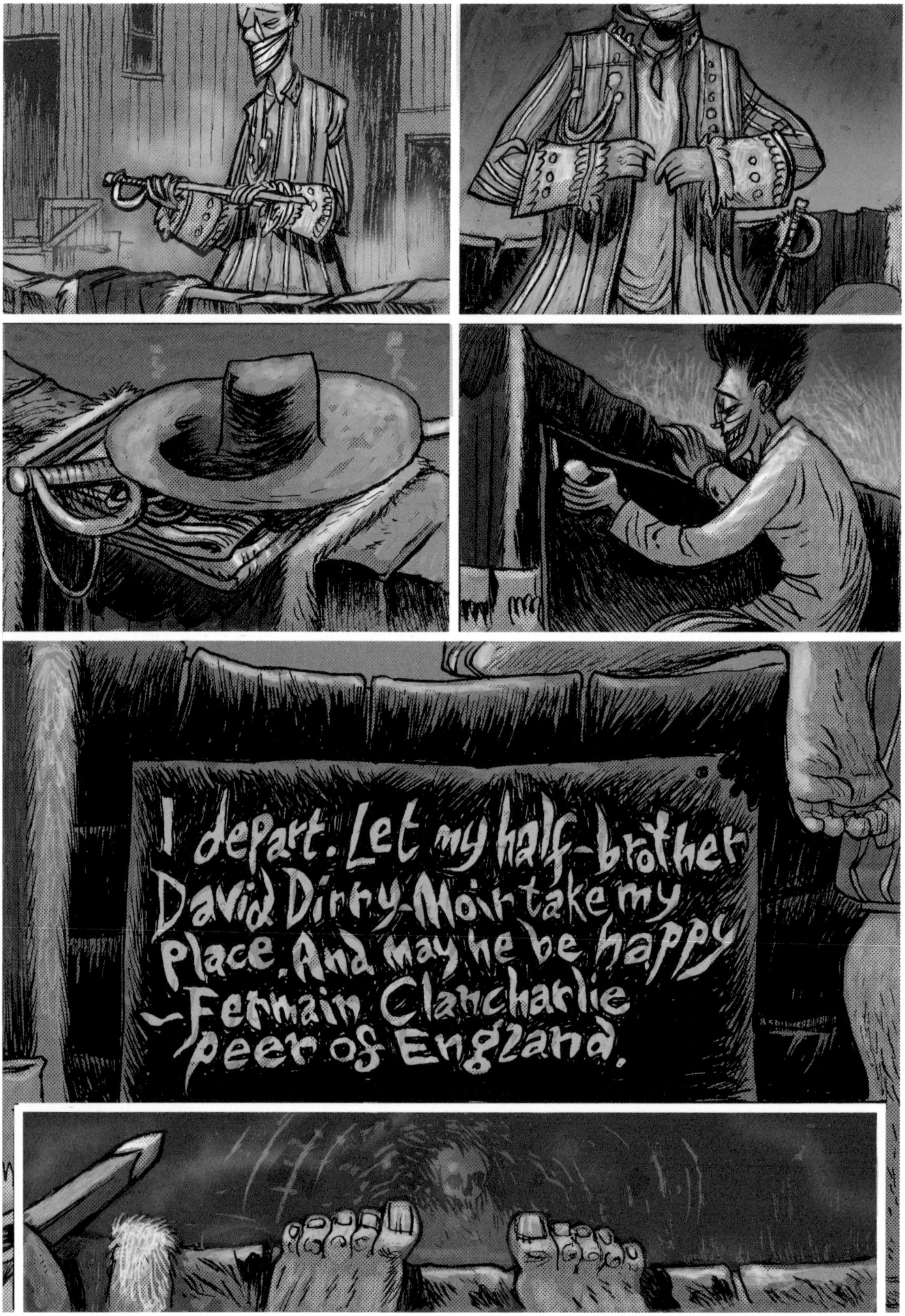
I depart. Let my half-brother
David Dirry-Moir take my
place. And may he be happy
~Fermain Clancharlie
peer of England.

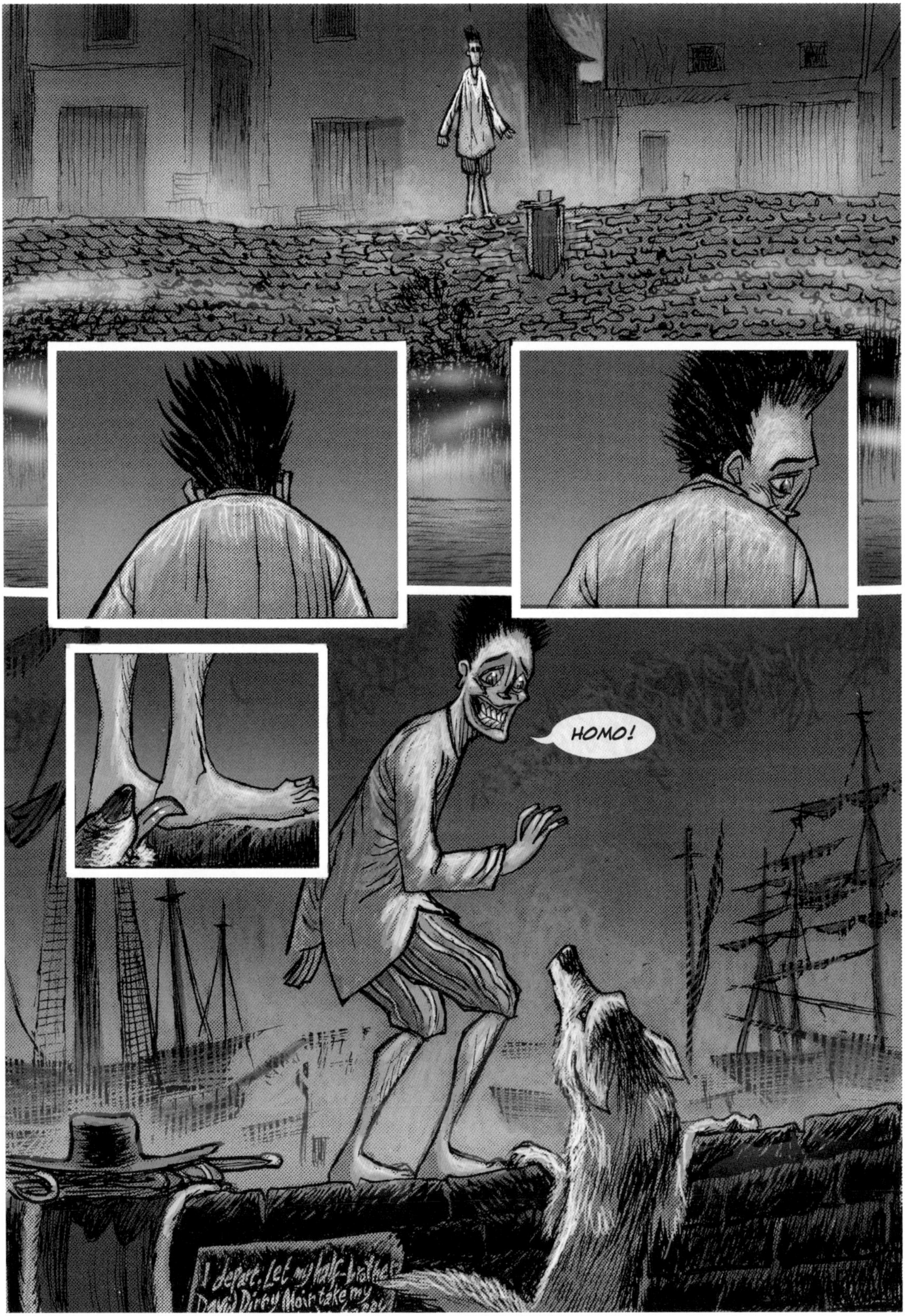
HOMO!
I depart. Let my half-brother
Dirry Moir take my

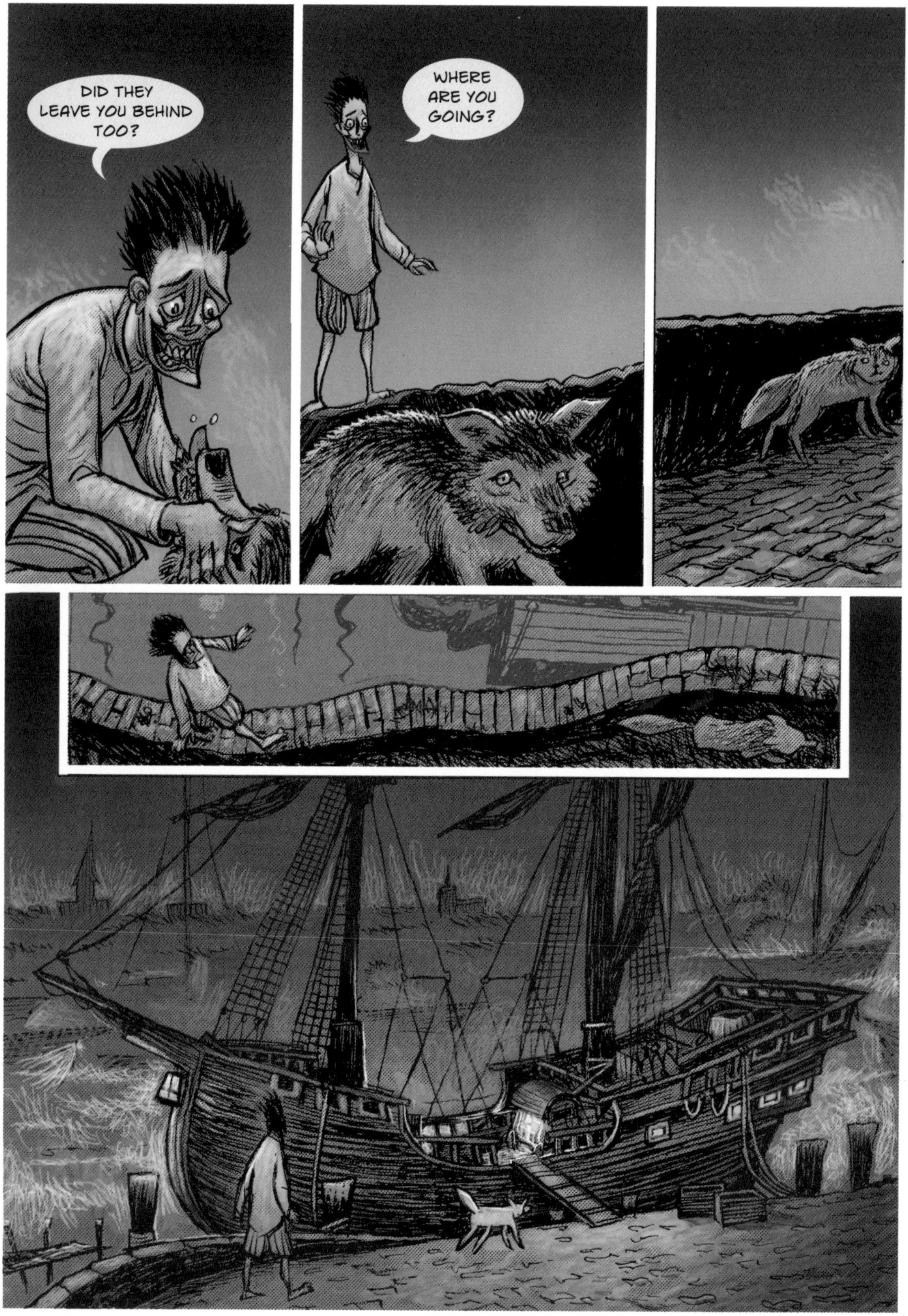
DID THEY LEAVE YOU BEHIND TOO?
WHERE ARE YOU GOING?

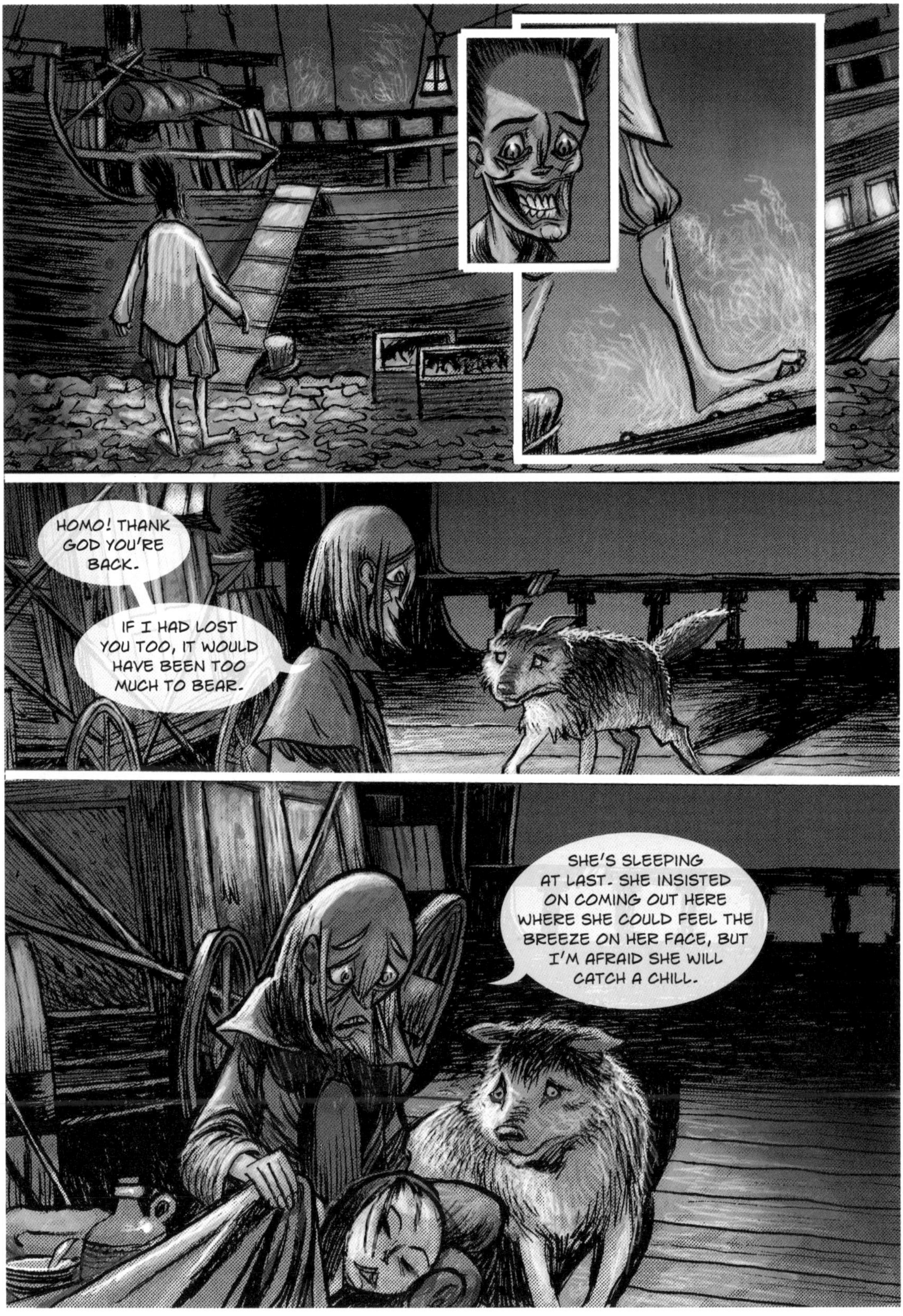
HOMO! THANK GOD YOU'RE BACK.
IF I HAD LOST YOU TOO, IT WOULD HAVE BEEN TOO MUCH TO BEAR.
SHE'S SLEEPING AT LAST. SHE INSISTED ON COMING OUT HERE WHERE SHE COULD FEEL THE BREEZE ON HER FACE, BUT I'M AFRAID SHE WILL CATCH A CHILL.

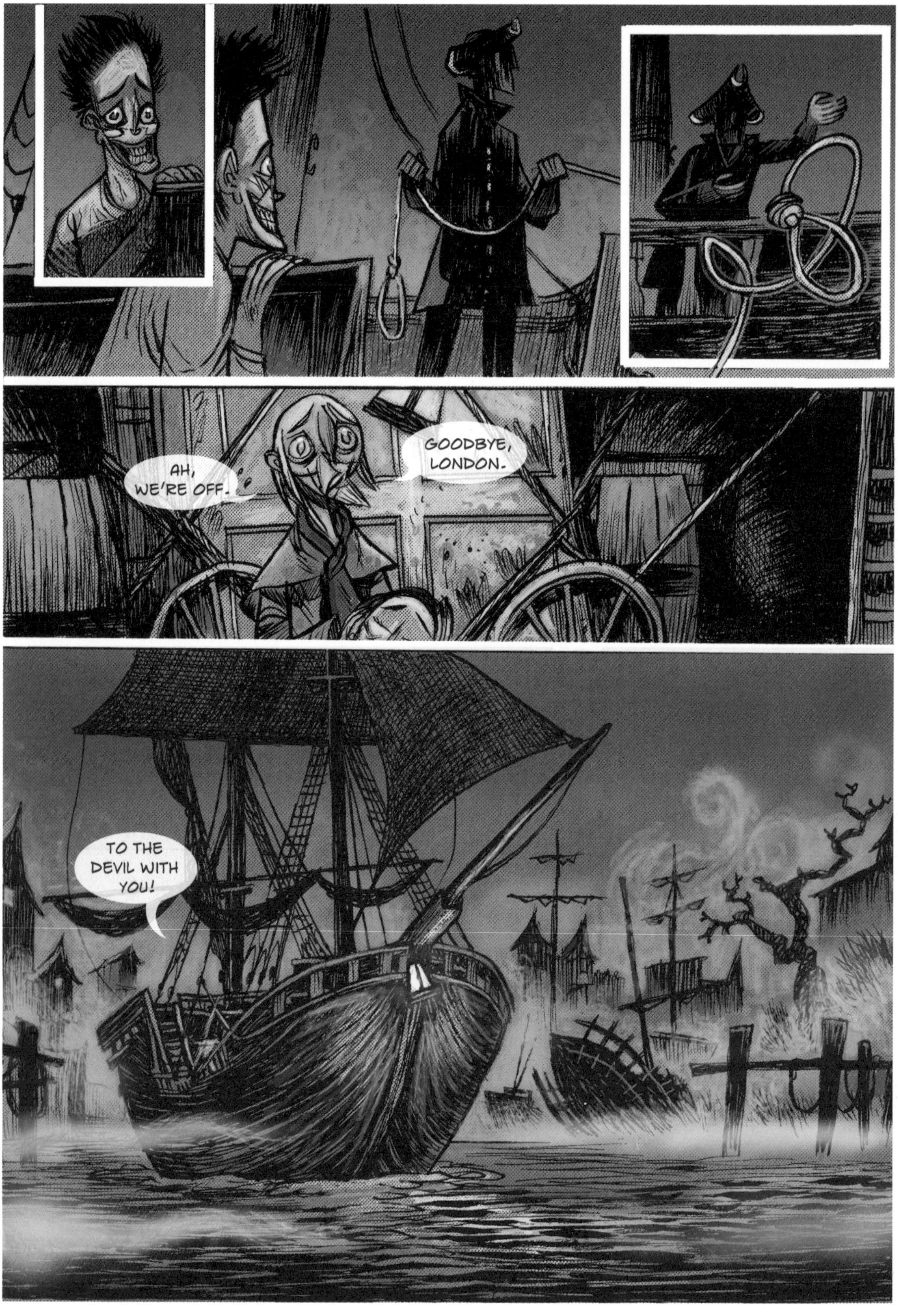
AH, WE'RE OFF.
GOODBYE, LONDON.
TO THE DEVIL WITH YOU!

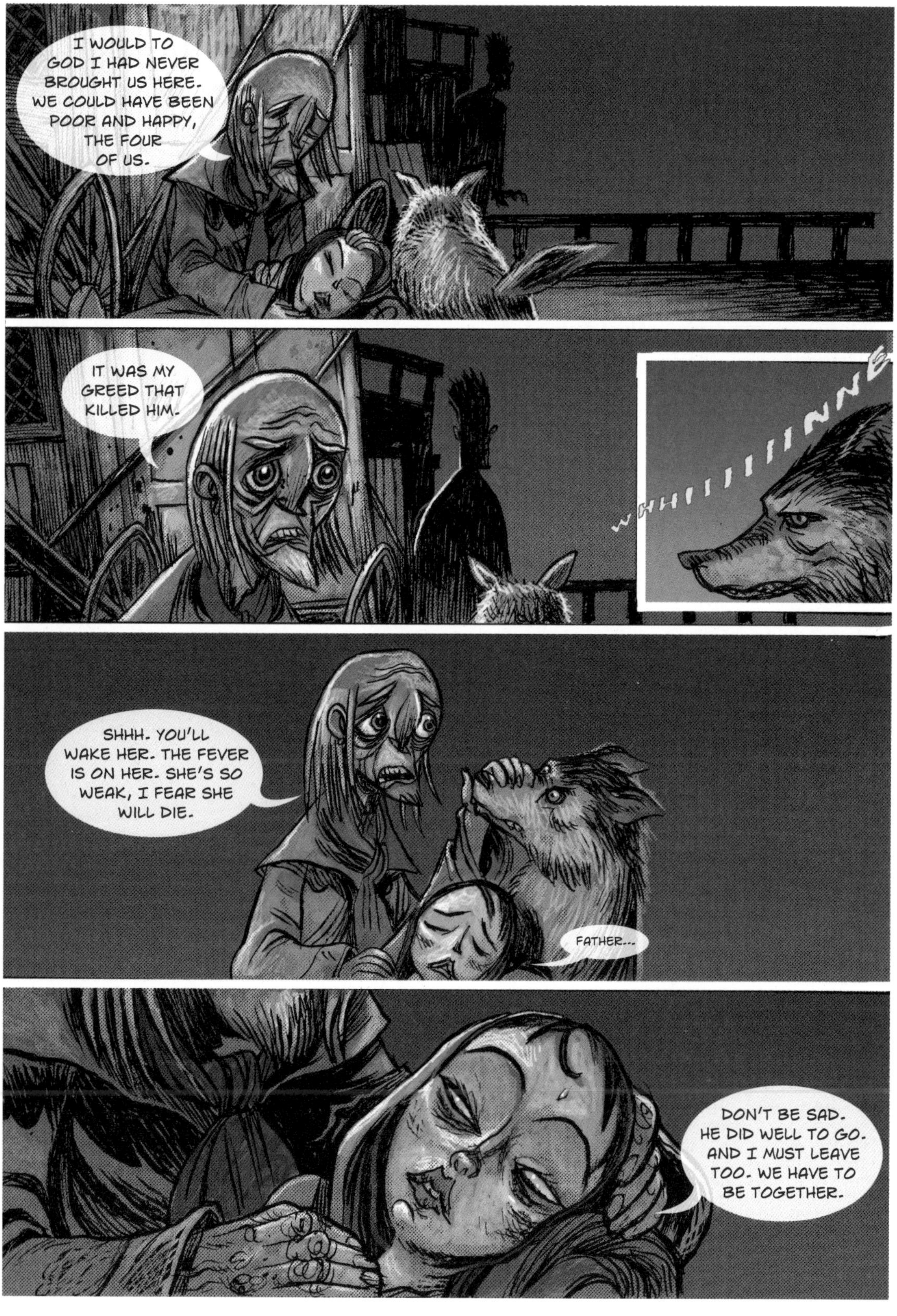
I WOULD TO GOD I HAD NEVER BROUGHT US HERE. WE COULD HAVE BEEN POOR AND HAPPY, THE FOUR OF US.
IT WAS MY GREED THAT KILLED HIM.
WHHIIIIIIIINNE
SHHH. YOU'LL WAKE HER. THE FEVER IS ON HER. SHE'S SO WEAK, I FEAR SHE WILL DIE.
FATHER...
DON'T BE SAD. HE DID WELL TO GO. AND I MUST LEAVE TOO. WE HAVE TO BE TOGETHER.

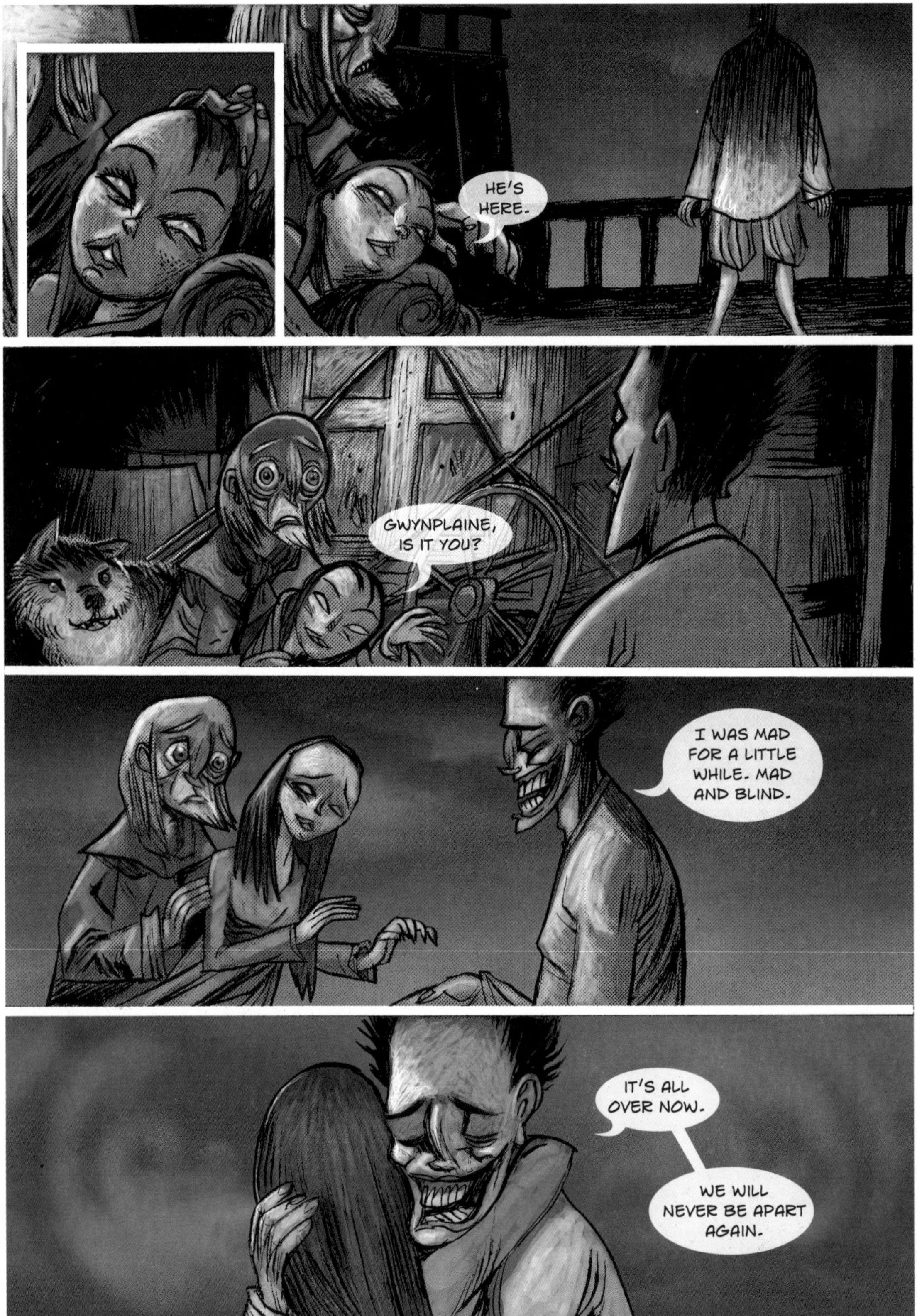
HE'S HERE.
GWYNPLAINE, IS IT YOU?
I WAS MAD FOR A LITTLE WHILE. MAD AND BLIND.
IT'S ALL OVER NOW.
WE WILL NEVER BE APART AGAIN.

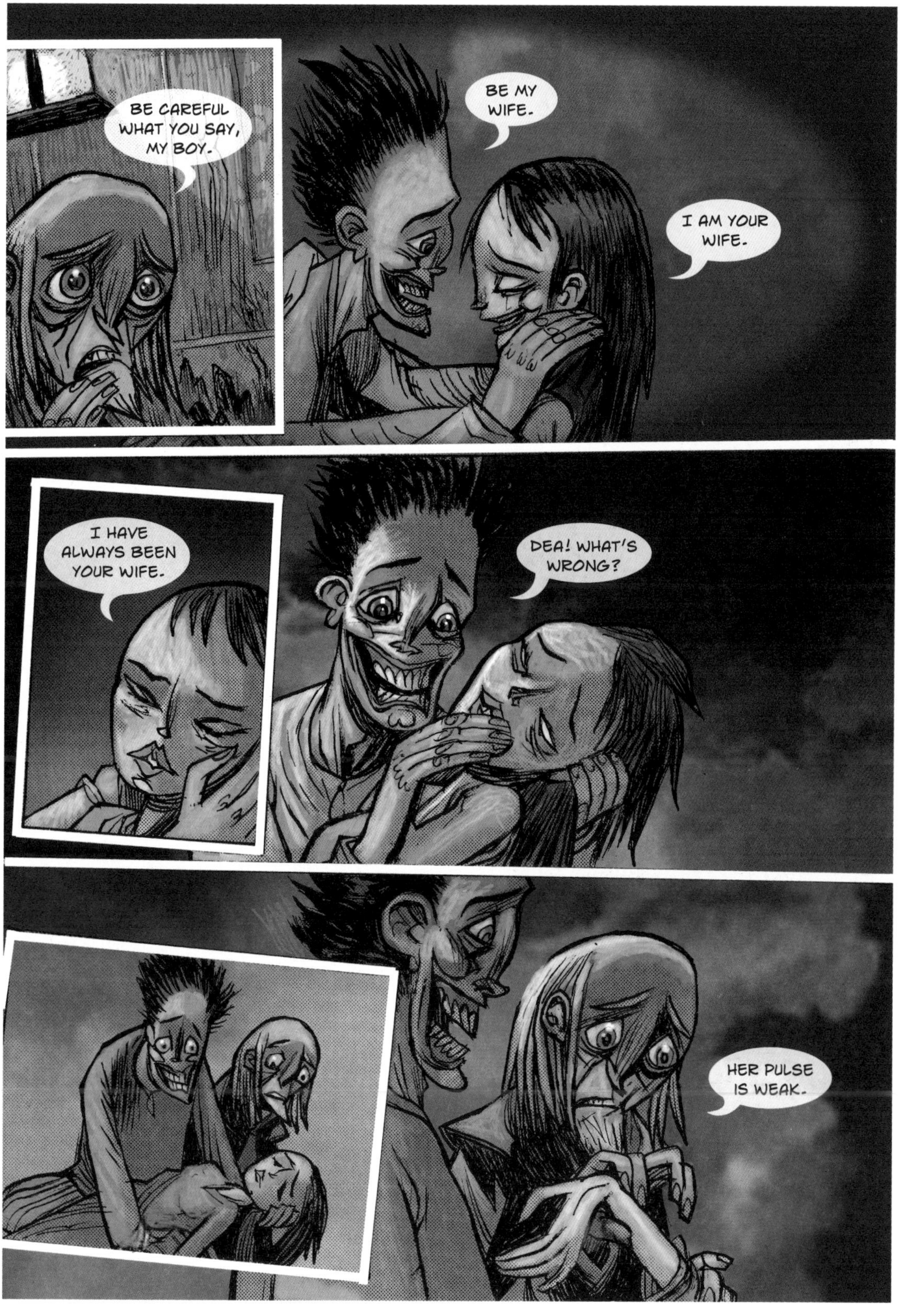
BE CAREFUL WHAT YOU SAY, MY BOY.
BE MY WIFE.
I AM YOUR WIFE.
I HAVE ALWAYS BEEN YOUR WIFE.
DEA! WHAT'S WRONG?
HER PULSE IS WEAK.

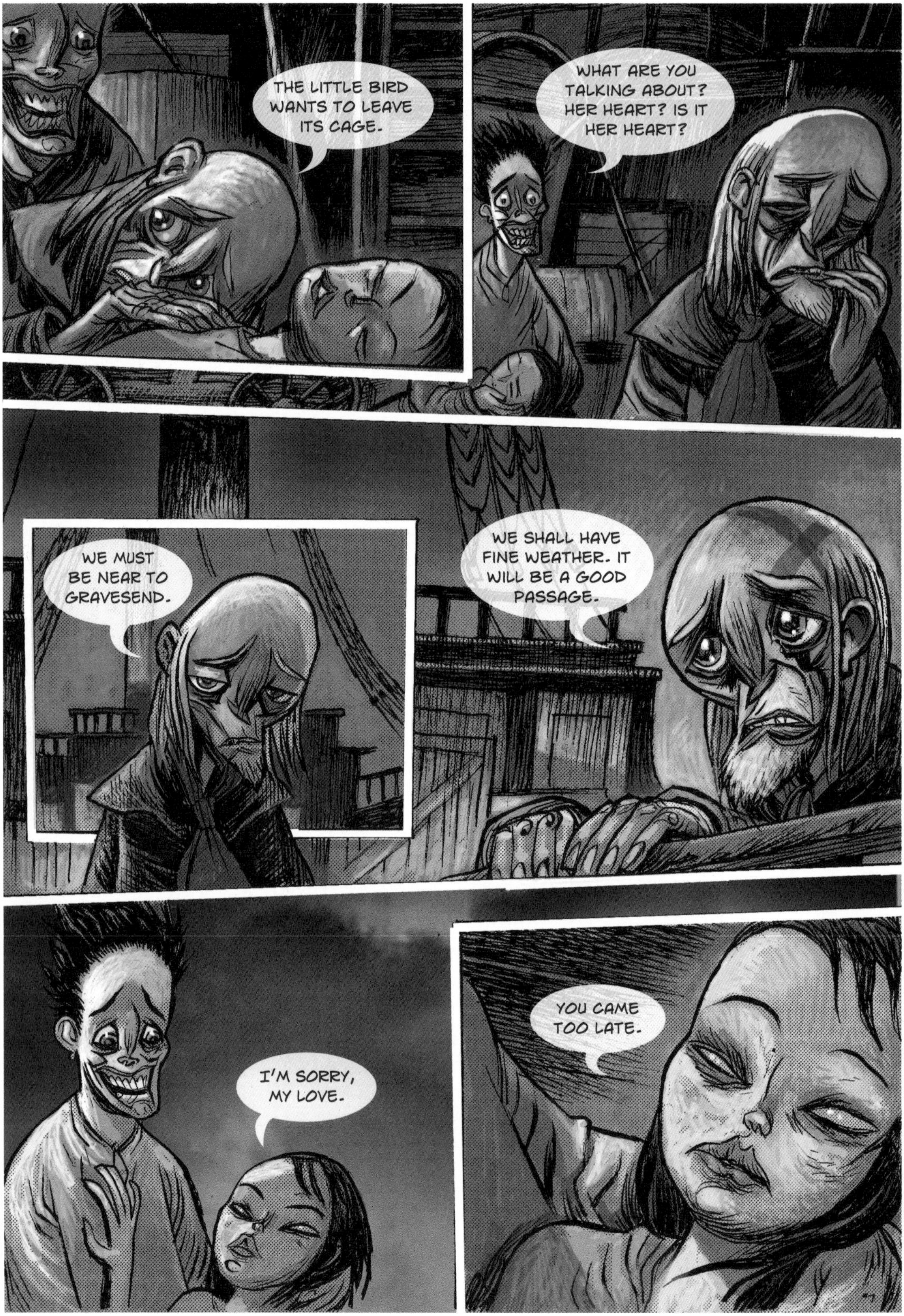
THE LITTLE BIRD WANTS TO LEAVE ITS CAGE.
WHAT ARE YOU TALKING ABOUT? HER HEART? IS IT HER HEART?
WE MUST BE NEAR TO GRAVESEND.
WE SHALL HAVE FINE WEATHER. IT WILL BE A GOOD PASSAGE.
I'M SORRY, MY LOVE.
YOU CAME TOO LATE.

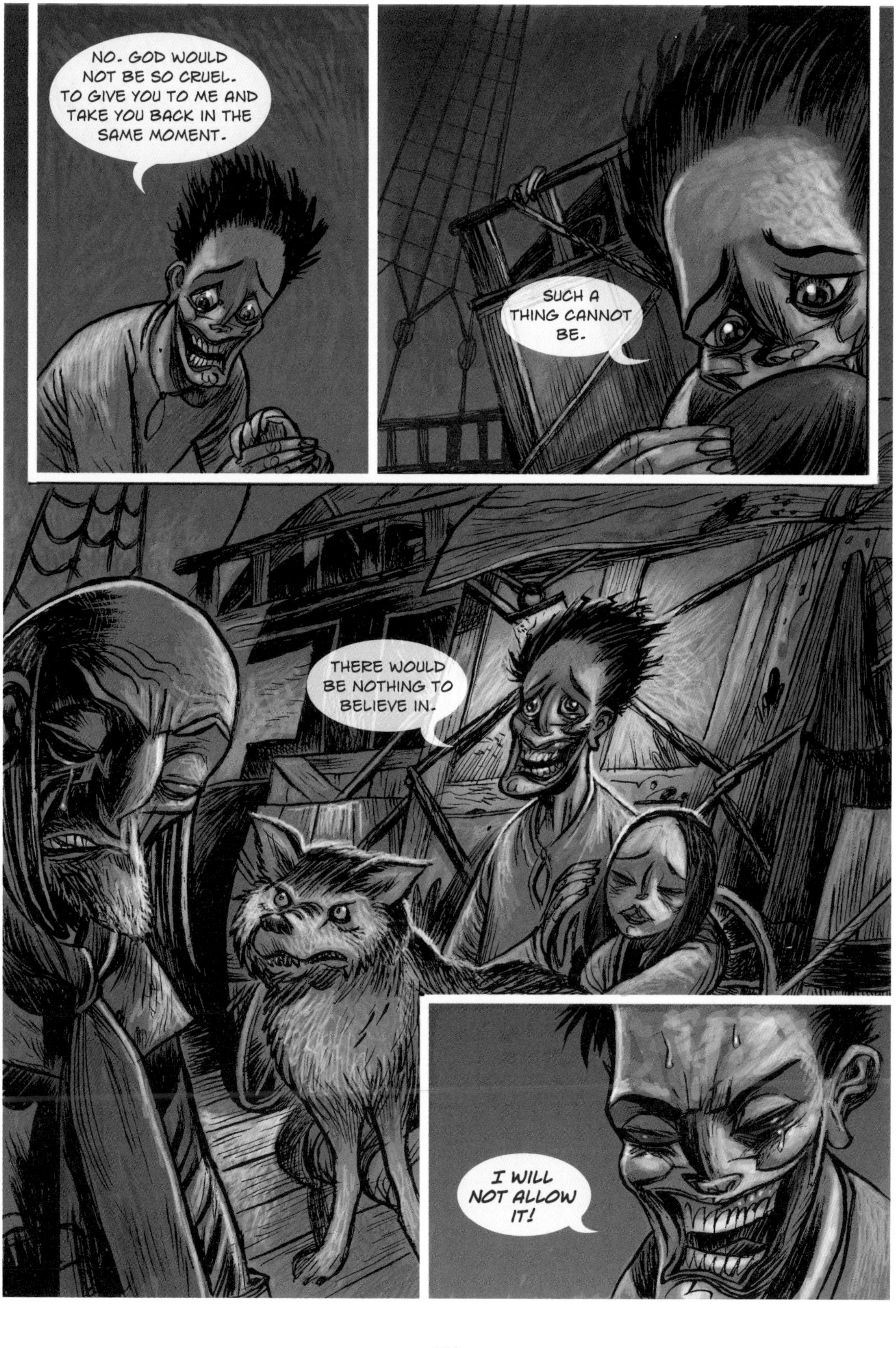
NO. GOD WOULD NOT BE SO CRUEL. TO GIVE YOU TO ME AND TAKE YOU BACK IN THE SAME MOMENT.
SUCH A THING CANNOT BE.
THERE WOULD BE NOTHING TO BELIEVE IN.
I WILL NOT ALLOW IT!

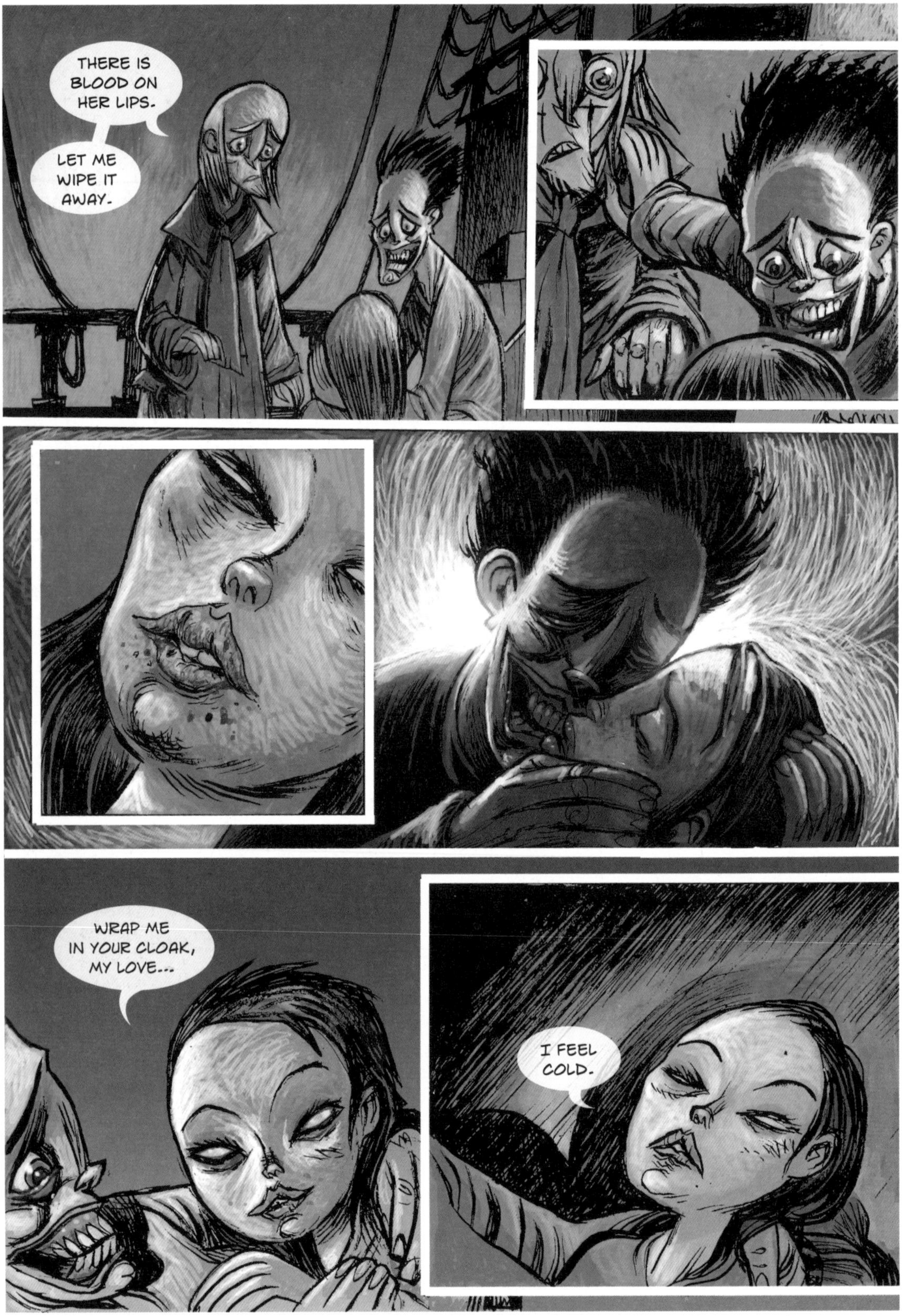
THERE IS BLOOD ON HER LIPS.
LET ME WIPE IT AWAY.
WRAP ME IN YOUR CLOAK, MY LOVE...
I FEEL COLD.

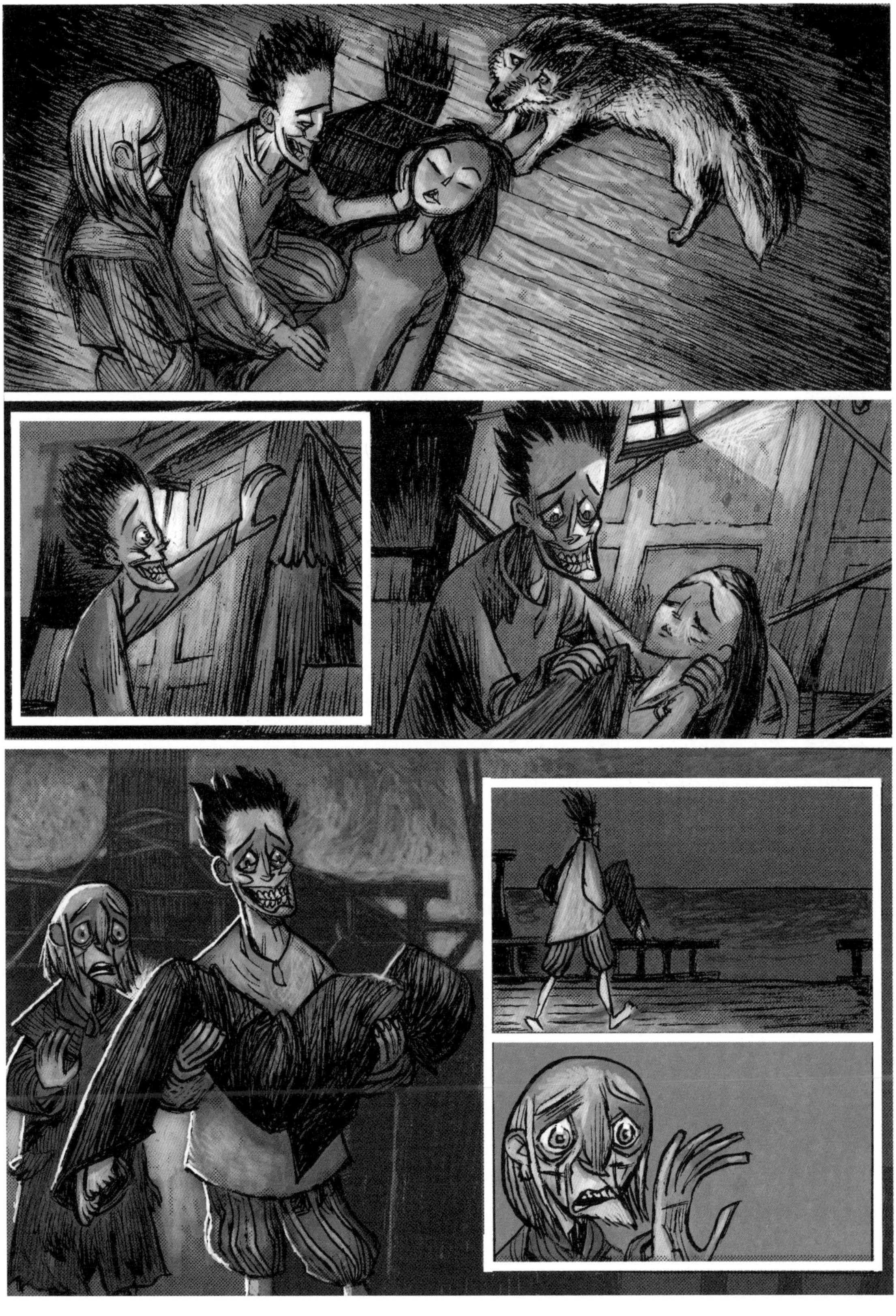

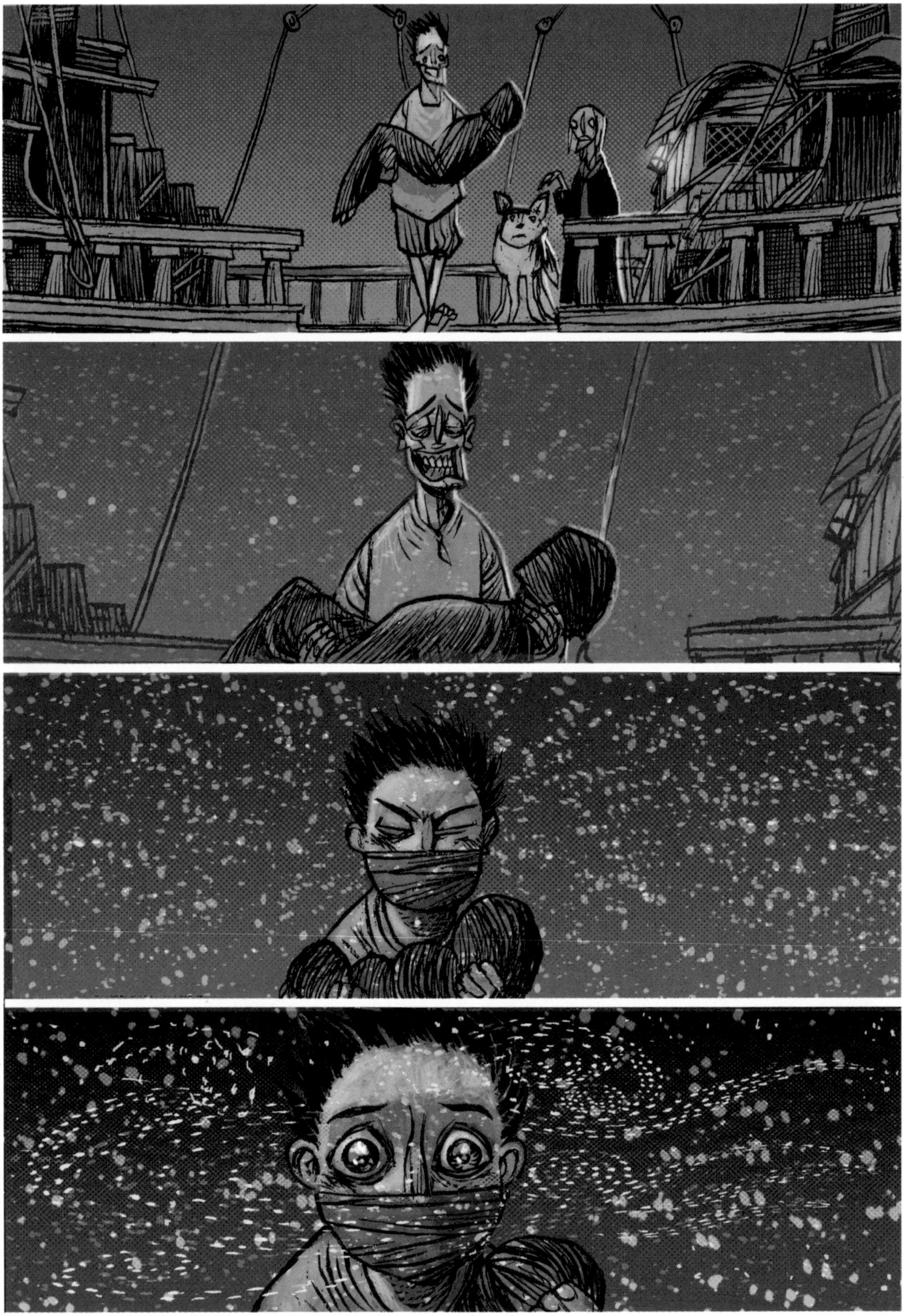

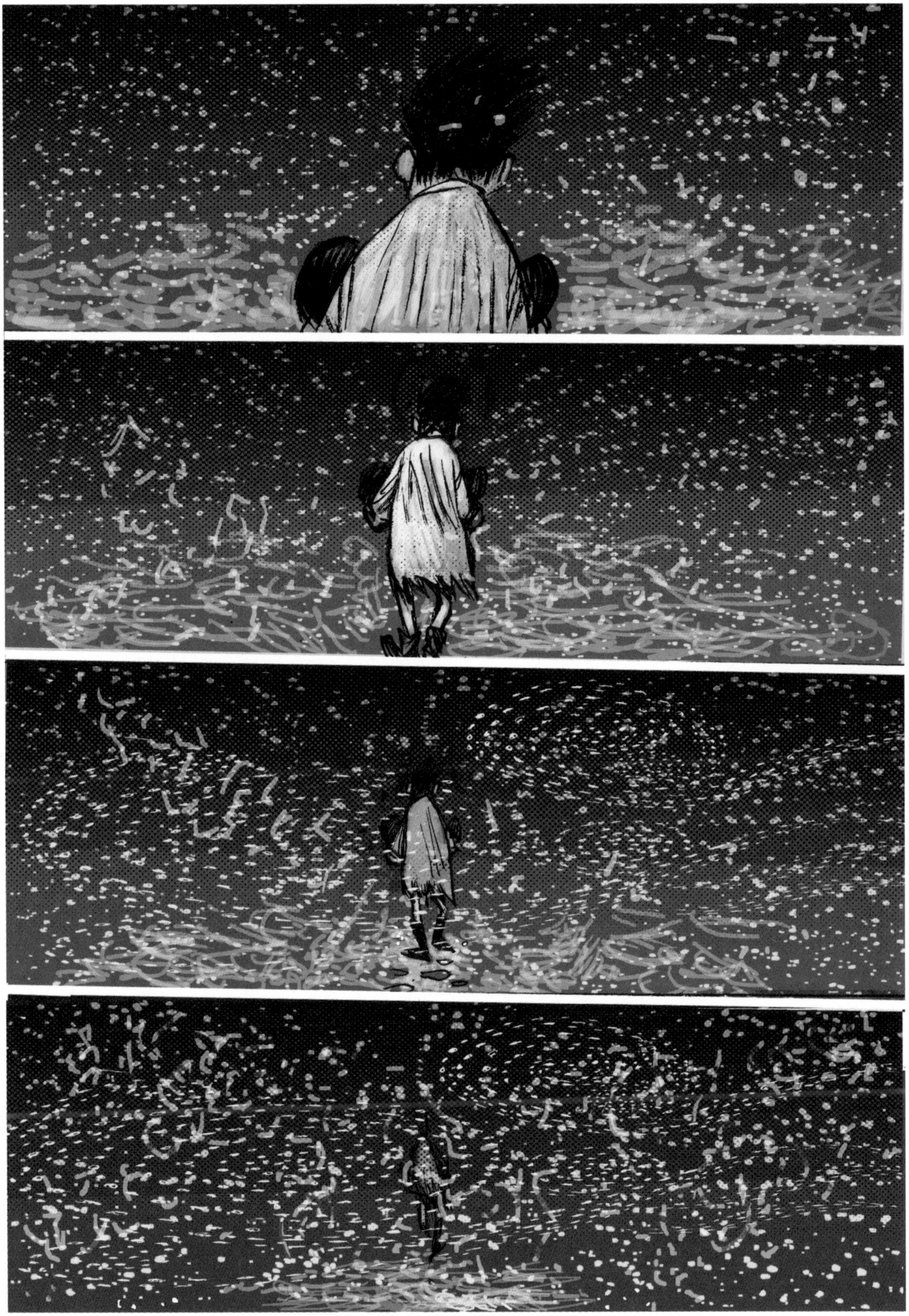

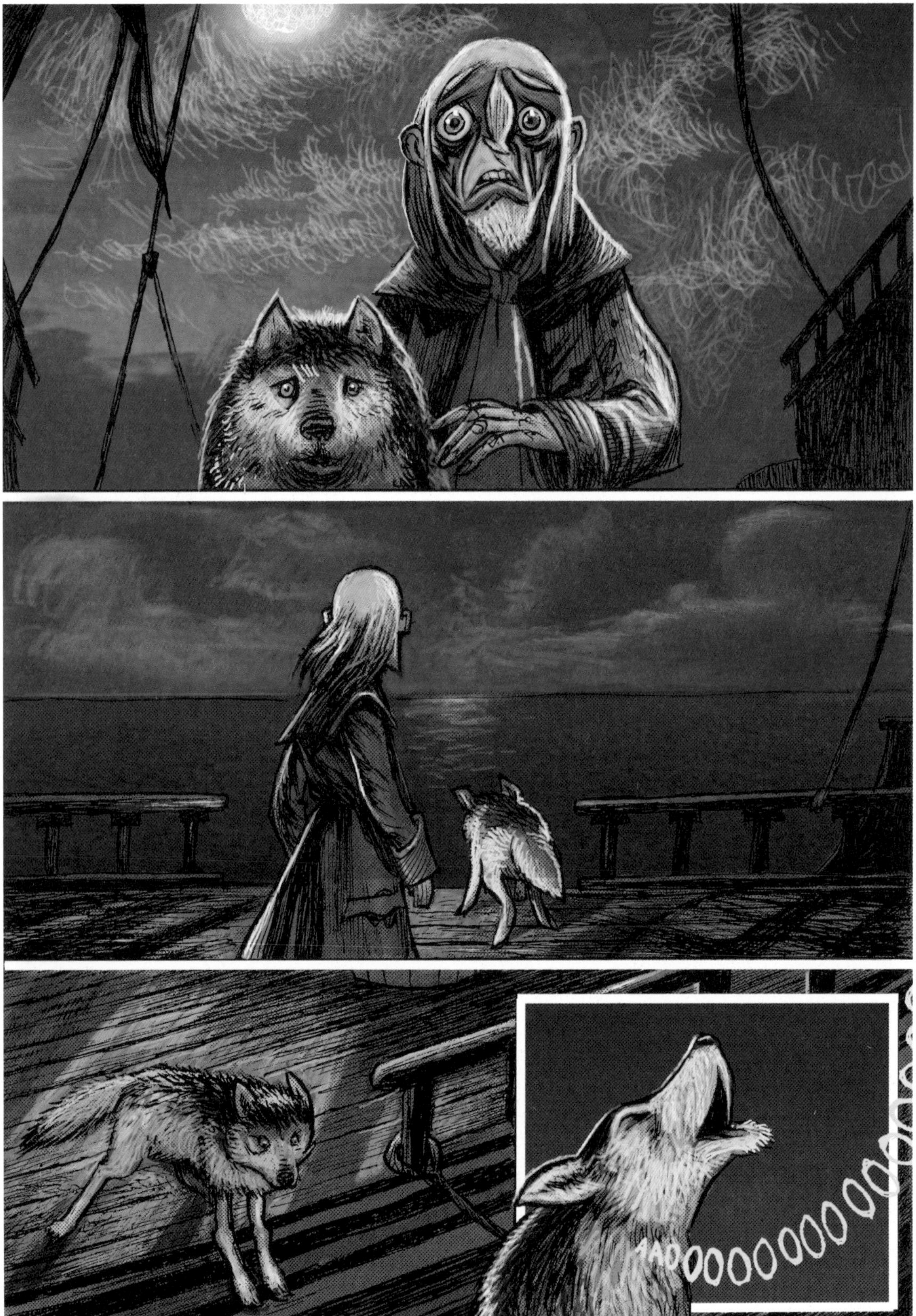
AAOOOOOOOOOOOOOOOOO

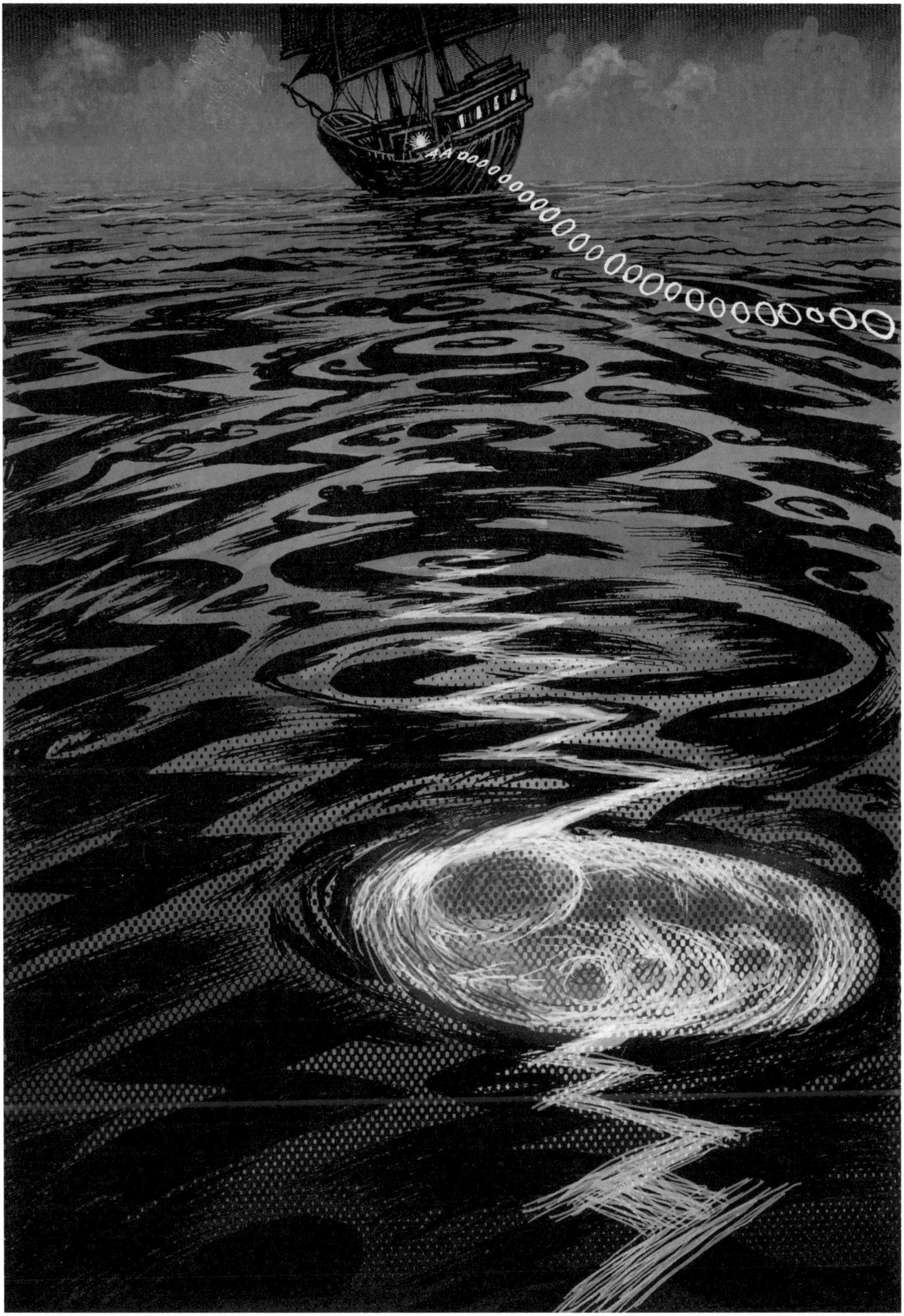
AAOOOOOOOOOOOOOOOOOOOOOOOO

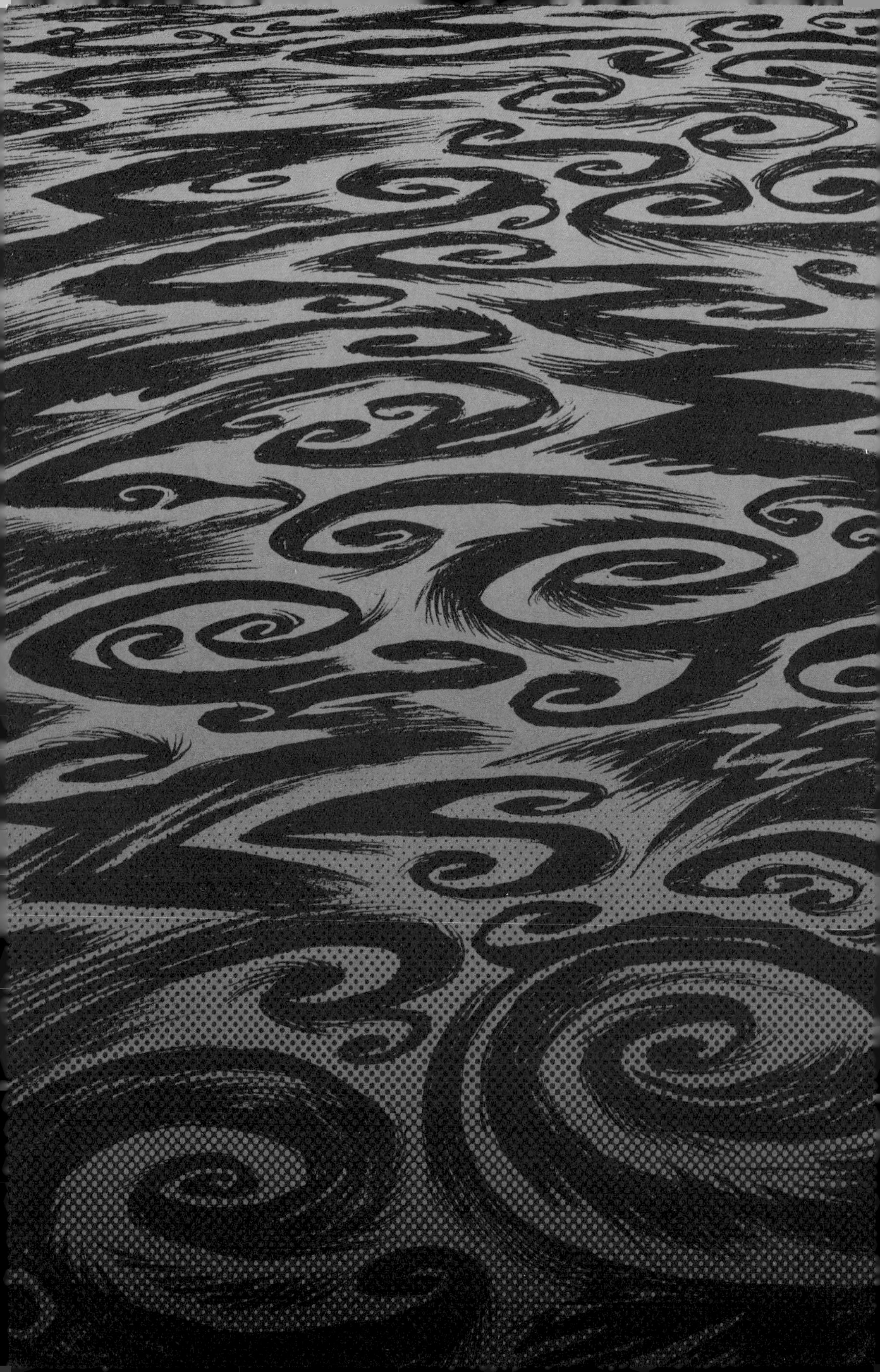

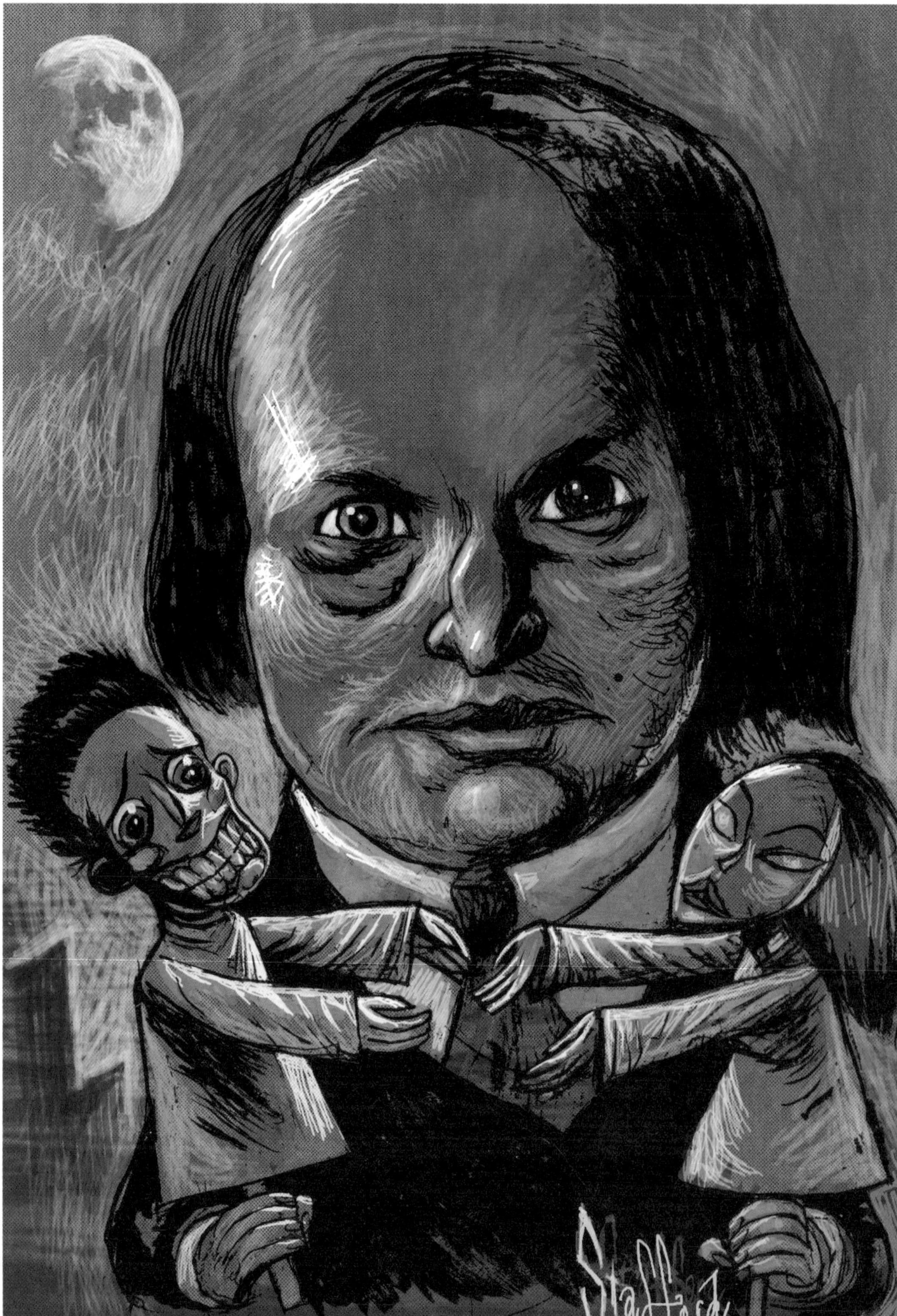
Stafford

The Man Who Laughs has left an indelible mark upon modern popular culture. When Heath Ledger's Joker says "Let's put a smile on that face" in the movie *The Dark Knight*, it's a twisted version of Victor Hugo's Gwynplaine who is speaking. In 1940, when Jerry Robinson, Bob Kane and Bill Finger were working on the first issue of the *Batman* comic, they saw a poster featuring Conrad Veidt in the 1928 movie of *The Man Who Laughs* and that image inspired them to create the Joker as Batman's nemesis. In 2011, I wrote an issue of *Batman and Robin* for DC Comics featuring a crazy Frenchman who mutilates his own son in a perverted homage to Victor Hugo.

The story was a tip of the hat to the man who inspired the Clown Prince of Crime, but like most people outside of France, I hadn't actually read *L'Homme Qui Rit*. It is nowhere near as popular as *Les Misérables* or *Notre-Dame de Paris*. When I finally managed to track down a copy of the book I soon realised why. Written in the latter part of Hugo's career, when he was living in exile in the Channel Islands, it is rambling and crammed with repetitive details of the workings of the British aristocracy and political system. But as I struggled through the more turgid passages I became entranced by the story that lay at the heart of the book – a story of love and humanity and the struggle against the workings of fate and a corrupt society. I found myself visualizing episodes and imagining them as scenes in a comic book: the Comprachicos sinking beneath the waves as they beg forgiveness for their sins, Gwynplaine struggling through the snow with the baby Dea in his arms, the first glimpse of his mutilated features, the fearful depths of Southwark Jail, the gothic maze of Gwynplaine's own castle.

To make the project viable, I knew I would have to take a knife to the original text, to cut drastically and also to rearrange the chronology of the story for dramatic effect. So I performed some radical surgery but not, I hope, a mutilation of the original. I added a couple of short scenes of my own: one where Ursus establishes his ability with ventriloquism and another where Gwynplaine wanders the streets of London and encounters a couple of bawds who unmask him to reveal "A monster!" Otherwise, the characters and events are faithful to the spirit of the novel.

There aren't many artists who could capture the grotesque aspects of the story and also convey the humanity of the characters and the black humour and irony of Hugo's prose. I worked with Mark Stafford once before on a story for SelfMadeHero's *Lovecraft Anthology: Volume I* and I knew he was the perfect artist to draw this book. I just had to convince him to spend a year adapting a long and near-unreadable 19th-century tome into a gripping graphic novel for a 21st-century audience. Miraculously, Mark became as enthusiastic as I was and I couldn't be happier with our collaboration.

There is no doubt that *L'Homme Qui Rit* has its flaws. When the literary historian George Saintsbury published his *History of the French Novel* in 1919, he described *L'Homme Qui Rit* as "probably the maddest book in recognized literature". He goes on to claim he could fill fifty pages enumerating the book's "absurdities". Yes, the Comprachicos are an invention of Hugo, as is the Wapentake, but as symbols of the impersonal workings of the state, they serve the writer's greater purpose. Victor Hugo devoted his political and literary life to attacking corruption and privilege and pursuing social justice. If he were alive today he would still be exposing the inequalities that allow a minority to control the wealth of the country by exploiting the labour of the majority. He would be exposing the secret torture carried out by agents of the British Government and warning of riots on the streets if the plight of the lower classes is not addressed.

I suspect that if Gwynplaine were to deliver his speech to the House of Lords today, it would ring as true now as it did then, and no doubt would be met with the same ridicule and laughter.

David Hine